ARCO CIVIL SERVICE ARITHMETIC AND VOCABULARY

15TH EDITION

PETERSON'S
A nelnet COMPANY

PETERSON'S
A nelnet COMPANY

An ARCO Book
ARCO is a registered trademark of Peterson's, and is used herein under license by Peterson's.

About Peterson's, a Nelnet company

Peterson's (www.petersons.com) is a leading provider of education information and advice, with books and online resources focusing on education search, test preparation, and financial aid. Its Web site offers searchable databases and interactive tools for contacting educational institutions, online practice tests and instruction, and planning tools for securing financial aid. Peterson's serves 110 million education consumers annually.

An American BookWorks Corporation Project

For more information, contact Peterson's, 2000 Lenox Drive, Lawrenceville, NJ 08648; 800-338-3282; or find us on the World Wide Web at: www.petersons.com/about.

Production Editor: Teresina Jonkoski; Manufacturing Manager: Ivona Skibicki; Composition Manager: Linda M. Williams.

ISBN-13: 978-0-7689-1697-3
ISBN-10: 0-7689-1697-6

Printed in the United States of America

10 9 8 7 6 09 08

Fifteenth edition

CONTENTS

PART THREE: VOCABULARY REVIEW

Petersons.com/publishing

Check out our Web site at www.petersons.com/publishing to see if there is any new information regarding civil service employment and any revisions or corrections to the content of this book. We've made sure the information in this book is accurate and up-to-date; however, the content may have changed since the time of publication.

INTRODUCTION

HOW TO USE THIS GUIDE

WHAT THIS BOOK WILL DO FOR YOU

Arco has followed testing trends and methods ever since the firm was founded in 1937. We *specialize* in books that prepare people for tests. Based on this experience, we have prepared the best possible book to help *you* score high.

To write this book we carefully analyzed every detail surrounding the forthcoming examinations. Since there is such variation in exams, we cannot predict exactly what your exam will be like. However, after studying many announcements and many exams, we have written this book to prepare you for the most probable question types. The review chapters will prepare you for questions that you are likely to face. The practice tests, while they are not actual exams, will give you excellent practice and preparation for your civil service exam. Other features of this book include details about:

- The job itself
- Official and unofficial announcements concerning the examination
- All the previous examinations, although many not available to the public
- Related examinations
- Technical literature that explains and forecasts the examination

CAN YOU PREPARE YOURSELF FOR YOUR TEST?

You want to pass this test. That's why you bought this book. Used correctly, your "self-tutor" will show you what to expect and will give you a speedy brush-up on the subjects tested in your exam. Some of these are subjects not taught in schools at all. Even if your study time is very limited, you should:

- Become familiar with the type of examination you will take
- Improve your test-taking skills
- Improve your skill in analyzing and answering questions involving reasoning, judgment, comparison, and evaluation
- Improve your speed and skill in reading and comprehension—an important part of your ability to learn and an important part of most tests

This book will:

- **Present every type of question you will encounter on the actual test.** This will put you at ease with the test format.
- **Find your weaknesses.** Once you know what subjects you're weak in, you can get right to work and concentrate on those areas. This kind of selective study yields maximum test results.

- **Give you confidence *now*.** It will build your self-confidence while you are preparing for the test. As you proceed, it will prevent the kind of test anxiety that causes low test scores.
- **Stress the multiple-choice type of question because that's the kind you'll see on your test.** You must not be satisfied with merely knowing the correct answer for each question. You must find out why the other choices are incorrect.

After testing yourself, you may find that you are weak in a particular area. You should concentrate on improving your skills by using the specific practice sections in this book that apply to you.

WHAT'S IN THIS BOOK?

If you already know what type of career you wish to pursue, this book will help you prepare for any of the major exams. If you don't know what type of job you'd like to apply for, this book will also help you. Not only will you be able to prepare for your exam, but you will also find information about various types of careers, and perhaps it will narrow down your choices. This book offers you an overview of the world of civil service, a brief introduction to federal, state, and city employers and their hiring requirements, and in-depth descriptions of a number of widely used examinations.

PART ONE

There are three parts to this book. Part One covers the major civil service employment sectors: federal, state, and municipal (city). There's more than enough for everyone here. Each sector has its own requirements and tests. However, as you will see, there are certain types of questions that will appear on most of these exams, regardless of the type of test you will take.

Also in this section is important information on test-taking techniques. This will give you guidelines to help you prepare for the actual test. Feeling anxious before you take a test is a normal reaction. We provide you with some relaxation tips so you can get a great test score.

PART TWO

Part Two is an overview of mathematics. If you haven't already been in the field, you will be surprised by the number of different civil service jobs that require mathematics skills as a part of standard examinations. This section gives you a good overview of the types of mathematical problems that routinely appear on certain civil service exams. Practice is provided for fractions, decimals, percents, powers and roots, statistics, distance problems, taxation, and more. Use this section to gain a full understanding of what your math strengths and weaknesses are. A special feature of this book is that all the correct answers are explained. If you find that you are getting several questions wrong in a particular section, review the *Answers and Explanations* and try those math problems again. Gaining familiarity with math problems that give you difficulty will save time and will better prepare you during the actual exam. Also included in this section are sample examinations that review your arithmetic skills. Level of difficulty, question styles, and scoring methods all conform closely to the examinations for which they are meant to prepare.

PART THREE

Part Three is designed to help you expand your vocabulary. It provides guidance on strengthening and developing your overall vocabulary skills in a variety of question formats that may appear on the civil service exam you are planning to take. Exercises are presented for synonyms and antonyms, sentence completions, and understanding word parts. A comprehensive A–Z word list of more than 1,000 words with definitions is also provided to help you broaden your vocabulary. And, as in the previous section, all correct answers are explained. Take time to read and understand the explanation given. By reading all of the explanations, you can gain greater insight into methods of answering questions and the reasoning behind the correct choices.

We strongly believe that regardless of the test that you think you're planning to take—or the career path you want to follow—try to take *all* of the exams in this book. It may seem like a lot of extra work, but you never know where you may end up. You may think you're interested in a job with the local city government, but end up working for a private company. Perhaps the exam you were hoping to take is not being given for another year, but some other test is being given next month. It is always better to be prepared.

PART ONE

LANDING CIVIL SERVICE JOBS

WHERE THE JOBS ARE

Government service is one of the nation's largest sources of employment. About one in every six people is employed by the government. Of those government employees, five out of six are employed by state or local governments, and the remainder work for the federal government.

As you can see, government employees represent a significant portion of the nation's work force. They work in large cities, small towns, and remote and isolated places such as lighthouses and forest ranger stations, and a small number of federal employees work overseas. In this chapter, we will outline the various types of government careers that are available at the federal, state, and local levels.

Almost every job in government service, at any level, will utilize some form of mathematics and/or vocabulary—either in the career itself or in a test for a specific job. If you have read and practiced the material in this book, you should be well prepared for any test that requires these skills. Now it's time to find the job that suits you. Very often, finding a job is a matter of luck. However, we'd like to take some of the luck out of it and make it more directive. Below are a variety of sources you can contact in your search for employment.

FEDERAL CIVILIAN EMPLOYMENT

The federal government is the nation's largest employer. It employs approximately 3 million civilian workers in the United States and an additional 150,000 civilian workers—half of them U.S. citizens—in U.S. territories and foreign countries. The headquarters of most government departments and agencies are in the Washington, D.C., area, but only one out of eight federal employees works there.

Federal employees work in occupations that represent nearly every kind of job in private employment as well as some unique to the federal government, such as regulatory inspectors, foreign service officers, and Internal Revenue agents. Most federal employees work for the executive branch of the government.

The executive branch includes the Office of the President, the cabinet departments, and about 100 independent agencies, commissions, and boards. This branch is responsible for activities such as administering federal laws, handling international relations, conserving natural resources, treating and rehabilitating disabled veterans, delivering the mail, conducting scientific research, maintaining the flow of supplies to the armed forces, and administering other programs to promote the health and welfare of the people of the United States.

The Department of Defense, which includes the Army, Navy, Air Force, Marine Corps, Coast Guard, and the newly formed Department of Homeland Security, is the largest department. It employs about one million civilian workers. The Departments of Agriculture, Health and Human Services, and the Treasury are also big employers. The two largest independent agencies are the U.S. Postal Service and the Department of Veterans Affairs.

There is also federal civilian employment available in the legislative branch, which includes Congress, the Government Printing Office, the General Accounting Office, and the

Library of Congress. The judicial branch, the smallest employer, hires people for work within the court system. Where should you begin your search?

FEDERAL JOBS

The Office of Personnel Management (OPM) is the place to start. It has a list of job openings that is updated daily. In addition, the office also publishes the *Federal Exam Announcement* each quarter during the year. Although staff members at the OPM are not responsible for hiring for jobs, they will provide you with access to each hiring agency, and there you can get the specific details about each job. You can reach OPM at 202-606-1800 or online at www.opm.gov.

You can find a complete application for federal employment along with instructions on how to fill it out at the OPM Web site. It also provides explanations of federal job categories and specific job descriptions. You can then search geographically and alphabetically to find out which jobs have current openings and exactly where the openings are located. The listings, in turn, refer you to full vacancy announcements, including qualifications, requirements, and application procedures and deadlines. With adequate equipment you can download the announcement. Or you can take notes from the information on your screen. Likewise, you can download application forms or even apply electronically using your computer. You can also follow instructions for getting the proper forms by telephone or mail.

Another excellent source is the *Federal Jobs Digest*, a biweekly newspaper that lists thousands of government jobs, both in the United States and in foreign countries. Its Web site features thousands of job listings at any one time. It can be reached at:

Federal Jobs Digest
Division of Breakthrough Publications
326 Main Street
Emmaus, PA 18049
Phone: 610-905-5825
Web site: www.jobsfed.com

You might also look under the heading "U.S. Government" in the blue pages of your telephone directory for a listing for Office of Personnel Management or Federal Job Information Center. A telephone call to this number may give you automated information pertinent to your own area or may direct you to a location at which you can pick up printed materials or conduct a search on a computer touch screen.

WHITE-COLLAR OCCUPATIONS

Because of its wide range of responsibilities, the federal government employs white-collar workers in many occupational fields. About 25 percent are administrative and clerical workers.

General clerical workers are employed in all federal departments and agencies. These include office machine operators, secretaries, clerk-typists, mail and file clerks, telephone operators, and workers in computer-related occupations. In addition, there are the half million postal clerks and mail carriers.

Many government workers are employed in engineering and related fields. The engineers represent virtually every branch and specialty of engineering. There are large numbers of technicians in areas such as engineering, electronics, surveying, and drafting. Nearly two thirds of all engineers work for the Department of Defense.

Of the more than 120,000 workers employed in accounting and budgeting work, 35,000 are professional accountants or Internal Revenue officers. Among technician and administrative occupations are accounting technicians, tax accounting technicians, and budget administrators. There are also large numbers of clerks in specialized accounting work. Accounting workers are employed throughout the government, particularly in the Departments of Defense and the Treasury and in the General Accounting Office.

Many federal employees work in hospitals or in medical, dental, and public health capacities. Three out of five are either professional nurses or nursing assistants. Other professional occupations in this field include physicians, dieticians, technologists, and physical therapists. Technician and aide jobs include medical technicians, medical laboratory aides, and dental assistants. Employees in this field work primarily for the Department of Veterans Affairs; others work for the Departments of Defense and Health and Human Services.

Other government workers are engaged in administrative work related to private business and industry. They arrange and monitor contracts with the private sector and purchase goods and services needed by the federal government. Administrative occupations include contract and procurement specialists, production control specialists, and Internal Revenue officers. Two out of three of these workers are employed by the Departments of Defense and the Treasury.

Another large group works in jobs concerned with the purchase, cataloging, storage, and distribution of supplies for the federal government. This field includes many managerial and administrative positions, such as supply management officers, purchasing officers, and inventory management specialists, as well as large numbers of specialized clerical positions. Most of these jobs are in the Department of Defense.

Throughout the federal government, many people are employed in the field of law. They fill professional positions, such as attorneys or law clerks, and administrative positions, such as passport and visa examiners or tax law specialists. There also are many clerical positions that involve examining claims.

The social sciences also employ many government workers. Economists are employed throughout the government; psychologists and social workers work primarily for the Department of Veterans Affairs; and foreign affairs and international relations specialists, for the Department of State. One third of the workers in this field are social insurance administrators employed largely in the Department of Health and Human Services.

About 50,000 biological and agricultural science workers are employed by the federal government, mostly in the Departments of Agriculture and Interior. Many of these work in forestry and soil conservation activities. Others administer farm assistance programs. The largest number is employed as biologists, forest and range fire controllers, soil conservationists, and forestry technicians.

The federal government employs another 50,000 people in investigative and inspection work. Large numbers of these are engaged in criminal investigation and health regulatory inspections, mostly in the Departments of the Treasury, Justice, and Agriculture.

Physical sciences is another area of government employment. Three out of four workers in the physical sciences are employed by the Departments of Defense, Interior, and Commerce. Professional workers include chemists, physicists, meteorologists, cartographers, and geologists. Aides and technicians include physical science technicians, meteorological technicians, and cartography technicians.

And in the mathematics field are professional mathematicians and statisticians and mathematics technicians and statistical clerks. They are employed primarily by the Departments of Defense, Agriculture, Commerce, and Health and Human Services.

Entrance requirements for white-collar jobs vary widely. A college degree in a specified field or equivalent work experience is usually required for professional occupations such as physicists and engineers.

Entrants into administrative and managerial occupations usually are not required to have knowledge of a specialized field, but must instead indicate a potential for future development by having a degree from a four-year college or responsible job experience. They usually begin as trainees and learn their duties on the job. Typical jobs in this group are budget analysts, claims examiners, purchasing specialists, administrative assistants, and personnel specialists.

Technician, clerical, and aide-assistant jobs have entry-level positions for people with a high school education or the equivalent. For many of these positions, no previous experience or training is required. The entry-level position is usually that of trainee. Workers who have junior college or technical school training or those who have specialized skills may enter these occupations at higher levels. Typical jobs are engineering technicians, supply clerks, clerk-typists, and nursing assistants.

BLUE-COLLAR OCCUPATIONS

Blue-collar occupations—craft, operative, laborer, and some service jobs—provide full-time employment for more than half a million federal workers. The Department of Defense employs about three fourths of these workers in establishments such as naval shipyards, arsenals, the Air or Army depots, as well as on construction, harbor, flood control, irrigation, or reclamation projects. Others work for the Department of Veterans Affairs, U.S. Postal Service, General Services Administration, Department of the Interior, and Tennessee Valley Authority.

The largest single blue-collar group consists of manual laborers. Large numbers also are employed in machine tool and metal work, motor vehicle operation, warehousing, and food preparation and serving. The federal government employs a wide variety of individuals in maintenance and repair work, such as electrical and electronic equipment installation and repair, and in vehicle and industrial equipment maintenance and repair. All these fields require a range of skill levels and include a variety of occupations comparable to the private sector.

Although the federal government employs blue-collar workers in many different fields, about half are concentrated in a small number of occupations. The largest group, the skilled mechanics, works as air-conditioning, aircraft, automobile, truck, electronics, sheet-metal, and general maintenance mechanics. Another large number of craft workers is employed as painters, pipefitters, carpenters, electricians, and machinists. A similar number serves as warehouse workers, truck drivers, and general laborers. An additional group of workers is employed as janitors and food service workers.

THE PRIVATE SECTOR

Most jobs in the private sector can be found in three ways—employment agencies, newspaper classified advertisements, and online job searches. Wherever you live there is certainly a local employment agency. Call to make an appointment and bring your resume. Keep in mind that they're the first interview that you will have in the line for employment, so you should dress appropriately and be somewhat informed about the types of jobs in which you would be interested. Reading through the section on various careers in this book will help you. Then, go to your local newspaper or, if you live in a small town, perhaps you can pick up a newspaper from a larger city near you. In many cases, you will be directed toward an employment agency to apply for a job. In others, you may be asked to call the company directly, write a letter, or send your resume to the company. Remember that just like an interview, your telephone call, letter, and/or resume are the first impressions someone makes of you, so be on your best behavior.

There are also dozens of career-oriented Web sites that will be helpful to you. Monster.com and CareerBuilder.com are two excellent online sources. You can post your resume online, as well as search for jobs on a state-by-state basis.

ENTRANCE REQUIREMENTS

People with previous training in a skilled trade may apply for a position with the federal government at the journey level. Those with no previous training may apply for appointment to one of several apprenticeship programs. Apprenticeship programs generally last four years; trainees receive both classroom and on-the-job training. After completing this training, a person is eligible for a position at the journey level. There are also a number of positions that require little or no prior training or experience, including janitors, maintenance workers, messengers, and many others.

THE MERIT SYSTEM

More than nine out of ten jobs in the federal government are merit-based. The Civil Service Act, administered by the U.S. Office of Personnel Management, covers six out of ten federal titles. This act was passed by Congress to ensure that federal employees are hired on the basis of individual merit and fitness. It provides for competitive examinations and the selection of new employees from among the most qualified applicants.

Some federal jobs are exempt from civil service requirements either by law or by action of the Office of Personnel Management. However, most of these positions are covered by separate merit systems of other agencies such as the Foreign Service of the Department of State, the Federal Bureau of Investigation, the Nuclear Regulatory Commission, and the Tennessee Valley Authority.

EARNINGS, ADVANCEMENT, AND WORKING CONDITIONS

Most federal civilian employees are paid according to one of three major pay systems: the **General Pay Schedule,** the **Wage System,** or the **Postal Service Schedule.**

GENERAL PAY SCHEDULE

More than half of all federal workers are paid under the General Schedule (GS), a pay scale for workers in professional, administrative, technical, and clerical jobs, and for workers such as guards and messengers. General Schedule jobs are classified by the U.S. Office of Personnel Management in one of fifteen grades, according to the difficulty of duties and responsibilities and the knowledge, experience, and skills required of the workers. GS pay rates are set by Congress and apply to government workers nationwide. They are reviewed annually to see whether they are comparable with salaries in private industry. They are generally subject to upwards adjustment for very high-cost-of-living regions. In low-cost areas, the GS pay scale may exceed that of most private-sector workers.

Most employees receive within-grade pay increases at one-, two-, or three-year intervals if their work is acceptable. Within-grade increases may also be given in recognition of high-quality service. Some managers and supervisors receive increases based on their job performance rather than on time in grade.

High school graduates who have no related work experience usually start in GS-2 jobs, but some who have special skills begin at grade GS-3. Graduates of two-year colleges and technical schools often can begin at the GS-4 level. Most people with bachelor's degrees appointed to professional and administrative jobs such as statisticians, economists, writers and editors, budget analysts, accountants, and physicists, can enter at grades GS-5 or GS-7, depending on experience

GENERAL PAY SCHEDULE (Range of Salaries)

Effective as of January 2004

GS Rating	Low	High
1	$15,625	$ 19,543
2	17,568	22,109
3	19,168	24,919
4	21,518	27,971
5	24,075	31,302
6	26,836	34,891
7	29,821	38,767
8	33,026	42,935
9	36,478	47,422
10	40,171	52,222
11	44,136	57,375
12	52,899	68,766
13	62,905	81,778
14	74,335	96,637
15	87,439	113,674

and academic record. Those who have a master's degree or Ph.D. or the equivalent education or experience may enter at the GS-9 or GS-11 level. Advancement to higher grades generally depends upon ability, work performance, and openings in jobs at higher grade levels.

FEDERAL WAGE SYSTEM

About one quarter of federal civilian workers are paid according to the Federal Wage System. Under this system, craft, service, and manual workers are paid hourly rates established on the basis of "prevailing" rates paid by private employers for similar work in the same locations. As a result, the federal government wage rate for an occupation varies by locality. This commitment to meeting the local wage scale allows the federal wage earner to bring home a weekly paycheck comparable to that which he or she would earn in the private sector and to enjoy the benefits and security of a government job at the same time. The federal wage earner has the best of all possible worlds in this regard.

Federal government employees work a standard 40-hour week. Employees who are required to work overtime may receive premium rates for the additional time or compensatory time off at a later date. Most employees work eight hours a day, five days a week, Monday through Friday, but in some cases, the nature of the work requires a different workweek. Annual earnings for most full-time federal workers are not affected by seasonal factors.

Federal employees earn 13 days of annual (vacation) leave each year during their first three years of service; 20 days each year until the end of fifteen years; after fifteen years, 26 days each year. Workers who are members of military reserve organizations also are granted up to 15 days of paid military leave a year for training purposes. A federal worker who is laid off, though federal layoffs are uncommon, is entitled to unemployment compensation similar to that provided for employees in private industry.

Other benefits available to most federal employees include a contributory retirement system, optional participation in low-cost group life and health insurance programs which are partly supported by the government (as the employer), and training programs to develop maximum job proficiency and help workers achieve their highest potential. These training programs may be conducted in government facilities or in private educational facilities at government expense.

STATE AND LOCAL EMPLOYMENT

State and local governments provide a very large and expanding source of job opportunities in a wide variety of occupational fields. About fifteen million people work for state and local government agencies; nearly three fourths of these work in units of local government such as counties, municipalities, towns, and school districts. The job distribution varies greatly from that in federal government service. Defense, international relations and commerce, immigration, and mail delivery are virtually non-existent in state and local governments. On the other hand, there is great emphasis on education, health, social services, transportation, construction, and sanitation.

STATE EMPLOYMENT

Almost every state has its own Web site. In order to access the state systems via the Internet, there's a very simple way to find each state, although it may take some searching once you're online.

To find the state Internet site, enter the following: www.state.____.us. In the blank, enter the two-letter abbreviation for that state. For Arizona, for example, you would enter www.state.az.us. For Wisconsin, enter www.state.wi.us. See the following list of the latest URLs for the state sites. Be aware, however, that the sites may change from time to time.

STATE INTERNET SITES

Alabama	www.state.al.us/	Montana	www.state.mt.gov/
Alaska	www.state.ak.us/	Nebraska	www.state.ne.us/
Arizona	www.state.az.us/	Nevada	www.state.nv.us/
Arkansas	www.state.ar.us/	New Hampshire	www.state.nh.us/
California	www.state.ca.us/	New Jersey	www.state.nj.us/
Colorado	www.state.co.us/	New Mexico	www.state.nm.us/
Connecticut	www.state.ct.us/	New York	www.state.ny.us/
Delaware	www.state.de.us/	North Carolina	www.state.nc.us/
District of Columbia	www.dchomepage.net/	North Dakota	www.state.nd.us/
Florida	www.state.fl.us/	Ohio	www.state.oh.us/
Georgia	www.state.ga.us/	Oklahoma	www.state.ok.us/
Hawaii	www.state.hi.us/	Oregon	www.state.or.us/
Idaho	www.state.id.us/	Pennsylvania	www.state.pa.us/
Illinois	www.state.il.us/	Rhode Island	www.state.ri.us/
Indiana	www.state.in.us/	South Carolina	www.state.sc.us/
Iowa	www.state.ia.us/	South Dakota	www.state.sd.us/
Kansas	www.state.ks.us/	Tennessee	www.state.tn.us/
Kentucky	www.state.ky.us/	Texas	www.state.tx.us/
Louisiana	www.state.la.us/	Utah	www.state.ut.us/
Maine	www.state.me.us/	Vermont	www.state.vt.us/
Maryland	www.state.md.us/	Virginia	www.state.va.us/
Massachusetts	www.state.ma.us/	Washington	www.wa.gov/
Michigan	www.state.mi.us/	West Virginia	www.state.wv.us/
Minnesota	www.state.mn.us/	Wisconsin	www.state.wi.us/
Mississippi	www.state.ms.us/	Wyoming	www.state.wy.us/
Missouri	www.state.mo.us/		

LOCAL EMPLOYMENT

You may find city and county employment information on the Internet through your state's home page. Or, if you're in a large city, it is likely that the city has its own Web site. Use some of the popular search vehicles such as Google.com, Yahoo.com, Ask.com, Altavista.com, and so on, to locate other job-related sites. Use search terms such as *jobs*, *employment*, *labor*, *business*, *help-wanted*, and so on. Add that to the specific city or state, and you'll be surprised at the number of suggested sites you'll get. You might enter into the search box something like *Miami+jobs*. The plus sign (+) indicates that you want both Miami and jobs to be in the same suggested sites.

You should also investigate to see if there is a local city Civil Service publication that lists upcoming job announcements. For example, in New York City, *The Chief-Leader* is the primary source for upcoming Civil Service jobs. You will also find information about state and federal jobs in the paper.

EDUCATIONAL SERVICES

About one half of all jobs in state and local government are in educational services. Educational employees work in public schools, colleges, and various extension services. About half of all education workers are instructional personnel. School systems, colleges, and universities also employ administrative personnel, librarians, guidance counselors, nurses, dieticians, clerks, and maintenance workers.

HEALTH SERVICES

The next largest field of state and local government employment is health services. Those employed in health and hospital work include physicians, nurses, medical laboratory technicians, dieticians, kitchen and laundry workers, and hospital attendants. Social services make up another aspect of health and welfare. Unfortunately, the need for welfare and human services has been increasing greatly. As the need grows, the opportunities for social workers and their affiliated administrative and support staff also grows.

GOVERNMENT CONTROL/FINANCIAL ACTIVITIES

Another million employees work in the areas of general governmental control and financial activities. These include chief executives and their staffs, legislative representatives, and persons employed in the administration of justice, tax enforcement and other financial work, and general administration. These functions require the services of individuals such as lawyers, judges and other court officers, city managers, property assessors, budget analysts, stenographers, and clerks.

STREETS AND HIGHWAYS

The movement of people is of great concern to both state and local governments. Street and highway construction and maintenance are of major importance. Highway workers include civil engineers, surveyors, operators of construction machinery and equipment, truck drivers, concrete finishers, carpenters, construction laborers, and, where appropriate, snow removers. Toll collectors are relatively few in number, but they too are state or county employees or employees of independent authorities of the states or counties. Mass transportation within municipalities and between the cities and their outlying suburbs is also the province of local government. Maintaining vehicles, roadbeds and signaling systems, and staffing the vehicles themselves, requires a large and varied work force.

POLICE AND FIRE PROTECTION SERVICES

Police and fire protection is another large field of employment. Along with uniformed officers, these services include extensive administrative, clerical, maintenance, and custodial personnel.

MISCELLANEOUS STATE AND LOCAL OCCUPATIONS

Other state and local government employees work in a wide variety of activities, including local utilities (water in most areas, electricity in some); natural resources; parks and recreation; sanitation; corrections; local libraries; sewage disposal; and housing and urban renewal. These activities require workers in diverse occupations such as economists, electrical engineers, electricians, pipefitters, clerks, foresters, and bus drivers.

CLERICAL, ADMINISTRATIVE, MAINTENANCE, AND CUSTODIAL WORKERS

A large percentage of employment in most government agencies is made up of clerical, administrative, maintenance, and custodial workers. Among the workers involved in these activities are word processors, secretaries, data processors, computer specialists, office managers, fiscal and budget administrators, bookkeepers, accountants, carpenters, painters, plumbers, guards, and janitors. The list is endless.

Most positions in state and local governments are filled by residents of the state or locality. Many localities have residency requirements. Exceptions are generally made for persons with skills that are in special demand.

EARNINGS

Job conditions and earnings of state and local government employees vary widely, depending upon occupation and locality. Salary differences from state to state and even within some states tend to reflect differences in the general wage level and cost of living in the various localities.

As with the federal government, a majority of state and local government positions are filled through some type of formal civil service test; that is, personnel are hired and promoted on the basis of merit. State and local government workers have the same protections as federal government workers: they cannot be refused employment because of their race; they cannot be denied promotion because someone else made a greater political contribution; and they cannot be fired because the boss's son needs a job. Jobs tend to be classified according to job description and pegged to a salary schedule that is based upon the job classifications. Periodic performance reviews also are standard expectations. Nearly every group of employees has some sort of union or organization, but the functions and powers of these units vary greatly.

Since states and local entities are independent, the benefits packages they offer their employees can be quite different. Most state and local government employees are covered by retirement systems or by the federal social security program. Most have some sort of health coverage. They usually work a standard week of 40 hours or less with overtime pay or compensatory time benefits for additional hours of work.

HOW TO GET A GOVERNMENT JOB

Now that you know where to look for a job, it's important to understand the procedure. The procedure you must follow to get a government job varies very little from job to job and from one level of government to another. There are variations in details, of course, but certain steps are common to all.

Once you have found a *Notice of Examination* (it may be called an Announcement), read it very carefully. If you can get a copy for yourself all the better. If not, then take lots of time to take notes. Make sure, you have written down all of the details. The *Notice of Examination* will give a brief job description. It will tell the title of the job and describe some of the job duties and responsibilities. On the basis of the job description, you will decide whether or not you want to try for this job. If the job appeals to you, you must concentrate on:

- **Education and experience requirements.** If you cannot meet these requirements, do not bother to apply. Government service is very popular; many people apply. The government has more than enough applicants from whom to choose. It will not waive requirements for you.

- **Age requirements.** Discrimination on the basis of age is illegal, but a number of jobs demand so much sustained physical effort that they require retirement at an early age. For these positions there is an entry age limit. If you are already beyond that age, do not apply. If you are still too young, inquire about the time lag until hiring. It may be that you will reach the minimum age by the time the position is to be filled.

- **Citizenship requirements.** Many jobs are open to all people who are eligible to work in the United States, but all law enforcement jobs and most federal jobs are limited to citizens. If you are well along the way toward citizenship and expect to be naturalized soon, inquire as to your exact status with respect to the job.

- **Residency requirements.** If there is a residency requirement, you must live within the prescribed limits or be willing to move. If you are not willing to live in the area, do not waste time applying.

- **What forms must be filed.** The Announcement of the position for which you are applying will specify the form of application requested. For most federal jobs, you may submit either the Optional Application for Federal Employment (OF 612) or a resume that fulfills the requirements set forth in the pamphlet *Applying for a Federal Job* (OF 510). For other than federal jobs, the Notice of Examination may tell you where you must go or write to get the necessary form or forms. Be sure you secure them all. The application might be a simple form asking nothing more than name, address, citizenship, and Social Security number or it may be a complex Experience Paper. An Experience Paper, as its title implies, asks a great deal about education, job training, job experience, and life experience. Typically, the Experience Paper permits no identification by name, sex, or race; the only identifying mark is your Social Security number. The purpose of this procedure is to avoid permitting bias of any sort to enter into the weighting of responses. The Experience Paper generally follows a short form of application which does include a name. When the rating process is completed, the forms are coordinated by means of the Social Security number.

- **Filing dates, place, and fee.** There is great variation in this area. For some positions you can file your application at any time. Others have a first day and last day for filing. If you file too early or too late, your application will not be considered. Sometimes it is sufficient to have your application postmarked by the last day for filing. More often, your application must be received by the last date. If you are mailing your application, allow five full business days for it to get there on time. Place of filing will be stated right on the Notice. Get the address right! Most applications may be filed by mail, but occasionally in-person filing is specified. Follow directions. Federal and postal positions require no filing fee. Most, but not all, government jobs do charge a fee for processing your application. The fee is not always the same. Be sure to check this out. If the Notice specifies "money order only," plan to purchase a money order. Be sure the money order is made out properly. If you send or present a personal check, your application will be rejected without consideration. If the announcement specifies "money order only," you cannot submit cash, even in person.
- **How to qualify.** This portion of the Notice will tell you the basis on which the candidate will be chosen. Some examination scores consist of a totaling up of weighted education and experience factors. This type of examination, called "an unassembled exam" because you do not come to one place to take the exam, is based upon your responses on the application and supplementary forms. Obviously, these must be very complete for you to get full credit for all you have learned and accomplished. The Notice may tell you of a qualifying exam, an exam that you must pass in addition to scoring high on an unassembled, written, or performance test. Or, the Notice may tell you of a competitive exam, written performance, or both. The competitive exam may be described in very general terms or in detail. It is even possible that a few sample questions will be attached. If the date of the exam has been set, that date will appear on the Notice. Write it down.

When you have the application forms in hand, photocopy them. Fill out the photocopies first. This way you can correct mistakes, change the order of information, add, or delete. You can work at fitting what you have to say into the space allowed. Do not exaggerate, but be sure to give yourself credit for responsibilities you have had, cost-saving ideas you gave your prior employer, or any accomplishments. Be clear and thorough in telling what you have learned and what you can do.

When you are satisfied with your draft, copy over the application onto the form(s). Be sure to include any backup material that is requested; by the same token, do not send more "evidence" than is truly needed to support your claims of qualification. Your application must be complete according to the requirements of the announcement, but must not be overwhelming. You want to command hiring attention by conforming exactly to requirements.

Check over all forms for neatness and completeness. Sign wherever indicated. Attach the fee, if required. Then mail or personally file the application on time.

If you are currently employed, *do not* give your notice now. Stay at your present job. If you are job hunting, continue your search. The time lag between application for a government job and actual employment is always many months; it may even be a year or two. Most people cannot afford to sit back and wait for the job.

If the Notice of Examination told you that there will be a competitive exam and told you about subjects of the examination, you can begin to study now. If not, just continue working and await notice of next steps.

When the Civil Service commission or personnel office to which you submitted your application receives it, the office will date, stamp, log, and open your file. The office may acknowledge receipt with more forms, sample exam questions, or a simple receipt slip. You may hear nothing at all for months.

Eventually you will receive a testing date or an interview appointment. Write these on your calendar in red so that you don't let the dates slip by. Write the address to which you are to report in the same place. If you receive an admission ticket for an exam, be sure to put it in a safe place; but keep it in sight so that you will not forget to take it with you to the exam. With an exam date, you should get information about the exam. Time may be short. Begin to study and prepare right away if you have not already done so.

If the next step is an exam, that exam might be either a paper-and-pencil exam or a performance exam. The exam depends on the nature of the job. The applicant for a locksmith's position might be asked to cut some complicated keys and to repair a broken lock; the track maintainer hopeful might have to replace ties or reset switches. The applicant for a position as a clerk-stenographer might have to take dictation and a typing test, along with a multiple-choice test of general clerical abilities. Applicants for most jobs will take only a written test. The written test is most frequently a multiple-choice test, one in which the test-taker chooses the best of four or five answer choices and marks the answer on a separate answer sheet. Multiple-choice tests are machine scored. Machine scoring insures accuracy and objectivity. No one can misinterpret your answers. Machine scoring also allows for many applicants to be rated at the same time.

Occasionally, the written test will consist of an essay portion along with or instead of the multiple-choice section. Essays usually appear at levels above initial entry level where there are fewer applicants and fewer papers to score. On an essay, the examiners are looking for indications that you can organize your thoughts and can express them effectively in writing.

If you are called for an exam, arrive promptly and dress appropriately. Neatness is always appropriate; however, you do not need to dress up for a performance exam or for a written exam. If you will do manual work for your performance exam, wear clean work clothes. For a written exam, neat, casual clothing is fine.

THE INTERVIEW

If there is no exam and you are called directly to an interview, what you wear is more important. Take special care to look businesslike and professional. You must not appear to be too casual, and certainly not sloppy. Overdressing is also inappropriate. A neat dress or skirted suit is fine for women; men should wear a shirt and tie with suit or slacks and a jacket. And pay attention to your grooming.

Interviews take up an interviewer's time. If you are called for an interview, you are under serious consideration. There may still be competition for the job; someone else may be more suited than you, but you are qualified and your skills and background have appealed to someone in the hiring office. The interview may be aimed at getting information about:

- **Your knowledge.** The interviewer wants to know what you know about the area in which you will work. For instance, if you will be doing data entry in a budget office, what do you know about the budget process? Are you at all interested in this area of financial planning? You may also be asked questions probing your knowledge of the agency for which you are interviewing. Do you care enough to have educated yourself about the functions and role of the agency, whether it's child welfare, pollution control, or international trade?

- **Your judgment.** You may be faced with hypothetical situations, job-related or interpersonal relations, and be asked "What would you do if . . . ?" questions. Think carefully before answering. You must be decisive but diplomatic. There are no "right answers." The interviewer is aware that you are being put on the spot. How well you can handle this type of question is an indication of your flexibility and maturity.
- **Your personality.** You will have to be trained and supervised. You will have to work with others. What is your attitude? How will you fit in? The interviewer will be trying to make judgments in these areas on the basis of general conversation with you and from your responses to specific lines of questioning. Be pleasant, polite, and open with your answers, but do not volunteer a great deal of extra information. Stick to the subjects introduced by the interviewer. Answer fully, but resist the temptation to ramble on.
- **Your attitude toward work conditions.** These are practical concerns: If the job will require frequent travel for extended periods, how do you feel about it? What is your family's attitude? If you will be very unhappy about the travel, you may leave the job and your training will have been a waste of the taxpayers' money. The interviewer also wants to know how you will react to overtime or irregular shifts.

Remember, working for the government is working for the people. Government revenues come from taxes. The hiring officers have a responsibility to put the right people into the right jobs in order to spend the taxpayers' money most effectively. And, as a government employee, you have a responsibility to give the people (including yourself) their money's worth.

Other steps along the hiring route may be a medical examination, physical performance testing, and psychological interviewing. If there is a written test, these steps do not occur until the written tests are scored and ranked. Steps that require the time of one examiner with one applicant are taken only when there is reasonable expectation of hiring.

MEDICAL EXAMINATION

A medical exam is self-explanatory. If there are eyesight or hearing requirements for the position, these must be checked against agency standards. If the job requires standing, lifting, or running, the applicant must be medically able to withstand the rigors. Since all government employers afford some sort of health coverage, there must be assurance of the general health of the employee or at least full awareness of current or potential problems. Drug testing is often included. Drug testing is legal if applied routinely and equally to all applicants and if notice of it is given beforehand.

PHYSICAL PERFORMANCE TEST

Physical performance testing is limited to applicants for physically demanding jobs. Police officers, firefighters, and correction officers, for example, must be able to run, climb, and carry, often under stress of personal danger as well as under the pressures of the immediate situation. Mail handlers and sanitation workers must be able to lift and carry many heavy loads, one after the other. Usually the physical performance test is a qualifying test—either you can do it or you can't. Sometimes, especially where speed may be a crucial element, the physical test is competitively scored and enters into the rating the candidate earns for placement on the certification list.

PSYCHOLOGICAL INTERVIEW

Finally, there is the psychological interview. This interview differs from the general information interview or the final hiring and placement interview in that it tries to assess your behavior under stress. Not all applicants for government jobs are subjected to a psychological interview. It is limited to persons who will carry guns, to people who must make very quick decisions at moments of danger, and to people who might find themselves under interrogation by hostile forces. In other words, police officers, firefighters, and CIA and DEA (Drug Enforcement Agency) agents, to name just a few, must be able to do their jobs without "cracking" under the pressure.

Reading all the applications and weeding out the unqualified ones takes time. Weighing education and experience takes time. Administering and scoring exams takes time. Interviews, medical exams, and physical performance tests take time. Verifying references takes time. Finally, the vacancies must occur, and the government agency must have the funds to fill the vacancies.

All of this clarifies why you must not leave a job or a job search at any step along the way. Wait until you are offered your government job before you cut other ties. But when you finally do get that job, you will have a good income, many benefits, and job security.

PREPARING YOURSELF FOR CIVIL SERVICE EMPLOYMENT

Most federal, state, and municipal units have recruitment procedures for filling civil service positions. They have developed a number of methods to make job opportunities known. Places where such information may be obtained include:

1. **The offices of the State Employment Services.** There are almost two thousand throughout the country. These offices are administered by the state in which they are located, with the financial assistance of the federal government. You will find the address of the one nearest you in your telephone book.
2. **Your state Civil Service Commission.** Address your inquiry to the capital city of your state.
3. **Your city Civil Service Commission.** It is sometimes called by another name, such as the Department of Personnel, but you will be able to identify it in your telephone directory under the listing of city departments.
4. **Your municipal building and your local library.**
5. **Complete listings are carried by such newspapers as *The Chief-Leader* (published in New York City), as well as by other city and state-wide publications devoted to civil service employees.** Many local newspapers run a section on regional civil service news.
6. **State and local agencies looking for competent employees will contact schools, professional societies, veterans organizations, unions, and trade associations.**
7. **School boards and boards of education, which employ the greatest proportion of all state and local personnel, should be asked directly for information about job openings.**

THE FORMAT OF THE JOB ANNOUNCEMENT

When a position is open and a civil service examination is to be given for it, a job announcement is drawn up. This generally contains everything an applicant has to know about the job.

The announcement begins with the job title and salary. A typical announcement then describes the work, the location of the position, the education and experience requirements, the kind of examination to be given, and the system of rating. It may also have something to say about veteran preference and the age limit. It tells which application form is to be filled out, where to get the form, and where and when to file it.

Study the job announcement carefully. It will answer many of your questions and help you decide whether you like the position and are qualified for it.

There is no point in applying for a position and taking the examination if you do not want to work where the job is. The job may be in your community or hundreds of miles away at the other end of the state. If you are not willing to work where the job is, study other announcements that will give you an opportunity to work in a place of your choice. A civil service job close to your home has an additional advantage since local residents usually receive preference in appointments.

The words **Optional Fields**—sometimes just the word **Options**—may appear on the front page of the announcement. You then have a choice to apply for that particular position in which you are especially interested. This is because the duties of various positions are quite different even though they bear the same broad title. A public relations clerk, for example, does different work from a payroll clerk, although they are considered broadly in the same general area.

Not every announcement has options. But whether or not it has them, the precise duties are described in detail, usually under the heading **Description of Work.** Make sure that these duties come within the range of your experience and ability.

Most job requirements give a **deadline for filing** an application. Others bear the words **No Closing Date** at the top of the first page; this means that applications will be accepted until the needs of the agency are met. In some cases a public notice is issued when a certain number of applications has been received. No application mailed past the deadline date will be considered.

Every announcement has a detailed section on **education and experience requirements** for the particular job and for the optional fields. Make sure that in both education and experience you meet the minimum qualifications. If you do not meet the given standards for one job, there may be others open where you stand a better chance of making the grade.

If the job announcement does not mention **veteran preference,** it would be wise to inquire if there is such a provision in your state or municipality. There may be none or it may be limited to disabled veterans. In some jurisdictions, surviving spouses of disabled veterans are given preference. All such information can be obtained through the agency that issues the job announcement.

Applicants may be denied examinations and eligible candidates may be denied appointments for any of the following reasons:

- Intentional false statements
- Deception or fraud in examination or appointment
- Use of intoxicating beverages to the extent that ability to perform the duties of the position is impaired
- Criminal, infamous, dishonest, immoral, or notoriously disgraceful conduct

The announcement describes the **kind of test** given for the particular position. Please pay special attention to this section. It tells what areas are to be covered in the written test and lists the specific subjects on which questions will be asked. Sometimes sample questions are given.

Usually the announcement states whether the examination is to be **assembled** or **unassembled.** In an assembled examination applicants assemble in the same place at the same time to take a written or performance test. The unassembled examination is one where an applicant does not take a test; instead, he or she is rated on his or her education and experience and whatever records of past achievement the applicant is asked to provide.

In the competitive examination, all applicants for a position compete with each other; the better the mark, the better the chance of being appointed. Also, competitive examinations are given to determine desirability for promotion among employees.

Civil service written tests are rated on a scale of 100, with 70 usually as the passing mark.

FILLING OUT THE APPLICATION FORM

Having studied the job announcement and having decided that you want the position and are qualified for it, your next step is to get an application form. The job announcement tells you where to send for it.

On the whole, civil service application forms differ little from state to state and locality to locality. The questions that have been worked out after years of experimentation are simple and direct, designed to elicit a maximal amount of information about you.

Many prospective civil service employees have failed to get a job because of slipshod, erroneous, incomplete, misleading, or untruthful answers. Give the application serious attention, for it is the first important step toward getting the job you want.

Here, along with some helpful comments, are the questions usually asked on the average application form, although not necessarily in this order.

- **Name of examination or kind of position applied for.** This information appears in large type on the first page of the job announcement.
- **Optional job** (if mentioned in the announcement). If you wish to apply for an option, simply copy the title from the announcement. If you are not interested in an option, write *None.*
- **Primary place of employment applied for.** The location of the position was probably contained in the announcement. You must consider whether you want to work there. The announcement may list more than one location where the job is open. If you would accept employment in any of the places, list them all; otherwise list the specific place or places where you would be willing to work.
- **Name and address.** Give in full, including your middle name if you have one, and your maiden name as well if you are a married woman.
- **Home and office phones.** If none, write *None.*
- **Legal or voting residence.** The state in which you vote is the one you list here.
- **Height without shoes, weight, sex.** Answer accurately.
- **Date of birth.** Give the exact day, month, and year.
- **Lowest grade or pay you will accept.** Although the salary is clearly stated in the job announcement, there may be a quicker opening in the same occupation but carrying less responsibility and thus a lower basic entrance salary. You will not be considered for a job paying less than the amount you give in answer to this question.
- **Will you accept temporary employment if offered you for (a) one month or less, (b) one to four months, (c) four to twelve months?** Temporary positions come up frequently and it is important to know whether you are available.
- **Will you accept less than full-time employment?** Part-time work comes up now and then. Consider whether you want to accept such a position while waiting for a full-time appointment.
- **Were you in active military service in the Armed Forces of the United States?** Veterans' preference, if given, is usually limited to active service during the following periods: 12/7/41–12/31/46; 6/27/50–1/31/55; 6/1/63–5/7/75; 6/1/83–12/1/87; 10/23/83–11/21/83; 12/20/89–1/3/90; 8/2/90 to end of current Persian Gulf hostilities.
- **Do you claim disabled veterans credit?** If you do, you have to show proof of a war-incurred disability compensable by at least 10 percent. This is done through certification by the Department of Veterans Affairs.
- **Special qualifications and skills.** Even though not directly related to the position for which you are applying, information about licenses and certificates obtained for teacher, pilot, registered nurse, and so on, is requested. List your experience in the use of machines and equipment and whatever other skills you have acquired. Also list published writings, public speaking experience, membership in professional societies, and honors and fellowships received.

- **Education.** List your entire educational history, including all diplomas, degrees, and special courses taken in any accredited or armed forces school. Also give your credits toward a college or a graduate degree.
- **References.** The names of people who can give information about you, with their occupations and business and home address, are often requested.
- **Your health.** Questions are asked concerning your medical record. You are expected to have the physical and psychological capacity to perform the job for which you are applying. Standards vary, of course, depending on the requirements of the position. A physical handicap usually will not bar an applicant from a job he can perform adequately unless the safety of the public is involved.
- **Work history.** Considerable space is allotted on the form for the applicant to tell about all his/her past employment. Examiners check all such answers closely. Do not embellish or falsify your record. If you were ever fired, say so. It is better for you to state this openly than for the examiners to find out the truth from your former employer.

On the following pages, you'll find samples of a New York City Application for Examination and a State of Louisiana Application.

NEW YORK CITY APPLICATION FOR EXAMINATION

DEPARTMENT OF CITYWIDE ADMINISTRATIVE SERVICES
DIVISION OF CITYWIDE PERSONNEL SERVICES
1 Centre Street, 14th floor New York, NY 10007

APPLICATION FOR EXAMINATION

(Directions for completing this application are on the *back* of this form. Additional information is on the Special Circumstances Sheet)

Download this form on-line: nyc.gov/html/dcas

FOLLOW DIRECTIONS ON BACK
Fill in all requested information clearly, accurately, and completely.

The City will only process applications with complete, correct, legible information which are accompanied by correct payment or waiver documentation.

All unprocessed applications will be returned to the applicant.

1. EXAM #:

Check One: ☐ Open Competitive ☐ Promotion

2. EXAM TITLE:

3. SOCIAL SECURITY NUMBER: - -

4. LAST NAME:

5. FIRST NAME:

6. MIDDLE INITIAL:

7. MAILING ADDRESS:

8. APT. #:

9. CITY OR TOWN:

10. STATE:

11. ZIP CODE: -

12. PHONE: - -

13. OTHER NAMES USED IN CITY SERVICE:

Questions 14& 15:
Discrimination on the basisof sex, sexual orientation, race, creed, color, age, disability status, veteran status or religious observance is prohibited by law. The City of New York is an equalopportunity employer. The identifying information requested on this form is to be used to determine the representation of protected groups among applicants. This information is voluntary and will not be made available to individualsmaking hiring decisions.

14. RACE/ETHNICITY (Check One):
☐ White ☐ American Indian/ Alaskan Native
☐ Black
☐ Hispanic ☐ Asian/Pacific Islander

15. SEX (Check One):
☐ Male
☐ Female

16. ARE YOU EMPLOYED BY HEALTH AND HOSPITALS CORPORATION? (Check One):
☐ YES ☐ NO

17. CHECK ALL BOXES THAT APPLY TO YOU: (Directions for this section are found on the "Special Circumstances" Sheet)

☐ I AM A SABBATH OBSERVER AND WILL REQUEST AN ALTERNATE TEST DATE (Verification required. See Item A on Special Circumstances Sheet)
☐ I HAVE A DISABILITY AND WILL REQUEST SPECIAL ACCOMMODATIONS (Verification required. See Item B on Special Circumstances Sheet).
☐ I CLAIM VETERANS' CREDIT (For qualifications see Item C on Special Circumstances Sheet)
☐ I CLAIM DISABLED VETERANS' CREDIT (For qualifications see Item C on Special Circumstances Sheet)
☐ I CLAIM PARENT LEGACY CREDIT (For qualifications see Item D on Special Circumstances Sheet)
☐ I CLAIM SIBLING LEGACY CREDIT (For qualifications see Item D on Special Circumstances Sheet)

18. Your Signature: ______________________ **Date:** __________

NEW YORK CITY APPLICATION—page 2

MICHAEL R. BLOOMBERG
Mayor

MARTHA K. HIRST
Commissioner

NOTE: *You should apply for an examination **only** if you meet the qualification requirements set forth in the Notice of Examination. Read the Notice of Examination carefully before completing the application form.*

Fill in all requested information clearly, accurately, and completely. ***The City will only process applications with complete, correct, legible information which are accompanied by correct payment or waiver documentation. All unprocessed applications will be returned to the applicant.***

Included in this material is a voter registration form. If you take this opportunity to register to vote, please mail the postage-paid form directly to the Board of Elections. The provision of government services is not conditioned on being registered to vote.

When appropriate the City will issue a refund for unprocessed applications after the close of the filing period.

DIRECTIONS FOR SUBMITTING APPLICATION FOR EXAMINATION

FORMS	All required forms which are listed in the upper-right-hand corner of the Notice of Examination must accompany your application. Failure to include these forms may result in your disqualification and you will not receive test scores.
FEE	The amount of the fee is stated in the Notice of Examination. Only a ***MONEY ORDER*** made out to ***D.C.A.S. (EXAMS)*** is acceptable payment (check or cash **are not** accepted). On the front of the money order you must clearly write your ***full name, social security number*** and ***the exam number.*** Keep your Money Order receipt as proof of filing.
FEE WAIVER	A filing fee is not charged if you are a New York City resident receiving public/cash assistance from the New York City Department of Social Services. To have the fee waived, you **must** be receiving full benefits and not partial benefits. If you are eligible, you must enclose a legible photocopy of your current Benefit Card (**formerly known as the Medicaid Card**) with your application. **The Food Coupon Photo Identification Card is *unacceptable*.** You must write your ***social security number*** and the ***exam number*** on the front of the photocopy of the Benefit Card. The name on your application must exactly match the name printed on your Benefit Card. **Fee Waivers are limited to persons who are recipients of Public Assistance at the time of submission of the application.** Any person who falsifies information concerning current receipt of Public Assistance in order to obtain a fee waiver may be banned from appointment to any position within the City of New York, and may be subject to criminal prosecution. All such violations will be referred to the Department of Investigation.
APPLICATION SUBMISSION	Your application must be postmarked no later than the last day of the application period indicated on the Notice of Examination. Mail the completed application, supporting documents, and required filing fee or fee waiver to: DCAS Application Section 1 Centre Street, 14th Floor, New York, NY 10007 C/O ***Exam #, Exam Title***

INSTRUCTIONS FOR COMPLETING APPLICATION FORM PROPERLY

To ensure proper processing of Application print all information *CLEARLY.* Failure to do so will delay or disqualify your application.

1. EXAM NO. / EXAM TITLE	See the Notice of Examination prior to filling in the exact exam number and exam title. Check either the Open Competitive (OC) or Promotion (PRO) box to indicate the type of examination you are applying for.
2. - 12. GENERAL INFORMATION	$ The address you give will be used as your mailing address for all official correspondence. $ Only one (1) address for each person is maintained in the files of this Department. $ If you change your mailing address after applying, see the Change Of Address section on Special Circumstances Sheet.
13. OTHER NAMES USED	If you have worked for a New York City agency under another name, write the other name in this section. If you have not used other names, skip this section.
14. - 15. ETHNICITY / SEX	Completing this information is voluntary. This information will not be made available to individuals making hiring decisions.
16. HHC EMPLOYEE	If you are employed by the Health and Hospitals Corporation, check the **YES** box in this section.
17. SPECIAL CIRCUMSTANCES	(Sabbath/Religious Observers, Special Accommodations because of a Disability, Veterans' or Disabled Veterans' Credit, Parent or Sibling Legacy Credit) Please see the "Special Circumstances" direction sheet for qualifications and definitions associated with this section.
18. SIGNATURE	Signing the application indicates that all statements you provided on this form and all other forms required for this examination are true and subject to the penalties of perjury.

Applicants who do not receive an admission card at least **4 days** prior to the tentative test date must obtain an admission card by coming to the Examining Service Section of the New York City Department of Citywide Administrative Services, 1 Centre Street, 14th Floor, Room 1448.

Rev. 05/2004

NEW YORK CITY APPLICATION—page 3

DEPARTMENT OF CITYWIDE ADMINISTRATIVE SERVICES
DIVISION OF CITYWIDE PERSONNEL SERVICES

Exam Support Group – Application Section
One Centre Street, 14th Floor
New York, NY 10007
Automated Telephone: (212) 669-1357 • Fax: (212) 669-4734

APPLICATION SUPPLEMENT

Exam Title: ______________________ **Exam No:** ______

Section 50-b of the New York State Civil Service Law requires that all applicants for Civil Service examinations be asked the following questions:

1. Do you have any loans made or guaranteed by the New York State Higher Education Services Corporation which are currently outstanding?

CHECK <u>ONLY</u> ONE: YES ☐ NO ☐

RETURN THIS SUPPLEMENT WITH YOUR APPLICATION FOR CIVIL SERVICE EXAMINATION <u>ONLY</u> IF YOU HAVE CHECKED THE YES BOX.

2. If you checked the YES box in *Question 1,* are you presently in default on such loan?

CHECK <u>ONLY</u> ONE: YES ☐ NO ☐

SOCIAL SECURITY NUMBER: ☐☐☐ - ☐☐ - ☐☐☐☐

<u>PLEASE PRINT CLEARLY:</u>

FULL NAME: ______________________
(Last Name, First Name, Middle Initial)

ADDRESS: ______________________
(Include the Apartment Number, Floor, and/or In Care of- C/O, if applicable)

CITY, STATE, ZIP: ______________________

COMPLETE THIS AFFIRMATION: I affirm under penalties of perjury that all statements made on this application and all supplementary information are true.

Signature: ______________________ **Date:** ___/___/___

DP-2512A (Rev. 05/2003)

The Official New York City Web Site
www.nyc.gov

STATE OF LOUISIANA APPLICATION—page 1

SF10
REV.10/03

APPLICANT: READ THE INSTRUCTIONS ON PAGE 2 BEFORE FILLING OUT THIS APPLICATION
Print clearly or type. Staple all loose pages before submitting application.

STATE PRE-EMPLOYMENT APPLICATION

STATE OF LOUISIANA
DEPARTMENT OF CIVIL SERVICE
P.O. BOX 94111, Capitol Station
Baton Rouge, Louisiana 70804-9111

AN EQUAL OPPORTUNITY EMPLOYER

FOR OFFICE USE

Action(s)______ JS NO.
Session______ V.P
Data Entry Completed______ S.R.
ISIS ______

LAST FIRST MI
Print Name Above

SEE INSTRUCTIONS ON PAGE 2

Parish of Residence | Are you 18 or older? ☐ Yes ☐ No | Other names ever used

Social Security Number

NAME – First | Middle | Last

Mailing Address

Work Telephone No. ( ) -

City | State | Zip Code

Home Telephone No. ( ) -

ARE YOU REQUESTING A REGRADE? ☐ **YES** ☐ **NO**

Email Address

Register, JobTitle(s) or Test Series Applied for	FOR OFFICE USE SER	CD	REJ	GRD	TR	ADDITIONAL TITLES	SER	CD	REJ	GRD	TR

ALL TITLES LISTED ABOVE MUST HAVE THE SAME SERIES NO.

JOB LOCATION AVAILABILITY – IMPORTANT: Mark at least one (1), but no more than twenty (20) parishes. Mark only the parish (es) where you are willing to work. If you fail to reply to an inquiry or decline an offer of employment in a parish you marked, you will be removed from the eligible list. Availability information on your most recent SF-10 will be your availability for all jobs for which you have applied.

☐ 01 Acadia	☐ 09 Caddo	☐ 17 E B R	☐ 25 Jackson	☐ 33 Madison	☐ 41 Red River	☐ 49 St Landry	☐ 57 Vermilion
☐ 02 Allen	☐ 10 Calcasieu	☐ 18 E. Carroll	☐ 26 Jefferson	☐ 34 Morehouse	☐ 42 Richland	☐ 50 St Martin	☐ 58 Vernon
☐ 03 Ascension	☐ 11 Caldwell	☐ 19 E. Feliciana	☐ 27 Jeff Davis	☐ 35 Natchitoches	☐ 43 Sabine	☐ 51 St Mary	☐ 59 Washington
☐ 04 Assumption	☐ 12 Cameron	☐ 20 Evangeline	☐ 28 Lafayette	☐ 36 Orleans	☐ 44 St Bernard	☐ 52 St. Tammany	☐ 60 Webster
☐ 05 Avoylles	☐ 13 Catahoula	☐ 21 Franklin	☐ 29 Lafourche	☐ 37 Ouachita	☐ 45 St Charles	☐ 53 Tangipahoa	☐ 61 WBR
☐ 06 Beauregard	☐ 14 Claiborne	☐ 22 Grant	☐ 30 LaSalle	☐ 38 Plaquemines	☐ 46 St Helena	☐ 54 Tensas	☐ 62 W Carroll
☐ 07 Bienville	☐ 15 Concordia	☐ 23 Iberia	☐ 31 Lincoln	☐ 39 Pte. Coupee	☐ 47 St James	☐ 55 Terrebonne	☐ 63 W. Feliciana
☐ 08 Bossier	☐ 16 DeSoto	☐ 24 Iberville	☐ 32 Livingston	☐ 40 Rapides	☐ 48 St John	☐ 56 Union	☐ 64 Winn

Please check the type of employment you will accept:
☐ **Permanent** ☐ **Temporary**

Note: Temporary Appointments are no more than 36 months.

Are you claiming Veteran's Preference points on this application?
☐ YES (If "Yes" complete military service information on Page 3)
☐ NO

AUTHORITY TO RELEASE INFORMATION: I consent to the release of information concerning my capacity and/or all aspects of prior job performance by employers, educational institutions, law enforcement agencies, and other individuals and agencies to duly accredited investigators, human resources staff, and other authorized employees of the state government for the purpose of determining my eligibility and suitability for employment.

I certify that all statements made on this application and any attached papers are true and complete to the best of my knowledge. I understand that information on this application may be subject to investigation and verification and that any misrepresentation or material omission may cause my application to be rejected, my name to be removed from the eligible register and/or subject me to dismissal from state service.

I HAVE READ THE STATEMENTS ABOVE CAREFULLY BEFORE SIGNING THIS APPLICATION:

Signature of Applicant: ______ **Social Security No. (For Verification):** ☐☐☐☐☐☐☐☐☐

Date:

1

STATE OF LOUISIANA APPLICATION—page 2

General Instructions

- Be sure you include your Social Security Number and Zip Code.
- Answer all questions and provide complete information about prior employment and education.
- List ALL prior employment. Attach additional sheets if needed.
- Keep a copy of your completed application for your own records.
- Do NOT submit a resume instead of this application.
- If responding to a vacancy posted on the web, follow the instructions in the posting carefully.

If you are applying to take a Civil Service Test:

- Bring a completed application; picture I.D. and proof of Social Security number with you to one of our testing centers.
- Visit our website at www.civilservice.louisiana.gov for test dates, times and locations.

Note: If you need special testing accommodations due to a disability, please contact the Civil Service Staffing Division at 225-342-8536 to make arrangements prior to testing.

If you wish to claim Veteran's Preference for wartime service or a campaign badge or medal:

- Attach a copy of your DD214 to your application.
- Complete Section on Active Military Service/Veteran's Preference.

Note: If you have already received veteran's preference points on Civil Service scores within the past year, you do not need to submit a DD214 with this application

See Veteran's Points Information on our website at www.civilservice.louisiana.gov for a list of qualifying service periods and information about additional preference for disabled veterans or their families. Click on "Applying For Jobs", or " Testing Information."

Definitions of terms used on application form.

Register: A group of jobs, which have identical Minimum Qualifications and use the same selection procedure (test). To apply for one or more jobs on a register, simply write the register title on the application rather than each of the individual job titles. For example, Administrative Specialist 4 and Administrative Manager 1 are both on the PET General Admin register. To apply for both jobs write "PET Gen Admin" under "REGISTER, JOB TITLE (S) OR TEST SERIES APPLIED FOR".

Series Number: A four-digit number identifying a test of selection procedure. Registers with the same series number can be applied for on one application form. **Registers with different series numbers require separate application forms.**

Regrade: The process used to apply for additional job titles using an already established Civil Service test grade record without re-taking the test.

Please ans wer the following questions,

☐ **Yes** ☐ **No** Do you possess a valid driver's license?

☐ **Yes** ☐ **No** Do you possess a valid commercial driver's license?

☐ **Yes** ☐ **No** Are you currently holding or running for an elective public office?

☐ **Yes** ☐ **No** Have you ever been on probation or sentenced to jail/prison as a result of a felony conviction or guilty plea to a felony charge? If "Yes", give the law enforcement authority (city police, sheriff, FBI, etc.) the offense, date of offense, place and disposition of case.

☐ **Yes** ☐ **No** Have you ever been fired from a job or resigned to avoid dismissal? If "YES" answer, please explain. A "YES" answer will not necessarily bar you from state employment.

If you are a male from the ages of 18 through 25, please answer the following question "YES" of "NO".

☐ Yes ☐ No Are you registered with the Selective Service System or exempted from such registration?

☐ **Does not Apply** If you are not a male in this age group, check "does not apply".

2

STATE OF LOUISIANA APPLICATION—page 3

NAME ____________________

ACTIVE MILITARY SERVICE/ VETERAN'S PREFERENCE

If you are a first time applicant, of if you are claiming Veteran's Preference for the first time, required PROOF MUST BE ATTACHED to this application to have preference points added to your score.

List the dates (month and year) and branch for all ACTIVE DUTY military service. Was this service performed on an active, full-time basis with full pay and allowances? (Check YES or NO for each period of service.)

FROM	TO	BRANCH OF SERVICE	YES	NO
			☐	☐
			☐	☐
			☐	☐

List all GRADES held and dates of each grade. Begin with highest grade. IMPORTANT: Use E-, or O-, or WO-grade.

FROM	TO	GRADE HELD	FROM	TO	GRADE HELD

TRAINING AND EDUCATION

Have you received a high school diploma or equivalency certificate?

☐ YES Date received ____________

☐ NO Highest grade and date completed ____________

A. LIST BUSINESS, VOCATIONAL OR TECHNICAL COLLEGES OR SCHOOLS ATTENDED	NAME/LOCATION OF SCHOOL	Dates Attended (Month & Year) FROM	TO	Did You Graduate? YES	NO	TITLE OF PROGRAM	SEM HRS	CLOCK HOURS PER WEEK
				☐	☐			
				☐	☐			
				☐	☐			

List any accounting Practice sets completed ____________________

B. LIST COLLEGES OR UNIVERSITIES ATTENDED (Include graduate or professional school)	NAME OF COLLEGE OR UNIVERSITY/ CITY AND STATE	Dates Attended (Month & Year) FROM	TO	Total Credit Hours Earned Sem	OR Qtr	Type of Degree Earned (BA,MA, etc)	Major Field of Study	Date Degree Received (Month & Year)

C. MAJOR SUBJECTS	CHIEF UNDERGRADUATE SUBJECTS (Show Major on Line 1.)	Total Credit Hours Earned Semester	OR Quarter	CHIEF GRADUATE SUBJECTS (Show Major on Line 1.)	Total Credit Hours Earned Semester	OR Quarter

LICENSES AND CERTIFICATION

List any job-related licenses or certificates that you have (CPA, Registered Nurse, P.E., etc.)

	TYPE OF PROFESSIONAL LICENSE OR CERTIFICATE (Specify Which One)	DATE ORIGINALLY LICENSED/OR CERTIFIED	EXPIRATION DATE	NAME AND ADDRESS OF LICENSING OR CERTIFYING AGENCY
1				
2				

TYPING SPEED

WPM

3

STATE OF LOUISIANA APPLICATION—page 4

IF YOU DO NOT ANSWER ALL QUESTIONS COMPLETELY, YOUR APPLICATION MAY BE REJECTED OR DELAYED SEVERAL WEEKS, AND YOU WILL MISS JOB OPPORTUNITIES.

NAME

WORK EXPERIENCE – IMPORTANT: List all jobs and activities including military service, part-time employment, self-employment, and volunteer work. BEGIN with your FIRST job in Block A; END with your MOST RECENT or PRESENT job.

A EMPLOYER/COMPANY NAME		KIND OF BUSINESS	
STREET ADDRESS		YOUR OFFICIAL JOB TITLE	
CITY AND STATE	TELEPHONE NUMBER ( )	BEGINNING SALARY	ENDING SALARY
DATES OF EMPLOYMENT (Mo/Da/YR) **FROM** / / **TO** / /	AVERAGE HRS. WORKED PER WEEK	REASON FOR LEAVING	NO. OF EMPLOYEES YOU DIRECTLY SUPERVISED
NAME / TITLE AND PHONE NO. OF YOUR SUPERVISOR		LIST JOB TITLES OF EMPLOYEES YOU DIRECTLY SUPERVISED	
NAME / TITLE OF PERSON WHO CAN VERIFY THIS EMPLOYMENT			

DUTIES: List the major duties involved with job and give an approximate percentage of time spent on each duty.

% OF TIME	MAJOR DUTIES
100%	

B EMPLOYER/COMPANY NAME		KIND OF BUSINESS	
STREET ADDRESS		YOUR OFFICIAL JOB TITLE	
CITY AND STATE	TELEPHONE NUMBER ( )	BEGINNING SALARY	ENDING SALARY
DATES OF EMPLOYMENT (Mo/Da/YR) **FROM** / / **TO** / /	AVERAGE HRS. WORKED PER WEEK	REASON FOR LEAVING	NO. OF EMPLOYEES YOU DIRECTLY SUPERVISED
NAME / TITLE AND PHONE NO. OF YOUR SUPERVISOR		LIST JOB TITLES OF EMPLOYEES YOU DIRECTLY SUPERVISED	
NAME / TITLE OF PERSON WHO CAN VERIFY THIS EMPLOYMENT			

DUTIES: List the major duties involved with job and give an approximate percentage of time spent on each duty.

% OF TIME	MAJOR DUTIES
100%	

4

STATE OF LOUISIANA APPLICATION—page 5

WORK EXPERIENCE – IMPORTANT: List all jobs and activities including military service, part-time employment, self-employment, and volunteer work. BEGIN with your FIRST job in Block A; END with your MOST RECENT or PRESENT job.

C EMPLOYER/COMPANY NAME	KIND OF BUSINESS
STREET ADDRESS	YOUR OFFICIAL JOB TITLE
CITY AND STATE / TELEPHONE NUMBER ( )	BEGINNING SALARY / ENDING SALARY
DATES OF EMPLOYMENT (Mo/Da/YR) **FROM** / / **TO** / / / AVERAGE HRS. WORKED PER WEEK	REASON FOR LEAVING / NO. OF EMPLOYEES YOU DIRECTLY SUPERVISED
NAME / TITLE AND PHONE NO. OF YOUR SUPERVISOR	LIST JOB TITLES OF EMPLOYEES YOU DIRECTLY SUPERVISED
NAME / TITLE OF PERSON WHO CAN VERIFY THIS EMPLOYMENT	

DUTIES: % OF TIME	**List the major duties involved with job and give an approximate percentage of time spent on each duty.** MAJOR DUTIES
100%	

D EMPLOYER/COMPANY NAME	KIND OF BUSINESS
STREET ADDRESS	YOUR OFFICIAL JOB TITLE
CITY AND STATE / TELEPHONE NUMBER ( )	BEGINNING SALARY / ENDING SALARY
DATES OF EMPLOYMENT (Mo/Da/YR) **FROM** / / **TO** / / / AVERAGE HRS. WORKED PER WEEK	REASON FOR LEAVING / NO. OF EMPLOYEES YOU DIRECTLY SUPERVISED
NAME / TITLE AND PHONE NO. OF YOUR SUPERVISOR	LIST JOB TITLES OF EMPLOYEES YOU DIRECTLY SUPERVISED
NAME / TITLE OF PERSON WHO CAN VERIFY THIS EMPLOYMENT	

DUTIES: % OF TIME	**List the major duties involved with job and give an approximate percentage of time spent on each duty.** MAJOR DUTIES
100%	

5

STATE OF LOUISIANA APPLICATION—page 6

WORK EXPERIENCE – IMPORTANT: List all jobs and activities including military service, part-time employment, self-employment, and volunteer work. BEGIN with your FIRST job in Block A; END with your MOST RECENT or PRESENT job.

E

EMPLOYER/COMPANY NAME		KIND OF BUSINESS	
STREET ADDRESS		YOUR OFFICIAL JOB TITLE	
CITY AND STATE	TELEPHONE NUMBER ( )	BEGINNING SALARY	ENDING SALARY
DATES OF EMPLOYMENT (Mo/Da/YR) **FROM** / / **TO** / /	AVERAGE HRS. WORKED PER WEEK	REASON FOR LEAVING	NO. OF EMPLOYEES YOU DIRECTLY SUPERVISED
NAME / TITLE AND PHONE NO. OF YOUR SUPERVISOR		LIST JOB TITLES OF EMPLOYEES YOU DIRECTLY SUPERVISED	
NAME / TITLE OF PERSON WHO CAN VERIFY THIS EMPLOYMENT			

DUTIES: **List the major duties involved with job and give an approximate percentage of time spent on each duty.**

% OF TIME	**MAJOR DUTIES**
100%	

F

EMPLOYER/COMPANY NAME		KIND OF BUSINESS	
STREET ADDRESS		YOUR OFFICIAL JOB TITLE	
CITY AND STATE	TELEPHONE NUMBER ( )	BEGINNING SALARY	ENDING SALARY
DATES OF EMPLOYMENT (Mo/Da/YR) **FROM** / / TO / /	AVERAGE HRS. WORKED PER WEEK	REASON FOR LEAVING	NO. OF EMPLOYEES YOU DIRECTLY SUPERVISED
NAME / TITLE PHONE NO. OF YOUR SUPERVISOR		LIST JOB TITLES OF EMPLOYEES YOU DIRECTLY SUPERVISED	
NAME / TITLE OF PERSON WHO CAN VERIFY THIS EMPLOYMENT			

DUTIES: **List the major duties involved with job and give an approximate percentage of time spent on each duty.**

% OF TIME	**MAJOR DUTIES**
100%	

FOR ADDITIONAL WORK EXPERIENCE OR INFORMATION, ATTACH SF10A OR 8 ½ X 11 PAPER. USE SAME FORMAT AS WORK EXPERIENCE ON THIS APPLICATION.

6

STATE OF LOUISIANA APPLICATION—page 7

State of Louisiana

Pre-employment Application
Standard Form 10(SF-10)
www.civilservice.louisiana.gov

APPLICANT EEO DATA FORM

Voluntary Applicant Information

The STATE OF LOUISIANA requests the data below so we may comply with federal Equal Employment Opportunity Law requirements. The information is strictly **VOLUNTARY** and in no way influences employment prospects.

Ethnic Origin:

☐ Hispanic or Latino ☐ Non-Hispanic or Non-Latino

Race: (Please check all that apply)

☐ White ☐ Asian

☐ American Indian / Alaskan Native ☐ Black or African American

☐ Native Hawaiian or Other Pacific Islander ☐ Other: ____________

Gender: **Date of Birth:**

☐ Male ☐ Female

How did you find out about this job?

☐ Civil Service Website ☐ Paper Announcement at Agency ☐ Newspaper Ad

☐ Flier ☐ Career Fair ☐ Word of Mouth ☐ Other: ____________

7

TEST-TAKING TECHNIQUES

Many factors enter into a high test score. The most important factor should be your ability to answer the questions, which in turn indicates the ability to learn and perform the duties of the job. Assuming that you have this ability, knowing what to expect on the exam and familiarity with techniques of effective test taking should give you the confidence you need to do your best on the exam.

There is no quick substitute for long-term study and development of your skills and abilities to prepare you for doing well on tests. However, there are some steps you can take to help you do the very best that you are prepared to do. Some of these steps are done before the test, and some are followed when you are taking the test. Knowing these steps is often called being "test-wise." Following these steps may help you feel more confident as you take the actual test.

"Test-wiseness" is a general term which simply means being familiar with some good procedures to follow when getting ready for and taking a test. The procedures fall into four major areas: (1) being prepared, (2) avoiding careless errors, (3) managing your time, and (4) guessing.

BE PREPARED

Don't make the test harder than it has to be by not preparing yourself. You are taking a very important step in preparation by reading this book and taking the sample tests which are included. This will help you to become familiar with the tests and the kinds of questions you will have to answer.

As you use this book, read the sample questions and directions for taking the test carefully. Then, when you take the sample tests, time yourself as you will be timed in the real test.

As you are working on the sample questions, don't look at the correct answers before you try to answer them on your own. This can fool you into thinking you understand a question when you really don't. Try it on your own first, then compare your answer with the one given. Remember, in a sample test, you are your own grader; you don't gain anything by pretending to understand something you really don't.

On the examination day assigned to you, allow the test itself to be the main attraction of the day. Do not squeeze it in between other activities. Be sure to bring the admission card, identification, and pencils, as instructed. Prepare these the night before so that you are not flustered by a last-minute search. Arrive rested, relaxed, and on time. In fact, plan to arrive a little bit early. Leave plenty of time for traffic tie-ups or other complications that might upset you and interfere with your test performance.

In the test room, the examiner will hand out forms for you to fill out. He or she will give you the instructions that you must follow in taking the examination. The examiner will tell you how to fill in the grids on the forms. Time limits and timing signals will be explained. If you do not understand any of the examiner's instructions, ASK QUESTIONS. It would be ridiculous to score less than your best because of poor communication.

At the examination, you must follow instructions exactly. Fill in the grids on the forms carefully and accurately. Misgridding may lead to loss of veterans' credits to which you may be entitled or misaddressing of your test results. Do not begin until you are told to begin. Stop as soon as the examiner tells you to stop. Do not turn pages until you are told to do so. Do not go back to parts you have already completed. Any infraction of the rules is considered cheating. If you cheat, your test paper will not be scored, and you will not be eligible for appointment.

The answer sheet for most multiple-choice exams is machine scored. You cannot give any explanations to the machine, so you must fill out the answer sheet clearly and correctly.

HOW TO MARK YOUR ANSWER SHEET

1. Blacken your answer space firmly and completely. ● is the only correct way to mark the answer sheet. ◐, ⊗, ⊘, and ∅ are all unacceptable. The machine might not read them at all.
2. Mark only one answer for each question. If you mark more than one answer, you will be considered wrong, even if one of the answers is correct.
3. If you change your mind, you must erase your mark. Attempting to cross out an incorrect answer like this ● will not work. You must erase any incorrect answer completely. An incomplete erasure might be read as a second answer.
4. All of your answering should be in the form of blackened spaces. The machine cannot read English. Do not write any notes in the margins.
5. MOST IMPORTANT: Answer each question in the right place. Question 1 must be answered in space 1; question 52 in space 52. If you skip an answer space and mark a series of answers in the wrong places, you must erase all those answers and do the questions over, marking your answers in the proper places. You cannot afford to use the limited time in this way. Therefore, as you answer *each* question, look at its number and check that you are marking your answer in the space with the same number.
6. For the typing tests, type steadily and carefully. Just don't rush, since that's when the errors occur. Keep in mind that each error subtracts 1 wpm (words per minute) from your final score.

AVOID CARELESS ERRORS

Don't reduce your score by making careless mistakes. Always read the instructions for each test section carefully, even when you think you already know what the directions are. It's why we stress throughout this book that it's important to fully understand the directions for these different question-types *before* you go into the actual exam. It will not only reduce errors, but it will save you time—time you will need for the questions.

What if you don't understand the directions? You will have risked getting the answers wrong for a whole test section. As an example, vocabulary questions can sometimes test synonyms (words that have similar meanings), and sometimes test antonyms (words with opposite meanings). You can easily see how a mistake in understanding in this case could make a whole set of answers incorrect.

If you have time, reread any complicated instructions after you do the first few questions to check that you really do understand them. Of course, whenever you are allowed to, ask the examiner to clarify anything you don't understand.

Other careless mistakes affect only the response to particular questions. This often happens with arithmetic questions, but can happen with other questions as well. This type of error, called a "response error," usually stems from a momentary lapse of concentration.

Example:

The question reads: "The capital of Massachusetts is . . . ." The answer is (D) Boston, but you mark (B) because "B" is the first letter of the word "Boston."

Example:

The question reads: "8 – 5 = ..." The answer is (A) 3, but you mark (C) thinking "third letter."

A common error in Reading Comprehension questions is bringing your own information into the subject. For example, you may encounter a passage that discusses a subject you know something about. While this can make the passage easier to read, it can also tempt you to rely on your own knowledge about the subject. You must rely on information within the passage for your answers—in fact, sometimes the "wrong answer" for the questions are based on true information about the subject *not* given in the passage. Since the test-makers are testing your reading ability, rather than your general knowledge of the subject, an answer based on information not contained in the passage is considered incorrect.

MANAGE YOUR TIME

Before you begin, take a moment to plan your progress through the test. Although you are usually not expected to finish all of the questions given on a test, you should at least get an idea of how much time you should spend on each question in order to answer them all. For example, if there are 60 questions to answer and you have 30 minutes, you will have about half a minute to spend on each question.

Keep track of the time on your watch or the room clock, but do not fixate on the time remaining. Your task is to answer questions. Do not spend too much time on any one question. If you find yourself stuck, do not take the puzzler as a personal challenge. Either guess and mark the question in the question booklet or skip the question entirely, marking the question as a skip and taking care to skip the answer space on the answer sheet. If there is time at the end of the exam or exam part, you can return and give marked questions another try.

MULTIPLE-CHOICE QUESTIONS

Almost all of the tests given on civil service exams are multiple-choice format. This means that you normally have four or five answer choices. But it's not something that should be overwhelming. There is a basic technique to answering these types of questions. Once you've understood this technique, it will make your test-taking far less stressful.

First, there should only be one correct answer. Since these tests have been given time and again, and the test-developers have a sense of which questions work and which questions don't work, it will be rare that your choices will be ambiguous. They may be complex, and somewhat confusing, but there will still be only one right answer.

The first step is to look at the question, without looking at the answer choices. Now select the correct answer. That may sound somewhat simplistic, but it's usually the case that your first choice is the correct one. If you go back and change it, redo it again and again, it's more likely that you'll end up with the wrong answer. Thus, follow your instinct. Once you have come up with the answer, look at the answer choices. If your answer is one of the choices, you're probably correct. It's not 100 percent infallible, but it's a strong possibility that you've selected the right answer.

With math questions you should first solve the problem. If your answer is among the choices, you're probably correct. Don't ignore things like the proper function signs (adding, subtracting, multiplying, and dividing), negative and positive numbers, and so on.

But suppose you don't know the correct answer. You then use the "process of elimination." It's a time-honored technique for test-takers. There is always one correct answer. There is usually one answer choice that is totally incorrect—a "distracter." If you look at that choice and it seems highly unlikely, then eliminate it. Depending on the number of choices (four or five), you've just cut down the number of choices to make. Now weigh the other choices. They may seem incorrect or they may be correct. If they seem incorrect, eliminate them. You've now increased your odds at getting the correct answer.

In the end, you may be left with only two choices. At that point, it's just a matter of guessing. But with only two choices left, you now have a 50 percent chance of getting it right. With four choices, you only have a 25 percent chance, and with five choices, only a 20 percent chance at guessing correctly. That's why the process of elimination is important.

Test-Taking Tips

1. **Get to the test center early.** Make sure you give yourself plenty of extra time to get there, park your car, if necessary, and even grab a healthy snack before the test.
2. **Listen to the test monitors and follow their instructions carefully.**
3. **Read every word of the instructions.** Read every word of every question.
4. **Mark your answers by completely darkening the answer space of your choice.** Do not use the test paper to work out your answers.
5. **Mark only ONE answer for each question, even if you think that more than one answer is correct.** You must choose only one. If you mark more than one answer, the scoring machine will consider you wrong.
6. **If you change your mind, erase completely.** Leave no doubt as to which answer you mean.
7. **If your exam permits you to use scratch paper or the margins of the test booklet for figuring, don't forget to mark the answer on the answer sheet.** Only the answer sheet is scored.
8. **Check often to be sure that the question number matches the answer space, that you have not skipped a space by mistake.**
9. **Guess according to the guessing suggestions we have made.**
10. **Stay alert.** Be careful not to mark a wrong answer just because you were not concentrating.
11. **Do not panic.** If you cannot finish any part before time is up, do not worry. If you are accurate, you can do well even without finishing. It is even possible to earn a scaled score of 100 without entirely finishing an exam part if you are very accurate. At any rate, do not let your performance on any one part affect your performance on any other part.
12. **Check and recheck, time permitting.** If you finish any part before time is up, use the remaining time to check that each question is answered in the right space and that there is only one answer for each question. If there are difficult questions you skipped, return to and rethink them.

SHOULD YOU GUESS?

You may be wondering whether or not it is wise to guess when you are not sure of an answer (even if you've reduced the odds to 50 percent) or whether it is better to skip the question when you are not certain. The wisdom of guessing depends on the scoring method for the particular examination part. If the scoring is "rights only," that is, one point for each correct answer and no subtraction for wrong answers, then by all means you should guess. Read the question and all of the answer choices carefully. Eliminate those answer choices that you are certain are wrong. Then guess from among the remaining choices. You cannot gain a point if you leave the answer space blank; you may gain a point with an educated guess or even with a lucky guess. In fact, it is foolish to leave any spaces blank on a test that counts "rights only." If it appears that you are about to run out of time before completing such an exam, mark all the remaining blanks with the same letter. According to the law of averages, you should get some portion of those questions right.

If the scoring method is "rights minus wrongs," such as the address checking test found on Postal Clerk Exam 470, DO NOT GUESS. A wrong answer counts heavily against you. On this type of test, do not rush to fill answer spaces randomly at the end. Work as quickly as possible while concentrating on accuracy. Keep working carefully until time is called. Then stop and leave the remaining answer spaces blank.

In guessing the answers to multiple-choice questions, take a second to eliminate those answers that are obviously wrong, then quickly consider and guess from the remaining choices. The fewer choices from which you guess, the better the odds of guessing correctly. Once you have decided to make a guess, be it an educated guess or a wild stab, do it right away and move on; don't keep thinking about it and wasting time. You should always mark the test questions at which you guess so that you can return later.

For those questions that are scored by subtracting a fraction of a point for each wrong answer, the decision as to whether or not to guess is really up to you.

A correct answer gives you one point; a skipped space gives you nothing at all, but costs you nothing except the chance of getting the answer right; a wrong answer costs you 1/4 point. If you are really uncomfortable with guessing, you may skip a question, BUT you must then remember to skip its answer space as well. The risk of losing your place if you skip questions is so great that we advise you to guess even if you are not sure of the answer. Our suggestion is that you answer every question in order, even if you have to guess. It is better to lose a few 1/4 points for wrong guesses than to lose valuable seconds figuring where you started marking answers in the wrong place, erasing, and re-marking answers. On the other hand, do not mark random answers at the end. Work steadily until time is up.

One of the questions you should ask in the testing room is what scoring method will be used on your particular exam. You can then guide your guessing procedure accordingly.

SCORING

If your exam is a short-answer exam such as those often used by companies in the private sector, your answers will be graded by a personnel officer trained in grading test questions. If you blackened spaces on the separate answer sheet accompanying a multiple-choice exam, your answer sheet will be machine-scanned or hand-scored using a punched card stencil. Then a raw score will be calculated using the scoring formula that applies to that test or test portion—rights only, rights minus wrongs, or rights minus a fraction of wrongs. Raw scores on test parts are then added together for a total raw score.

A raw score is *not* a final score. The raw score is not the score that finds its way onto an eligibility list. The civil service testing authority, Postal Service, or other testing body converts raw scores to a scaled score according to an unpublicized formula of its own. The scaling formula allows for slight differences in difficulty of questions from one form of the exam to another and allows for equating the scores of all candidates. Regardless of the number of questions and possible different weights of different parts of the exam, most civil service clerical test scores are reported on a scale of 1 to 10. The entire process of conversion from raw to scaled score is confidential information. The score you receive is not your number right, is not your raw score, and, despite being on a scale of 1 to 100, is not a percentage. It is a scaled score. If you are entitled to veterans' service points, these are added to your passing scaled score to boost your rank on the eligibility list. Veterans' points are added only to passing scores. A failing score cannot be brought to passing level by adding veterans' points. The score earned plus veterans' service points, if any, is the score that finds its place on the rank order eligibility list. Highest scores go to the top of the list.

PART TWO

ARITHMETIC REVIEW

SOLVING ARITHMETIC PROBLEMS

In order to solve a mathematical problem, it is essential to know the mathematical meaning of the words used. There are many expressions that have the same meanings in mathematics. These expressions may indicate a relationship between quantities, or an operation (addition, subtraction, multiplication, or division) to be performed. This chapter will help you to recognize some of the mathematical terms commonly found in word problems.

EQUALITY

The following expressions all indicate that two quantities are equal (=):

is equal to
is the same as
the result is
yields
gives

ADDITION

The following expressions all indicate that the numbers A and B are to be added:

A + B	2 + 3
the sum of A and B	the sum of 2 and 3
the total of A and B	the total of 2 and 3
A added to B	2 added to 3
A increased by B	2 increased by 3
B more than A	3 more than 2
B greater than A	3 greater than 2

SUBTRACTION

The following all indicate that the number B is to be subtracted from the number A:

A − B	10 − 3
A minus B	10 minus 3
A less B	10 less 3
the difference between A and B	the difference between 10 and 3
from A subtract B	from 10 subtract 3
A take away B	10 take away 3
A decreased by B	10 decreased by 3
A diminished by B	10 diminished by 3
B is subtracted from A	3 is subtracted from 10
B less than A	3 less than 10

MULTIPLICATION

If the numbers A and B are to be multiplied (A × B), the following expressions may be used:

A × B	2 × 3
A multiplied by B	2 multiplied by 3
the product of A and B	the product of 2 and 3

The parts of a multiplication problem are indicated in the example below:

$$\begin{array}{rl} 15 & \text{(multiplicand)} \\ \times\ 10 & \text{(multiplier)} \\ \hline 150 & \text{(product)} \end{array}$$

DIVISION

Division of the numbers A and B (in the order A ÷ B) may be indicated in the following ways:

A ÷ B	14 ÷ 2
A divided by B	14 divided by 2
the quotient of A and B	the quotient of 14 and 2

The parts of a division problem are indicated in the example below:

$$\begin{array}{rl} & 5 \ \text{(quotient)} \\ \text{(divisor) } 7 & \overline{)36} \ \text{(dividend)} \\ & 35 \\ \hline & 1 \ \text{(remainder)} \end{array}$$

FACTORS AND DIVISORS

The relationship A × B = C, for any whole numbers A, B, and C, may be expressed as:

A × B = C	2 × 3 = 6
A and B are factors of C	2 and 3 are factors of 6
A and B are divisors of C	2 and 3 are divisors of 6
C is divisible by A and B	6 is divisible by 2 and 3
C is a multiple of A and of B	6 is a multiple of 2 and of 3

FRACTIONS

FRACTIONS AND MIXED NUMBERS

1. A **fraction** is part of a unit.
   a. A fraction has a **numerator** and a **denominator.**

      Example: In the fraction $\frac{3}{4}$, 3 is the numerator and 4 is the denominator.

   b. In any fraction, the numerator is being divided by the denominator.

      Example: The fraction $\frac{2}{7}$ indicates that 2 is being divided by 7

c. In a fraction problem, the whole quantity is 1, which may be expressed by a fraction in which the numerator and denominator are the same number.

Example: If the problem involves $\frac{1}{8}$ of a quantity, then the whole quantity is $\frac{8}{8}$, or 1

2. A **mixed number** is a whole number, or integer, together with a fraction, such as $2\frac{3}{5}$, $7\frac{3}{8}$, etc. The integer is the integral part and the fraction is the fractional part.

3. An **improper fraction** is one in which the numerator is equal to or greater than the denominator, such as $\frac{19}{6}$, $\frac{25}{4}$, or $\frac{10}{10}$.

4. To rename a mixed number as an improper fraction:

   a. Multiply the denominator of the fraction by the integer.

   b. Add the numerator to the product.

   c. Place this sum over the denominator of the fraction.

Problem: Rename $3\frac{4}{7}$ as an improper fraction.

SOLUTION: $7 \times 3 = 21$

$21 + 4 = 25$

$3\frac{4}{7} = \frac{25}{7}$

Answer: $\frac{25}{7}$

5. To rename an improper fraction as a mixed number:

   a. Divide the numerator by the denominator. The quotient, disregarding the remainder, is the integral part of the mixed number.

   b. Place the remainder, if any, over the denominator. This is the fractional part of the mixed number.

Problem: Rename $\frac{36}{13}$ as a mixed number.

SOLUTION:

$$\begin{array}{r} 2 \\ 13\overline{)36} \\ 26 \\ \hline 10 \end{array}$$ remainder

$\frac{36}{13} = 2\frac{10}{13}$

Answer: $2\frac{10}{13}$

6. The numerator and denominator of a fraction may be changed by multiplying both by the same number, without affecting the value of the fraction.

   Example: The value of the fraction $\frac{2}{5}$ is not altered if the numerator and the denominator are multiplied by 2, obtaining a result of $\frac{4}{10}$.

7. The numerator and denominator of a fraction may be changed by dividing both by the same number without affecting the value of the fraction. This process is called **simplifying the fraction.** A fraction that has been simplified as much as possible is said to be in **simplest form.**

   Example: The value of the fraction $\frac{3}{12}$ is not altered if the numerator and denominator are divided by 3, obtaining a result of $\frac{1}{4}$.

   Example: If $\frac{6}{30}$ is simplified to simplest form (by dividing both numerator and denominator by 6), the result is $\frac{1}{5}$.

8. As a final answer to a problem:

   a. Improper fractions should be renamed as mixed numbers.

   b. Fractions should be written in simplest terms.

ADDITION OF FRACTIONS

9. Fractions cannot be added unless all of the denominators are all the same.

   a. If the denominators are the same, add all the numerators and place this sum over the common denominator. In the case of mixed numbers, follow the above rule for the fractions and then add the integers.

   Example: The sum of $2\frac{3}{8} + 3\frac{1}{8} + \frac{3}{8} = 5\frac{7}{8}$.

   b. If the denominators are not the same, the fractions, in order to be added, must be renamed as ones having the same denominator. To do this, it is first necessary to find the least common denominator.

10. The **least common denominator** (henceforth called the LCD) is the least number that can be divided evenly by all the given denominators. If no two of the given denominators can be divided by the same number, then the LCD is the product of all the denominators.

   Example: The LCD of $\frac{1}{2}$, $\frac{1}{3}$, and $\frac{1}{5}$ is $2 \times 3 \times 5 = 30$.

11. To find the LCD when two or more of the given denominators can be divided by the same number:

   a. Write down the denominators, leaving plenty of space between the numbers.

   b. Select the least number (other than 1) by which one or more of the denominators can be divided evenly.

   c. Divide the denominators by this number, copying down those that cannot be divided evenly. Place this number to one side.

d. Repeat this process, placing each divisor to one side until there are no longer any denominators that can be divided evenly by any selected number.

e. Multiply all the divisors to find the LCD.

Problem: Find the LCD of $\frac{1}{5}, \frac{1}{7}, \frac{1}{10}$, and $\frac{1}{14}$.

SOLUTION:

$$\begin{array}{r|rrrr} 2 & 5 & 7 & 10 & 14 \\ 5 & 5 & 7 & 5 & 7 \\ 7 & 1 & 7 & 1 & 7 \\ \hline & 1 & 1 & 1 & 1 \end{array}$$

Answer: $7 \times 5 \times 2 = 70$

12. To add the fractions having different denominators:

a. Find the LCD of the denominators.

b. Rename each fraction as an equivalent fraction having the LCD as its denominator.

c. When all of the fractions have the same denominator, they may be added, as in the example following item 9a.

Problem: Add $\frac{1}{4}, \frac{3}{10}$, and $\frac{2}{5}$.

SOLUTION: Find the LCD:

$$\begin{array}{r|rrr} 2 & 4 & 10 & 5 \\ 2 & 2 & 5 & 5 \\ 5 & 1 & 5 & 5 \\ \hline & 1 & 1 & 1 \end{array}$$

LCD $= 2 \times 2 \times 5 = 20$

$$\frac{1}{4} = \frac{5}{20}$$

$$\frac{3}{10} = \frac{6}{20}$$

$$+\frac{2}{5} = +\frac{8}{20}$$

$$\frac{19}{20}$$

Answer: $\frac{19}{20}$

13. To add mixed numbers in which the fractions have different denominators, add the fractions by following the rules in item 12 and then add the integers.

Problem: Add $2\frac{5}{7}$, $5\frac{1}{2}$, and 8

SOLUTION: LCD = 14

$$2\frac{5}{7} = 2\frac{10}{14}$$
$$5\frac{1}{2} = 5\frac{7}{14}$$
$$+8 = +8$$
$$15\frac{17}{14} = 16\frac{3}{14}$$

Answer: $16\frac{3}{14}$

SUBTRACTION OF FRACTIONS

14. a. Unlike addition, which may involve adding more than two numbers at the same time, subtraction involves only two numbers.

b. In subtraction, as in addition, the denominators must be the same.

15. To subtract fractions:

a. Find the LCD.

b. Rename both fractions so that each has the LCD as the denominator.

c. Subtract the numerator of the second fraction from the numerator of the first, and place this difference over the LCD.

d. Simplify, if possible.

Problem: Find the difference of $\frac{5}{8}$ and $\frac{1}{4}$.

SOLUTION: LCD = 8

$$\frac{5}{8} = \frac{5}{8}$$
$$-\frac{1}{4} = -\frac{2}{8}$$
$$\frac{3}{8}$$

Answer: $\frac{3}{8}$

16. To subtract mixed numbers:

a. It may be necessary to "borrow," so that the fractional part of the first term is greater than the fractional part of the second term.

b. Subtract the fractional parts of the mixed numbers and simplify.

c. Subtract the integers.

Problem: Subtract $16\frac{4}{5}$ from $29\frac{1}{3}$

SOLUTION: LCD = 15

$$29\frac{1}{3} = 29\frac{5}{15}$$
$$-16\frac{4}{5} = -16\frac{12}{15}$$

Note that $\frac{5}{15}$ is less than $\frac{12}{15}$. Borrow 1 from 29, and rename the 1 as $\frac{15}{15}$.

$$29\frac{5}{15} = 28\frac{20}{15}$$
$$-16\frac{12}{15} = -16\frac{12}{15}$$
$$12\frac{8}{15}$$

Answer: $12\frac{8}{15}$

MULTIPLICATION OF FRACTIONS

17. a. To be multiplied, fractions need not have the same denominators.

b. A whole number can be written with a denominator of 1.

18. To multiply fractions:

a. Rename the mixed numbers, if any, as improper fractions.

b. Multiply all the numerators, and place this product over the product of the denominators.

c. Simplify, if possible.

Problem: Multiply $\frac{2}{3} \times 2\frac{4}{7} \times \frac{5}{9}$.

$$2\frac{4}{7} = \frac{18}{7}$$

SOLUTION: $\frac{2}{3} \times \frac{18}{7} \times \frac{5}{9} = \frac{180}{189}$

$$= \frac{20}{21}$$

Answer: $\frac{20}{21}$

19. a. Dividing common factors is a method to facilitate multiplication. To divide common factors means to divide a numerator and a denominator by the same number in a multiplication problem.

Example: In the problem $\frac{4}{7} \times \frac{5}{6}$, the numerator 4 and the denominator 6 may be divided by 2.

$$\frac{\overset{2}{\cancel{4}}}{7} \times \frac{5}{\underset{3}{\cancel{6}}} = \frac{10}{21}$$

b. The word "of" is often used to mean "multiply."

Example: $\frac{1}{2}$ of $\frac{1}{2} = \frac{1}{2} \times \frac{1}{2} = \frac{1}{4}$

20. To multiply a whole number by a mixed number:

a. Multiply the whole number by the fractional part of the mixed number.

b. Multiply the whole number by the integral part of mixed number.

c. Add both products.

Problem: Multiply $23\frac{3}{4}$ by 95

$$\frac{95}{1} \times \frac{3}{4} = \frac{285}{4}$$

$$= 71\frac{1}{4}$$

SOLUTION: $95 \times 23 = 2185$

$$2185 + 71\frac{1}{4} = 2256\frac{1}{4}$$

Answer: $2256\frac{1}{4}$

DIVISION OF FRACTIONS

21. The **reciprocal** of a fraction is obtained by "switching" the numerator and the denominator.

a. Thus, when finding the reciprocal of a fraction, the numerator becomes the denominator and the denominator becomes the numerator.

Example: The reciprocal of $\frac{3}{8}$ is $\frac{8}{3}$.

Example: The reciprocal of $\frac{1}{3}$ is $\frac{3}{1}$, or simply 3.

b. Since every whole number can be written with a denominator of 1, the reciprocal of a whole number is a fraction having 1 as the numerator and the whole number itself as the denominator.

Example: The reciprocal of 5 (expressed fractionally as $\frac{5}{1}$) is $\frac{1}{5}$.

22. To divide fractions:

   a. Rename all the mixed numbers, if any, as improper fractions.

   b. Multiply by the reciprocal of the second fraction.

   c. Simplify, if possible.

Problem: Divide $\frac{2}{3}$ by $2\frac{1}{4}$.

$$2\frac{1}{4} = \frac{9}{4}$$

SOLUTION: $\frac{2}{3} \div \frac{9}{4} = \frac{2}{3} \times \frac{4}{9}$

$$= \frac{8}{27}$$

Answer: $\frac{8}{27}$

23. A **complex fraction** is one that has a fraction as the numerator, as the denominator, or as both.

Example: $\dfrac{\frac{2}{3}}{5}$ is a complex fraction.

24. To simplify a complex fraction:

   a. Divide the numerator by the denominator.

   b. Simplify, if possible.

Problem:

Simplify $\dfrac{\frac{3}{7}}{\frac{5}{14}}$.

SOLUTION: $\frac{3}{7} \div \frac{5}{14} = \frac{3}{7} \times \frac{14}{5} = \frac{42}{35}$

$$= \frac{6}{5}$$

$$= 1\frac{1}{5}$$

Answer: $1\frac{1}{5}$

COMPARING FRACTIONS

25. If two fractions have the same denominator, the one having the greater numerator is the greater fraction.

Example: $\frac{3}{7}$ is greater than $\frac{2}{7}$.

26. If two fractions have the same numerator, the one having the greater denominator is the lesser fraction.

Example: $\frac{5}{12}$ is less than $\frac{5}{11}$.

27. To compare two fractions having different numerators and different denominators:

a. Rename the fractions as equivalent fractions having their LCD as their new denominators.

b. Compare, as in the example following item 25.

Problem: Compare $\frac{4}{7}$ and $\frac{5}{8}$.

SOLUTION: LCD = 7 × 8 = 56

$\frac{4}{7} = \frac{32}{56}$

$\frac{5}{8} = \frac{35}{56}$

Answer: Since $\frac{35}{56}$ is greater than $\frac{32}{56}$, $\frac{5}{8}$ is greater than $\frac{4}{7}$.

FRACTION PROBLEMS

28. Most fraction problems can be arranged in the form: "What fraction of a number is another number?" This form contains three important parts:

1. The fraction part
2. The number following "of"
3. The number following "is"

a. If the fraction and the "of" number are given, multiply them to find the "is" number.

Problem: What is $\frac{3}{4}$ of 20?

SOLUTION: Write the question as "$\frac{3}{4}$ of 20 is what number?"

Then multiply the fraction $\frac{3}{4}$ by the "of" number, 20

$$\frac{3}{\not{4}_1} \times \not{20}^{5} = 15$$

Answer: 15

b. If the fractional part and the "is" number are given, divide the "is" number by the fraction to find the "of" number.

Problem: $\frac{4}{5}$ of what number is 40?

SOLUTION: To find the "of" number, divide 40 by $\frac{4}{5}$.

$$40 \div \frac{4}{5} = \frac{\not{40}^{10}}{1} \times \frac{5}{\not{4}_1}$$

$$= 50$$

Answer: 50

c. To find the fractional part when the other two numbers are known, divide the "is" number by the "of" number.

Problem: What part of 12 is 9?

SOLUTION: $9 \div 12 = \frac{9}{12}$

$= \frac{3}{4}$

Answer: $\frac{3}{4}$

PRACTICE TEST

1. Simplify to simplest form: $\frac{60}{108}$

(A) $\frac{1}{48}$
(B) $\frac{1}{3}$
(C) $\frac{5}{9}$
(D) $\frac{10}{18}$

2. Rename $\frac{27}{7}$ as a mixed number.

(A) $2\frac{1}{7}$
(B) $3\frac{6}{7}$
(C) $6\frac{1}{3}$
(D) $7\frac{1}{2}$

3. Rename $4\frac{2}{3}$ as an improper fraction.

(A) $\frac{10}{3}$
(B) $\frac{11}{3}$
(C) $\frac{14}{3}$
(D) $\frac{42}{3}$

4. Find the LCD of $\frac{1}{6}$, $\frac{1}{10}$, $\frac{1}{18}$, and $\frac{1}{21}$.

(A) 160
(B) 330
(C) 630
(D) 1260

5. Add $16\frac{3}{8}$, $4\frac{4}{5}$, $12\frac{3}{4}$, and $23\frac{5}{6}$.

(A) $57\frac{91}{120}$
(B) $57\frac{1}{4}$
(C) 58
(D) 59

6. Subtract $27\frac{5}{14}$ from $43\frac{1}{6}$.

(A) 15
(B) 16
(C) $15\frac{8}{21}$
(D) $15\frac{17}{21}$

7. Multiply $17\frac{5}{8}$ by 128.

(A) 2200
(B) 2305
(C) 2356
(D) 2256

8. Divide $1\frac{2}{3}$ by $1\frac{1}{9}$.

(A) $\frac{2}{3}$

(B) $1\frac{1}{2}$

(C) $1\frac{23}{27}$

(D) 6

9. What is the value of $12\frac{1}{6} - 2\frac{3}{8} - 7\frac{2}{3} + 19\frac{3}{4}$?

(A) 21

(B) $21\frac{7}{8}$

(C) $21\frac{1}{8}$

(D) 22

10. Simplify the complex fraction $\frac{\frac{4}{9}}{\frac{2}{5}}$.

(A) $\frac{1}{2}$

(B) $\frac{9}{10}$

(C) $\frac{2}{5}$

(D) $1\frac{1}{9}$

11. Which fraction is the greatest?

(A) $\frac{9}{16}$

(B) $\frac{7}{10}$

(C) $\frac{5}{8}$

(D) $\frac{4}{5}$

12. One brass rod measures $3\frac{5}{16}$ inches long and another brass rod measures $2\frac{3}{4}$ inches long. Together, their length is

(A) $6\frac{9}{16}$ in.

(B) $5\frac{1}{8}$ in.

(C) $6\frac{1}{16}$ in.

(D) $5\frac{1}{16}$ in.

13. The number of half-pound packages of tea that can be weighed out of a box that holds $10\frac{1}{2}$ lb. of tea is

(A) 5

(B) $10\frac{1}{2}$

(C) $20\frac{1}{2}$

(D) 21

14. If each bag of tokens weighs $5\frac{3}{4}$ pounds, how many pounds do three bags weigh?

(A) $7\frac{1}{4}$

(B) $15\frac{3}{4}$

(C) $16\frac{1}{2}$

(D) $17\frac{1}{4}$

15. During one week, a man traveled $3\frac{1}{2}$, $1\frac{1}{4}$, $1\frac{1}{6}$, and $2\frac{3}{8}$ miles. The next week he traveled $\frac{1}{4}$, $\frac{3}{8}$, $\frac{9}{16}$, $3\frac{1}{16}$, $2\frac{5}{8}$, and $3\frac{3}{16}$ miles. How many more miles did he travel the second week than the first week?

(A) $1\frac{37}{48}$
(B) $1\frac{1}{2}$
(C) $1\frac{3}{4}$
(D) 1

16. A certain type of board is sold only in lengths of multiples of 2 feet. The shortest board sold is 6 feet and the longest is 24 feet. A builder needs a large quantity of this type of board in $5\frac{1}{2}$-foot lengths. For minimum waste, the lengths to be ordered should be

(A) 6 ft.
(B) 12 ft.
(C) 22 ft.
(D) 24 ft.

17. A man spent $\frac{15}{16}$ of his entire fortune in buying a car for $7,500. How much money did he possess?

(A) $6,000
(B) $6,500
(C) $7,000
(D) $8,000

18. The population of a town was 54,000 in the last census. It has increased by $\frac{2}{3}$ since then. Its present population is

(A) 18,000
(B) 36,000
(C) 72,000
(D) 90,000

19. If one third of the liquid contents of a can evaporates on the first day and three fourths of the remainder evaporates on the second day, the fractional part of the original contents remaining at the close of the second day is

(A) $\frac{5}{12}$
(B) $\frac{7}{12}$
(C) $\frac{1}{6}$
(D) $\frac{1}{2}$

20. A car is run until the gas tank is $\frac{1}{8}$ full. The tank is then filled to capacity by putting in 14 gallons. The capacity of the gas tank of the car is

(A) 14 gal.
(B) 15 gal.
(C) 16 gal.
(D) 17 gal.

ANSWERS AND EXPLANATIONS

1. C	**6.** D	**11.** D	**16.** C
2. B	**7.** D	**12.** C	**17.** D
3. C	**8.** B	**13.** D	**18.** D
4. C	**9.** B	**14.** D	**19.** C
5. A	**10.** D	**15.** A	**20.** C

1. **The correct answer is (C).** Divide the numerator and denominator by 12:

$$\frac{60 \div 12}{108 \div 12} = \frac{5}{9}$$

One alternate method (there are several) is to divide the numerator and denominator by 6 and then by 2:

$$\frac{60 \div 6}{108 \div 6} = \frac{10}{18}$$

$$\frac{10 \div 2}{18 \div 2} = \frac{5}{9}$$

2. **The correct answer is (B).** Divide the numerator (27) by the denominator (7):

$$7\overline{)27}\ \text{quotient } 3$$

$$\underline{21}$$

$$6 \text{ remainder}$$

$$\frac{27}{7} = 3\frac{6}{7}$$

3. **The correct answer is (C).**

$$4 \times 3 = 12$$

$$12 + 2 = 14$$

$$4\frac{2}{3} = \frac{14}{3}$$

4. **The correct answer is (C).**

2)	6	10	18	21	(2 is a divisor of 6, 10, and 18)
3)	3	5	9	21	(3 is a divisor of 3, 9, and 21)
3)	1	5	3	7	(3 is a divisor of 3)
5)	1	5	1	7	(5 is a divisor of 5)
7)	1	1	1	7	(7 is a divisor of 7)
	1	1	1	1	

$$\text{LCD} = 2 \times 3 \times 3 \times 5 \times 7 = 630$$

5. The correct answer is (A). LCD = 120

$$16\frac{3}{8} = 16\frac{45}{120}$$
$$4\frac{4}{5} = 4\frac{96}{120}$$
$$12\frac{3}{4} = 12\frac{90}{120}$$
$$+23\frac{5}{6} = +23\frac{100}{120}$$
$$55\frac{331}{120} = 57\frac{91}{120}$$

6. The correct answer is (D). LCD = 42

$$43\frac{1}{6} = 43\frac{7}{42} = 42\frac{49}{42}$$
$$-27\frac{5}{14} = -27\frac{15}{42} = -27\frac{15}{42}$$
$$15\frac{34}{42} = 15\frac{17}{21}$$

7. The correct answer is (D).

$$17\frac{5}{8} = \frac{141}{8}$$
$$\frac{141}{\cancel{8}_1} \times \frac{\cancel{128}^{16}}{1} = 2256$$

8. The correct answer is (B).

$$1\frac{2}{3} \div 1\frac{1}{9} = \frac{5}{3} \div \frac{10}{9}$$
$$= \frac{\cancel{5}^{1}}{\cancel{3}_{1}} \times \frac{\cancel{9}^{3}}{\cancel{10}_{2}} = \frac{3}{2} = 1\frac{1}{2}$$

9. **The correct answer is (B).** LCD = 24

$$12\frac{1}{6} = 12\frac{4}{24} = 11\frac{28}{24}$$
$$-2\frac{3}{8} = -2\frac{9}{24} = -2\frac{9}{24}$$
$$9\frac{19}{24} = 9\frac{19}{24}$$
$$-7\frac{2}{3} = -7\frac{16}{24}$$
$$2\frac{3}{24} = 2\frac{3}{24}$$
$$+19\frac{3}{4} = +19\frac{18}{24}$$
$$21\frac{21}{24}$$
$$21\frac{21}{24} = 21\frac{7}{8}$$

10. **The correct answer is (D).** To simplify a complex fraction, divide the numerator by the denominator:

$$\frac{4}{9} \div \frac{2}{5} = \frac{\overset{2}{\cancel{4}}}{9} \times \frac{5}{\underset{1}{\cancel{2}}}$$
$$= \frac{10}{9} = 1\frac{1}{9}$$

11. **The correct answer is (D).** Write all of the fractions with the same denominator. LCD = 80

$$\frac{9}{16} = \frac{45}{80}$$
$$\frac{7}{10} = \frac{56}{80}$$
$$\frac{5}{8} = \frac{50}{80}$$
$$\frac{4}{5} = \frac{64}{80}$$

Therefore, $\frac{4}{5}$ is the greatest fraction.

12. The correct answer is (C).

$$\begin{aligned} 3\frac{5}{16} &= 3\frac{5}{16} \\ +2\frac{3}{4} &= +2\frac{12}{16} \\ &= 5\frac{17}{16} \\ &= 6\frac{1}{16} \end{aligned}$$

13. The correct answer is (D).

$$10\frac{1}{2} \div \frac{1}{2} = \frac{21}{2} \div \frac{1}{2}$$

$$= \frac{21}{\cancel{2}_{1}} \times \frac{\cancel{2}^{1}}{1}$$

$$= 21$$

14. The correct answer is (D).

$$5\frac{3}{4} \times 3 = \frac{23}{4} \times \frac{3}{1}$$

$$= \frac{69}{4}$$

$$= 17\frac{1}{4}$$

15. The correct answer is (A).

First week: LCD = 24

$$\begin{aligned} 3\frac{1}{2} &= 3\frac{12}{24} \text{ miles} \\ 1\frac{1}{4} &= 1\frac{6}{24} \\ 1\frac{1}{6} &= 1\frac{4}{24} \\ +2\frac{3}{8} &= +2\frac{9}{24} \end{aligned}$$

$$7\frac{31}{24} = 8\frac{7}{24} \text{ miles}$$

Second week: LCD = 16

$$\frac{1}{4} = \frac{4}{16} \text{ miles}$$
$$\frac{3}{8} = \frac{6}{16}$$
$$\frac{9}{16} = \frac{9}{16}$$
$$3\frac{1}{16} = 3\frac{1}{16}$$
$$2\frac{5}{8} = 2\frac{10}{16}$$
$$+3\frac{3}{16} = +3\frac{3}{16}$$
$$8\frac{33}{16} = 10\frac{1}{16} \text{ miles}$$

LCD = 48

$$10\frac{1}{16} = 9\frac{51}{48} \text{ miles second week}$$
$$-8\frac{7}{24} = -8\frac{14}{48} \text{ miles first week}$$
$$1\frac{37}{48} \text{ more miles traveled}$$

16. The correct answer is (C).

Each 6-foot board yields one $5\frac{1}{2}$-foot board with $\frac{1}{2}$ foot of waste.

Each 12-foot board yields two $5\frac{1}{2}$-foot boards with 1 foot of waste.

($2 \times 5\frac{1}{2} = 11$; $12 - 11 = 1$ foot of waste)

Each 24-foot board yields four $5\frac{1}{2}$-foot boards with 2 feet of waste.

($4 \times 5\frac{1}{2} = 22$; $24 - 22 = 2$ feet of waste)

Each 22-foot board may be divided into four $5\frac{1}{2}$-foot boards with no waste.

($4 \times 5\frac{1}{2} = 22$ feet exactly)

17. The correct answer is (D). $\frac{15}{16}$ of the man's fortune is \$7,500. Therefore, his fortune

$$= 7{,}500 \div \frac{15}{16}$$
$$= \frac{\overset{500}{\cancel{7{,}500}}}{1} \times \frac{16}{\underset{1}{\cancel{15}}}$$
$$= 8{,}000$$

18. The correct answer is (D). $\frac{2}{3}$ of 54,000 = increase

$$\text{Increase} = \frac{2}{\not{3}_1} \times \not{54,000}^{18,000}$$

$$= 36,000$$

$$\text{Present population} = 54,000 + 36,000$$

$$= 90,000$$

19. The correct answer is (C).

First day: $\frac{1}{3}$ evaporates

$\frac{2}{3}$ remains

Second day: $\frac{3}{4}$ of $\frac{2}{3}$ evaporates

$\frac{1}{4}$ of $\frac{2}{3}$ remains

The amount remaining is $\frac{1}{\not{4}_2} \times \frac{\not{2}^1}{3} = \frac{1}{6}$ of original contents

20. The correct answer is (C). $\frac{7}{8}$ of capacity = 14 gal. Therefore,

$$\text{capacity} = 14 \div \frac{7}{8}$$

$$= \frac{\not{14}^2}{1} \times \frac{8}{\not{7}_1}$$

$$= 16 \text{ gal.}$$

DECIMALS

1. A **decimal,** which is a number with a decimal point (.), is actually a fraction, the denominator of which is understood to be 10 or some power of 10.

   a. The number of digits, or places, after a decimal point determines which power of 10 the denominator is. If there is one digit, the denominator is understood to be 10; if there are two digits, the denominator is understood to be 100, etc.

   Example: $.3 = \frac{3}{10}, .57 = \frac{57}{100}, .643 = \frac{643}{1,000}$

   b. The addition of zeros after a decimal point does not change the value of the decimal. The zeros may be removed without changing the value of the decimal.

   Example: $.7 = .70 = .700$ and vice versa, $.700 = .70 = .7$

   c. Since a decimal point is understood to exist after any whole number, the addition of any number of zeros after such a decimal point does not change the value of the number.

   Example: $2 = 2.0 = 2.00 = 2.000$

ADDITION OF DECIMALS

2. Decimals are added in the same way that whole numbers are added, with the provision that the decimal points must be kept in a vertical line, one under the other. This determines the place of the decimal point in the answer.

   Problem: Add 2.31, .037, 4, and 5.0017

   SOLUTION:

   $$\begin{array}{r} 2.3100 \\ .0370 \\ 4.0000 \\ +\ 5.0017 \\ \hline 11.3487 \end{array}$$

   Answer: 11.3487

SUBTRACTION OF DECIMALS

3. Decimals are subtracted in the same way that whole numbers are subtracted, with the provision that, as in addition, the decimal points must be kept in a vertical line, one under the other. This determines the place of the decimal point in the answer.

   Problem: Subtract 4.0037 from 15.3

   SOLUTION:

   $$\begin{array}{r} 15.3000 \\ -\ 4.0037 \\ \hline 11.2963 \end{array}$$

   Answer: 11.2963

MULTIPLICATION OF DECIMALS

4. Decimals are multiplied in the same way that whole numbers are multiplied.

   a. The number of decimal places in the product equals the sum of the number of decimal places in the multiplicand and in the multiplier.

   b. If there are fewer places in the product than this sum, then a sufficient number of zeros must be added in front of the product so as to equal the number of places required, and a decimal point is then written in front of the zeros.

   Problem: Multiply 2.372 by .012

   SOLUTION:

   ```
      2.372   (3 decimal places)
   ×   .012   (3 decimal places)
   ---------
       4744
      2372
   ---------
    .028464   (6 decimal places)
   ```

   Answer: .028464

5. A decimal can be multiplied by a power of 10 by moving the decimal point to the right as many places as indicated by the power. If multiplied by 10, the decimal point is moved one place to the right; if multiplied by 100, the decimal point is moved two places to the right; etc.

   Example: $.235 \times 10 = 2.35$
   $.235 \times 100 = 23.5$
   $.235 \times 1000 = 235$

DIVISION OF DECIMALS

6. There are four types of division involving decimals:

   1. When the dividend only is a decimal.
   2. When the divisor only is a decimal.
   3. When both are decimals.
   4. When neither dividend nor divisor is a decimal.

   a. When the dividend only is a decimal, the division is the same as that of whole numbers, except that a decimal point must be placed in the quotient exactly above the decimal point in the dividend.

   Problem: Divide 12.864 by 32

   SOLUTION:

   ```
          .402
    32)12.864
        128
        ---
          64
          64
          --
   ```

   Answer: .402

b. When the divisor only is a decimal, the decimal point in the divisor is omitted and as many zeros are placed to the right of the dividend as there were decimal places in the divisor.

Problem: Divide 211,327 by 6.817

```
                                     31000
SOLUTION:   6.817)211327 = 6817)211327000
           (3 decimal places)    20451  (3 zeros added)
                                  6817
                                  6817
```

Answer: 31,000

c. When both the divisor and dividend are decimals, the decimal point in the divisor is omitted and the decimal point in the dividend must be moved to the right as many decimal places as there were in the divisor. If there are not enough places in the dividend, zeros must be added to the end of the dividend to make up the difference.

Problem: Divide 2.62 by .131

```
                               20
SOLUTION:   .131)2.62 = 131)2620
                            262
```

Answer: 20

d. In instances when neither the divisor nor the dividend is a decimal, a problem may still involve decimals. This occurs in two cases: when the dividend is a lesser number than the divisor, and when it is required to work out a division to a certain number of decimal places. In either case, write in a decimal point after the dividend, add as many zeros as necessary, and place a decimal point in the quotient above that in the dividend.

Problem: Divide 7 by 50

```
              .14
SOLUTION:  50)7.00
              50
              200
              200
```

Answer: .14

Problem: What is 155 divided by 40, carried out to 3 decimal places?

```
              3.875
SOLUTION:  40)155.000
              120
               350
               320
                300
                280
                 200
```

Answer: 3.875

7. A decimal can be divided by a power of 10 by moving the decimal point to the *left* as many places as indicated by the power. If divided by 10, the decimal point is moved one place to the left; if divided by 100, the decimal point is moved two places to the left; etc. If there are not enough places, add zeros in front of the number to make up the difference and add a decimal point.

Example: .4 divided by 10 = .04
.4 divided by 100 = .004

ROUNDING DECIMALS

8. To round a number to a given decimal place:

   a. Locate the given place.
   b. If the digit to the right is less than 5, omit all digits following the given place.
   c. If the digit to the right is 5 or more, increase the given place by 1 and omit all digits following the given place.

Examples: 4.27 = 4.3 to the nearest tenth
.71345 = .713 to the nearest thousandth

9. In problems involving money, answers are usually rounded to the nearest cent (hundredth).

RENAMING OF FRACTIONS AS DECIMALS

10. A fraction can be renamed as a decimal by dividing the numerator by the denominator and working out the division to as many decimal places as required.

Problem: Rename $\frac{5}{11}$ to a decimal of 2 places.

SOLUTION: $\frac{5}{11} = 11\overline{)5.00}$

```
        .45
11)5.00
   4.44
     60
     55
      5
```

Answer: .45

11. To simplify fractions containing a decimal in either the numerator or the denominator, or in both, divide the numerator by the denominator.

Problem: What is the value of $\frac{2.34}{.6}$?

SOLUTION: $\frac{2.34}{.6} = .6\overline{)2.34} = 6\overline{)23.4}$

```
      3.9
  6)23.4
    18
     54
     54
```

Answer: 3.9

RENAMING OF DECIMALS AS FRACTIONS

12. Since a decimal point indicates a number having a denominator that is a power of 10, a decimal can be expressed as a fraction, the numerator of which is the number itself and the denominator of which is the power indicated by the number of decimal places in the decimal.

Example: $.3 = \frac{3}{10}, .47 = \frac{47}{100}$

13. When to rename decimals as fractions:

a. When dealing with whole numbers, do not rename the decimal.

Example: In the problem $12 \times .14$, it is better to keep the decimal: $12 \times .14 = 1.68$

b. When dealing with fractions, rename the decimal as a fraction.

Example: In the problem $\frac{3}{5} \times .17$, it is better to rename the decimal as a fraction:

$$\frac{3}{5} \times .17 = \frac{3}{5} \times \frac{17}{100} = \frac{51}{500}$$

14. Because the decimal equivalents of fractions are often used, it is helpful to be familiar with the most common equivalences.

$\frac{1}{2} = .5$	$\frac{1}{3} = .3333$
$\frac{1}{4} = .25$	$\frac{2}{3} = .6667$
$\frac{3}{4} = .75$	$\frac{1}{6} = .1667$
$\frac{1}{5} = .2$	$\frac{1}{7} = .1429$
$\frac{1}{8} = .125$	$\frac{1}{9} = .1111$
$\frac{1}{16} = .0625$	$\frac{1}{12} = .0833$

Note that the left column contains exact values. The values in the right column have been rounded to the nearest ten-thousandth.

PRACTICE TEST

1. Add 37.03, 11.5627, 3.4005, 3423, and 1.141.

(A) 3476.1342
(B) 3500
(C) 3524.4322
(D) 3424.1342

2. Subtract 4.64324 from 7.

(A) 3.35676
(B) 2.35676
(C) 2.45676
(D) 2.36676

3. Multiply 27.34 by 16.943.

(A) 463.22162
(B) 453.52162
(C) 462.52162
(D) 462.53162

4. What is 19.6 divided by 3.2, carried out to 3 decimal places?

(A) 6.125
(B) 6.124
(C) 6.123
(D) 5.123

5. What is $\frac{5}{11}$ in decimal form (to the nearest hundredth)?

(A) .44
(B) .55
(C) .40
(D) .45

6. What is .64 in simplest fraction form?

(A) $\frac{16}{50}$
(B) $\frac{16}{25}$
(C) $\frac{64}{25}$
(D) $\frac{64}{100}$

7. What is the difference between $\frac{3}{5}$ and $\frac{9}{8}$ expressed as a decimal?

(A) .525
(B) .425
(C) .520
(D) .500

8. A boy saved up $4.56 the first month, $3.82 the second month, and $5.06 the third month. How much did he save up altogether?

(A) $12.86
(B) $13.28
(C) $13.44
(D) $14.02

9. The diameter of a certain rod is required to be 1.51 $\pm$ .015 inches. The rod would not be acceptable if the diameter measured

(A) 1.490 in.
(B) 1.500 in.
(C) 1.510 in.
(D) 1.525 in.

10. After an employer figures out an employee's salary of $190.57, he deducts $3.05 for Social Security and $5.68 for pension. What is the amount of the check after these deductions?

(A) $181.84
(B) $181.92
(C) $181.93
(D) $181.99

11. If the outer diameter of a metal pipe is 2.84 inches and the inner diameter is 1.94 inches, then the thickness of the metal is

(A) .45 in.
(B) .90 in.
(C) 1.94 in.
(D) 2.39 in.

12. A boy earns $20.56 on Monday, $32.90 on Tuesday, and $20.78 on Wednesday. He spends half of all that he earned during the three days. How much does he have left?

(A) $29.19
(B) $31.23
(C) $34.27
(D) $37.12

13. The total cost of $3\frac{1}{2}$ pounds of meat at $1.69 a pound and twenty lemons at $.60 a dozen is

(A) $6.00
(B) $6.40
(C) $6.52
(D) $6.92

14. A reel of cable weighs 1,279 lb. If the empty reel weighs 285 lb. and the cable weighs 7.1 lb. per foot, the number of feet of cable on the reel is

(A) 220
(B) 180
(C) 140
(D) 100

15. A total of 345 fasteners at $4.15 per 100 fasteners costs

(A) $.1432
(B) $1.4320
(C) $14.32
(D) $143.20

ANSWERS AND EXPLANATIONS

1. A	**4.** A	**7.** A	**10.** A	**13.** D
2. B	**5.** D	**8.** C	**11.** A	**14.** C
3. A	**6.** B	**9.** A	**12.** D	**15.** C

1. **The correct answer is (A).** Line up all the decimal points one under the other. Then add:

$$\begin{array}{r} 37.03 \\ 11.5627 \\ 3.4005 \\ 3423.0000 \\ +\ \ 1.141 \\ \hline 3476.1342 \end{array}$$

2. **The correct answer is (B).** Add a decimal point and five zeros to the 7. Then subtract:

$$\begin{array}{r} 7.00000 \\ -\ 4.64324 \\ \hline 2.35676 \end{array}$$

3. **The correct answer is (A).** Since there are two decimal places in the multiplicand and three decimal places in the multiplier, there will be five (2 + 3 = 5) decimal places in the product.

$$\begin{array}{r} 27.34 \\ \times\ 16.943 \\ \hline 8202 \\ 1\ 0936\ \ \\ 24\ 606\ \ \ \ \\ 164\ 04\ \ \ \ \ \ \\ 273\ 4\ \ \ \ \ \ \ \ \\ \hline 463.22162 \end{array}$$

4. **The correct answer is (A).** Eliminate the decimal point from the divisor by moving it one place to the right. Move the decimal point in the dividend one place to the right and add three zeros in order to carry your answer out to three decimal places, as instructed in the problem.

$$\begin{array}{r} 6.125 \\ 3.2.\overline{)19.6.000} \\ 19\ 2\ \ \ \ \ \ \\ \hline 40\ \ \ \ \\ 32\ \ \ \ \\ \hline 80\ \ \\ 64\ \ \\ \hline 160 \\ 160 \\ \hline \end{array}$$

5. **The correct answer is (D).** To rename a fraction as a decimal, divide the numerator by the denominator:

$$\begin{array}{r} .454 \\ 11\overline{)5.000} \\ \underline{44} \\ 60 \\ \underline{55} \\ 50 \\ \underline{44} \\ 6 \end{array}$$

= 0.45 to the nearest hundredth.

6. **The correct answer is (B).** To rename a decimal as a fraction, divide by the power of 10 indicated by the number of decimal places:

$$64 \div 100 = \frac{64}{100}$$
$$= \frac{16}{25}$$

7. **The correct answer is (A).** Rename each fraction as a decimal and subtract to find the difference:

$$\frac{9}{8} = 1.125 \qquad \frac{3}{5} = .60$$

$$\begin{array}{r} 1.125 \\ -\ \ .60 \\ \hline 0.525 \end{array}$$

8. **The correct answer is (C).** Add the savings for each month:

$$\begin{array}{r} 4.56 \\ 3.82 \\ +\ \ 5.06 \\ \hline \$13.44 \end{array}$$

9. **The correct answer is (A).**

$$\begin{array}{r} 1.510 \\ +\ .015 \\ \hline 1.525 \end{array}$$

$$\begin{array}{r} 1.510 \\ -\ .015 \\ \hline 1.495 \end{array}$$

The rod may have a diameter of from 1.495 inches to 1.525 inches inclusive. So the answer is 1.490 in.

10. **The correct answer is (A).** Add to find the final total deductions:

$$\begin{array}{r} \$3.05 \\ +\ \ 5.68 \\ \hline \$8.73 \end{array}$$

Subtract total deductions from salary to find amount of check:

$$\begin{array}{r} \$190.57 \\ -\ \ \ \ 8.73 \\ \hline \$181.84 \end{array}$$

11. **The correct answer is (A).** Outer diameter minus inner diameter divided by 2 equals thickness of metal:

$$\begin{array}{r} 2.84 \\ -\ 1.94 \\ \hline .90 \end{array}$$

$0.90 \div 2 = 0.45$ in.

12. **The correct answer is (D).** Add the daily earnings to find total earnings:

$$\begin{array}{r} \$20.56 \\ 32.90 \\ +\ \ 20.78 \\ \hline \$74.24 \end{array}$$

Divide total earnings by 2 to find out what he has left:

$$2\overline{)\$74.24}\quad = \$37.12$$

13. **The correct answer is (D).** Find the cost of $3\frac{1}{2}$ pounds of meat:

$$\begin{array}{r} \$1.69 \\ \times\ \ \ 3.5 \\ \hline 845 \\ 507\ \\ \hline \$5.915 \end{array}$$

$\$5.915 = \$5.92$ to the nearest cent

Find the cost of 20 lemons:

$\$.60 \div 12 = \$.05$ (for 1 lemon)

$\$.05 \times 20 = \$1.00$ (for 20 lemons)

Add cost of meat and cost of lemons:

$$\begin{array}{r} \$5.92 \\ +\ \ 1.00 \\ \hline \$6.92 \end{array}$$

14. The correct answer is (C). Subtract weight of empty reel from total weight to find weight of cable:

$$\begin{array}{r} 1279 \text{ lb.} \\ -\ 285 \text{ lb.} \\ \hline 994 \text{ lb.} \end{array}$$

Each foot of cable weighs 7.1 lb. Therefore to find the number of feet of cable on the reel, divide 994 by 7.1:

$$\begin{array}{r} 140. \\ 7.1.\overline{)994.0.} \\ 71 \\ \hline 284 \\ 284 \\ \hline 00 \end{array}$$

15. The correct answer is (C).

Each fastener costs:

$\$4.15 \div 100 = \$.0415$

345 fasteners cost:

$$\begin{array}{r} 345 \\ \times\ .0415 \\ \hline 1725 \\ 345\ \ \\ 13\,80\ \ \ \ \\ \hline 14.3175 \end{array}$$

So, the correct answer rounded to the nearest cent is $14.32

PERCENTS

1. The percent symbol (%) means "parts of a hundred." Some problems involve expressing a fraction or a decimal as a percent. In other problems, it is necessary to express a percent as a fraction or a decimal in order to perform the calculations.

2. To rename a whole number or a decimal as a percent:

   a. Multiply the number by 100.

   b. Affix a % sign.

Problem: Rename 3 as a percent.

SOLUTION: $3 \times 100 = 300$

$3 = 300\%$

Answer: 300%

Problem: Rename .67 as a percent.

SOLUTION: $.67 \times 100 = 67$

$= 67\%$

Answer: 67%

Problem: Rename $4\frac{2}{3}$ as a percent.

SOLUTION: $4\frac{2}{3} \times 100 = \frac{14}{3} \times 100 = \frac{1,400}{3}$

$= 466\frac{2}{3}$

$4\frac{2}{3} = 466\frac{2}{3}\%$

Answer: $466\frac{2}{3}\%$

3. To remove a % sign attached to a decimal, divide the decimal by 100. If necessary, the resulting decimal may then be renamed as a fraction.

Problem: Rename .5% as a decimal and as a fraction.

SOLUTION: $.5\% = .5 \div 100 = .005$

$.005 = \frac{5}{1,000} = \frac{1}{200}$

Answer: $.5\% = .005$

$.5\% = \frac{1}{200}$

4. To remove a % sign attached to a fraction or mixed number, divide the fraction or mixed number by 100, and simplify, if possible. If necessary, the resulting fraction may then be renamed as a decimal.

Problem: Rename $\frac{3}{4}\%$ as a fraction and as a decimal.

SOLUTION: $\frac{3}{4}\% = \frac{3}{4} \div 100 = \frac{3}{4} \times \frac{1}{100}$

$= \frac{3}{400}$

$\frac{3}{400} = 400\overline{)3.0000}$ = .0075

Answer: $\frac{3}{4}\% = \frac{3}{400}$

$\frac{3}{4}\% = .0075$

5. Some fraction percent equivalents are used so frequently that it is helpful to be familiar with them.

$\frac{1}{25} = 4\%$	$\frac{1}{5} = 20\%$
$\frac{1}{20} = 5\%$	$\frac{1}{4} = 25\%$
$\frac{1}{12} = 8\frac{1}{3}\%$	$\frac{1}{3} = 33\frac{1}{3}\%$
$\frac{1}{10} = 10\%$	$\frac{1}{2} = 50\%$
$\frac{1}{8} = 12\frac{1}{2}\%$	$\frac{2}{3} = 66\frac{2}{3}\%$
$\frac{1}{6} = 16\frac{2}{3}\%$	$\frac{3}{4} = 75\%$

SOLVING PERCENT PROBLEMS

6. Most percent problems involve three quantities:

1. The rate (R), which is followed by a % sign.
2. The base (B), which follows the word "of."
3. The amount or percentage (P), which usually follows the word "is."

a. If the rate (R) and the base (B) are known, then the percentage (P) = R × B.

Problem: Find 15% of 50.

SOLUTION: Rate = 15%

Base = 50

P = R × B

P = 15% × 50

= .15 × 50

= 7.5

Answer: 15% of 50 is 7.5.

b. If the rate (R) and the percentage (P) are known, then the base (B) $= \frac{P}{R}$.

Problem: 7% of what number is 35?

SOLUTION:

$$\text{Rate} = 7\%$$
$$\text{Percentage} = 35$$
$$B = \frac{P}{R}$$
$$B = \frac{35}{7\%}$$
$$= 35 \div .07$$
$$= 500$$

Answer: 7% of 500 is 35

c. If the percentage (P) and the base (B) are known, then the rate (R) $= \frac{P}{B}$.

Problem: There are 96 men in a group of 150 people. What percent of the group are men?

SOLUTION:

$$\text{Base} = 150$$
$$\text{Percentage (amount)} = 96$$
$$\text{Rate} = \frac{96}{150}$$
$$= .64$$
$$= 64\%$$

Answer: 64% of the group are men.

Problem: In a tank holding 20 gallons of solution, 1 gallon is alcohol. What is the strength of the solution in percent?

SOLUTION:

$$\text{Percentage (amount)} = 1 \text{ gallon}$$
$$\text{Base} = 20 \text{ gallons}$$
$$\text{Rate} = \frac{1}{20}$$
$$= .05$$
$$= 5\%$$

Answer: The solution is 5% alcohol.

7. In a percent problem, the whole is 100%.

Example: If a problem involves 10% of a quantity, the rest of the quantity is 90%.

Example: If a quantity has been increased by 5%, the new amount is 105% of the original quantity.

Example: If a quantity has been decreased by 15%, the new amount is 85% of the original quantity.

PRACTICE TEST

1. 10% written as a decimal is
   (A) 1.0
   (B) 0.01
   (C) 0.001
   (D) 0.1

2. What is 5.37% in fraction form?
   (A) $\frac{537}{10,000}$
   (B) $5\frac{537}{10,000}$
   (C) $\frac{537}{1,000}$
   (D) $5\frac{37}{100}$

3. What percent of $\frac{5}{6}$ is $\frac{3}{4}$?
   (A) 75%
   (B) 60%
   (C) 80%
   (D) 90%

4. What percent is 14 of 24?
   (A) $62\frac{1}{4}\%$
   (B) $58\frac{1}{3}\%$
   (C) $41\frac{2}{3}\%$
   (D) $33\frac{3}{5}\%$

5. 200% of 800 equals
   (A) 2,500
   (B) 16
   (C) 1,600
   (D) 4

6. If John must have a mark of 80% to pass a test of 35 items, the number of items he may miss and still pass the test is
   (A) 7
   (B) 8
   (C) 11
   (D) 28

7. The regular price of a TV set that sold for $118.80 at a 20% reduction sale is
   (A) $148.50
   (B) $142.60
   (C) $138.84
   (D) $95.04

8. A circle graph of a budget shows the expenditure of 26.2% for housing, 28.4% for food, 12% for clothing, 12.7% for taxes, and the balance for miscellaneous items. The percent for miscellaneous items is
   (A) 31.5%
   (B) 79.3%
   (C) 20.7%
   (D) 68.5%

9. Two dozen shuttlecocks and four badminton rackets are to be purchased for a playground. The shuttlecocks are priced at $.35 each and the rackets at $2.75 each. The playground receives a discount of 30% from these prices. The total cost of this equipment is
   (A) $7.29
   (B) $11.43
   (C) $13.58
   (D) $18.60

10. A piece of wood weighing 10 ounces is found to have a weight of 8 ounces after drying. The moisture content was
    (A) 25%
    (B) $33\frac{1}{3}\%$
    (C) 20%
    (D) 40%

11. A bag contains 800 coins. Of these, 10% are dimes, 30% are nickels, and the rest are quarters. The amount of money in the bag is
    (A) less than $150
    (B) between $150 and $300
    (C) between $301 and $450
    (D) more than $450

12. Six quarts of a 20% solution of alcohol in water are mixed with 4 quarts of a 60% solution of alcohol in water. The alcoholic strength of the mixture is

(A) 80%
(B) 40%
(C) 36%
(D) 72%

13. A man insures 80% of his property and pays a $2\frac{1}{2}\%$ premium amounting to $348. What is the total value of his property?

(A) $17,000
(B) $18,000
(C) $18,400
(D) $17,400

14. A clerk divides his 35-hour work week as follows: $\frac{1}{5}$ of his time was spent in sorting mail; $\frac{1}{2}$ of his time in filing letters; and $\frac{1}{7}$ of his time in reception work. The rest of his time was devoted to messenger work. The percent of time spent on messenger work by the clerk during the week was most nearly

(A) 6%
(B) 10%
(C) 14%
(D) 16%

15. In a school in which 40% of the enrolled students are boys, 80% of the boys are present on a certain day. If 1,152 boys are present, the total school enrollment is

(A) 1,440
(B) 2,880
(C) 3,600
(D) 5,400

ANSWERS AND EXPLANATIONS

1. D	**4.** B	**7.** A	**10.** C	**13.** D
2. A	**5.** C	**8.** C	**11.** A	**14.** D
3. D	**6.** A	**9.** C	**12.** C	**15.** C

1. The correct answer is (D). 10% = .10 = .1

2. The correct answer is (A). $5.37\% = .0537 = \frac{537}{10{,}000}$

3. The correct answer is (D).

$$\text{Base (number following "of")} = \frac{5}{6}$$

$$\text{Percentage (number following "is")} = \frac{3}{4}$$

$$\text{Rate} = \frac{\text{Percentage}}{\text{Base}}$$

$$= \text{Percentage} \div \text{Base}$$

$$\text{Rate} = \frac{3}{4} \div \frac{5}{6}$$

$$= \frac{3}{\cancel{4}_{2}} \times \frac{\cancel{6}^{3}}{5}$$

$$= \frac{9}{10}$$

$$\frac{9}{10} = .9 = 90\%$$

4. The correct answer is (B).

Base (number following "of") = 24
Percentage (number following "is") = 14
Rate = Percentage ÷ Base
Rate = 14 ÷ 24

$$= .58\frac{1}{3}$$

$$= 58\frac{1}{3}\%$$

5. The correct answer is (C).

$$200\% \text{ of } 800 = 2.00 \times 800$$
$$= 1{,}600$$

6. The correct answer is (A). He must answer 80% of 35 correctly. Therefore, he may miss 20% of 35.

$$20\% \text{ of } 35 = .20 \times 35$$
$$= 7$$

7. **The correct answer is (A).** Since $118.80 represents a 20% reduction, $118.80 = 80% of the regular price.

$$\text{Regular price} = \frac{\$188.80}{80\%}$$
$$= \$118.80 \div .80$$
$$= \$148.50$$

8. **The correct answer is (C).** All the items in a circle graph total 100%. Add the figures given for housing, food, clothing, and taxes:

$$\begin{array}{r} 26.7\% \\ 28.4\% \\ 12\ \ \ \% \\ +\ 12.7\% \\ \hline 79.3\% \end{array}$$

Subtract this total from 100% to find the percent for miscellaneous items:

$$\begin{array}{r} 100.0\% \\ -\ \ 79.3\% \\ \hline 20.7\% \end{array}$$

9. **The correct answer is (C).**

$$\begin{array}{rcrcr} \text{Price of shuttlecocks} & = & 24 \times \$.35 & = & \$8.40 \\ \text{Price of rackets} & = & 4 \times \$2.75 & = & \$11.00 \\ \hline \text{Total price} & = & & & \$19.40 \end{array}$$

Discount is 30%, and 100% − 30% = 70%

$$\text{Actual cost} = 70\% \text{ of } \$19.40$$
$$= .70 \times \$19.40$$
$$= \$13.58$$

10. **The correct answer is (C).** Subtract the weight of wood after drying from original weight of wood to find amount of moisture in wood:

$$\begin{array}{r} 10 \\ -\ \ 8 \\ \hline 2 \end{array}$$ ounces of moisture in wood

$$\text{Moisture content} = \frac{2 \text{ ounces}}{10 \text{ ounces}} = .2 = 20\%$$

11. **The correct answer is (A).**

Find the number of each kind of coin:

$$10\% \text{ of } 800 = .10 \times 800 = 80 \text{ dimes}$$
$$30\% \text{ of } 800 = .30 \times 800 = 240 \text{ nickels}$$
$$60\% \text{ of } 800 = .60 \times 800 = 480 \text{ quarters}$$

Find the value of the coins:

$$\begin{array}{rcrcr} 80 \text{ dimes} & = & 80 \times .10 & = & \$\ \ 8.00 \\ 240 \text{ nickels} & = & 240 \times .05 & = & 12.00 \\ 480 \text{ quarters} & = & 480 \times .25 & = & 120.00 \\ \hline & & & \text{Total} & \$140.00 \end{array}$$

The total amount is less than $150, choice (A).

12. The correct answer is (C).

The first solution contains 20% of 6 quarts of alcohol.

$$\text{Alcohol content} = .20 \times 6 = 1.2 \text{ quarts}$$

The second solution contains 60% of 4 quarts of alcohol.

$$\text{Alcohol content} = .60 \times 4 = 2.4 \text{ quarts}$$

$$\text{Mixture contains: } 1.2 + 2.4 = 3.6 \text{ quarts alcohol}$$

$$6 + 4 = 10 \text{ quarts liquid}$$

$$\text{Alcoholic strength of mixture} = \frac{3.6}{10} = 36\%$$

13. The correct answer is (D).

$$2\tfrac{1}{2}\% \text{ of insured value} = \$348$$

$$\text{Insured value} = \frac{348}{2\frac{1}{2}\%} = 348 \div .025 = \$13{,}920$$

$13,920 is 80% of the total value

$$\text{Total value} = \frac{\$13{,}920}{80\%} = \$13{,}920 \div .80 = \$17{,}400$$

14. The correct answer is (D).

$$\frac{1}{5} = 20\% \text{ sorting mail}$$

$$\frac{1}{2} = 50\% \text{ filing}$$

$$+\frac{1}{7} = 14.3\% \text{ reception}$$

84.3% accounted for

$$\begin{array}{r} 100.0\% \\ -\ 84.3\% \\ \hline 15.7\% \end{array}$$

So the correct answer is most nearly 16%, choice (D).

15. The correct answer is (C).

$$80\% \text{ of the boys} = 1{,}152$$

$$\text{Number of boys} = \frac{1{,}152}{80\%} = 1{,}152 \div .80 = 1{,}440$$

$$40\% \text{ of students} = 1{,}440$$

$$\text{Total number of students} = \frac{1{,}440}{40\%} = 1{,}440 \div .40 = 3{,}600$$

DROPPING FINAL ZEROS

1. a. A zero in a whole number is considered a "final zero" if it appears in the units column or if all columns to its right are filled with zeros. A final zero may be omitted in certain kinds of problems.

   b. In decimal numbers, a zero appearing in the extreme right column may be dropped with no effect on the solution of a problem.

2. In multiplying whole numbers, the final zero(s) may be dropped during computation and simply transferred to the answer.

Examples:

$$\begin{array}{r} 2310 \\ \times\ 150 \\ \hline 1155 \\ 231 \\ \hline 346500 \end{array}$$

$$\begin{array}{r} 129 \\ \times\ 210 \\ \hline 129 \\ 258 \\ \hline 27090 \end{array}$$

$$\begin{array}{r} 1760 \\ \times\ 205 \\ \hline 880 \\ 352 \\ \hline 360800 \end{array}$$

PRACTICE TEST

1. $\begin{array}{r} 230 \\ \times\ 12 \\ \hline \end{array}$

2. $\begin{array}{r} 175 \\ \times\ 130 \\ \hline \end{array}$

3. $\begin{array}{r} 203 \\ \times\ 14 \\ \hline \end{array}$

4. $\begin{array}{r} 621 \\ \times\ 140 \\ \hline \end{array}$

5. $\begin{array}{r} 430 \\ \times\ 360 \\ \hline \end{array}$

6. $\begin{array}{r} 132 \\ \times\ 310 \\ \hline \end{array}$

7. $\begin{array}{r} 350 \\ \times\ 24 \\ \hline \end{array}$

8. $\begin{array}{r} 520 \\ \times\ 410 \\ \hline \end{array}$

9. $\begin{array}{r} 634 \\ \times\ 120 \\ \hline \end{array}$

10. $\begin{array}{r} 430 \\ \times\ 230 \\ \hline \end{array}$

ANSWERS AND EXPLANATIONS

1.
```
  230
× 12
   46
  23
 2760
```

2.
```
  175
× 130
  525
 175
22750
```

3.
```
  203
×  14
  812
 203
 2842
```

4.
```
  621
× 140
 2484
 621
86940
```

5.
```
   430
 × 360
   258
  129
154800
```

6.
```
  132
× 310
  132
 396
40920
```

7.
```
  350
×  24
  140
  70
 8400
```

8.
```
   520
 × 410
    52
  208
213200
```

9.
```
  634
× 120
 1268
 634
76080
```

10.
```
  430
× 230
  129
  86
98900
```

MULTIPLYING WHOLE NUMBERS BY DECIMALS

1. In multiplying a whole by a decimal number, if there are one or more final zeros in the multiplicand, move the decimal point in the multiplier to the right the same number of places as there are final zeros in the multiplicand. Then cross out the final zero(s) in the multiplicand. The new problem will have the same answer as the original problem.

Examples:

$$\begin{array}{r} 27500 \\ \times\ .15 \\ \hline \end{array} = \begin{array}{r} 275 \\ \times\ 15 \\ \hline \end{array} \qquad \begin{array}{r} 1250 \\ \times\ .345 \\ \hline \end{array} = \begin{array}{r} 125 \\ \times\ 3.45 \\ \hline \end{array}$$

PRACTICE TEST

Rewrite and solve the following problems, dropping the final zeros and moving decimal points the appropriate number of spaces. Then compute the answers.

1. $\begin{array}{r} 2400 \\ \times\ .02 \\ \hline \end{array}$

2. $\begin{array}{r} 620 \\ \times\ .04 \\ \hline \end{array}$

3. $\begin{array}{r} 800 \\ \times\ .005 \\ \hline \end{array}$

4. $\begin{array}{r} 600 \\ \times\ .002 \\ \hline \end{array}$

5. $\begin{array}{r} 340 \\ \times\ .08 \\ \hline \end{array}$

6. $\begin{array}{r} 480 \\ \times\ .4 \\ \hline \end{array}$

7. $\begin{array}{r} 400 \\ \times\ .04 \\ \hline \end{array}$

8. $\begin{array}{r} 5300 \\ \times\ .5 \\ \hline \end{array}$

9. $\begin{array}{r} 930 \\ \times\ .3 \\ \hline \end{array}$

10. $\begin{array}{r} 9000 \\ \times\ .001 \\ \hline \end{array}$

ANSWERS AND EXPLANATIONS

1. $\begin{array}{r} 24 \\ \times\ 2 \\ \hline 48 \end{array}$

2. $\begin{array}{r} 62 \\ \times\ .4 \\ \hline 24.8 \end{array}$

3. $\begin{array}{r} 8 \\ \times\ .5 \\ \hline 4.0 \end{array}$

4. $\begin{array}{r} 6 \\ \times\ .2 \\ \hline 1.2 \end{array}$

5. $\begin{array}{r} 34 \\ \times\ .8 \\ \hline 27.2 \end{array}$

6. $\begin{array}{r} 48 \\ \times\ 4 \\ \hline 192 \end{array}$

7. $\begin{array}{r} 4 \\ \times\ 4 \\ \hline 16 \end{array}$

8. $\begin{array}{r} 53 \\ \times\ 50 \\ \hline 2650 \end{array}$

9. $\begin{array}{r} 93 \\ \times\ 3 \\ \hline 279 \end{array}$

10. $\begin{array}{r} 9 \\ \times\ 1 \\ \hline 9 \end{array}$

DIVIDING BY WHOLE NUMBERS

1. a. When there are final zeros in the divisor but no final zeros in the dividend, move the decimal point in the dividend to the left as many places as there are final zeros in the divisor, then omit the final zeros.

   Example: $2700.\overline{)37523.} = 27.\overline{)375.23}$

   b. When there are fewer final zeros in the divisor than there are in the dividend, drop the same number of final zeros from the dividend as there are final zeros in the divisor.

   Example: $250.\overline{)45300.} = 25.\overline{)4530.}$

   c. When there are more final zeros in the divisor than there are in the dividend, move the decimal point in the dividend to the left as many places as there are final zeros in the divisor, then omit the final zeros.

   Example: $2300.\overline{)690.} = 23.\overline{)6.9}$

   d. When there are no final zeros in the divisor, no zeros can be dropped in the dividend.

   Example: $23.\overline{)690.} = 23.\overline{)690}$

PRACTICE TEST

Rewrite and solve the following problems, dropping the final zeros and moving the decimal points the appropriate number of places.

1. $600.\overline{)72.}$

2. $310.\overline{)6200.}$

3. $7600.\overline{)1520.}$

4. $46.\overline{)920.}$

5. $11.0\overline{)220.}$

6. $700.\overline{)84.}$

7. $90.\overline{)8100.}$

8. $8100.\overline{)1620.}$

9. $25.\overline{)5250.}$

10. $41.0\overline{)820.}$

11. $800.\overline{)96.}$

12. $650.\overline{)1300.}$

13. $5500.\overline{)110.}$

14. $36.\overline{)720.}$

15. $87.0\overline{)1740.}$

ANSWERS AND EXPLANATIONS

1.
$$\begin{array}{r} .12 \\ 6.\overline{).72} \end{array}$$

2.
$$\begin{array}{r} 20 \\ 31.\overline{)620.} \\ \underline{62} \\ 00 \end{array}$$

3.
$$\begin{array}{r} .2 \\ 76.\overline{)15.2} \\ \underline{15\ 2} \\ 0\ 0 \end{array}$$

4.
$$\begin{array}{r} 20. \\ 46.\overline{)920.} \\ \underline{92} \\ 00 \end{array}$$

5.
$$\begin{array}{r} 20 \\ 11.\overline{)220.} \\ \underline{22} \\ 00 \end{array}$$

6.
$$\begin{array}{r} .12 \\ 7.\overline{).84} \end{array}$$

7. $\begin{array}{r} 90 \\ 9.\overline{)810.} \end{array}$

8. $\begin{array}{r} .2 \\ 81.\overline{)16.2} \\ \underline{16\ 2} \\ 0\ 0 \end{array}$

9. $\begin{array}{r} 210 \\ 25.\overline{)5250.} \\ \underline{50} \\ 25 \\ \underline{25} \\ 00 \end{array}$

10. $\begin{array}{r} 20 \\ 41.\overline{)820.} \\ \underline{82} \\ 00 \end{array}$

11. $\begin{array}{r} .12 \\ 8.\overline{).96} \end{array}$

12. $\begin{array}{r} 2 \\ 65.\overline{)130.} \\ \underline{130} \\ 00 \end{array}$

13. $\begin{array}{r} .02 \\ 55.\overline{)1.10} \\ \underline{1\ 10} \\ 00 \end{array}$

14. $\begin{array}{r} 20 \\ 36.\overline{)720.} \\ \underline{72} \\ 00 \end{array}$

15. $\begin{array}{r} 20 \\ 87.\overline{)1740.} \\ \underline{174} \\ 00 \end{array}$

DIVISION BY MULTIPLICATION

1. Instead of dividing by a particular number, the same answer is obtained by multiplying by the equivalent multiplier.
2. To find the equivalent multiplier of a given divisor, divide 1 by the divisor.

   Example: The equivalent multiplier of $12\frac{1}{2}$ is $1 \div 12\frac{1}{2}$ or .08. The division problem $100 \div 12\frac{1}{2}$ may be more easily solved as the multiplication problem $100 \times .08$. The answer will be the same.
3. Common divisors and their equivalent multipliers are shown below:

Divisor	*Equivalent Multiplier*
$11\frac{1}{9}$	.09
$12\frac{1}{2}$	.08
$14\frac{2}{7}$	.07
$16\frac{2}{3}$	.06
20	.05
25	.04
$33\frac{1}{3}$	.03
50	.02

4. A divisor may be multiplied or divided by any power of 10, and the only change in its equivalent multiplier will be in the placement of the decimal point, as may be seen in the following table:

Divisor	*Equivalent Multiplier*
.025	40.
.25	4.
2.5	.4
25.	.04
250	.004
2500.	.0004

PRACTICE TEST

Rewrite and solve each of the following problems by using equivalent multipliers. Drop the final zeros where appropriate.

1. $100 \div 16\frac{2}{3} =$
2. $200 \div 25 =$
3. $300 \div 33\frac{1}{3} =$
4. $250 \div 50 =$
5. $80 \div 12\frac{1}{2} =$
6. $800 \div 14\frac{2}{7} =$
7. $620 \div 20 =$
8. $500 \div 11\frac{1}{9} =$
9. $420 \div 16\frac{2}{3} =$
10. $1200 \div 33\frac{1}{3}$
11. $955 \div 50 =$
12. $300 \div 25 =$
13. $275 \div 12\frac{1}{2} =$
14. $625 \div 25 =$
15. $244 \div 20 =$
16. $350 \div 16\frac{2}{3} =$
17. $400 \div 33\frac{1}{3} =$
18. $375 \div 25 =$
19. $460 \div 20 =$
20. $250 \div 12\frac{1}{2} =$

ANSWERS AND EXPLANATIONS

1. $100 \times .06 = 1 \times 6 = 6$
2. $200 \times .04 = 2 \times 4 = 8$
3. $300 \times .03 = 3 \times 3 = 9$
4. $250 \times .02 = 25 \times .2 = 5$
5. $80 \times .08 = 8 \times .8 = 6.4$
6. $800 \times .07 = 8 \times 7 = 56$
7. $620 \times .05 = 62 \times .5 = 31$
8. $500 \times .09 = 5 \times 9 = 45$
9. $420 \times .06 = 42 \times .6 = 25.2$
10. $1200 \times .03 = 12 \times 3 = 36$
11. $955 \times .02 = 19.1$
12. $300 \times .04 = 3 \times 4 = 12$
13. $275 \times .08 = 22$
14. $625 \times .04 = 25$
15. $244 \times .05 = 12.2$
16. $350 \times .06 = 35 \times .6 = 21$
17. $400 \times .03 = 4 \times 3 = 12$
18. $375 \times .04 = 15$
19. $460 \times .05 = 46 \times .5 = 23$
20. $250 \times .08 = 25 \times .8 = 20$

MULTIPLICATION BY DIVISION

1. Just as some division problems are made easier by changing them to equivalent multiplication problems, certain multiplication problems are made easier by changing them to equivalent division problems.
2. Instead of arriving at an answer by multiplying by a particular number, the same answer is obtained by dividing by the equivalent divisor.
3. To find the equivalent divisor of a given multiplier, divide 1 by the multiplier.
4. Common multipliers and their equivalent divisors are show below:

Multiplier	*Equivalent Divisor*
$11\frac{1}{9}$	.09
$12\frac{1}{2}$	.08
$14\frac{2}{7}$	.07
$16\frac{2}{3}$	.06
20	.05
25	.04
$33\frac{1}{3}$	.03
50	.02

Notice that the multiplier-equivalent divisor pairs are the same as the divisor-equivalent multiplier pairs given earlier.

PRACTICE TEST

Rewrite and solve each of the following problems by using division. Drop the final zeros where appropriate.

1. $77 \times 14\frac{2}{7} =$

2. $81 \times 11\frac{1}{9} =$

3. $475 \times 20 =$

4. $42 \times 50 =$

5. $36 \times 33\frac{1}{3} =$

6. $96 \times 12\frac{1}{2} =$

7. $126 \times 16\frac{2}{3} =$

8. $48 \times 25 =$

9. $33 \times 33\frac{1}{3} =$

10. $84 \times 14\frac{2}{7} =$

11. $99 \times 11\frac{1}{9} =$

12. $126 \times 33\frac{1}{3} =$

13. $168 \times 12\frac{1}{2} =$

14. $654 \times 16\frac{2}{3} =$

15. $154 \times 14\frac{2}{7} =$

16. $5250 \times 50 =$

17. $324 \times 25 =$

18. $625 \times 20 =$

19. $198 \times 11\frac{1}{9} =$

20. $224 \times 14\frac{2}{7} =$

ANSWERS AND EXPLANATIONS

1. $.07\overline{)77.} = \begin{array}{r}1100.\\ 7\overline{)7700.}\end{array}$

2. $.09\overline{)81.} = \begin{array}{r}900.\\ 9\overline{)8100.}\end{array}$

3. $.05\overline{)475.} = \begin{array}{r}9500.\\ 5\overline{)47500.}\end{array}$

4. $.02\overline{)42.} = \begin{array}{r}2100.\\ 2\overline{)4200.}\end{array}$

5. $.03\overline{)36.} = \begin{array}{r}1200.\\ 3\overline{)3600.}\end{array}$

6. $.08\overline{)96.} = \begin{array}{r}1200\\ 8\overline{)9600.}\end{array}$

7. $.06\overline{)126.} = \begin{array}{r}2100.\\ 6\overline{)12600.}\end{array}$

8. $.04\overline{)48.} = \begin{array}{r}1200.\\ 4\overline{)4800.}\end{array}$

9. $.03\overline{)33.} = \begin{array}{r}1100.\\ 3\overline{)3300.}\end{array}$

10. $.07\overline{)84.} = \begin{array}{r}1200.\\ 7\overline{)8400.}\end{array}$

11. $.09\overline{)99.} = \begin{array}{r}1100.\\ 9\overline{)9900.}\end{array}$

12. $.03\overline{)126.} = \begin{array}{r}4200.\\ 3\overline{)12600.}\end{array}$

13. $.08\overline{)168.} = \begin{array}{r}2100.\\ 8\overline{)16800.}\end{array}$

14. $.06\overline{)654.} = \begin{array}{r}10900.\\ 6\overline{)65400.}\end{array}$

15. $.07\overline{)154.} = \begin{array}{r}2200.\\ 7\overline{)15400.}\end{array}$

16. $.02\overline{)5250.} = \begin{array}{r}262500.\\ 2\overline{)525000.}\end{array}$

17. $.04\overline{)324.} = \begin{array}{r}8100.\\ 4\overline{)32400.}\end{array}$

18. $.05\overline{)625.} = \begin{array}{r}12500.\\ 5\overline{)62500.}\end{array}$

19. $.09\overline{)198.} = \begin{array}{r}2200.\\ 9\overline{)19800.}\end{array}$

20. $.07\overline{)224.} = \begin{array}{r}3200.\\ 7\overline{)22400.}\end{array}$

POWERS AND ROOTS

1. The numbers that are multiplied to give a product are called the **factors** of the product.

   Example: In $2 \times 3 = 6$, 2 and 3 are factors of 6.

2. If the factors are the same, an **exponent** may be used to indicate the number of times the factor appears.

   Example: In $3 \times 3 = 3^2$, the number 3 appears as a factor twice, as is indicated by the exponent 2.

3. When a product is written in exponential form, the number the exponent refers to is called the **base.** The exponent itself is called the **power.**

   Example: In 2^5, the number 2 is the base and 5 is the exponent (or power). $2^5 = 2 \times 2 \times 2 \times 2 \times 2 = 32$, so 32 is the product.

4. a. If the exponent used is 2, we say that the base has been squared, or raised to the second power.

   Example: 6^2 is read "six squared" or "six to the second power."

   b. If the exponent used is 3, we say that the base has been cubed, or raised to the third power.

   Example: 5^3 is read "five cubed" or "five to the third power."

   c. If the exponent is 4, we say that the base has been raised to the fourth power. If the exponent is 5, we say that the base has been raised to the fifth power, etc.

   Example: 2^8 is read "two to the eighth power."

5. A number that is the product of a number squared is called a **perfect square.**

   Example: 25 is a perfect square because $25 = 5^2$.

6. a. If a number has exactly two equal factors, each factor is called the **square root** of the number.

   Example: $9 = 3 \times 3$; therefore, 3 is the square root of 9.

   b. The symbol $\sqrt{}$ is used to indicate square root.

   Example: $\sqrt{9} = 3$ means that the square root of 9 is 3, or $3 \times 3 = 9$.

7. The square root of the most common perfect squares may be found by using the following table, or by trial and error; that is, by finding the number that, when squared, yields the given perfect square.

Number	*Perfect Square*	*Number*	*Perfect Square*
1	1	10	100
2	4	11	121
3	9	12	144
4	16	13	169
5	25	14	196
6	36	15	225
7	49	20	400
8	64	25	625
9	81	30	900

   Example: To find $\sqrt{81}$, note that 81 is the perfect square of 9, or $9^2 = 81$. Therefore, $\sqrt{81} = 9$.

8. To find the square root of a fraction, find the square root of its numerator and of its denominator.

Example: $\sqrt{\frac{4}{9}} = \frac{\sqrt{4}}{\sqrt{9}} = \frac{2}{3}$

9. a. If a number has exactly three equal factors, each factor is called the cube root of the number.

b. The symbol $\sqrt[3]{}$ is used to indicate the cube root.

Example: $8 = 2 \times 2 \times 2$; therefore, $\sqrt[3]{8} = 2$.

PRACTICE TEST

1. The square of 10 is

(A) 1
(B) 2
(C) 5
(D) 100

2. The cube of 9 is

(A) 3
(B) 27
(C) 81
(D) 729

3. The fourth power of 2 is

(A) 2
(B) 4
(C) 8
(D) 16

4. In exponential form, the product of $7 \times 7 \times 7 \times 7 \times 7$ may be written

(A) 5^7
(B) 7^5
(C) 2^7
(D) 7^2

5. The value of 3^5 is

(A) 243
(B) 125
(C) 35
(D) 15

6. The square root of 1,175, to the nearest whole number, is

(A) 32
(B) 33
(C) 34
(D) 35

7. Find $\sqrt{503}$ to the nearest 10th.

(A) 22.4
(B) 22.5
(C) 22.6
(D) 22.7

8. Find $\sqrt{\frac{1}{4}}$.

(A) 2
(B) $\frac{1}{2}$
(C) $\frac{1}{8}$
(D) $\frac{1}{16}$

9. Find $\sqrt[3]{64}$.

(A) 3
(B) 4
(C) 8
(D) 32

10. The sum of 2^2 and 2^3 is

(A) 9
(B) 10
(C) 12
(D) 32

ANSWERS AND EXPLANATIONS

1. D	**3.** D	**5.** A	**7.** A	**9.** B
2. D	**4.** B	**6.** C	**8.** B	**10.** C

1. **The correct answer is (D).** $10^2 = 10 \times 10 = 100$
2. **The correct answer is (D).**

$$\begin{aligned} 9^3 &= 9 \times 9 \times 9 \\ &= 81 \times 9 \\ &= 729 \end{aligned}$$

3. **The correct answer is (D).**

$$\begin{aligned} 2^4 &= 2 \times 2 \times 2 \times 2 \\ &= 4 \times 2 \times 2 \\ &= 8 \times 2 \\ &= 16 \end{aligned}$$

4. **The correct answer is (B).** $7 \times 7 \times 7 \times 7 \times 7 = 7^5$
5. **The correct answer is (A).**

$$\begin{aligned} 3^5 &= 3 \times 3 \times 3 \times 3 \times 3 \\ &= 243 \end{aligned}$$

6. **The correct answer is (C).** Try all possible answers.

$$\begin{aligned} 32^2 &= 1{,}024 \\ 33^2 &= 1{,}089 \\ 34^2 &= 1{,}156 \\ 35^2 &= 1{,}225 \end{aligned}$$

Since 1,175 is closest to 1,156, its square root must be closest to 34.

7. **The correct answer is (A).** Try all possible answers.

$$\begin{aligned} (22.4)^2 &= 501.76 \\ (22.5)^2 &= 506.25 \end{aligned}$$

You can stop here since $(22.6)^2$ and $(22.7)^2$ will both be greater than 506.25. Since 501.76 is closest to 503, its square root must be closest to 22.4.

8. **The correct answer is (B).**

$$\sqrt{\frac{1}{4}} = \frac{\sqrt{1}}{\sqrt{4}} = \frac{1}{2}$$

9. **The correct answer is (B).** Since $4 \times 4 \times 4 = 64$, $\sqrt[3]{64} = 4$
10. **The correct answer is (C).** $2^2 + 2^3 = 4 + 8 = 12$

TABLE OF MEASURES

AMERICAN MEASURES	
Length	**Liquid Measure**
1 foot (ft. or ′) = 12 inches (in. or ″) 1 yard (yd.) = 36 inches 1 yard = 3 feet 1 rod (rd.) = 16½ feet 1 mile (mi.) = 5,280 feet 1 mile = 1,760 yards 1 mile = 320 rods	1 cup (c.) = 8 fluid ounces (fl. oz.) 1 pint (pt.) = 2 cups 1 pint = 4 gills (gi.) 1 quart (qt.) = 2 pints 1 gallon (gal.) = 4 quarts 1 barrel (bl., bbl.) = 31½ gallons
Weight	**Dry Measure**
1 pound (lb.) = 16 ounces (oz.) 1 hundredweight (cwt.) = 100 pounds 1 ton (T) = 2,000 pounds	1 quart (qt.) = 2 pints (pt.) 1 peck (pk.) = 8 quarts 1 bushel (bu) = 4 pecks
Area	**Volume**
1 square foot (ft^2 or sq. ft.) = 144 square inches (in^2 or sq. in.) 1 square yard (yd^2 or sq. yd.) = 9 square feet	1 cubic foot (ft^3 or cu. ft.) = 1,728 cubic inches ($in.^3$ or cu. in.) 1 cubic yard (yd^3 or cu. yd.) = 27 cubic feet 1 gallon = 231 cubic inches

GENERAL MEASURES		
Time	**Angles and Arcs**	**Counting**
1 minute (min.) = 60 seconds (sec.) 1 hour (hr.) = 60 minutes 1 day = 24 hours 1 week = 7 days 1 year = 52 weeks 1 calendar year = 365 days	1 minute (′) = 60 seconds (″) 1 degree (°) = 60 minutes 1 circle = 360 degrees	1 dozen (doz.) = 12 units 1 gross (gr.) = 12 dozen 1 gross = 144 units

TABLE OF AMERICAN—METRIC CONVERSIONS (Approximate)		
American to Metric	**Metric to American**	**Table of Metric Conversions***
1 inch = 2.54 centimeters 1 yard = .9 meter 1 mile = 1.6 kilometers 1 ounce = 28 grams 1 pound = 454 grams 1 fluid ounce = 30 milliliters 1 liquid quart = .95 liters	1 centimeter = .39 inch 1 meter = 1.1 yards 1 kilometer = .6 mile 1 kilogram = 2.2 pounds 1 liter = 1.06 liquid quart	1 liter = 1,000 cubic centimeters (cm^3) 1 milliliter = 1 cubic centimeter 1 liter of water has a mass of 1 kilogram 1 milliliter of water has a mass of 1 gram

* These conversions are exact only under specific conditions. If the conditions are not met, the conversions are approximate.

THE METRIC SYSTEM

LENGTH		
Unit	**Abbreviation**	**Number of Meters**
myriameter	mym	10,000
kilometer	km	1,000
hectometer	hm	100
dekameter	dam	10
meter	m	1
decimeter	dm	0.1
centimeter	cm	0.01
millimeter	mm	0.001
AREA		
Unit	**Abbreviation**	**Number of Square Meters**
square kilometer	sq km *or* km^2	1,000,000
hectare	ha	10,000
are	a	100
centare	ca	1
square centimeter	sq cm *or* cm^2	0.0001
VOLUME		
Unit	**Abbreviation**	**Number of Cubic Meters**
dekastere	das	10
stere	s	1
decistere	ds	0.10
cubic centimeter	cu cm *or* cm^3 *or* cc	0.000001
CAPACITY		
Unit	**Abbreviation**	**Number of Liters**
kiloliter	kl	1,000
hectoliter	hl	100
dekaliter	dal	10
liter	l	1
deciliter	dl	0.10
centiliter	cl	0.01
milliliter	ml	0.001
MASS AND WEIGHT		
Unit	**Abbreviation**	**Number of Grams**
metric ton	MT *or* t	1,000,000
quintal	q	100,000
kilogram	kg	1,000
hectogram	hg	100
dekagram	dag	10
gram	g *or* gm	1
decigram	dg	0.10
centigram	cg	0.01
milligram	mg	0.001

DENOMINATE NUMBERS (MEASUREMENT)

1. A **denominate number** is a number that specifies a given measurement. The unit of measure is called the **denomination.**

   Example: 7 miles, 3 quarts, and 5 grams are denominate numbers.

2. a. The American system of measurement uses such denominations as pints, ounces, pounds, and feet.

   b. The metric system of measurement uses such denominations as grams, liters, and meters.

AMERICAN SYSTEM OF MEASUREMENT

3. To convert from one unit of measure to another, find in the Table of Measures how many units of the smaller denomination equal one unit of the larger denomination. This number is called the **conversion number.**

4. To convert from one unit of measure to a smaller unit, multiply the given number of units by the conversion number.

   Problem: Convert 7 yards to inches.

   SOLUTION: 1 yard = 36 inches (conversion number)
   7 yards = 7 × 36 inches
   = 252 inches

   Answer: 252 in.

   Problem: Convert 2 hours 12 minutes to minutes.

   SOLUTION: 1 hour = 60 minutes (conversion number)
   2 hr 12 min = 2 hr + 12 min
   2 hr = 2 × 60 min = 120 min
   2 hr 12 min = 120 min + 12 min
   = 132 min

   Answer: 132 min.

5. To convert from one unit of measure to a larger unit:

   a. Divide the given number of units by the conversion number.

   Problem: Convert 48 inches to feet.

   SOLUTION: 1 foot = 12 inches (conversion number)
   48 in ÷ 12 = 4 ft

   Answer: 4 ft.

b. If there is a remainder, it is expressed in terms of the smaller unit of measure.

Problem: Convert 35 ounces to pounds and ounces.

SOLUTION: 1 pound = 16 ounces (conversion number)

$$35 \text{ oz} \div 16 = 16\overline{)35 \text{ oz}} \quad \text{quotient } 2\text{lb}$$

$$\begin{array}{r} 32 \\ \hline 3 \text{ oz} \end{array}$$

$$= 2 \text{ lb } 3 \text{ oz}$$

Answer: 2 lb. 3 oz.

6. To add denominate numbers, arrange them in columns by common unit, then add each column. If necessary simplify the answer, starting with the smallest unit.

Problem: Add 1 yd. 2 ft. 8 in., 2 yd. 2 ft. 10 in., and 3 yd. 1 ft. 9 in.

SOLUTION:

$$\begin{array}{l} 1 \text{ yd } 2 \text{ ft } 8 \text{ in} \\ 2 \text{ yd } 2 \text{ ft } 10 \text{ in} \\ +\,3 \text{ yd } 1 \text{ ft } 9 \text{ in} \\ \hline 6 \text{ yd } 5 \text{ ft } 27 \text{ in} \\ = 6 \text{ yd } 7 \text{ ft } 3 \text{ in (since 27 in = 2 ft 3 in)} \\ = 8 \text{ yd } 1 \text{ ft } 3 \text{ in (since 7 ft = 2 yd 1 ft)} \end{array}$$

Answer: 8 yd. 1 ft. 3 in.

7. To subtract denominate numbers, arrange them in columns by common unit, then subtract each column starting with the smallest unit. If necessary, borrow to increase the number of a particular unit.

Problem: Subtract 2 gal. 3 qt. from 7 gal. 1 qt.

SOLUTION:

$$\begin{array}{rcr} 7 \text{ gal } 1 \text{ qt} & = & 6 \text{ gal } 5 \text{ qt} \\ -2 \text{ gal } 3 \text{ qt} & = & -2 \text{ gal } 3 \text{ qt} \\ \hline & & 4 \text{ gal } 2 \text{ qt} \end{array}$$

Note that 1 gal. was borrowed from 7 gal.

1 gal = 4 qt

Therefore, 7 gal 1 qt = 6 gal 5 qt

Answer: 4 gal. 2 qt.

8. To multiply a denominate number by a given number:

a. If the denominate number contains only one unit, multiply the numbers and write the unit.

Example: 3 oz × 4 = 12 oz

b. If the denominate number contains more than one unit of measurement, multiply the number of each unit by the given number and simplify the answer, if necessary.

Problem: Multiply 4 yd. 2 ft. 8 in. by 2.

SOLUTION:

$$\begin{array}{l} 4 \text{ yd } 2\text{ft } 8 \text{ in} \\ \times \qquad\qquad 2 \\ \hline 8 \text{ yd } 4 \text{ ft } 16 \text{ in} \\ = 8 \text{ yd } 5 \text{ ft } 4 \text{ in (since 16 in = 1 ft 4 in)} \\ = 9 \text{ yd } 2 \text{ ft } 4 \text{ in (since 5 ft = 1 yd 2 ft)} \end{array}$$

Answer: 9 yd. 2 ft. 4 in.

9. To divide a denominate number by a given number, convert all units to the smallest unit, then divide. Simplify the answer, if necessary.

Problem: Divide 5 lb. 12 oz. by 4

SOLUTION:

$$\begin{aligned} 1 \text{ lb} &= 16 \text{ oz, therefore} \\ 5 \text{ lb } 12 \text{ oz} &= 92 \text{ oz} \\ 92 \text{ oz} \div 4 &= 23 \text{ oz} \\ &= 1 \text{ lb } 7 \text{ oz} \end{aligned}$$

Answer: 1 lb. 7 oz.

10. Alternate method of division:

a. Divide the number of the largest unit by the given number.

b. Convert any remainder to the next largest unit.

c. Divide the total number of that unit by the given number.

d. Again convert any remainder to the next unit and divide.

e. Repeat until no units remain.

Problem: Divide 9 hr. 21 min. 40 sec. by 4.

SOLUTION:

```
          2 hr  20 min  25 sec
       4)9 hr  21 min  40sec
         8 hr
         1 hr = 60 min
                81 min
                80 min
                 1 min =  60 sec
                         100 sec
                         100 sec
                           0 sec
```

Answer: 2 hr. 20 min. 25 sec.

METRIC MEASUREMENT

11. The basic units of the metric system are the meter (m), which is used to measure length; the gram (g), which is used to measure weight; and the liter (l) which is used to measure capacity or volume.

12. The prefixes that are used with the basic units, and their meanings, are:

Prefix	Abbreviation	Meaning
micro	μ	one millionth of (.000001)
milli	m	one thousandth of (.001)
centi	c	one hundredth of (.01)
deci	d	one tenth of (.1)
deka	da or dk	ten times (10)
hecto	h	one hundred times (100)
kilo	k	one thousand times (1,000)
mega	M	one million times (1,000,000)

13. To convert *to* a basic metric unit from a prefixed metric unit, multiply by the number indicated in the prefix.

Example: Convert 72 millimeters to meters.

72 millimeters = 72 × .001 meter
= .072 meter

Example: Convert 4 kiloliters to liters.

4 kiloliters = 4 × 1000 liters
= 4,000 liters

14. To convert *from* a basic unit to a prefixed unit, divide by the number indicated in the prefix.

Example: Convert 300 liters to hectoliters.

300 liters = 300 ÷ 100 hectoliters
= 3 hectoliters

Example: Convert 4.5 meters to decimeters.

4.5 meters = 4.5 ÷ .1 decimeter
= 45 decimeters

15. To convert from any prefixed metric unit to another prefixed metric unit, first convert to a basic unit, then convert the basic unit to the desired unit.

Problem: Convert 420 decigrams to kilograms.

SOLUTION: 420 dg = 420 × .1 g = 42 g
42 g = 42 ÷ 1,000 kg = .042 kg

Answer: .042 kg

16. To add, subtract, multiply, or divide using metric measurement, first convert all units to the same unit, then perform the desired operation.

Problem: Subtract 1,200 g from 2.5 kg.

SOLUTION:

$$\begin{array}{rcr} 2.5 \text{ kg} & = & 2{,}500 \text{ g} \\ -\ 1{,}200 \text{ g} & = & -\ 1{,}200 \text{ g} \\ \hline & & 1{,}300 \text{ g} \end{array}$$

Answer: 1,300 g or 1.3 kg

17. To convert from a metric measure to an American measure, or the reverse:

a. In the Table of American–Metric Conversions, find how many units of the desired measure are equal to one unit of the given measure.

b. Multiply the given number by the number found in the table.

Problem: Find the number of pounds in 4 kilograms.

SOLUTION: From the table, 1 kg = 2.2 lb.
4 kg = 4 × 2.2 lb
= 8.8 lb

Answer: 8.8 lb.

Problem: Find the number of meters in 5 yards.

SOLUTION: 1 yd = .9 m
5 yd = 5 × .9 m
= 4.5 m

Answer: 4.5 m

TEMPERATURE MEASUREMENT

18. The temperature measurement used in the United States is the degree Fahrenheit (°F). The metric measurement for temperature is the degree Celsius (°C), also called degree Centigrade.

19. Degrees Celsius may be converted to degrees Fahrenheit by the formula:

$$°F = \frac{9}{5}°C + 32°$$

Problem: Water boils at 100°C. Convert this to °F.

SOLUTION:
$$°F = \frac{9}{\cancel{5}_1} \times \cancel{100°}^{20} + 32°$$
$$= 180° + 32°$$
$$= 212°$$

Answer: 100°C = 212°F

20. Degrees Fahrenheit may be converted to degrees Celsius by the formula:

$$°C = \frac{5}{9}(°F - 32°)$$

In using this formula, perform the subtraction in the parenthesis first, then multiply by $\frac{5}{9}$.

Problem: If normal body temperature is 98.6°F, what is normal body temperature on the Celsius scale?

SOLUTION:
$$°C = \frac{5}{9}(98.6° - 32°)$$
$$= \frac{5}{9} \times 66.6°$$
$$= \frac{333}{9}°$$
$$= 37°$$

Answer: Normal body temperature = 37°C.

PRACTICE TEST

1. A carpenter needs boards for 4 shelves, each 2′ 9″ long. How many feet of board should he buy?

(A) 11
(B) $11\frac{1}{6}$
(C) 13
(D) $15\frac{1}{2}$

2. The number of half-pints in 19 gallons of milk is

(A) 76
(B) 152
(C) 304
(D) 608

3. The product of 8 ft. 7 in. multiplied by 8 is

(A) 69 ft. 6 in.
(B) 68.8 ft.
(C) $68\frac{2}{3}$ ft.
(D) 68 ft. 2 in.

4. $\frac{1}{3}$ of 7 yards is

(A) 2 yd.
(B) 4 ft.
(C) $2\frac{1}{2}$ yd.
(D) 7 ft.

5. Six gross of special drawing pencils were purchased for use in an office. If the pencils were used at the rate of 24 a week, the maximum number of weeks that the 6 gross of pencils would last is

(A) 6 weeks
(B) 12 weeks
(C) 24 weeks
(D) 36 weeks

6. If 7 ft. 9 in. are cut from a piece of wood that is 9 ft. 6 in., then the piece that is left is

(A) 1 ft. 9 in.
(B) 1 ft. 10 in.
(C) 2 ft. 2 in.
(D) 2 ft. 5 in.

7. Subtract 3 hours 49 minutes from 5 hours 13 minutes.

(A) 1 hr. 5 min.
(B) 1 hr. 10 min.
(C) 1 hr. 18 min.
(D) 1 hr. 24 min.

8. An entire piece of wood 35 feet 6 inches long was used to make four shelves of equal lengths. The length of each shelf was

(A) 8.9 in.
(B) 8 ft. 9 in.
(C) 8 ft. $9\frac{1}{2}$ in.
(D) 8 ft. $10\frac{1}{2}$ in.

9. The number of yards equal to 126 inches is

(A) 3.5
(B) 10.5
(C) 1260
(D) 1512

10. If there are 231 cubic inches in 1 gallon, the number of cubic inches in 3 pints is closest to which one of the following?

(A) 24
(B) 29
(C) 57
(D) 87

11. The sum of 5 feet $2\frac{3}{4}$ inches, 8 feet $\frac{1}{2}$ inch, and $12\frac{1}{2}$ inches is

(A) 14 ft. $3\frac{3}{4}$ in.
(B) 14 ft. $5\frac{3}{4}$ in.
(C) 14 ft. $9\frac{1}{4}$ in.
(D) 15 ft. $\frac{1}{2}$ in.

12. Add 5 hr. 13 min., 3 hr. 49 min., and 14 min.

(A) 8 hr. 16 min.
(B) 9 hr. 16 min.
(C) 9 hr. 76 min.
(D) 8 hr. 6 min.

13. Assuming that 2.54 centimeters = 1 inch, a metal rod that measures $1\frac{1}{2}$ feet would most nearly equal which one of the following?

(A) 380 cm
(B) 46 cm
(C) 30 cm
(D) 18 cm

14. A micromillimeter is defined as one millionth of a millimeter. A length of 17 micromillimeters may be represented as

(A) .00017 mm
(B) .0000017 mm
(C) .000017 mm
(D) .00000017 mm

15. How many liters are equal to 4,200 ml?

(A) .42
(B) 4.2
(C) 420
(D) 420,000

16. Add 26 dg, .4 kg, 5 g, 184 cg.

(A) 215.4 g
(B) 319.34 g
(C) 409.44 g
(D) 849.00 g

17. Four full bottles of equal size contain a total of 1.28 liters of cleaning solution. How many milliliters are in each bottle?

(A) 3.20
(B) 5.12
(C) 320
(D) 512

18. How many liters of water can be held in a 5-gallon jug? (See Conversion Table.)

(A) 19
(B) 38
(C) 40
(D) 50

19. To the nearest degree, what is a temperature of 12°C equal to on the Fahrenheit scale?

(A) 19°
(B) 54°
(C) 57°
(D) 79°

20. A company requires that the temperature in its offices be kept at 68°F. What is this in °C?

(A) 10°
(B) 15°
(C) 20°
(D) 25°

ANSWERS AND EXPLANATIONS

1. A	**5.** D	**9.** A	**13.** B	**17.** C
2. C	**6.** A	**10.** D	**14.** C	**18.** A
3. C	**7.** D	**11.** A	**15.** B	**19.** B
4. D	**8.** D	**12.** B	**16.** C	**20.** C

1. **The correct answer is (A).**

$$\begin{array}{r} 2\text{ ft } \ 9\text{ in} \\ \times \qquad 4 \\ \hline 8\text{ ft } 36\text{ in} = 11\text{ ft} \end{array}$$

2. **The correct answer is (C).** Find the number of half-pints in 1 gallon:

$$1\text{ gal} = 4\text{ qts}$$
$$4\text{ qts} = 4 \times 2\text{ pts} = 8\text{ pts}$$
$$8\text{ pts} = 8 \times 2 = 16\text{ half-pints}$$

Multiply to find the number of half-pints in 19 gallons:

$$19\text{ gallons} = 19 \times 16\text{ half-pints}$$
$$= 304\text{ half-pints}$$

3. **The correct answer is (C).**

$$\begin{array}{r} 8\text{ ft } \ 7\text{ in} \\ \times \qquad 8 \\ \hline 64\text{ ft } 56\text{ in} = 68\text{ ft } 8\text{ in} \end{array}$$

(since 56 in = 4 ft 8 in)

$$8\text{ in} = \frac{8}{12}\text{ ft} = \frac{2}{3}\text{ ft}$$

$$68\text{ ft } 8\text{ in} = 68\frac{2}{3}\text{ ft}$$

4. **The correct answer is (D).**

$$\frac{1}{3} \times 7\text{ yd} = 2\frac{1}{3}\text{ yd}$$
$$= 2\text{ yd } 1\text{ ft}$$
$$= (2 \times 3\text{ ft}) + 1\text{ ft}$$
$$= 7\text{ ft.}$$

5. **The correct answer is (D).** Find the number of units in 6 gross:

$$1\text{ gross} = 144\text{ units}$$
$$6\text{ gross} = 6 \times 144\text{ units}$$
$$= 864\text{ units}$$

Divide units by rate of use:

$$864 \div 24 = 36\text{ weeks}$$

6. **The correct answer is (A).**

$$\begin{array}{rcr} 9\text{ ft } 6\text{ in} = & & 8\text{ ft } 18\text{ in.} \\ -\ 7\text{ ft } 9\text{ in} = & - & 7\text{ ft } \ 9\text{ in.} \\ \hline & & 1\text{ ft } \ 9\text{ in.} \end{array}$$

7. The correct answer is (D).

$$\begin{array}{rr} \text{5 hours 13 minutes} = & \text{4 hours 73 minutes} \\ -\ \text{3 hours 49 minutes} = & -\ \text{3 hours 49 minutes} \\ \hline & \text{1 hour 24 minutes} \end{array}$$

8. The correct answer is (D).

$$\begin{array}{l} \text{8 feet 10 inches} + \frac{2}{4}\text{ inches} = \text{8 ft } 10\frac{1}{2}\text{ in} \\ 4\overline{)35\text{ feet} \quad 6\text{ inches}} \\ \underline{32\text{ feet}} \\ 3\text{ feet} = \underline{36\text{ inches}} \\ \qquad 42\text{ inches} \\ \qquad \underline{40\text{ inches}} \\ \qquad 2\text{ inches} \end{array}$$

9. The correct answer is (A).

$1 \text{ yd} = 36 \text{ in}$

$126 \div 36 = 3.5$

10. The correct answer is (D).

$$\begin{aligned} 1\text{gal} &= 4 \text{ qt} = 8 \text{ pt} \\ \text{Therefore, } 1 \text{ pt} &= 231 \text{ cubic inches} \div 8 \\ &= 28.875 \text{ cubic inches} \\ 3 \text{ pts} &= 3 \times 28.875 \text{ cubic inches} \\ &= 86.625 \text{ inches} \end{aligned}$$

11. The correct answer is (A).

$$\begin{array}{rr} \text{5 feet} & 2\frac{3}{4}\text{ inches} \\ \text{8 feet} & \frac{1}{2}\text{ inches} \\ + & 12\frac{1}{2}\text{ inches} \\ \hline \text{13 feet} & 15\frac{3}{4}\text{ inches} \\ = \text{14 feet} & 3\frac{3}{4}\text{ inches} \end{array}$$

12. The correct answer is (B).

$$\begin{array}{r} \text{5 hr 13 min} \\ \text{3 hr 49 min} \\ +\quad \text{14 min} \\ \hline \text{8 hr 76 min} \\ = \text{9 hr 16 min} \end{array}$$

13. The correct answer is (B).

$$1 \text{ foot} = 12 \text{ inches}$$
$$1\frac{1}{2} \text{ feet} = 1\frac{1}{2} \times 12 \text{ inches} = 18 \text{ inches}$$
$$1 \text{ inch} = 2.54 \text{ cm}$$
$$\text{Therefore, } 18 \text{ inches} = 18 \times 2.54 \text{ cm} = 45.72 \text{ cm}$$

So, the correct answer is 46 cm.

14. The correct answer is (C).

$$1 \text{ micromillimeter} = .000001 \text{ mm}$$
$$17 \text{ micromillimeters} = 17 \times .000001 \text{ mm} = .000017 \text{ mm}$$

15. The correct answer is (B).

$$4200 \text{ ml} = 4200 \times .001 \text{ l} = 4.200 \text{ l}$$

16. The correct answer is (C). Convert all of the units to grams:

$$\begin{aligned} 26 \text{ dg} &= 26 \times .1 \text{ g} = 2.6 \text{ g} \\ .4 \text{ kg} &= .4 \times 1000 \text{ g} = 400 \text{ g} \\ 5 \text{ g} &= 5 \text{ g} \\ 184 \text{ cg} &= 184 \times .01 \text{ g} = \underline{1.84 \text{ g}} \\ & \qquad 409.44 \text{ g} \end{aligned}$$

17. The correct answer is (C).

$$1.28 \text{ liters} \div 4 = .32 \text{ liters}$$
$$.32 \text{ liters} = .32 \div .001 \text{ ml} = 320 \text{ ml}$$

18. The correct answer is (A). Find the number of liters in 1 gallon:

$$1 \text{ qt} = .95 \text{ l}$$
$$1 \text{ gal} = 4 \text{ qts}$$
$$1 \text{ gal} = 4 \times .95 \text{ l} = 3.8 \text{ l}$$

Multiply to find the number of liters in 5 gallons:

$$5 \text{ gal} = 5 \times 3.8 \text{ l} = 19 \text{ l}$$

19. The correct answer is (B).

$$°F = \frac{9}{5} \times 12° + 32° = \frac{108°}{5} + 32° = 21.6° + 32° = 53.6°$$

So the correct answer is 54°.

20. The correct answer is (C).

$$°C = \frac{5}{9}(68° - 32°) = \frac{5}{\cancel{9}_{1}} \times \cancel{36°}^{4} = 20°$$

GEOMETRY

ANGLES

1. a. An **angle** is the figure formed by two lines meeting at a point.

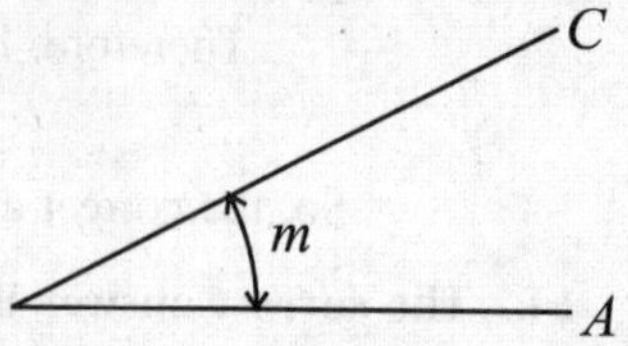

b. The point B is the vertex of the angle and the lines BA and BC are the **sides** of the angle.

2. There are three common ways of naming an angle:

a. By a small letter or figure written within the angle as $\angle m$.

b. By the capital letter at its vertex, as $\angle B$.

c. By three capital letters, the middle letter being the vertex letter, as $\angle ABC$ or $\angle CBA$.

3. a. When two straight lines intersect (cut each other), four angles are formed. If these four angles are equal, each angle is called a **right angle** and contains 90°. The symbol ⌉ is used to indicate a right angle.

Example:

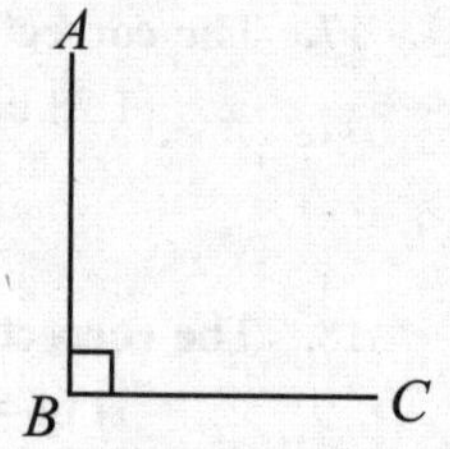

$\angle ABC$ is a right angle.

b. An angle measuring less than 90° is called an **acute angle.**

c. If the two sides of an angle extend in opposite directions forming a straight line, the angle is called a **straight angle** and measures 180°.

d. An angle measuring more than 90° but less than 180° is called an **obtuse angle.**

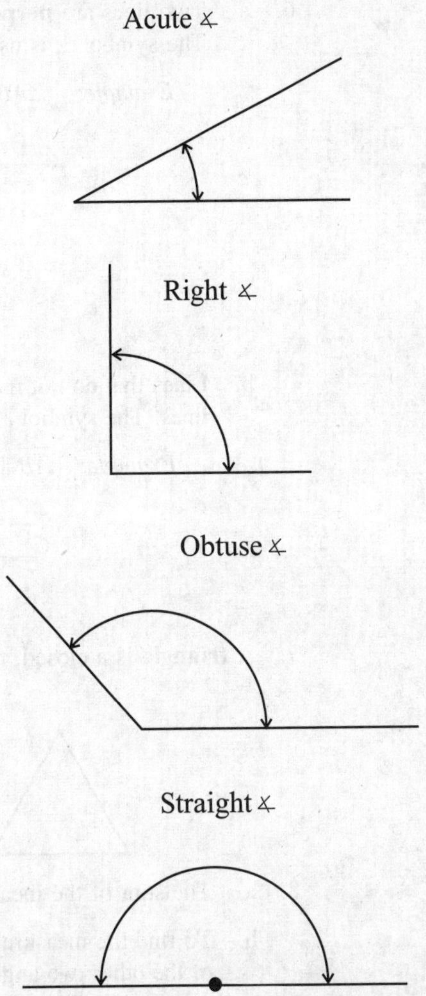

4. a. Two angles are **complementary** if the sum of their measures is 90°.

   b. To find the **complement** of an angle, subtract the measure of the given angle from 90°.

   Example: The complement of 60° is 90° − 60° = 30°

5. a. Two angles are **supplementary** if the sum of their measures is 180°.

   b. To find the **supplement** of an angle, subtract the measure of the given angle from 180°.

   Example: The supplement of 60° is 180° − 60° = 120°.

LINES

6. a. Two lines are **perpendicular** to each other if they meet to form a right angle. The symbol ⊥ is used to indicate that the lines are perpendicular.

Example: $\angle ABC$ is a right angle. Therefore $\overline{AB} \perp \overline{BC}$.

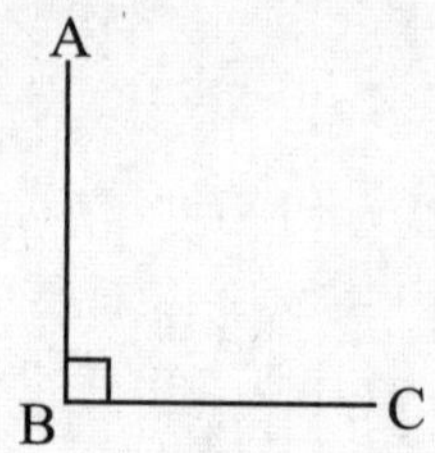

b. Lines that do not meet no matter how far they are extended are called **parallel** lines. The symbol ∥ is used to indicate that the two lines are parallel.

Example: $\overline{AB} \parallel \overline{CD}$.

TRIANGLES

7. A **triangle** is a closed, three-sided figure. The figures below are all triangles.

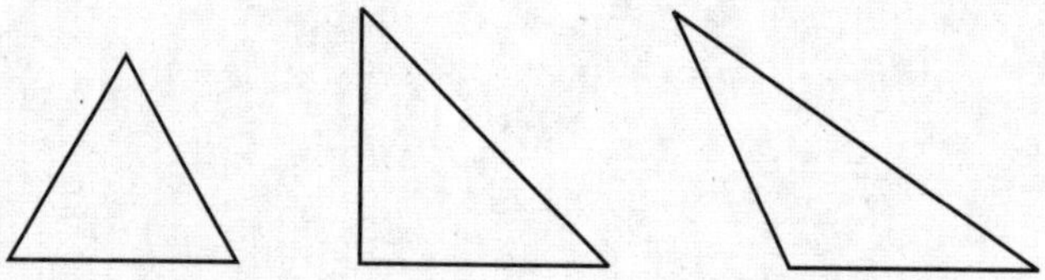

8. a. The sum of the measures of three angles of a triangle is 180°.

b. To find the measure of an angle of a triangle when you are given the measures of the other two angles, add the measures of the given angles and subtract their sum from 180°.

Problem: The measures of two angles of a triangle are 60° and 40°. Find the measure of the third angle.

SOLUTION:
$$60° + 40° = 100°$$
$$180° - 100° = 80°$$

Answer: The measure of the third angle is 80°.

9. a. A triangle that has two congruent sides is called an **isosceles triangle.**

b. In an isosceles triangle, the angles opposite the congruent sides are also congruent.

10. a. A triangle that has all three sides congruent is called an **equilateral triangle.**

b. Each angle of an equilateral triangle measures 60°.

11. a. A triangle that has a right angle is called a **right triangle.**

b. In a right triangle, the two acute angles are complementary.

c. In a right triangle, the side opposite the right angle is called the **hypotenuse** and is the longest side. The other two sides are called **legs.**

Example: $\overline{AC}$ is the hypotenuse.
$\overline{AB}$ and $\overline{BC}$ are the legs.

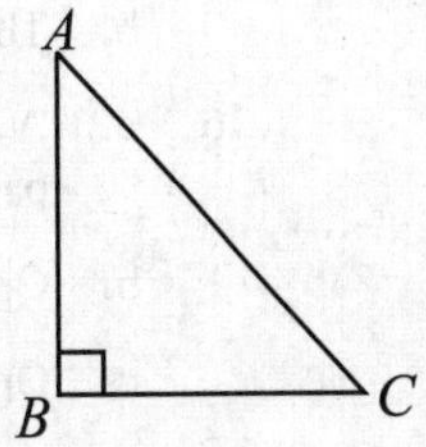

12. The **Pythagorean theorem** states that in a right triangle, the square of the hypotenuse equals the sum of the squares of the legs.

13. To find the hypotenuse of a right triangle when given the legs:

a. Square each leg.

b. Add the squares.

c. Compute the square root of this sum.

Problem: In a right triangle the legs are 6 inches and 8 inches. Find the hypotenuse.

SOLUTION: $6^2 = 36 \quad 8^2 = 64$

$36 + 64 = 100$

$\sqrt{100} = 10$

Answer: The hypotenuse is 10 inches.

14. To find a leg when given the other leg and the hypotenuse of a right triangle:

a. Square the hypotenuse and the given leg.

b. Subtract the square of the leg from the square of the hypotenuse.

c. Compute the square root of the difference.

Problem: One leg of a right triangle is 12 feet and the hypotenuse is 20 feet. Find the other leg.

SOLUTION: $12^2 = 144 \quad 20^2 = 400$

$400 - 144 = 256$

$\sqrt{256} = 16$

Answer: The other leg is 16 feet.

QUADRILATERALS

15. a. A **quadrilateral** is a closed, four-sided figure in two dimensions. Common quadrilaterals are the **parallelogram, rectangle,** and **square.**

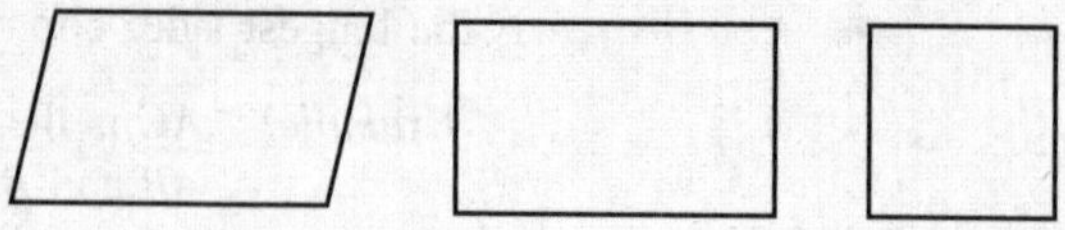

b. The sum of the measures of the four angles of a quadrilateral is 360°.

16. a. A **parallelogram** is a quadrilateral in which both pairs of opposite sides are parallel.

b. Opposite sides of a parallelogram are congruent.

c. Opposite angles of a parallelogram are congruent.

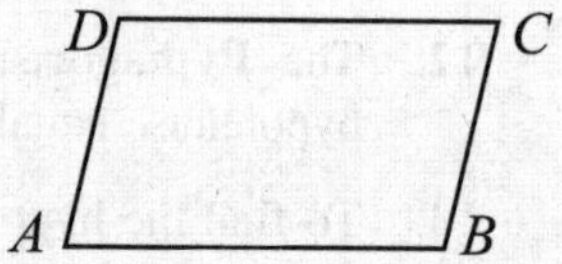

In parallelogram $ABCD$,

$$\overline{AB} \parallel \overline{CD},\quad \overline{AD} \parallel \overline{BC}$$
$$AB = CD,\quad AD = BC$$
$$m\angle A = m\angle C,\ m\angle B = m\angle D$$

17. A **rectangle** has all of the properties of a parallelogram. In addition, all four of its angles are right angles.

18. A **square** is a rectangle with the additional property that all four of its sides are congruent.

CIRCLES

19. A **circle** is a closed-plane curve, all points of which are equidistant from a point within called the **center.**

20. a. A **complete circle** contains 360°.

b. A **semicircle** contains 180°.

21. a. A **chord** is a line segment connecting any two points on the circle.

b. A **radius** of a circle is a line segment connecting the center with any point on the circle.

c. A **diameter** is a chord passing through the center of the circle.

d. A **secant** is a chord extended outside of the circle in either one or both directions.

e. A **tangent** is a line touching a circle at one and only one point.

f. The **circumference** is the length of the curved line bounding the circle.

g. An **arc** of a circle is any part of the circumference.

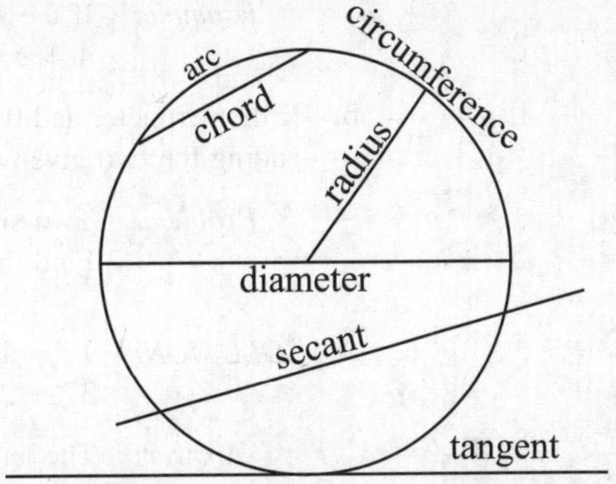

22. a. A **central angle**, as $\angle AOB$ in the figure below, is an angle whose vertex is the center of the circle and whose sides are radii. A central angle is equal to, or has the same number of degrees as, its intercepted arc.

b. An **inscribed angle**, as $\angle MNP$, is an angle whose vertex is on the circle and whose sides are chords. An inscribed angle has half the number of degrees as its intercepted arc. $\angle MNP$ intercepts arc MP and has half the degrees of arc MP.

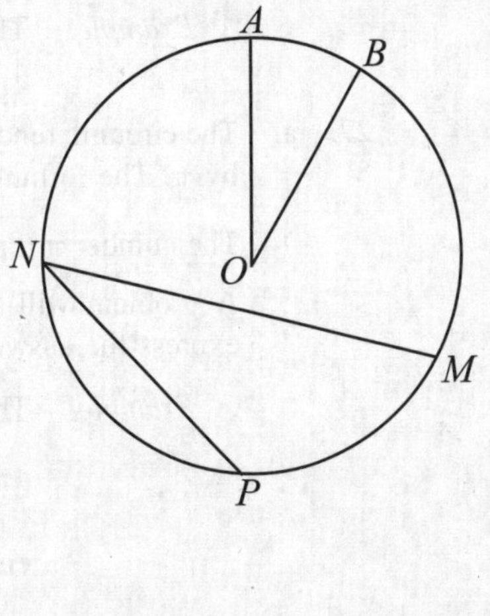

PERIMETER

23. The **perimeter** of a two-dimensional figure is the distance around the figure.

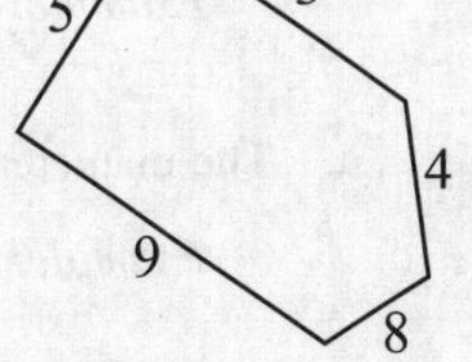

Example: The perimeter of the figure above is $9 + 8 + 4 + 3 + 5 = 29$.

24. a. The perimeter of a triangle is found by adding the length of all of its sides.

Example: If the sides of a triangle are 4, 5, and 7, its perimeter is $4 + 5 + 7 = 16$.

b. If the perimeter and two sides of a triangle are given, the third side is found by adding the two given sides and subtracting this sum from the perimeter.

Problem: Two sides of a triangle are 12 and 15, and the perimeter is 37. Find the other side.

SOLUTION: $12 + 15 = 27$
$37 - 27 = 10$

Answer: The length of the third side is 10.

25. The perimeter of a rectangle equals twice the sum of the length and the width. The formula is $P = 2(l + w)$.

Example: The perimeter of a rectangle whose length is 7 feet and width is 3 feet equals $2 \times 10 = 20$ feet.

26. The perimeter of a square equals the length of its side multiplied by 4. The formula is $P = 4s$.

Example: The perimeter of a square, one side of which is 5 feet, is 4×5 feet $= 20$ feet.

27. a. The circumference of a circle is equal to the product of the diameter multiplied by π. The formula is $C = \pi d$.

b. The number π ("pi") is approximately $\frac{22}{7}$, or 3.14 (3.1416 for greater accuracy). A problem will usually state which approximation for π to use; otherwise, express the answer in terms of "pi," π.

Example: The circumference of a circle whose diameter is 4 inches is 4π inches; or, if it is approximated by $\frac{22}{7}$, then the circumference would be $4 \times \frac{22}{7} = \frac{88}{7} = 12\frac{4}{7}$ inches.

c. Since the diameter is twice the radius, the circumference equals twice the radius multiplied by π. The formula is $C = 2\pi r$.

Example: If the radius of a circle is 3 inches, then the circumference is 6π inches.

d. The diameter of a circle equals the circumference divided by π.

Example: If the circumference of a circle is 11 inches, then assuming $\pi = \frac{22}{7}$

$$\text{diameter} = 11 \div \frac{22}{7} \text{ inches}$$
$$= \overset{1}{\cancel{11}} \times \frac{7}{\underset{2}{\cancel{22}}} \text{ inches}$$
$$= \frac{7}{2} \text{ inches, or } 3\frac{1}{2} \text{ inches.}$$

AREA

28. a. In a figure of two dimensions, the total space within the figure is called the **area.**

b. Area is expressed in square units, such as square inches, square centimeters, and square miles.

c. In computing area, all dimensions must be expressed in the same units.

29. The area of a square is equal to the square of the length of its side. The formula is $A = s^2$.

Example: The area of a square, one side of which is 6 inches, is $6 \times 6 =$ 36 square inches.

30. a. The area of a rectangle equals the product of the length and the width. The length is any side; the width is a side next to the length. The formula is $A = l \times w$.

Example: If the length of a rectangle is 6 feet and its width 4 feet, then the area is $6 \times 4 = 24$ square feet.

b. If given the area of a rectangle and one dimension, divide the area by the given dimension to find the other dimension.

Example: If the area of a rectangle is 48 square feet and one dimension is 4 feet, then the other dimension is $48 \div 4 = 12$ feet.

31. a. The altitude, or height, of a parallelogram is a line drawn from a vertex perpendicular to the opposite side or base.

Example: $\overline{DE}$ is the height.
$\overline{AB}$ is the base.

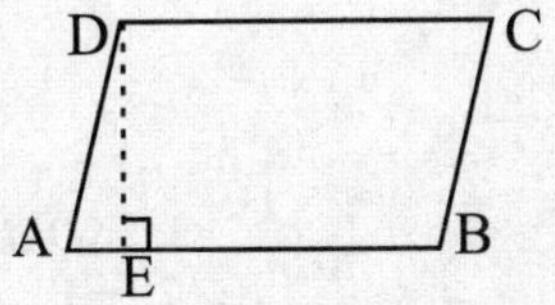

b. The area of a parallelogram is equal to the product of its base and its height: $A = b \times h$.

Example: If the base of a parallelogram is 10 centimeters and its height is 5 centimeters, its area is $5 \times 10 = 50$ square centimeters.

c. If given one of these dimensions and the area, divide the area by the given dimension to find the other dimension of a parallelogram.

Example: If the area of a parallelogram is 40 square inches and its height is 8 inches, its base is $40 \div 8 = 5$ inches.

32. a. The altitude, or height, of a triangle is a line drawn from a vertex perpendicular to the line containing the opposite side, called the base.

b. The area of a triangle is equal to one half the product of the base and the height: $A = \frac{1}{2}b \times h$.

Example: The area of a triangle having a height of 5 inches and a base of 4 inches is $\frac{1}{2} \times 5 \times 4 = \frac{1}{2} \times 20 = 10$ square inches.

c. In a right triangle, one leg may be considered the height and the other leg the base. Therefore, the area of a right triangle is equal to one half the product of the legs.

Example: The legs of a right triangle are 3 and 4. Its area is $\frac{1}{2} \times 3 \times 4 =$ 6 square units.

33. a. The area of a circle is equal to the radius squared, multiplied by π: $A = \pi r^2$.

Example: If the radius of a circle is 6 inches, then the area = 36π square inches.

b. To find the radius of a circle given the area, divide the area by π and find the square root of the quotient.

Example: To find the radius of a circle of area 100π,

$$\frac{100\pi}{\pi} = 100$$

$$\sqrt{100} = 10 = \text{radius.}$$

34. Some figures are composed of several geometric shapes. To find the area of such a figure it is necessary to find the area of each of its parts.

Problem: Find the area of the figure below.

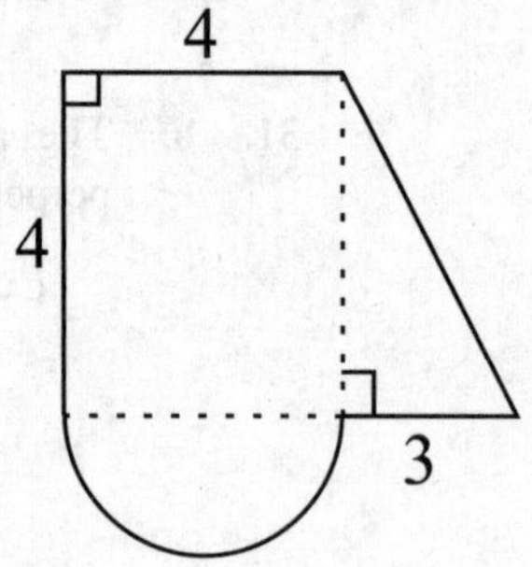

SOLUTION: The figure is composed of three parts: a square of side 4, a semicircle of diameter 4 (attached to the lower side of the square), and a right triangle with legs 3 and 4 (attached to the right side of the square).

$$\text{Area of square} = 4^2 = 16$$

$$\text{Area of triangle} = \frac{1}{4} \times 3 \times 4 = 6$$

$$\text{Area of semicircle is } \frac{1}{2} \text{ area of the circle} = \frac{1}{2}\pi r^2$$

$$\text{Radius} = \frac{1}{2} \times 4 = 2$$

$$\text{Area} = \frac{1}{2}\pi r^2$$

$$= \frac{1}{2} \times \pi \times 2^2$$

$$= 2\pi$$

Answer: Total area = $16 + 6 + 2\pi = 22 + 2\pi$

THREE-DIMENSIONAL FIGURES

35. a. In a three-dimensional figure, the total space contained within the figure is called the **volume;** it is expressed in **cubic units.**

b. The total outside surface is called the **surface area;** it is expressed in **square units.**

c. In computing volume and surface area, all dimensions must be expressed in the same units.

36. a. A **rectangular solid** is a figure of three dimensions having six rectangular faces meeting each other at right angles. The three dimensions are length, width, and height.

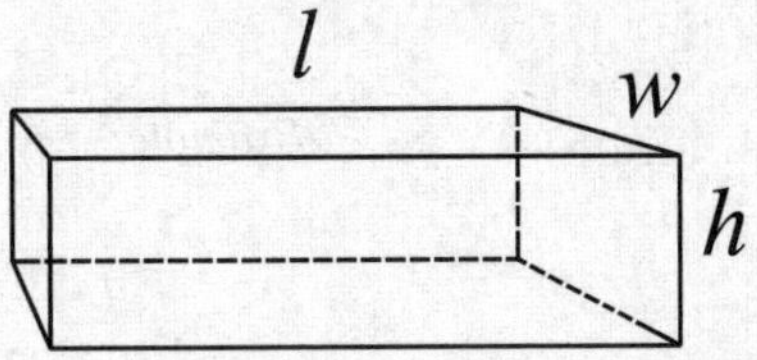

The figure above is a rectangular solid; "*l*" is the length, "*w*" is the width, and "*h*" is the height.

b. The volume of a rectangular solid is the product of the length, width, and height: $V = l \times w \times h$.

Example: The volume of a rectangular solid whose length is 6 feet, width 3 feet, and height 4 feet is $6 \times 3 \times 4 = 72$ cubic feet.

37. a. A **cube** is a rectangular solid whose edges are congruent. The figure below is a cube; the length, width, and height are all equal to "*e*."

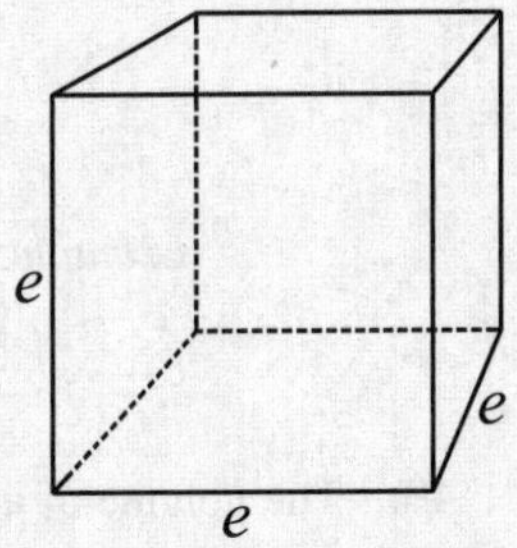

b. The volume of a cube is equal to the edge cubed: $V = e^3$.

Example: The volume of a cube whose height is 6 inches equals $6^3 = 6 \times 6 \times 6 = 216$ cubic inches.

c. The surface area of a cube is equal to the area of any side multiplied by 6.

Example: The surface area of a cube whose length is 5 inches $= 5^2 \times 6 = 25 \times 6 = 150$ square inches.

38. The volume of a **circular cylinder** is equal to the product of π, the radius squared, and the height: $V = \pi r^2 h$.

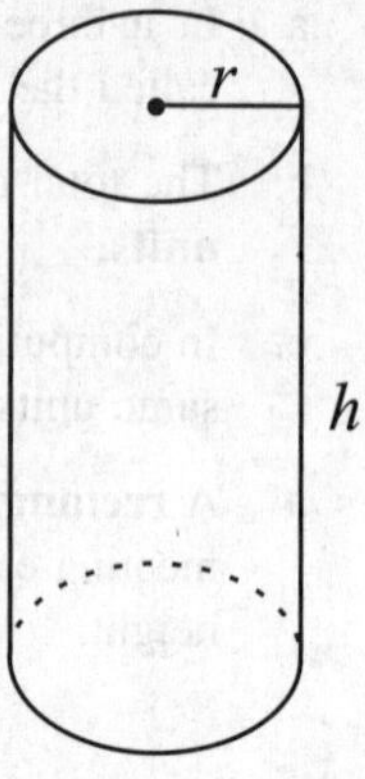

Example: A circular cylinder has a radius of 7 inches and a height of $\frac{1}{2}$ inch. Using $\pi = \frac{22}{7}$, its volume is

$$\frac{22}{7} \times 7 \times 7 \times \frac{1}{2} = 77 \text{ cubic inches}$$

39. The volume of a **sphere** is equal to $\frac{4}{3}$ the product of π and the radius cubed: $V = \frac{4}{3}\pi r^3$.

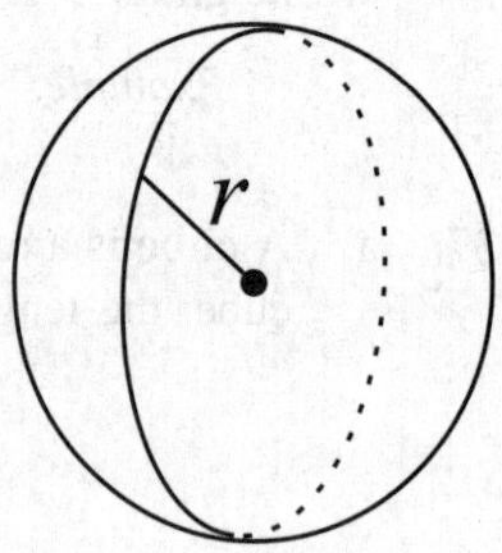

Example: If the radius of a sphere is 3 cm, its volume in terms of π is

$$\frac{4}{3} \times \pi \times 3 \text{ cm} \times 3 \text{ cm} \times 3 \text{ cm} = 36\pi \text{ cm}^3$$

40. The volume of a **cone** is given by the formula $V = \frac{1}{3}\pi r^2 h$, where r is the radius and h is the height.

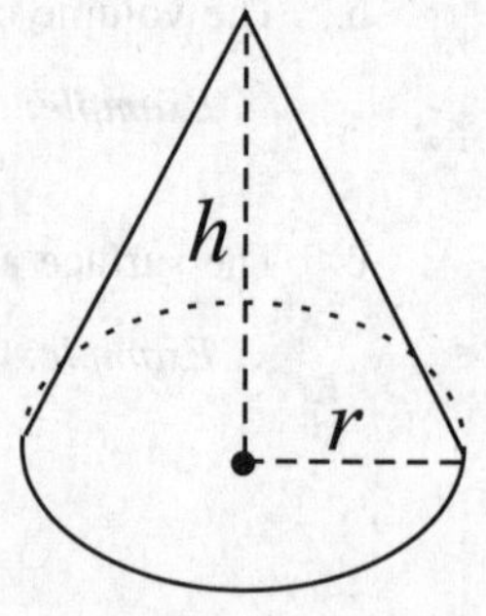

Example: In the cone shown, if $h = 9$ cm, $r = 10$ cm, and $\pi = 3.14$, then the volume is

$$\frac{1}{3} \times 3.14 \times 10 \times 10 \times 9 = 3.14 \times 300 \text{ cm}^3$$
$$= 942 \text{ cm}^3$$

41. The volume of a **pyramid** is given by the formula $V = \frac{1}{3}Bh$, where B is the area of the base, and h is the height.

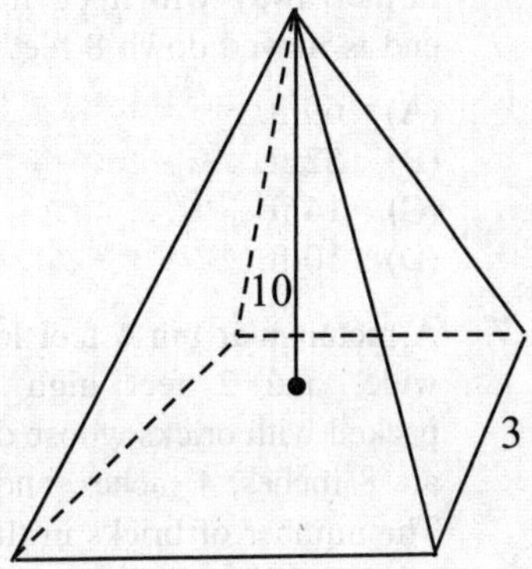

Example: In the pyramid shown, the height is 10″ and the sides of the base are 3″. Since the base is a square, $B = 3^2 = 9$ square inches.

$V = \frac{1}{3} \times 9 \times 10 = 30$ cubic inches.

PRACTICE TEST

1. If the perimeter of a rectangle is 68 yards and the width is 48 feet, the length is

(A) 10 yd.
(B) 18 yd.
(C) 20 ft.
(D) 56 ft.

2. The total length of fencing needed to enclose a rectangular area 46 feet by 34 feet is

(A) 26 yd. 1 ft.
(B) $26\frac{2}{3}$ yd.
(C) 52 yd. 2 ft.
(D) $53\frac{1}{3}$ yd.

3. An umbrella 50″ long can lie diagonally on the bottom of a trunk whose length and width are, respectively,

(A) 36″, 30″
(B) 42″, 24″
(C) 42″, 36″
(D) 39″, 30″

4. A road runs 1,200 ft. from A to B, and then makes a right angle going to C, a distance of 500 ft. A new road is being built directly from A to C. How much shorter will the new road be?

(A) 400 ft.
(B) 609 ft.
(C) 850 ft.
(D) 1,300 ft.

5. A certain triangle has sides that are, respectively, 6 inches, 8 inches, and 10 inches long. A rectangle equal in area to that of the triangle has a width of 3 inches. The perimeter of the rectangle, expressed in inches, is

(A) 11
(B) 16
(C) 22
(D) 24

6. A ladder 65 feet long is leaning against the wall. Its lower end is 25 feet away from the wall. How much farther away will it be if the upper end is moved down 8 feet?

(A) 60 ft.
(B) 52 ft.
(C) 14 ft.
(D) 10 ft.

7. A rectangular bin 4 feet long, 3 feet wide, and 2 feet high is solidly packed with bricks whose dimensions are 8 inches, 4 inches, and 2 inches. The number of bricks in the bin is

(A) 54
(B) 648
(C) 1,296
(D) None of these

8. If the cost of digging a trench is \$2.12 a cubic yard, what would be the cost of digging a trench 2 yards by 5 yards by 4 yards?

(A) \$21.20
(B) \$40
(C) \$64
(D) \$84.80

9. A piece of wire is shaped to enclose a square, whose area is 121 square inches. It is then reshaped to enclose a rectangle whose length is 13 inches. The area of the rectangle, in square inches, is

(A) 64
(B) 96
(C) 117
(D) 144

10. The area of a 2-foot-wide walk around a garden that is 30 feet long and 20 feet wide is

(A) 104 sq. ft.
(B) 216 sq. ft.
(C) 680 sq. ft.
(D) 704 sq. ft.

11. The area of a circle is 49π. Find its circumference in terms of π.

(A) 14π
(B) 28π
(C) 49π
(D) 98π

12. In two hours, the minute hand of a clock rotates through an angle of

(A) 90°
(B) 180°
(C) 360°
(D) 720°

13. A box is 12 inches in width, 6 inches in length, and 6 inches in height. How many square inches of paper would be required to cover it on all sides?

(A) 192
(B) 360
(C) 720
(D) 1,440

14. If the volume of a cube is 64 cubic inches, the sum of its edges is

(A) 48 in.
(B) 32 in.
(C) 16 in.
(D) 24 in.

15. The diameter of a conical pile of cement is 30 feet and its height is 14 feet. If $\frac{3}{4}$ cubic yard of cement weighs 1 ton, then the number of tons of cement in the cone to the nearest ton is

(Volume of cone $= \frac{1}{3}\pi r^2 h$;

use $\pi = \frac{22}{7}$)

(A) 92
(B) 163
(C) 489
(D) 652

ANSWERS AND EXPLANATIONS

1. B	**4.** A	**7.** B	**10.** B	**13.** C
2. D	**5.** C	**8.** D	**11.** A	**14.** A
3. C	**6.** C	**9.** C	**12.** D	**15.** B

1. The correct answer is (B).

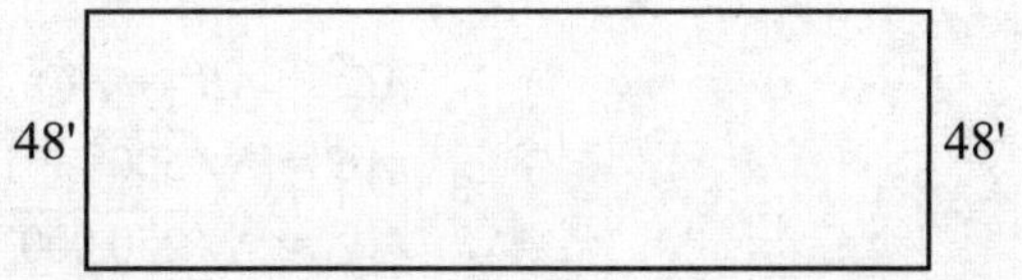

Perimeter = 68 yards
Each width = 48 feet = 16 yards
Both widths = 16 yd + 16 yd = 32 yd
Perimeter = sum of all sides
Remaining two sides must total 68 − 32 = 36 yards
Since the remaining two sides are equal, they are each 36 ÷ 2 = 18 yards

2. The correct answer is (D).

$$\text{Perimeter} = 2(46 + 34)\text{ feet}$$
$$= 2 \times 80\text{ feet}$$
$$= 160\text{ feet}$$

$$160\text{ feet} = 160 \div 3\text{ yards} = 53\frac{1}{3}\text{ yards}$$

3. The correct answer is (C). The umbrella would be the hypotenuse of a right triangle whose legs are the dimension of the trunk.

The Pythagorean theorem states that in a right triangle, the square of the hypotenuse equals the sum of the squares of the legs. Therefore, the sum of the dimensions of the trunk squared must at least equal the length of the umbrella squared, which is 50^2, or 2,500. The only set of dimensions filling this condition is choice (C):

$$(42)^2 + (36)^2 = 1{,}764 + 1{,}296$$
$$= 3{,}060$$

4. **The correct answer is (A).** The new road is the hypotenuse of a right triangle, whose legs are the old road.

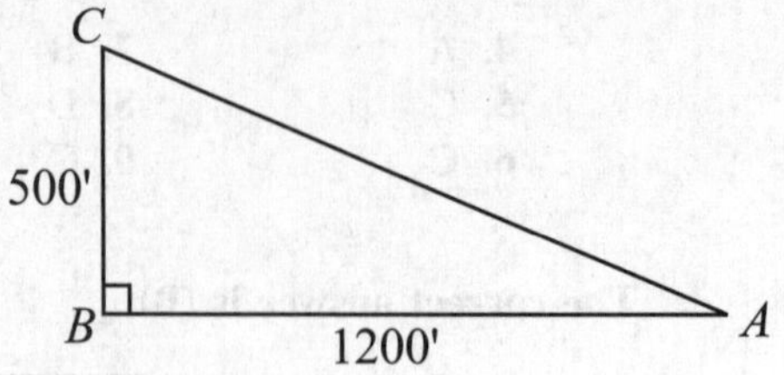

$$AC^2 = AB^2 + BC^2$$
$$AC = \sqrt{500^2 + 1200^2}$$
$$= \sqrt{250{,}000 + 1{,}440{,}000}$$
$$= \sqrt{1{,}690{,}000}$$
$$= 1{,}300 \text{ feet}$$
$$\text{Old Road} = 1{,}200 + 500 \text{ feet}$$
$$= 1{,}700 \text{ feet}$$
$$\text{New road} = 1{,}300 \text{ feet}$$
$$\text{Difference} = 400 \text{ feet}$$

5. **The correct answer is (C).** Since $6^2 + 8^2 = 10^2$ ($36 + 64 = 100$), the triangle is a right triangle. The area of the triangle is $\frac{1}{2} \times 6 \times 8 = 24$ square inches. If the width of the rectangle is 3 inches, the length is $24 \div 3 = 8$ inches. Then the perimeter of the rectangle is $2(3 + 8) = 2 \times 11 = 22$ inches.

6. **The correct answer is (C).** The ladder forms a right triangle with the wall and the ground.

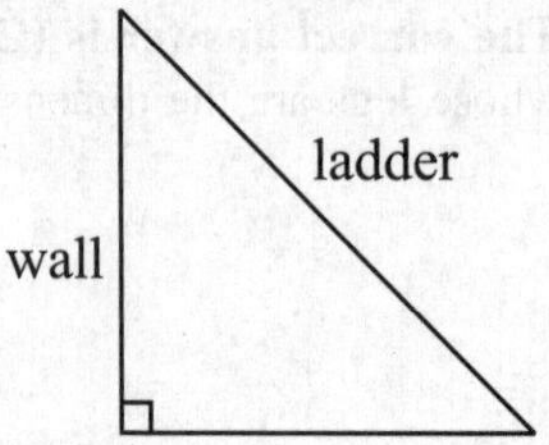

First, find the height that the ladder reaches when the lower end of the ladder is 25 feet from the wall:

$$65^2 = 4{,}225$$
$$25^2 = 625$$
$$65^2 - 25^2 = 3{,}600$$
$$\sqrt{3{,}600} = 60$$

The ladder reaches 60 feet up the wall when its lower end is 25 feet from the wall.

If the upper end is moved down 8 feet, the ladder will reach a height of $60 - 8 = 52$ feet. The new triangle formed has a hypotenuse of 65 feet and one leg of 52 feet. Find the other leg:

$$65^2 = 4{,}225$$
$$52^2 = 2{,}704$$
$$65^2 - 52^2 = 1{,}521$$
$$\sqrt{1{,}521} = 39$$

The lower end of the ladder is now 39 feet from the wall. This is $39 - 25 = 14$ feet farther than it was before.

7. The correct answer is (B). Convert the dimensions of the bin to inches:

$$\begin{aligned} 4 \text{ feet} &= 48 \text{ inches} \\ 3 \text{ feet} &= 36 \text{ inches} \\ 2 \text{ feet} &= 24 \text{ inches} \\ \text{Volume of bin} &= 48 \times 36 \times 24 \text{ cubic inches} \\ &= 41{,}472 \text{ cubic inches} \\ \text{Volume of each brick} &= 8 \times 4 \times 2 \text{ cubic inches} \\ &= 64 \text{ cubic inches} \\ 41{,}472 \div 64 &= 648 \text{ bricks} \end{aligned}$$

8. The correct answer is (D). The trench contains

$$\begin{aligned} 2 \text{ yd} \times 5 \text{ yd} \times 4 \text{ yd} &= 40 \text{ cubic yards} \\ 40 \times \$2.12 &= \$84.80 \end{aligned}$$

9. The correct answer is (C). Find the dimensions of the square: If the area of the square is 121 square inches, each side is $\sqrt{121} = 11$ inches, and the perimeter is $4 \times 11 = 44$ inches. Next, find the dimensions of the rectangle: The perimeter of the rectangle is the same as the perimeter of the square, since the same length of wire is used to enclose either figure. Therefore, the perimeter of the rectangle is 44 inches. If the two lengths are each 13 inches, their total is 26 inches, and $44 - 26$ inches, or 18 inches, remain for the two widths. Each width is equal to $18 \div 2 = 9$ inches. The area of a rectangle with length 13 in and width 9 in is $13 \times 9 = 117$ sq in.

10. The correct answer is (B).

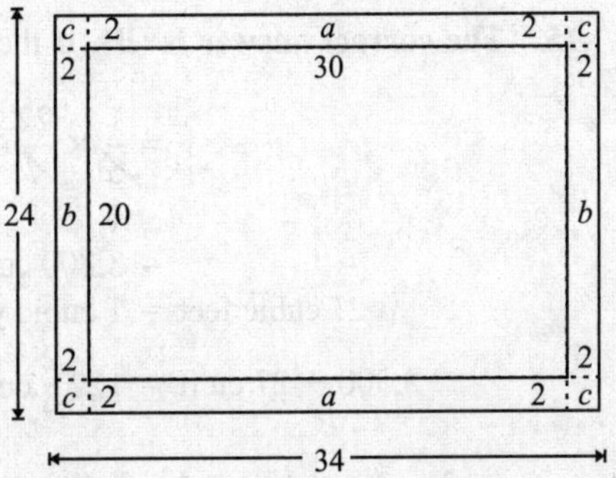

The walk consists of:

a. Two rectangles, each having a length of 30 feet and a width of 2 feet.

$$\begin{aligned} \text{Area of each rectangle} &= 2 \times 30 = 60 \text{ sq. ft.} \\ \text{Area of both rectangles} &= 120 \text{ sq. ft.} \end{aligned}$$

b. Two rectangles, each having a length of 20 feet and a width of 2 feet.

$$\begin{aligned} \text{Area of each rectangle} &= 2 \times 20 = 40 \text{ sq. ft.} \\ \text{Area of both rectangles} &= 80 \text{ sq. ft.} \end{aligned}$$

c. Four squares, each having sides measuring 2 feet.

$$\begin{aligned} \text{Area of each square} &= 2^2 = 4 \text{ sq. ft.} \\ \text{Area of four squares} &= 16 \text{ sq. ft.} \\ \text{Total area of walk} &= 120 + 80 + 16 \\ &= 216 \text{ sq. ft.} \end{aligned}$$

Alternate solution:

$$\begin{aligned} \text{Area of walk} &= \text{Area of large rectangle} - \text{Area of small rectangle} \\ &= (34 \times 24) - (30 \times 20) \\ &= 816 - 600 \\ &= 216 \text{ sq. ft.} \end{aligned}$$

11. **The correct answer is (A).** If the area of a circle is 49π, its radius is $\sqrt{49} = 7$. Then, the circumference is equal to $2 \times 7 \times \pi = 14\pi$.

12. **The correct answer is (D).** In 1 hour, the minute hand rotates through 360°. In 2 hours, it rotates through $2 \times 360° = 720°$.

13. **The correct answer is (C).** Find the area of each surface:

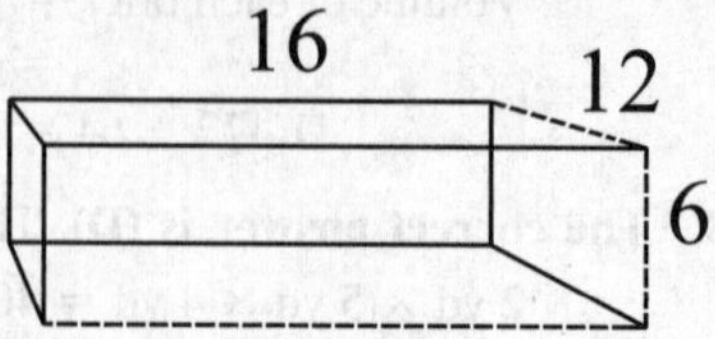

$$\begin{aligned}
\text{Area of top} &= 12 \times 16 = 192 \text{ sq. in.}\\
\text{Area of bottom} &= 12 \times 16 = 192 \text{ sq. in.}\\
\text{Area of front} &= 6 \times 16 = 96 \text{ sq. in.}\\
\text{Area of back} &= 6 \times 16 = 96 \text{ sq. in.}\\
\text{Area of right side} &= 12 \times 6 = 72 \text{ sq. in.}\\
\text{Area of left side} &= 12 \times 6 = 72 \text{ sq. in.}\\
\text{Total surface area} &= 720 \text{ sq. in.}
\end{aligned}$$

14. **The correct answer is (A).** For a cube, $V = e^3$. If the volume is 64 cubic inches, each edge is $\sqrt[3]{64} = 4$ inches. A cube has 12 edges. If each edge is 4 inches, the sum of the edges is $4 \times 12 = 48$ inches.

15. **The correct answer is (B).** If the diameter = 30 feet, then the radius = 15 feet.

$$V = \frac{1}{\not{3}_1} \times \frac{22}{\not{7}_1} \times \not{15}^{\,5} \times 15 \times \not{14}^{\,2}$$

$$= 3{,}300 \text{ cubic feet}$$

$$27 \text{ cubic feet} = 1 \text{ cubic yard}$$

$$3{,}300 \div 27 \text{ cu ft} = 122\frac{2}{9} \text{ cu yd}$$

$$122\frac{2}{9} \div \frac{3}{4} = \frac{1{,}100}{9} \times \frac{4}{3} = \frac{4{,}400}{27} = 163 \text{ tons to the nearest ton}$$

STATISTICS AND PROBABILITY

STATISTICS

1. The **averages** used in statistics include the **arithmetic mean**, the **median,** and the **mode.**

2. a. The most commonly used average of a group of numbers is the **arithmetic mean.** It is found by adding the numbers given and then dividing this sum by the number of items being averaged.

   Problem: Find the arithmetic mean of 2, 8, 5, 9, 6, and 12.

   SOLUTION: There are six numbers.

   $$\text{Arithmetic mean} = \frac{2 + 8 + 5 + 9 + 6 + 12}{6}$$

   $$= \frac{42}{6}$$

   $$= 7$$

   Answer: The arithmetic mean is 7.

   b. If a problem calls for simply the "average" or the "mean," it is referring to the arithmetic mean.

3. If a group of numbers is arranged in order, the number in the middle is called the **median.** If there is no single middle number (this occurs when there is an even number of items), the median is found by computing the arithmetic mean of the two middle numbers.

   Example: The median of 6, 8, 10, 12, and 14 is 10.

   Example: The median of 6, 8, 10, 12, 14, and 16 is the arithmetic mean of 10 and 12.

   $$\frac{10 + 12}{2} = \frac{22}{2} = 11$$

4. The **mode** of a group of numbers is the number that appears most often.

   Example: The mode of 10, 5, 7, 9, 12, 5, 10, 5, and 9 is 5.

5. To obtain the average of quantities that are weighted:

   a. Set up a table listing the quantities, their respective weights, and their respective values.

   b. Multiply the value of each quantity by its respective weight.

   c. Add up these products.

   d. Add up the weights.

   e. Divide the sum of the products by the sum of the weights.

Problem: Assume that the weights for the following subjects are English 3, history 2, mathematics 2, foreign languages 2, and art 1. What would be the average of a student who marks are: English 80, history 85, algebra 84, Spanish 82, and art 90?

SOLUTION:

Subject	Weight	Mark
English	3	80
History	2	85
Algebra	2	84
Spanish	2	82
Art	1	90

English	$3 \times 80 =$	240
History	$2 \times 85 =$	170
Algebra	$2 \times 84 =$	168
Spanish	$2 \times 82 =$	164
Art	$1 \times 90 =$	90
		832

Sum of the weights: $3 + 2 + 2 + 2 + 1 =$ 10

$832 \div 10 = 83.2$

Answer: Average $= 83.2$

PROBABILITY

6. The study of probability deals with predicting the outcome of chance events; that is, events in which one has no control over the results.

   Example: Tossing a coin, rolling dice, and drawing concealed objects from a bag are chance events.

7. The probability of a particular outcome is equal to the number of ways that outcome can occur, divided by the total number of possible outcomes.

   Example: In tossing a coin, there are two possible outcomes: heads or tails. The probability that the coin will turn up heads is $1 \div 2$, or $\frac{1}{2}$.

   Example: If a bag contains five balls of which three are red, the probability of drawing a red ball is $\frac{3}{5}$. The probability of drawing a ball that is not red is $\frac{2}{5}$.

8. a. If an event is certain, its probability is 1.

   Example: If a bag contains only red balls, the probability of drawing a red ball is 1.

   b. If an event is impossible, its probability is 0.

   Example: If a bag contains only red balls, the probability of drawing a green ball is 0.

9. Probability may be expressed in fractional, decimal, or percent form.

   Example: An event having a probability of $\frac{1}{2}$ is said to be 50% probable.

10. A probability determined by random sampling of a group of items is assumed to apply to other items in that group and in other similar groups.

Problem: A random sampling of 100 items produced in a factory shows that 7 are defective. How many items of the total production of 50,000 can be expected to be defective?

SOLUTION: The probability of an item's being defective is $\frac{7}{100}$, or 7%. Of the total production, 7% can be expected to be defective.

7% × 50,000 = .07 × 50,000 = 3,500

Answer: 3,500 items.

PRACTICE TEST

1. The arithmetic mean of 73.8, 92.2, 64.7, 43.8, 56.5, and 46.4 is

(A) 60.6
(B) 62.9
(C) 64.48
(D) 75.48

2. The median of the numbers 8, 5, 7, 5, 9, 9, 1, 8, 10, 5, and 10 is

(A) 5
(B) 7
(C) 8
(D) 9

3. The mode of the numbers 16, 15, 17, 12, 15, 15, 18, 19, and 18 is

(A) 15
(B) 16
(C) 17
(D) 18

4. A clerk filed 73 forms on Monday, 85 forms on Tuesday, 54 on Wednesday, 92 on Thursday, and 66 on Friday. What was the average number of forms filed per day?

(A) 60
(B) 72
(C) 74
(D) 92

5. The grades received on a test by 20 students were: 100, 55, 75, 80, 65, 65, 85, 90, 80, 45, 40, 50, 85, 85, 85, 80, 80, 70, 65, and 60. The average of these grades is

(A) 70
(B) 72
(C) 77
(D) 80

6. A buyer purchased 75 six-inch rulers costing 15¢ each, 100 one-foot rulers costing 30¢ each, and 50 one-yard rulers costing 72¢ each. What was the average price per ruler?

(A) $26\frac{1}{8}$¢
(B) $34\frac{1}{3}$¢
(C) 39¢
(D) 42¢

7. What is the average of a student who received 90 in English, 84 in algebra, 75 in French, and 76 in music, if the subjects have the following weights: English 4, algebra 3, French 3, and music 1?

(A) 81
(B) $81\frac{1}{2}$
(C) 82
(D) 83

Questions 8–11 refer to the following information:

A census shows that on a certain block the number of children in each family is 3, 4, 4, 0, 1, 2, 0, 2, and 2, respectively.

8. Find the average number of children per family.

(A) 2

(B) $2\frac{1}{2}$

(C) 3

(D) $3\frac{1}{2}$

9. Find the median number of children.

(A) 1
(B) 2
(C) 3
(D) 4

10. Find the mode of the number of children.

(A) 0
(B) 1
(C) 2
(D) 4

11. What is the probability that a family chosen at random on this block will have 4 children?

(A) $\frac{4}{9}$

(B) $\frac{2}{9}$

(C) $\frac{4}{7}$

(D) $\frac{2}{1}$

12. What is the probability that an even number will come up when a single die is thrown?

(A) $\frac{1}{6}$

(B) $\frac{1}{3}$

(C) $\frac{1}{2}$

(D) 1

13. A bag contains three black balls, two yellow balls, and four red balls. What is the probability of drawing a black ball?

(A) $\frac{1}{2}$

(B) $\frac{1}{3}$

(C) $\frac{2}{3}$

(D) $\frac{4}{9}$

14. In a group of 1,000 adults, 682 are women. What is the probability that a person chosen at random from this group will be a man?

(A) .318
(B) .682
(C) .5
(D) 1

15. In a balloon factory, a random sampling of 100 balloons showed that 3 had pinholes in them. In a sampling of 2,500 balloons, how many may be expected to have pinholes?

(A) 30
(B) 75
(C) 100
(D) 750

ANSWERS AND EXPLANATIONS

1. B	**4.** C	**7.** D	**10.** C	**13.** B
2. C	**5.** B	**8.** A	**11.** B	**14.** A
3. A	**6.** B	**9.** B	**12.** C	**15.** B

1. The correct answer is (B). Find the sum of the values:

$$73.8 + 92.2 + 64.7 + 43.8 + 56.5 + 46.4 = 377.4$$

There are six values.

$$\text{Arithmetic mean} = \frac{377.4}{6} = 62.9$$

2. The correct answer is (C). Arrange the numbers in order:

1, 5, 5, 5, 7, 8, 8, 9, 9, 10, 10

The middle number, or median is 8.

3. The correct answer is (A). The mode is that number appearing most frequently. The number 15 appears three times.

4. The correct answer is (C).

$$\text{Average} = \frac{73 + 85 + 54 + 92 + 66}{5}$$

$$= \frac{370}{5}$$

$$= 74$$

5. The correct answer is (B). Sum of the grades = 1,440

$$\frac{1,440}{20} = 72$$

6. The correct answer is (B).

$$\begin{array}{rcl} 75 \times 15¢ &=& 1,125¢ \\ 100 \times 30¢ &=& 3,000¢ \\ \underline{50} \times 72¢ &=& \underline{3,600¢} \\ 225 & & 7,725¢ \end{array}$$

$$\frac{7,725¢}{225} = 34\frac{1}{3}¢$$

7. The correct answer is (D).

Subject	Grade	Weight
English	90	4
Algebra	84	3
French	75	3
Music	76	1

$(90 \times 4) + (84 \times 3) + (75 \times 3) + (76 \times 1)$
$360 + 252 + 225 + 76 = 913$
$\text{Weight} = 4 + 3 + 3 + 1 = 11$
$913 \div 11 = 83$ average

8. **The correct answer is (A).**

$$\text{Average} = \frac{3 + 4 + 4 + 0 + 1 + 2 + 0 + 2 + 2}{9}$$
$$= \frac{18}{9}$$
$$= 2$$

9. **The correct answer is (B).** Arrange the numbers in order:

   0, 0, 1, 2, 2, 2, 3, 4, 4

   Of the nine numbers, the fifth (middle) number is 2.

10. **The correct answer is (C).** The number appearing the most often is 2.

11. **The correct answer is (B).** There are nine families, two of which have 4 children. The probability is $\frac{2}{9}$.

12. **The correct answer is (C).** Of the six possible numbers, three are even (2, 4, and 6). The probability is $\frac{3}{6}$, or $\frac{1}{2}$.

13. **The correct answer is (B).** There are nine balls in all. The probability of drawing a black ball is $\frac{3}{9}$, or $\frac{1}{3}$.

14. **The correct answer is (A).** If 682 people of the 1,000 are women, the number of men is $1{,}000 - 682 = 318$. Then, the probability of choosing a man is $\frac{318}{1{,}000} = .318$.

15. **The correct answer is (B).** There is a probability of $\frac{3}{100} = 3\%$ that a balloon may have a pinhole.

   $3\% \times 2{,}500 = 75$

GRAPHS

1. **Graphs** illustrate comparisons and trends in statistical information. The most commonly used graphs are **bar graphs, line graphs, circle graphs**, and **pictographs.**

BAR GRAPHS

2. **Bar graphs** are used to compare various quantities. Each bar may represent a single quantity or may be divided to represent several quantities.

3. Bar graphs may have horizontal or vertical bars.

Problem:

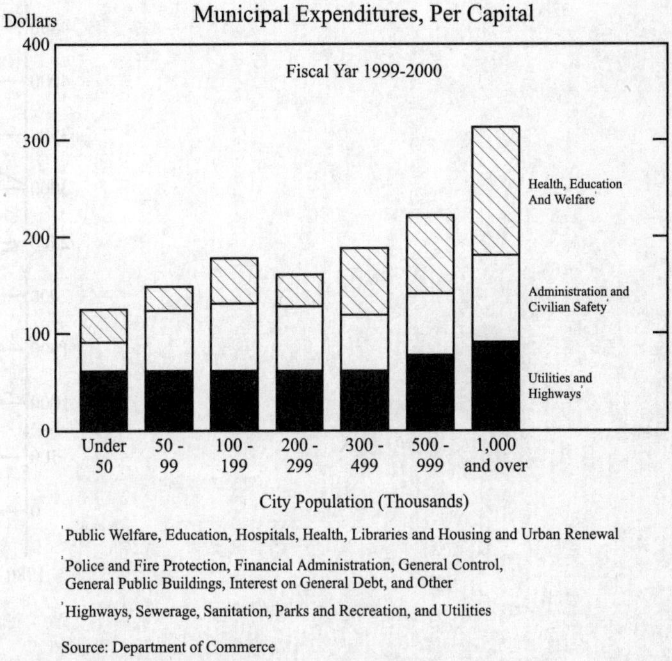

Question 1: What was the approximate municipal expenditure per capita in cities having populations of 200,000 to 299,000?

Answer: The middle bar of the seven shown represents cities having populations from 200,000 to 299,000. This bar reaches about halfway between 100 and 200. Therefore, the per capita expenditure was approximately $150.

Question 2: Which cities spent the most per capita on health, education, and welfare?

Answer: The bar for cities having populations of 1,000,000 or more has a larger striped section than the other bars. Therefore, those cities spent the most.

Question 3: Of the three categories of expenditures, which was least dependent on city size?

Answer: The expenditures for utilities and highways, the darkest part of each bar, varied least as city size increases.

LINE GRAPHS

4. **Line graphs** are used to show trends, often over a period of time.
5. A line graph may include more than one line, with each line representing a different item.

Problem: The graph below indicates at five-year intervals the number of citations issued for various offenses from the year 1980 to the year 2000.

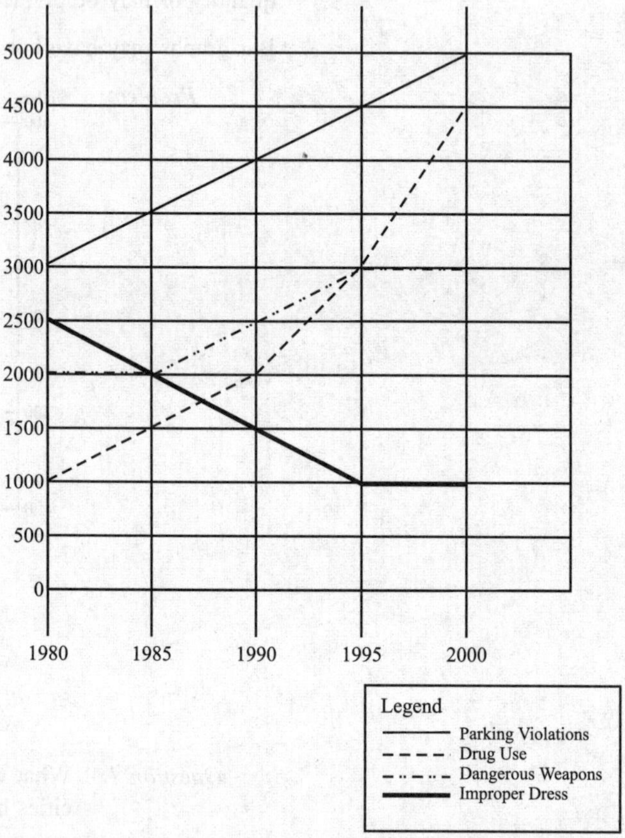

Question 4: Over the twenty-year period, which offense shows an average rate of increase of more than 150 citations per year?

Answer: Drug use citations increased from 1,000 in 1980 to 4,500 in 2000. The average increase over the twenty-year period is $\frac{3500}{20} = 170$

Question 5: Over the twenty-year period, which offense shows a constant rate of increase or decrease?

Answer: A straight line indicates a constant rate of increase or decrease. Of the four lines, the one representing parking violations is the only straight one.

Question 6: Which offense shows a total increase or decrease of 50 percent for the full twenty-year period?

Answer: Dangerous weapons citations increased from 2,000 in 1980 to 3,000 in 2000, which is an increase of 50 percent.

CIRCLE GRAPHS

6. **Circle graphs** are used to show the relationship of various parts of a quantity to each other and to the whole quantity.
7. Percents are often used in circle graphs. The 360 degrees of the circle represent 100%.
8. Each part of the circle graph is called a **sector.**

Problem: The following circle graph shows how the federal budget of $300.4 billion was spent.

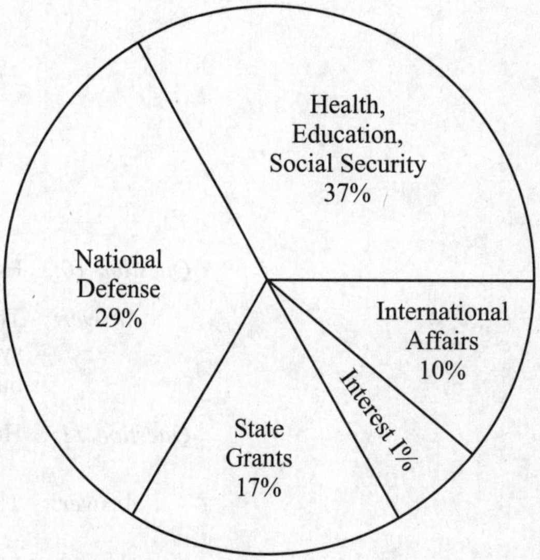

Question 7: What is the value of I?

Answer: There must be a total of 100% in a circle graph. The sum of the other sectors is:

$$17\% + 29\% + 37\% + 10\% = 93\%$$

Therefore, $I\% = 100\% - 93\% = 7\%$, so $I = 7$.

Question 8: How much money was actually spent on national defense?

Answer: $29\% \times \$300.4 \text{ billion} = \$87.116 \text{ billion}$
$= \$87{,}116{,}000{,}000$

Question 9: How much more money was spent on state grants than on interest?

Answer: $17\% - 7\% = 10\%$
$10\% \times 300.4 \text{ billion} = \$30.04 \text{ billion}$
$= \$30{,}040{,}000{,}000$

PICTOGRAPHS

9. **Pictographs** allow comparisons of quantities by using symbols. Each symbol represents a given number of a particular item.

Problem:

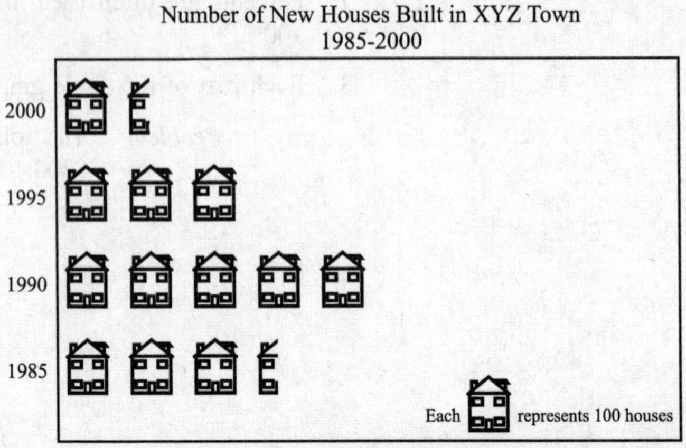

Question 10: How many more new houses were built in 1990 than in 1995?

Answer: There are two more symbols for 1990 than for 1995. Each symbol represents 100 houses. Therefore, 200 more houses were built in 1990.

Question 11: How many new houses were built in 1985?

Answer: There are $3\frac{1}{2}$ symbols shown for 1985; $3\frac{1}{2} \times 100 = 350$ houses.

Question 12: In which year were half as many houses built as in 1995?

Answer: In 1995, $3 \times 100 = 300$ houses were built. Half of 300, or 150, houses were built in 2000.

PRACTICE TEST

Questions 1–4 refer to the following graph.

Yearly Incidence of Major Crimes for Community Z 1998-2000

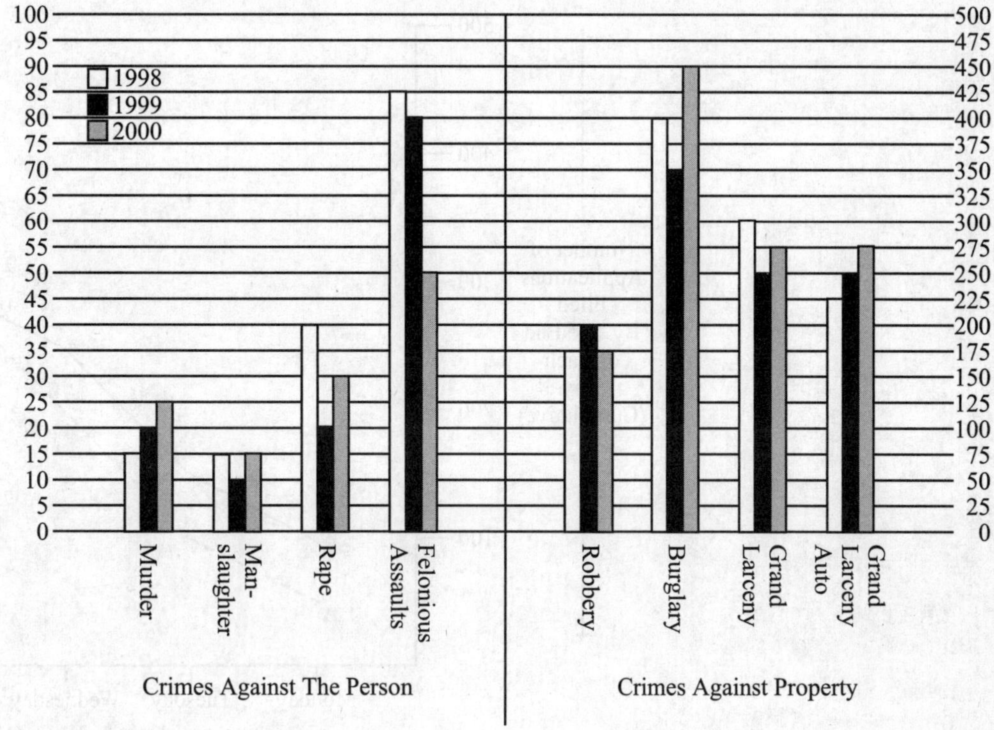

1. In 2000, the incidence of which of the following crimes was greater than in both of the previous two years?

(A) Grand larceny
(B) Murder
(C) Rape
(D) Robbery

2. If the incidence of burglary in 2001 increases over 2000 by the same number as it had increased in 2000 over 1999, then the average for this crime for the four-year period from 1998 through 2001 would be most nearly

(A) 100
(B) 400
(C) 425
(D) 440

3. The above graph indicates that the *percentage* increase in grand larceny auto from 1999 to 2000 was

(A) 5%
(B) 10%
(C) 15%
(D) 20%

4. Which of the following cannot be determined because there is not enough information in the above graph to do so?

(A) For the three-year period, what percentage of all "Crimes Against the Person" involved murders committed in 1999?
(B) For the three-year period, what percentage of all "Major Crimes" was committed in the first six months of 1999?
(C) Which major crimes followed a pattern of continuing yearly increases for the three-year period?
(D) For 2000, what was the ratio of robbery, burglary, and grand larceny crimes?

Questions 5–7 refer to the following graph.

In the graph below, the lines "A" and "B" represent the cumulative progress in the work of two file clerks, each of whom was given 500 consecutively numbered applications to file in the proper cabinets over a five-day work week.

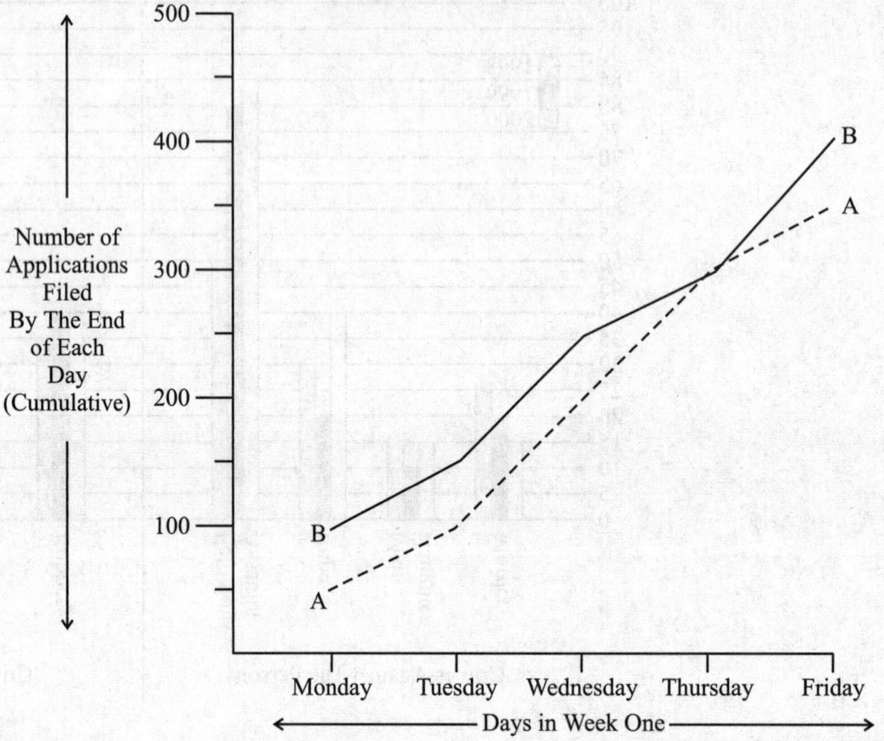

5. The day during which the greatest number of applications was filed by both clerks was

(A) Monday
(B) Tuesday
(C) Wednesday
(D) Friday

6. At the end of the second day, the percentage of applications still to be filed was

(A) 25%
(B) 50%
(C) 66%
(D) 75%

7. Assuming that the production pattern is the same the following week as the week shown in the chart, the day on which Clerk B will finish this assignment will be

(A) Monday
(B) Tuesday
(C) Wednesday
(D) Friday

Questions 8–11 refer to the following graph.

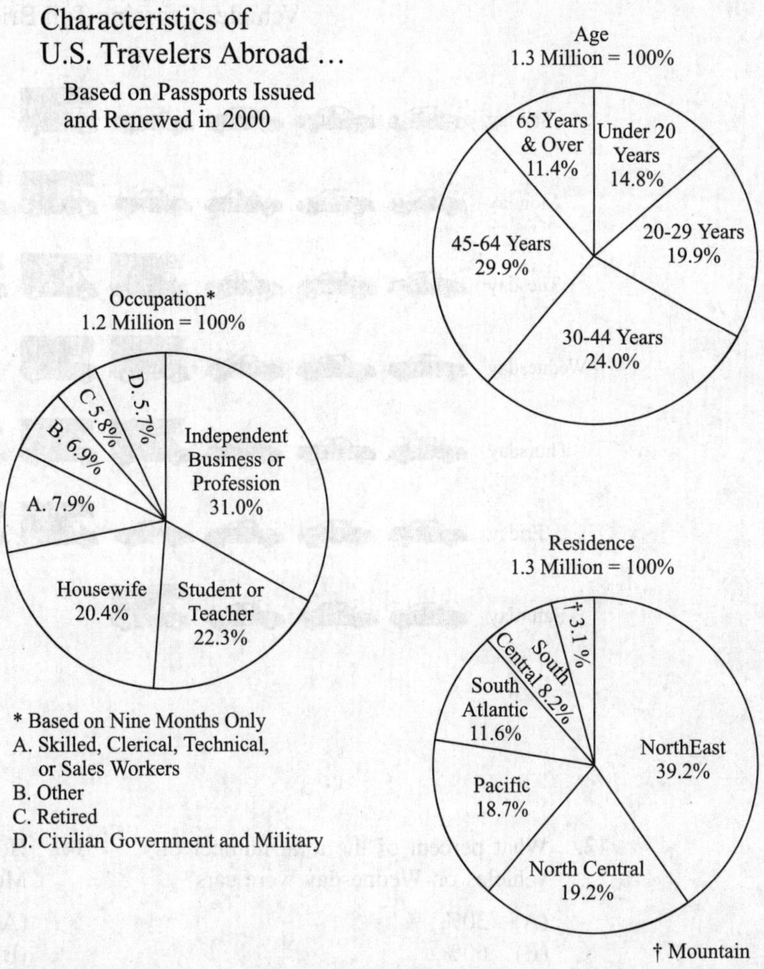

Note: Due to rounding, figures may not add up to 100%

8. Approximately how many persons aged 29 or younger traveled abroad in 2000?

(A) 175,000
(B) 245,000
(C) 385,000
(D) 450,000

9. Of the people who did NOT live in the North East, approximately what percent came from the North Central states?

(A) 19.2%
(B) 19.9%
(C) 26.5%
(D) 31.6%

10. The fraction of travelers from the four smallest occupation groups is most nearly equal to the fraction of travelers

(A) under age 20, and 65 and over, combined.
(B) from the North Central and Mountain states.
(C) between 45 and 64 years of age.
(D) from the Housewife and Other categories.

11. If the South Central, Mountain, and Pacific sections were considered as a single classification, how many degrees would its sector include?

(A) 30°
(B) 67°
(C) 108°
(D) 120°

Questions 12–15 refer to the following graph.

Vehicles Crossing Toll Bridge

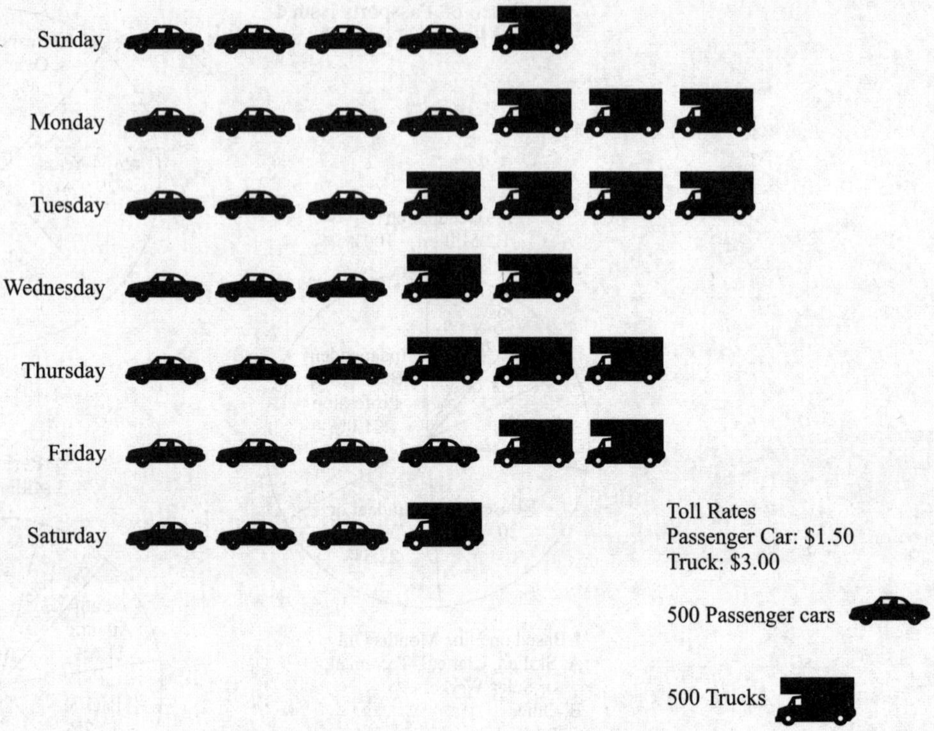

12. What percent of the total number of vehicles on Wednesday were cars?

(A) 30%
(B) 60%
(C) 20%
(D) 50%

13. What was the total number of vehicles crossing the bridge on Tuesday?

(A) 7
(B) 700
(C) 1,100
(D) 3,500

14. How many more trucks crossed on Monday than on Saturday?

(A) 200
(B) 1,000
(C) 1,500
(D) 2,000

15. How much money was collected in tolls on Friday?

(A) $1,200
(B) $1,800
(C) $6,000
(D) $7,500

ANSWERS AND EXPLANATIONS

1. B	**4.** B	**7.** A	**10.** A	**13.** D
2. D	**5.** C	**8.** D	**11.** C	**14.** B
3. B	**6.** D	**9.** D	**12.** B	**15.** C

1. **The correct answer is (B).** The incidence of murder increased from 15 in 1998, to 20 in 1999, to 25 in 2000.

2. **The correct answer is (D).** The incidence of burglary in 1998 was 400; in 1999 it was 350; and in 2000 it was 450. The increase from 1999 to 2000 was 100. An increase of 100 from 2000 gives 550 in 2001.

   The average of 400, 350, 450, and 550 is

   $$\frac{400 + 350 + 450 + 550}{4} = \frac{1750}{4} = 437.5$$

   So the correct answer is (D), 440.

3. **The correct answer is (B).** The incidence of grand larceny auto went from 250 in 1999 to 275 in 2000, an increase of 25. The percent increase is

   $$\frac{25}{250} = .10 = 10\%$$

4. **The correct answer is (B).** This graph gives information by year, not month. It is impossible to determine from the graph the percentage of crimes committed during the first six months of any year.

5. **The correct answer is (C).** For both A and B, the greatest increase in the cumulative totals occurred from the end of Tuesday until the end of Wednesday. Therefore, the largest number of applications was filed on Wednesday.

6. **The correct answer is (D).** By the end of Tuesday, A had filed 100 applications and B had filed 150, for a total of 250. This left 750 of the original 1,000 applications.

   $$\frac{750}{1,000} = .75 = 75\%$$

7. **The correct answer is (A).** During Week One, Clerk B files 100 applications on Monday, 50 on Tuesday, 100 on Wednesday, 50 on Thursday, and 100 on Friday, for a total of 400. On Monday of Week Two, he will file numbers 401 to 500.

8. **The correct answer is (D).**

   $$\begin{aligned} \text{20 − 29 yrs.:} &\quad 19.9\% \\ \text{Under 20 yrs.:} &\quad +14.8\% \\ &\quad \overline{34.7\%} \end{aligned}$$

   $$\begin{aligned} 34.7\% \times 13 \text{ million} &= .4511 \text{ million} \\ &= 451,100 \end{aligned}$$

   So the correct answer is (D) 450,000.

9. The correct answer is (D). 100% − 39.2 % = 60.8% did not live in North East. 19.2% lived in North Central.

$$\frac{19.2}{60.8} = .316 \text{ approximately}$$

So the correct answer is (D) 31.6%.

10. The correct answer is (A). Four of the smallest groups of occupation:

7.9% + 6.9% + 5.8% + 5.7% = 26.3%

Age groups under 20 and 65 and over:

14.8% + 11.4% = 26.2%

11. The correct answer is (C).

South Central:	8.2%
Mountain:	3.1%
Pacific:	18.7%
	30.0%

30% × 360° = 108°

12. The correct answer is (B). There are five vehicle symbols, of which three are cars.

$$\frac{3}{5} = 60\%$$

13. The correct answer is (D). On Tuesday, there were 3 × 500 = 1,500 cars and 4 × 500 = 2,000 trucks. The total number of vehicles was 3,500.

14. The correct answer is (B). The graph shows two more truck symbols on Monday than on Saturday. Each symbol represents 500 trucks, so there were 2 × 500 = 1,000 more trucks on Monday.

15. The correct answer is (C). On Friday there were

4 × 500 = 2,000 cars
2 × 500 = 1,000 trucks

Car tolls: 2,000 × $1.50 =	$3,000
Truck tolls: 1,000 × $3.00 =	+ $3,000
Total tolls:	$6,000

RATIO AND PROPORTION

RATIO

1. A **ratio** expresses the relationship between two (or more) quantities in terms of numbers. The mark used to indicate ratio is the colon (:) and is read "to."

   Example: The ratio 2:3 is read "2 to 3."

2. A ratio also represents division. Therefore, any ratio of two terms may be written as a fraction, and any fraction may be written as a ratio.

   Example: $3{:}4 = \frac{3}{4}$

   $\frac{5}{6} = 5{:}6$

3. To simplify any complicated ratio of two terms containing fractions, decimals, or percents:

   a. Divide the first term by the second.

   b. Write as a fraction in simplest form.

   c. Write the fraction as a ratio.

   Problem: Simplify the ratio $\frac{5}{6} : \frac{7}{8}$

   SOLUTION: $\frac{5}{6} \div \frac{7}{8} = \frac{5}{6} \times \frac{8}{7} = \frac{40}{42} = \frac{20}{21}$

   $\frac{20}{21} = 20{:}21$

   Answer: 20:21

4. To solve problems in which the ratio is given:

   a. Add the terms in the ratio.

   b. Divide the total amount that is to be put into a ratio by this sum.

   c. Multiply each term in the ratio by this quotient.

   Problem: The sum of $360 is divided among 3 people according to the ratio 3:4:5. How much does each person receive?

   SOLUTION:
   3 + 4 + 5 = 12
   $360 ÷ 12 = $30
   $30 × 3 = $90
   $30 × 4 = $120
   $30 × 5 = $150

   Answer: The money is divided thus: $90, $120, $150.

PROPORTION

5. a. A **proportion** indicates the equality of two ratios.

Example: 2:4 = 5:10 is a proportion. This is read "2 is to 4 as 5 is to 10."

b. In a proportion, the two outside terms are called the **extremes**, and the two inside terms are called the **means.**

Example: In the proportion 2:4 = 5:10, 2 and 10 are the extremes, and 4 and 5 are the means.

c. Proportions are often written in fractional form.

Example: The proportion 2:4 = 5:10 may be written $\frac{2}{4} = \frac{5}{10}$

d. In any proportion, the product of the means equals the product of the extremes. If the proportion is in fractional form, the products may be found by cross-multiplication.

Example: In $\frac{2}{4} = \frac{5}{10}$, $4 \times 5 = 2 \times 10$

e. The product of the extremes divided by one mean equals the other mean; the products of the means divided by one extreme equals the other extreme.

6. Many problems in which three terms are given and one term is unknown can be solved by using proportions. To solve such problems:

a. Formulate the proportion very carefully according to the facts given. (If any term is misplaced, the solution will be incorrect.) Any symbol may be written in place of the missing term.

b. Determine by inspection whether the means or the extremes are known. Multiply the pair that has both terms given.

c. Divide this product by the third term given to find the unknown term.

Problem: The scale on the map shows that 2 cm represent 30 miles of actual length. What is the actual length of a road that is represented by 7 cm on the map?

SOLUTION: The map lengths and the actual lengths are in proportion; that is, they have equal ratios. If m stands for the unknown length, the proportion is:

$$\frac{2}{7} = \frac{30}{m}$$

As the proportion is written, m is an extreme and is equal to the product of the means, divided by the other extreme:

$$m = \frac{7 \times 30}{2}$$

$$m = \frac{210}{2}$$

$$m = 105$$

Answer: 7 cm on the map represent 105 miles.

Problem: If a money bag containing 500 nickels weighs 6 pounds, how much will a money bag containing 1,600 nickels weigh?

SOLUTION: The weights of the bags and the number of coins in them are proportional. Suppose w represents the unknown weight. Then

$$\frac{6}{w} = \frac{500}{1{,}600}$$

The unknown is a mean and is equal to the product of the extremes, divided by the other mean:

$$w = \frac{6 \times 1{,}600}{500}$$

$$w = 19.2$$

Answer: A bag containing 1,600 nickels weighs 19.2 pounds.

PRACTICE TEST

1. The ratio of 24 to 64 is

(A) 8:3
(B) 24:100
(C) 3:8
(D) 64:100

2. The Baltimore Ravens won eight games and lost three. The ratio of games won to games played is

(A) 8:11
(B) 3:11
(C) 8:3
(D) 3:8

3. The ratio of $\frac{1}{4}$ to $\frac{3}{5}$ is

(A) 1 to 3
(B) 3 to 20
(C) 5 to 12
(D) 3 to 4

4. If there are 16 boys and 12 girls in a class, the ratio of the number of girls to the number of children in the class is

(A) 3 to 4
(B) 3 to 7
(C) 4 to 7
(D) 4 to 3

5. 259 is to 37 as

(A) 5 is to 1
(B) 63 is to 441
(C) 84 is to 12
(D) 130 is to 19

6. Two dozen cans of dog food at the rate of three cans for $1.45 would cost

(A) $10.05
(B) $11.20
(C) $11.60
(D) $11.75

7. A snapshot measures $2\frac{1}{2}$ inches by $1\frac{7}{8}$ inches. It is to be enlarged so that the longer dimension will be 4 inches. The length of the enlarged shorter dimension will be

(A) $2\frac{1}{2}$ in.
(B) 3 in.
(C) $3\frac{3}{8}$ in.
(D) None of these

8. Men's white handkerchiefs cost $2.29 for three. The cost per dozen handkerchiefs is

(A) $27.48
(B) $13.74
(C) $9.16
(D) $6.87

9. A certain pole casts a shadow 24 feet long. At the same time another pole 3 feet high casts a shadow 4 feet long. How high is the first pole, given that the heights and shadows are in proportion?

(A) 18 ft.
(B) 19 ft.
(C) 20 ft.
(D) 21 ft.

10. The actual length represented by $3\frac{1}{2}$ inches on a drawing having a scale of $\frac{1}{8}$ inch to the foot is

(A) 3.75 ft.
(B) 28 ft.
(C) 360 ft.
(D) 120 ft.

11. Aluminum bronze consists of copper and aluminum, usually in the ratio of 10:1 by weight. If an object made of this alloy weighs 77 pounds, how many pounds of aluminum does it contain?

(A) 7.7
(B) 7
(C) 70
(D) 62.3

12. It costs 31 cents per square foot to lay vinyl flooring. To lay 180 square feet of flooring, it will cost

(A) $16.20
(B) $18.60
(C) $55.80
(D) $62.00

13. If a per diem worker earns $352 in sixteen days, the amount that he will earn in 117 days, at the same rate, is most nearly

(A) $3,050
(B) $2,575
(C) $2,285
(D) $2,080

14. Assuming that on a blueprint $\frac{1}{8}$ inch equals 12 inches of actual length, the actual length in inches of a steel bar represented on the blueprint by a line $3\frac{3}{4}$ inches long is

(A) $3\frac{3}{4}$
(B) 30
(C) 450
(D) 360

15. A, B, and C invested $9,000, $7,000 and $6,000, respectively. Their profits were to be divided according to the ratio of their investment. If B uses his share of the firm's profit of $825 to pay a personal debt of $230, how much will he have left?

(A) $30.50
(B) $32.50
(C) $34.50
(D) $36.50

ANSWERS AND EXPLANATIONS

1. C	**4.** B	**7.** B	**10.** B	**13.** B
2. A	**5.** C	**8.** C	**11.** B	**14.** D
3. C	**6.** C	**9.** A	**12.** C	**15.** B

1. **The correct answer is (C).** The ratio of 24 to 64 may be written 24:64 or $\frac{24}{64}$. In fraction form, the ratio can be simplified:

$$\frac{24}{64} = \frac{3}{8} \text{ or } 3:8$$

2. **The correct answer is (A).** The number of games played was 3 + 8 = 11. The ratio of games won to games played is 8:11.

3. **The correct answer is (C).**

$$\begin{aligned} \frac{1}{4} : \frac{3}{5} &= \frac{1}{4} \div \frac{3}{5} \\ &= \frac{1}{4} \times \frac{5}{3} \\ &= \frac{5}{12} \\ &= 5:12 \end{aligned}$$

4. **The correct answer is (B).** There are 16 + 12 = 28 children in the class. The ratio of number of girls to number of children is 12:28.

$$\frac{12}{28} = \frac{3}{7} = 3 \text{ to } 7$$

5. **The correct answer is (C).** The ratio $\frac{259}{37}$ simplifies by 37 to $\frac{7}{1}$. The ratio $\frac{84}{12}$ also simplifies to $\frac{7}{1}$. Therefore, $\frac{259}{37} = \frac{84}{12}$ is a proportion.

6. **The correct answer is (C).** The number of cans is proportional to the price. Let p represent the unknown price:

$$\begin{aligned} \frac{3}{24} &= \frac{1.45}{p} \\ p &= \frac{1.45 \times 24}{3} \\ p &= \frac{34.80}{3} \\ &= \$11.60 \end{aligned}$$

7. **The correct answer is (B).** Let s represent the unknown shorter dimension:

$$\frac{2\frac{1}{2}}{4} = \frac{1\frac{7}{8}}{s}$$

$$s = \frac{4 \times 1\frac{7}{8}}{2\frac{1}{2}}$$

$$= \frac{\overset{1}{\cancel{4}} \times \frac{15}{\underset{2}{\cancel{8}}}}{\frac{5}{2}}$$

$$= \frac{15}{2} \div \frac{5}{2}$$

$$= \frac{15}{2} \times \frac{2}{5}$$

$$= 3 \text{ in.}$$

8. **The correct answer is (C).** If p is the cost per dozen (12):

$$\frac{3}{12} = \frac{2.29}{p}$$

$$p = \frac{\overset{4}{\cancel{12}} \times 2.29}{\underset{1}{\cancel{3}}}$$

$$= \$9.16$$

9. **The correct answer is (A).** If f is the height of the first pole, the proportion is:

$$\frac{f}{24} = \frac{3}{4}$$

$$f = \frac{\overset{6}{\cancel{24}} \times 3}{\underset{1}{\cancel{4}}}$$

$$= 18 \text{ ft.}$$

10. The correct answer is (B). If y is the unknown length:

$$\frac{3\frac{1}{2}}{\frac{1}{8}} = \frac{y}{1}$$

$$y = \frac{3\frac{1}{2} \times 1}{\frac{1}{8}}$$

$$= 3\frac{1}{2} \div \frac{1}{8}$$

$$= \frac{7}{2} \times \frac{8}{1}$$

$$= 28 \text{ ft.}$$

11. The correct answer is (B). Since only two parts of a proportion are known (77 pounds is total weight), the problem must be solved by the ratio method. The ratio 10:1 means that if the alloy were separated into equal parts, ten of those parts would be copper and one would be aluminum, for a total of 10 + 1 = 11 parts.

$77 \div 11 = 7$ lb per part

The alloy has one part aluminum.

$7 \times 1 = 7$ lb aluminum

12. The correct answer is (C). The cost (c) is proportional to the number of square feet.

$$\frac{\$.31}{c} = \frac{1}{180}$$

$$c = \frac{\$.31 \times 180}{1}$$

$$= \$55.80$$

13. The correct answer is (B). The amount earned is proportional to the number of days worked. If a is the unknown amount:

$$\frac{\$352}{a} = \frac{16}{117}$$

$$a = \frac{\$352 \times 117}{16}$$

$$a = \$2{,}574$$

14. The correct answer is (D). If (*n*) is the unknown length:

$$\frac{\frac{1}{8}}{3\frac{3}{4}} = \frac{12}{n}$$

$$n = \frac{12 \times 3\frac{3}{4}}{\frac{1}{8}}$$

$$= \frac{\overset{3}{\cancel{12}} \times \frac{15}{\underset{1}{\cancel{4}}}}{\frac{1}{8}}$$

$$= \frac{45}{\frac{1}{8}}$$

$$= 45 \div \frac{1}{8}$$

$$= 45 \times \frac{8}{1}$$

$$= 360$$

15. The correct answer is (B). The ratio of investment is:

9,000:7,000:6,000 or 9:7:6

9 + 7 + 6 = 22

\$825 ÷ 22 = \$37.50 each share of profit

7 × \$37.50 = \$262.50 B's share of profit

	\$262.50
−	230.00
	\$32.50 amount B has left

WORK AND TANK

WORK

1. a. In work problems, there are three items involved: the number of people working, the time spent working, and the amount of work done.

   b. The number of people working is directly proportional to the amount of work done; that is, the more people on the job, the more of the work will be done, and vice versa.

   c. The number of people working is inversely proportional to the time needed to finish the job; that is, the more people on the job, the less time it will take to finish it, and vice versa.

   d. The time expended on a job is directly proportional to the amount of work done; that is, the more time expended on a job, the more work that is done, and vice versa.

WORKING AT THE SAME RATES

2. a. When given the time required by a number of people working at same rates to complete a job, multiply the number of people by the time required to find the time required by one person to do the complete job.

   Example: If it takes 4 people working at equal rates 30 days to finish a job, then 1 person will take $30 \times 4 = 120$ days.

   b. When given the time required by 1 person to complete a job, to find the time required by a number of people working at equal rates to complete the same job, divide the time by the number of people.

   Example: If 1 person can do a job in 20 days, it will take 4 people working at the same rate $20 \div 4 = 5$ days to finish.

3. To solve problems involving people who work at the same rates:

   a. Multiply the number of people by the time to find the time required by 1 person.

   b. Divide this time by the number of people actually working.

   Problem: Four workers can do a job in 48 days. How long will it take 3 workers to finish the job?

   SOLUTION: One worker can do the job in $48 \times 4 = 192$ days.
   Three workers can do the job in $192 \div 3 = 64$ days.

   Answer: It would take 3 workers 64 days.

4. In some work problems, the rates, though unequal, can be equalized by comparison. To solve such problems:

   a. Determine from the facts given how many equal rates there are.

   b. Multiply the number of equal rates by the time given.

   c. Divide this by the number of equal rates.

Problem: Three workers can do a job in 12 days. Two of the workers work twice as fast as the third. How long would it take one of the faster workers to do the job himself?

SOLUTION: There are 2 fast workers and 1 slow worker. The amount of time required, therefore, would be the same as the amount of time required by 5 slow workers working at equal rates.

One slow worker will take $12 \times 5 = 60$ days.

One fast worker = 2 slow workers; therefore he will take $60 \div 2 = 30$ days to complete the job.

Answer: It will take 1 fast worker 30 days to complete the job.

5. Unit time is time expressed in terms of 1 minute, 1 hour, 1 day, etc.

6. The rate at which a person works is the amount of work he can do in unit time.

7. If given the time it will take one person to do a job, then the reciprocal of the time is the part done in unit time.

Example: If a worker can do a job in 6 days, then he can do $\frac{1}{6}$ of the work in 1 day.

8. The reciprocal of the work done in unit time is the time it will take to do the complete job.

Example: If a worker can do $\frac{3}{7}$ of the work in 1 day, then he can do the whole job in $\frac{7}{3}$, or $2\frac{1}{3}$, days.

9. If given the various times in which each of a number of people can complete a job, to find the time it will take to do the job if all work together:

   a. Find the reciprocal of the time of each to find how much each can do in unit time.

   b. Add these reciprocals to find what part of the job all working together can do in unit time.

   c. Find the reciprocal of this sum to find the time it will take all of them together to do the whole job.

Problem: If it takes ***A*** 3 days to dig a certain ditch, whereas ***B*** can dig it in 6 days, and ***C*** in 12, how long would it take all three to do the job together?

SOLUTION: **A** can do it in 3 days; therefore, he can do $\frac{1}{3}$ of the job in 1 day.

B can do it in 6 days; therefore he can do $\frac{1}{6}$ of the job in 1 day.

C can do it in 12 days; therefore, he can do $\frac{1}{12}$ of the job in 1 day.

$$\frac{1}{3}+\frac{1}{6}+\frac{1}{12}=\frac{7}{12}$$

A, **B**, and **C** can do $\frac{7}{12}$ of the work in 1 day; therefore, it will take them $\frac{12}{7}$, or $1\frac{5}{7}$, days to complete the job.

Answer: **A**, **B**, and **C**, working together, can complete the job in $1\frac{5}{7}$ days.

10. If given the total time it requires a number of people working together to complete a job, and the times of all but 1 are known, to find the missing time:

    a. Find the reciprocal of the given times to find how much each can do in unit time.

    b. Add the reciprocals to find how much is done in unit time by those whose rates are known.

    c. Subtract this sum from the reciprocal of the total time to find the missing rate.

    d. Find the reciprocal of this rate to find the unknown time.

Problem: **A**, **B**, and **C** can do a job, working together, in 2 days. **B** can do it in 5 days, and **C** can do it in 4 days. How long would it take **A** to do it himself?

SOLUTION: **B** can do it in 5 days; therefore he can do $\frac{1}{5}$ in 1 day. **C** can do it in 4 days; therefore, he can do $\frac{1}{4}$ in 1 day. The part that can be done by **B** and **C** together in 1 day is:

$$\frac{1}{5}+\frac{1}{4}=\frac{9}{20}$$

The total time is 2 days; therefore, all together can do $\frac{1}{2}$ in 1 day.

$$\frac{1}{2}-\frac{9}{20}=\frac{1}{20}$$

A can do $\frac{1}{20}$ in 1 day; therefore, he can do the whole job in 20 days.

Answer: It would take **A** 20 days to complete the job himself.

11. In some work problems, certain values are given for the three factors—number of workers, the amount of work done, and the time. It is then usually required to find the changes that occur when one or two of the factors are given different values.

One of the best methods of solving such problems is by directly making the necessary divisions and multiplications.

In the following problem, it is easily seen that more workers will be required since more houses are to be built in a shorter time.

Problem: If 60 workers can build four houses in 12 months, how many workers would be required to build six houses in 4 months?

SOLUTION: To build six houses instead of four in the same amount of time, we would need $\frac{6}{4}$ of the number of workers.

$\frac{6}{4} \times 60 = 90$

Since we now have 4 months where previously we needed 12, we must triple the number of workers.

$90 \times 3 = 270$

Answer: 270 workers will be needed to build six houses in 4 months.

TANK PROBLEMS

12. Solving tank problems is similar to solving work problems. Completely filling (or emptying) a tank may be thought of as completing a job.

13. If given the time it takes a pipe to fill or empty a tank, the reciprocal of the time will represent that part of the tank that is filled or emptied in unit time.

Example: If it takes a pipe 4 minutes to fill a tank, then $\frac{1}{4}$ of the tank is filled in 1 minute.

14. If given the part of a tank that a pipe or a combination of pipes can fill or empty in unit time, find the reciprocal of the part to find the total time required to fill or empty the whole tank.

Example: If a pipe can fill $\frac{2}{5}$ of a tank in 1 minute, then it will take $\frac{5}{2}$, or $2\frac{1}{2}$, minutes to fill the entire tank.

15. To solve tank problems in which only one action (filling or emptying) is going on:

    a. Find the reciprocal of the time of each pipe to find how much each can do in unit time.

    b. Add the reciprocals to find how much all can do in unit time.

    c. Find the reciprocal of this sum to find the total time.

Problem: Pipe A can fill a tank in 3 minutes, whereas B can fill it in 4 minutes. How long would it take both pipes, working together, to fill it?

SOLUTION: Pipe A can fill it in 3 minutes; therefore, it can fill $\frac{1}{3}$ of the tank in 1 minute. Pipe B can fill it in 4 minutes; therefore, it can fill $\frac{1}{4}$ of the tank in 1 minute.

$$\frac{1}{3} + \frac{1}{4} = \frac{7}{12}$$

Pipe A and Pipe B can fill $\frac{7}{12}$ of the tank in 1 minute; therefore they can fill the tank in $\frac{12}{7}$, or $1\frac{5}{7}$, minutes.

Answer: Pipes A and B, working together, can fill the tank in $1\frac{5}{7}$ minutes.

16. In problems in which both filling and emptying actions are occurring:
    a. Determine which process has the faster rate.
    b. The difference between the filling rate and the emptying rate is the part of the tank that is actually being filled or emptied in unit time. The fraction representing the slower action is subtracted from the fraction representing the faster process.

Problem: A certain tank can be filled by Pipe A in 12 minutes. Pipe B can empty the tank in 18 minutes. If both pipes are open, how long will it take to fill or empty the tank?

SOLUTION: Pipe A fills $\frac{1}{12}$ of the tank in 1 minute.

Pipe B empties $\frac{1}{18}$ of the tank in 1 minute.

$$\frac{1}{12} = \frac{3}{36}$$

$$\frac{1}{18} = \frac{2}{36}$$

Since $\frac{1}{12}$ is greater than $\frac{1}{18}$, the tank will ultimately be filled. In 1 minute, $\frac{3}{36} - \frac{2}{36} = \frac{1}{36}$ of the tank is actually filled. Therefore, the tank will be completely filled in 36 minutes.

Answer: It will take 36 minutes to completely fill the tank if both pipes are open.

PRACTICE TEST

1. If 314 clerks filed 6,594 papers in 10 minutes, what is the number filed per minute by the average clerk?

(A) 2
(B) 2.4
(C) 2.1
(D) 2.5

2. Four men working together can dig a ditch in 42 days. They begin, but 1 man works only half-days. How long will it take to complete the job?

(A) 48 days
(B) 45 days
(C) 43 days
(D) 44 days

3. A clerk is requested to file 800 cards. If he can file cards at the rate of 80 cards an hour, the number of cards remaining to be filed after 7 hours of work is

(A) 140
(B) 240
(C) 260
(D) 560

4. If it takes 4 days for three machines to do a certain job, it will take two machines

(A) 6 days
(B) $5\frac{1}{2}$ days
(C) 5 days
(D) $5\frac{1}{3}$ days

5. A stenographer has been assigned to place entries on 500 forms. She places entries on 25 forms by the end of half an hour, when she is joined by another stenographer. The second stenographer places entries at the rate of 45 an hour. Assuming that both stenographers continue to work at their respective rates of speed, the total number of hours required to carry out the entire assignment is

(A) 5
(B) $5\frac{1}{2}$
(C) $6\frac{1}{2}$
(D) 7

6. If, in five days, a clerk can copy 125 pages, of thirty-six lines each, with eleven words to the line, how many pages of thirty lines each and twelve words to the line can he copy in six days?

(A) 145
(B) 155
(C) 160
(D) 165

7. ***A*** and ***B*** do a job together in 2 hours. Working alone, ***A*** does the job in 5 hours. How long will it take ***B*** to do the job alone?

(A) $3\frac{1}{3}$ hours
(B) $2\frac{1}{4}$ hours
(C) 3 hours
(D) 2 hours

8. A stenographer transcribes her notes at the rate of one line typed in 10 seconds. At this rate, how long (in minutes and seconds) will it take her to transcribe notes, which will require seven pages of typing, twenty-five lines to the page?

(A) 29 min 10 sec
(B) 17 min 50 sec
(C) 40 min 10 sec
(D) 20 min 30 sec

9. A group of 5 clerks has been assigned to insert 24,000 letters into envelopes. The clerks perform this work at the following rates of speed: Clerk A, 1,100 letters an hour; Clerk B, 1,450 letters an hour; Clerk C, 1,200 letters an hour; Clerk D, 1,300 letters an hour; Clerk E, 1,250 letters an hour. At the end of 2 hours of work, Clerks C and D are assigned to another task. From the time that clerks C and D were taken off the assignment, the number of hours required for the remaining clerks to complete this assignment is

(A) less than 3 hours
(B) 3 hours
(C) more than 3 hours, but less than 4 hours
(D) more than 4 hours

10. If a certain job can be performed by 18 workers in 26 days, the number of workers needed to perform the job in 12 days is

(A) 24
(B) 30
(C) 39
(D) 52

11. A steam shovel excavates 2 cubic yards every 40 seconds. At this rate, the amount excavated in 45 minutes is

(A) 90 cu. yd.
(B) 135 cu. yd.
(C) 900 cu. yd.
(D) 3,600 cu. yd.

12. If a plant making bricks turns out 1,250 bricks in 5 days, the number of bricks that can be made in 20 days is

(A) 5,000
(B) 6,250
(C) 12,500
(D) 25,000

13. A tank is $\frac{3}{4}$ full. Pipe A can fill the tank in 12 minutes. Pipe B can empty it in 8 minutes. If both pipes are open, how long will it take to empty the tank?

(A) 14 min.
(B) 22 min.
(C) 16 min.
(D) 18 min.

14. A tank that holds 400 gallons of water can be filled by one pipe in 15 minutes and emptied by another in 40 minutes. How long would it take to fill the tank if both pipes were open?

(A) 20 min.
(B) 21 min.
(C) 23 min.
(D) 24 min.

15. An oil burner in a housing development burns 76 gallons of fuel oil per hour. At 9 a.m. on a very cold day, the superintendent asks the housing manager to put in an emergency order for more fuel oil. At that time, he reports that he has on hand 266 gallons. At noon, he again comes to the manager, notifying him than no oil has been delivered. The maximum amount of time that he can continue to furnish heat without receiving more oil is

(A) $\frac{1}{2}$ hour
(B) 1 hour
(C) $1\frac{1}{2}$ hours
(D) 2 hours

ANSWERS AND EXPLANATIONS

1. C	**4.** A	**7.** A	**10.** C	**13.** D
2. A	**5.** B	**8.** A	**11.** B	**14.** D
3. B	**6.** D	**9.** B	**12.** A	**15.** A

1. **The correct answer is (C).** 6,594 papers ÷ 314 clerks = 21 papers per clerk in 10 minutes

   21 papers ÷ 10 minutes = 2.1 papers per minute filed by the average clerk

2. **The correct answer is (A).** It would take 1 man 42 × 4 = 168 days to complete the job, working alone. If $3\frac{1}{2}$ men are working (1 man works half-days, the other 3 work full days), the job would take $168 \div 3\frac{1}{2} = 48$ days.

3. **The correct answer is (B).** In 7 hours, the clerk files 7 × 80 = 560 cards. Since 800 cards must be filed, there are 800 − 560 = 240 remaining.

4. **The correct answer is (A).** It would take one machine 3 × 4 = 12 days to do the job. Two machines could do the job in 12 ÷ 2 = 6 days.

5. **The correct answer is (B).** At the end of the first half-hour, there are 500 − 25 = 475 forms remaining. If the first stenographer completed 25 forms in half an hour, her rate is 25 × 2 = 50 forms per hour. The combined rate of the two stenographers is 50 + 45 = 95 forms per hour. The remaining can be completed in 475 ÷ 95 = 5 hours. Adding the first half-hour, the entire job requires $5\frac{1}{2}$ hours.

6. **The correct answer is (D).** 36 lines × 11 words = 396 words on each page, 125 pages × 396 words = 49,500 words in 5 days.

   49,500 ÷ 5 = 9,900 words in 1 day
   12 words × 30 lines = 360 words on each page

   $$9{,}900 \div 360 = 27\frac{1}{2} \text{ pages in 1 day}$$

   $$27\frac{1}{2} \times 6 = 165 \text{ pages in 6 days.}$$

7. **The correct answer is (A).** If ***A*** can do the job alone in 5 hours, ***A*** can do $\frac{1}{5}$ of the job in 1 hour. Working together, ***A*** and ***B*** can do the job in 2 hours, therefore in 1 hour they do $\frac{1}{2}$ the job. In 1 hour, ***B*** alone does

   $$\frac{1}{2} - \frac{1}{5} = \frac{5}{10} - \frac{2}{10}$$

   $$= \frac{3}{10}$$

   It would take ***B*** $\frac{10}{3}$ hours $= 3\frac{1}{3}$ hours to do the whole job alone.

8. **The correct answer is (A).** She must type 7 × 25 = 175 lines. At the rate of 1 line per 10 seconds, it will take 175 × 10 = 1,750 seconds.

   1,750 seconds ÷ 60 = 29 min. 10 sec.

9. The correct answer is (B).

Clerk	Number of Letters per hour
A	1,100
B	1,450
C	1,200
D	1,300
E	+1,250
Total	6,300

All 5 clerks working together process a total of 6,300 letters per hour. After 2 hours, they have processed $6{,}300 \times 2 = 12{,}600$. Of the original 24,000 letters, there are

$$\begin{array}{r} 24{,}000 \\ -\ 12{,}600 \\ \hline 11{,}400 \text{ letters remaining} \end{array}$$

Clerks A, B, and E working together process a total of 3,800 letters per hour. It will take them

$$11{,}400 \div 3{,}800 = 3 \text{ hours}$$

to process the remaining letters.

10. The correct answer is (C). The job could be performed by 1 worker in 18×26 days = 468 days. To perform the job in 12 days would require $468 \div 12 = 39$ workers.

11. The correct answer is (B). The shovel excavates 1 cubic yard in 20 seconds. There are $45 \times 60 = 2{,}700$ seconds in 45 minutes. In 2,700 seconds, the shovel can excavate $2{,}700 \div 20 = 135$ cu. yd.

12. The correct answer is (A). In 20 days, the plant can produce four times as many bricks as in 5 days.

$$1{,}250 \times 4 = 5{,}000 \text{ bricks}$$

13. The correct answer is (D). Pipe A can fill the tank in 12 min or fill $\frac{1}{12}$ of the tank in 1 minute. Pipe B can empty the tank in 8 minutes or empty $\frac{1}{8}$ of the tank in 1 minute. In 1 minute, $\frac{1}{8} - \frac{1}{12}$ of the tank is emptied (since $\frac{1}{8}$ is greater than $\frac{1}{12}$).

$$\begin{array}{rcl} \frac{1}{8} & = & \frac{3}{24} \\ -\frac{1}{12} & = & -\frac{2}{24} \\ \hline & & \frac{1}{24} \text{ of the tank is emptied per minute} \end{array}$$

It would take 24 minutes to empty the whole tank, but it is only $\frac{3}{4}$ full:

$$\frac{3}{\not{4}_{1}} \times \not{24}^{6} = 18 \text{ minutes}$$

14. The correct answer is (D). The first pipe can fill $\frac{1}{15}$ of the tank in 1 minute. The second pipe can empty $\frac{1}{40}$ of the tank in 1 minute. With both pipes open $\frac{1}{15} - \frac{1}{40}$ of the tank will be filled per minute.

$$\frac{1}{15} = \frac{8}{120}$$
$$\frac{1}{40} = -\frac{3}{120}$$
$$\frac{5}{120} = \frac{1}{24}$$

In 1 minute, $\frac{1}{24}$ of the tank is filled; therefore it will take 24 minutes for the entire tank to be filled.

15. The correct answer is (A). If 76 gallons are used per hour, it will take $266 \div 76 = 3\frac{1}{2}$ hours to use 266 gallons. From 9 a.m. to noon is 3 hours; therefore, there is only fuel for $\frac{1}{2}$ hour more.

DISTANCE

1. In distance problems, there are usually three quantities involved; the distance (in miles), the rate (in miles per hour—mph), and the time (in hours).

   a. To find the distance, multiply the rate by the time.

   Example: A man traveling 40 miles an hour for 3 hours travels 40 × 3 = 120 miles.

   b. The rate is the distance traveled in unit time. To find the rate, divide the distance by the time.

   Example: If a car travels 100 miles in 4 hours, the rate is 100 ÷ 4 = 25 miles an hour.

   c. To find the time, divide the distance by the rate.

   Example: If a car travels 150 miles at the rate of 30 miles an hour, the travel time is 150 ÷ 30 = 5 hours.

COMBINED RATES

2. a. When 2 people or objects are traveling towards each other, the rate at which they are approaching each other is the sum of their respective rates.

   b. When 2 people or objects are traveling in directly opposite directions, the rate at which they are separating is the sum of their respective rates.

3. To solve problems involving combined rates:

   a. Determine which of the three factors is to be found.

   b. Combine the rates and find the unknown factor.

   Problem: **A** and **B** are walking towards each other over a road 120 miles long. **A** walks at a rate of 6 miles an hour, and **B** walks at a rate of 4 miles an hour. How soon will they meet?

   SOLUTION: The factor to be found is the time.

   Time = Distance ÷ Rate
   Distance = 120 miles
   Rate = 6 + 4 = 10 miles an hour
   Time = 120 ÷ 10 = 12 hours

   Answer: They will meet in 12 hours.

   Problem: Joe and Sam are walking in opposite directions. Joe walks at the rate of 5 miles an hour, and Sam walks at the rate of 7 miles an hour. How far apart will they be at the end of 3 hours?

   SOLUTION: The factor to be found is distance.

   Distance = Time × Rate
   Time = 3 hours
   Rate = 5 + 7 = 12 miles an hour
   Distance = 12 × 3 = 36 miles

   Answer: They will be 36 miles apart at the end of 3 hours.

4. To find the time it takes a faster person or object to catch up with a slower person or object:

   a. Determine how far ahead the slower person or object is.

   b. Subtract the slower rate from the faster rate to find the gain in rate per unit time.

   c. Divide the distance that has been gained by the difference in rates.

Problem: Two automobiles are traveling along the same road. The first one, which travels at the rate of 30 miles an hour, starts out 6 hours ahead of the second one, which travels at the rate of 50 miles an hour. How long will it take the second one to catch up with the first one?

SOLUTION: The first automobile starts out 6 hours ahead of the second. Its rate is 30 miles an hour. Therefore, it has traveled $6 \times 30 = 180$ miles by the time the second one starts. The second automobile travels at the rate of 50 miles an hour. Therefore, its gain is $50 - 30 = 20$ miles an hour. The second auto has to catch up 180 miles. Therefore, it will take $180 \div 20 = 9$ hours to catch up with the first automobile.

Answer: It will take the faster auto 9 hours to catch up with the slower one.

AVERAGE OF TWO RATES

5. In some problems, two or more rates must be averaged. When the times are the same for two or more different rates, add the rates and divide by the number of rates.

Example: If a man travels for 2 hours at 30 miles an hour, at 40 miles an hour for the next 2 hours, and at 50 miles an hour for the next 2 hours, then his average rate for the 6 hours is $(30 + 40 + 50) \div 3 = 40$ miles an hour.

6. When the times are not the same, but the distances are the same:

   a. Assume the distance to be a convenient length.

   b. Find the time at the first rate.

   c. Find the time at the second rate.

   d. Find the time at the third rate, if any.

   e. Add up all the distances and divide by the total time to find the average rate.

Problem: A boy travels a certain distance at the rate of 20 miles an hour and returns at the rate of 30 miles an hour. What is his average rate for both trips?

SOLUTION: The distance is the same for both trips. Assume that it is 60 miles. The time for the first trip is $60 \div 20 = 3$ hours. The time for the second trip is $60 \div 30 = 2$ hours. The total distance is 120 miles. The total time is 5 hours. Average rate is $120 \div 5 = 24$ miles an hour.

Answer: The average rate is 24 miles an hour.

7. When the times are not the same and the distances are not the same:
   a. Find the time for the first distance.
   b. Find the time for the second distance.
   c. Find the time for the third distance, if any.
   d. Add up all the distances and divide by the total time to find the average rate.

Problem: A man travels 100 miles at 20 miles an hour, 60 miles at 30 miles an hour, and 80 miles at 10 miles an hour. What is his average rate for the three trips?

SOLUTION: The time for the first trip is 100 ÷ 20 = 5 hours. The time for the second trip is 60 ÷ 30 = 2 hours. The time for the third trip is 80 ÷ 10 = 8 hours. The total distance is 240 miles. The total time is 15 hours. Average rate is 240 ÷ 15 = 16 miles an hour.

Answer: The average rate for the three trips is 16 miles an hour.

GASOLINE PROBLEMS

8. Problems involving miles per gallon (mpg) of gasoline are solved in the same way as those involving miles per hour. The word "gallon" simply replaces the word "hour."

9. Miles per gallon = Distance in miles ÷ No. of gallons.

Example: If a car can travel 100 miles using 4 gallons of gasoline, then its gasoline consumption is 100 ÷ 4 = 25 mpg.

PRACTICE TEST

1. A ten-car train took 6 minutes to travel between two stations that are 3 miles apart. The average speed of the train was

(A) 20 mph
(B) 25 mph
(C) 30 mph
(D) 35 mph

2. A police car is ordered to report to the scene of a crime 5 miles away. If the car travels at an average rate of 40 miles per hour, then the time it will take to reach its destination is

(A) 3 min.
(B) 7.5 min.
(C) 10 min.
(D) 13.5 min.

3. If the average speed of a train between two stations is 30 miles per hour and the two stations are $\frac{1}{2}$ mile apart, then the time it takes the train to travel from one station to the other is

(A) 1 min.
(B) 2 min.
(C) 3 min.
(D) 4 min.

4. A car completes a 10-mile trip in 20 minutes. If it does one half the distance at a speed of 20 miles an hour, then its speed for the remainder of the distance must be

(A) 30 mph
(B) 40 mph
(C) 50 mph
(D) 60 mph

5. An express train leaves one station at 9:02 and arrives at the next station at 9:08. If the distance traveled is $2\frac{1}{2}$ miles, the average speed of the train is

(A) 15 mph
(B) 20 mph
(C) 25 mph
(D) 30 mph

6. A motorist averaged 60 miles per hour in going a distance of 240 miles. He made the return trip over the same distance in 6 hours. What was his average speed for the entire trip?

(A) 40 mph
(B) 48 mph
(C) 50 mph
(D) 60 mph

7. A city has been testing various types of gasoline for economy and efficiency. It has been found that a police radio patrol car can travel 18 miles on a gallon of Brand A gasoline, costing \$1.30 a gallon, and 15 miles on a gallon of Brand B gasoline, costing \$1.25 a gallon. For a distance of 900 miles, Brand B will cost

(A) \$10 more than Brand A.
(B) \$10 less than Brand A.
(C) \$100 more than Brand A.
(D) the same as Brand A.

8. A suspect arrested in New Jersey is being turned over by New Jersey authorities to 2 New York City police officers for a crime committed in New York City. The New York City officers receive their prisoner at a point $18\frac{1}{2}$ miles from their precinct station house, and travel directly toward their destination at an average speed of 40 miles an hour except for a delay of 10 minutes at one point because of a traffic tie-up. The time it should take the officers to reach their destination is most nearly

(A) 18 min.
(B) 22 min.
(C) 32 min.
(D) 38 min.

9. The Mayflower sailed from Plymouth, England, to Plymouth Rock, a distance of approximately 2,800 miles, in 63 days. The average speed was closest to which one of the following?

(A) $\frac{1}{2}$ mph
(B) 1 mph
(C) 2 mph
(D) 3 mph

10. If a vehicle is to complete a 20-mile trip at an average rate of 30 miles per hour, it must complete the trip in

(A) 20 min.
(B) 30 min.
(C) 40 min.
(D) 50 min.

11. A car began a trip with 12 gallons of gasoline in the tank and ended with $7\frac{1}{2}$ gallons. The car traveled 17.3 miles for each gallon of gasoline. During the trip, gasoline was bought for \$10, at a cost of \$1.25 per gallon. The total number of miles traveled during this trip was most nearly

(A) 79
(B) 196
(C) 216
(D) 229

12. A man travels a total of 4.2 miles each day to and from work. The traveling consumes 72 minutes each day. How many hours (to the nearest hundredth of an hour) would he save in 129 working days if he moved to another residence so that he would travel only 1.7 miles each day, assuming he travels at the same rate?

(A) 92.11 hours
(B) 93.62 hours
(C) 95.35 hours
(D) 98.08 hours

13. A man can travel a certain distance at the rate of 25 miles an hour by automobile. He walks back the same distance on foot at the rate of 10 miles an hour. What is his average rate for both trips?

(A) $14\frac{2}{7}$ mph
(B) $15\frac{1}{3}$ mph
(C) $17\frac{1}{2}$ mph
(D) 35 mph

14. Two trains running on the same track travel at the rates of 25 and 30 miles an hour. If the first train starts out an hour earlier, how long will it take the second train to catch up with it?

(A) 2 hr.
(B) 3 hr.
(C) 4 hr.
(D) 5 hr.

15. Two ships are 1,550 miles apart sailing towards each other. One sails at the rate of 85 miles per day and the other at 65 miles per day. How far apart will they be at the end of nine days?

(A) 180 mi.
(B) 200 mi.
(C) 220 mi.
(D) 240 mi.

ANSWERS AND EXPLANATIONS

1. C	**4.** D	**7.** A	**10.** C	**13.** A
2. B	**5.** C	**8.** D	**11.** C	**14.** D
3. A	**6.** B	**9.** C	**12.** A	**15.** B

1. The correct answer is (C).

$$6 \text{ min} = \frac{6}{60} \text{ hr} = .1 \text{ hr}$$

$$\text{Speed (Rate)} = \text{Distance} \div \text{Time}$$
$$\text{Speed} = 3 \div .1 = 30 \text{ mph}$$

2. The correct answer is (B).

$$\text{Time} = \text{Distance} \div \text{Rate}$$
$$\text{Time} = 5 \div 40 = .125 \text{ hr}$$
$$.125 \text{ hr} = .125 \times 60 \text{ min}$$
$$= 7.5 \text{ min.}$$

3. The correct answer is (A).

$$\text{Time} = \text{Distance} \div \text{Rate}$$

$$\text{Time} = \frac{1}{2} \text{ mi} \div 30 \text{ mph}$$
$$= \frac{1}{60}$$
$$\frac{1}{60} \text{ hr} = 1 \text{min.}$$

4. The correct answer is (D). First part of trip $= \frac{1}{2}$ of 10 miles $=$ 5 miles

$$\text{Time for first part} = 5 \div 20$$
$$= \frac{1}{4} \text{ hour}$$
$$= 15 \text{ minutes}$$

Second part of trip was 5 miles, completed in 20 − 15 minutes = 5 minutes.

$$5 \text{ minutes} = \frac{1}{12} \text{ hour}$$

$$\text{Rate} = 5 \text{ mi} \div \frac{1}{12} \text{ hr}$$
$$= 60 \text{ mph}$$

5. The correct answer is (C). Time is 6 minutes, or .1 hour

$$\text{Speed} = \text{Distance} \div \text{Time}$$
$$= 2\frac{1}{2} \div .1$$
$$= 2.5 \div .1$$
$$= 25 \text{ mph}$$

6. The correct answer is (B).

$$\begin{aligned}\text{Time for first 240 mi} &= 240 \div 60\\ &= 4 \text{ hours}\\ \text{Time for return trip} &= 6 \text{ hours}\\ \text{Total time for round trip} &= 10 \text{ hours}\\ \text{Total distance for round trip} &= 480 \text{ mi}\\ \text{Average rate} &= 480 \text{ mi} \div 10 \text{ hr}\\ &= 48 \text{ mph}\end{aligned}$$

7. The correct answer is (A).

$$\begin{aligned}\text{Brand A requires } 900 \div 18 &= 50 \text{ gal}\\ 50 \text{ gal} \times \$1.30 \text{ per gal} &= \$65\\ \text{Brand B requires } 900 \div 15 &= 60 \text{ gal}\\ 60 \text{ gal} \times \$1.25 \text{ per gal} &= \$75\end{aligned}$$

Brand B will cost $10 more than Brand A.

8. The correct answer is (D).

$$\begin{aligned}\text{Time} &= \text{Distance} \div \text{Rate}\\ \text{Time} &= 18.5 \text{ mi} \div 40 \text{ mph}\\ &= .4625 \text{ hours}\\ &= .4625 \times 60 \text{ minutes}\\ &= 27.75 \text{ minutes}\\ 27.75 + 10 &= 37.75 \text{ minutes}\end{aligned}$$

So the correct answer is (D), 38 min.

9. The correct answer is (C).

$$\begin{aligned}63 \text{ days} &= 63 \times 24 \text{ hours}\\ &= 1{,}512 \text{ hours}\\ \text{Speed} &= 2{,}800 \text{ mi} \div 1{,}512 \text{ hr}\\ &= 1.85 \text{ mph}\end{aligned}$$

The correct answer is (C), 2 mph.

10. The correct answer is (C).

$$\begin{aligned}\text{Time} &= 20 \text{ mi} \div 30 \text{ mph}\\ &= \frac{2}{3} \text{ hr}\end{aligned}$$

$$\frac{2}{3} \text{ hr} = \frac{2}{3} \times 60 \text{ min} = 40 \text{ min}$$

11. The correct answer is (C). The car used

$$12 - 7\frac{1}{2} = 4\frac{1}{2} \text{ gal, plus}$$

$$\$10.00 \div \$1.25 = 8 \text{ gal}$$

for a total of $12\frac{1}{2}$ gal, or 12.5 gal.

$$12.5 \text{ gal} \times 17.3 \text{ mpg} = 216.25 \text{ mi}$$

The correct answer is (C), 216.

12. The correct answer is (A).

$$72 \text{ min} = \frac{72}{60} \text{ hr} = 1.2 \text{ hr}$$

$$\text{Rate} = 4.2 \text{ mi} \div 1.2 \text{ hr} = 3.5 \text{ mph}$$

At this rate it would take 1.7 mi ÷ 3.5 mph = .486 hours (approx.) to travel 1.7 miles. The daily savings in time is 1.2 hr − .486 hr = .714 hr

$$.714 \text{ hr} \times 129 \text{ days} = 92.106 \text{ hr}$$

The correct answer is (A), 92.11 hr

13. The correct answer is (A). Assume a convenient distance, say, 50 mi.

$$\begin{aligned} \text{Time by automobile} &= 50 \text{ mi} \div 25 \text{ mph} \\ &= 2 \text{ hr} \\ \text{Time walking} &= 50 \text{ mi} \div 10 \text{ mph} \\ &= 5 \text{ hr} \\ \text{Total time} &= 7 \text{ hours} \\ \text{Total distance} &= 100 \text{ mi} \\ \text{Average rate} &= 100 \text{ mi} \div 7 \text{ hr} \\ &= 14\tfrac{2}{7} \text{ mph} \end{aligned}$$

14. The correct answer is (D). 30 mi − 25 mi = 5 mi gain per 1 hr.

During the first hour, the first train travels 25 miles.

$$25 \text{ mi} \div 5 \text{ mph} = 5 \text{ hr}$$

15. The correct answer is (B).

$$\begin{aligned} 85 \text{ mi} \times 9 \text{ days} &= 765 \text{ mi} \\ 65 \text{ mi} \times 9 \text{ days} &= \underline{585 \text{ mi}} \\ & 1{,}350 \text{ mi} \end{aligned}$$

1,550 mi − 1,350 mi = 200 miles apart at the end of nine days.

INTEREST

1. **Interest** (I) is the price paid for the use of money. There are three items considered in interest problems:

   a. The **principal** (p), which is the amount of money bearing interest.

   b. The **interest rate** (r), expressed in percent on an annual basis.

   c. The **time** (t) during which the principal is used, expressed in terms of a year.

2. The basic formulas used in interest problems are:

   a. $I = prt$

   b. $p = \frac{I}{rt}$

   c. $r = \frac{I}{pt}$

   d. $t = \frac{I}{pr}$

3. a. For most interest problems, the year is considered to have 360 days. Months are considered to have thirty days, unless a particular month is specified.

   b. To use the interest formulas, time must be expressed as part of a year.

   Examples: 5 months $= \frac{5}{12}$ year

   36 days $= \frac{36}{360}$ year, or $\frac{1}{10}$ year

   1 year 3 months $= \frac{15}{12}$ year

   c. In reference to time, the prefix "semi" means "every half." The prefix "bi" means "every two."

   Examples: Semiannually means every half-year (every six months).

   Biannually means every two years.

   Semimonthly means every half-month (every fifteen days, unless the month is specified).

   Biweekly means every two weeks (every fourteen days).

4. There are two types of interest problems:

   a. **Simple interest**, in which the interest is calculated only once over a given period of time.

   b. **Compound interest**, in which interest is recalculated at given time periods based on previously earned interest.

SIMPLE INTEREST

5. To find the interest when the principal, rate, and time are given:

   a. Rename the interest rate as a fraction.

   b. Express the time as a fractional part of a year.

   c. Multiply all three items.

   Problem: Find the interest on \$400 at $11\frac{1}{4}\%$ for three months and sixteen days.

   SOLUTION: $11\frac{1}{4}\% = \frac{45}{4}\% = \frac{45}{400}$

   3 months and 16 days = 106 days (30 days per month)

   106 days $= \frac{106}{360}$ of a year $= \frac{53}{180}$ year (360 days per year)

   $$\overset{1}{\cancel{400}} \times \frac{\overset{1}{\cancel{45}}}{\underset{1}{\cancel{400}}} \times \frac{53}{\underset{4}{\cancel{180}}} = \frac{53}{4}$$

   $$= 13.25$$

   Answer: Interest = \$13.25

6. To find the principal if the interest, interest rate, and time are given:

   a. Rename the interest rate as a fraction.

   b. Express the time as a fractional part of year.

   c. Multiply the rate by the time.

   d. Divide the interest by this product.

   Problem: What amount of money invested at 6% would receive interest of \$18 over $1\frac{1}{2}$ years?

   SOLUTION:

   $$6\% = \frac{6}{100}$$

   $$1\frac{1}{2}\text{ years} = \frac{3}{2}\text{ years}$$

   $$\frac{\overset{3}{\cancel{6}}}{100} \times \frac{3}{\underset{1}{\cancel{2}}} = \frac{9}{100}$$

   $$\$18 \div \frac{9}{100} = \overset{2}{\cancel{\$18}} \times \frac{100}{\underset{1}{\cancel{9}}}$$

   $$= \$200$$

   Answer: Principal = \$200

7. To find the rate if the principal, time, and interest are given:

   a. Express the time as a fractional part of a year.

   b. Multiply the principal by the time.

   c. Divide the interest by this product.

   d. Rename as a percent.

   Problem: At what interest rate should \$300 be invested for forty days to accrue \$2 in interest?

   SOLUTION: $40\text{ days} = \frac{40}{360}\text{ of a year}$

   $$\overset{5}{\cancel{300}} \times \frac{\overset{20}{\cancel{40}}}{\underset{\underset{3}{\cancel{6}}}{\cancel{360}}} = \frac{100}{3}$$

   $$\$2 \div \frac{100}{3} = \overset{1}{\cancel{2}} \times \frac{3}{\underset{50}{\cancel{100}}}$$

   $$= \frac{3}{50}$$

   $$\frac{3}{50} = 6\%$$

   Answer: Interest rate = 6%

8. To find the time (in years) if the principal, interest, and interest rate are given:

   a. Rename the interest rate as a fraction (or decimal).

   b. Multiply the principal by the rate.

   c. Divide the interest by this product.

Problem: Find the length of time for which \$240 must be invested at 5% to accrue \$16 in interest.

SOLUTION:

$5\% = .05$

$240 \times .05 = 12$

$16 \div 12 = 1\frac{1}{3}$

Answer: Time $= 1\frac{1}{3}$ years

COMPOUND INTEREST

9. Interest may be computed on a compound basis; that is, the interest at the end of a certain period (half year, full year, or whatever time stipulated) is added to the principal for the next period. The interest is then computed on the new increased principal, and for the next period the interest is again computed on the new increased principal. Since the principal constantly increases, compound interest yields more than simple interest.

10. To find the compound interest when given the principal, the rate, and time period:

    a. Calculate the interest as for simple interest problems, using the period of compounding for the time.

    b. Add the interest to the principal.

    c. Calculate the interest on the new principal over the period of compounding.

    d. Add this interest to form a new principal.

    e. Continue the same procedure until all periods required have been accounted for.

    f. Subtract the original principal from the final principal to find the compound interest.

Problem: Find the amount that \$200 will become if compounded semiannually at 8% for $1\frac{1}{2}$ years.

SOLUTION: Since it is to be compounded semiannually for $1\frac{1}{2}$ years, the interest will have to be computed three times.

Interest for the first period:	$.08 \times \frac{1}{2} \times \$200 = \$8$
First new principal:	$\$200 + \$8 = \$208$
Interest for the second period:	$.08 \times \frac{1}{2} \times \$208 = \$8.32$
Second new principal:	$\$208 + \$8.32 = \$216.32$
Interest for the third period:	$.08 \times \frac{1}{2} \times \$216.32 = \$8.6528$
Final principal:	$\$216.32 + \$8.6528 = \$224.9728$

Answer: \$224.97 to the nearest cent

BANK DISCOUNTS

11. A promissory note is a commitment to pay a certain amount of money on a given date, called the date of maturity.

12. When a promissory note is cashed by a bank in advance of its date of maturity, the bank deducts a discount from the principal and pays the rest to the depositor.

13. To find the bank discount:

    a. Find the time between the date the note is deposited and its date of maturity, and express this time as a fractional part of a year.

    b. Rename the rate as a fraction.

    c. Multiply the principal by the time and the rate to find the bank discount.

    d. If required, subtract the bank discount from the original principal to find the amount the bank will pay the depositor.

Problem: A $400 note drawn up on August 12, 2004, for ninety days is deposited at a bank on September 17, 2004. The bank charges a $6\frac{1}{2}\%$ discount on notes. How much will the depositor receive?

SOLUTION: From August 12, 2004 to September 17, 2004, is thirty-six days. This means that the note has fifty-four days to run.

$$54 \text{ days} = \frac{54}{360} \text{ of a year}$$

$$6\frac{1}{2}\% = \frac{13}{2}\% = \frac{13}{200}$$

$$\$400 \times \frac{13}{200} \times \frac{54}{360} = \frac{39}{10}$$

$$= \$3.90$$

$$\$400 - \$3.90 = \$396.10$$

Answer: The depositor will receive $396.10

PRACTICE TEST

1. What is the simple interest on $460 for two years at $8\frac{1}{2}$%?
   (A) $46.00
   (B) $52.75
   (C) $78.20
   (D) $96.00

2. For borrowing $300 for one month, a man was charged $6. The rate of interest was
   (A) $\frac{1}{5}$%
   (B) 12%
   (C) 24%
   (D) 2%

3. At a simple interest rate of 5% a year, the principal that will give $12.50 interest in six months is
   (A) $250
   (B) $500
   (C) $625
   (D) $650

4. Find the interest on $480 at $10\frac{1}{2}$% for two months and fifteen days.
   (A) $ 9.50
   (B) $10.50
   (C) $13.25
   (D) $14.25

5. The interest on $300 at 6% for ten days is
   (A) $ .50
   (B) $1.50
   (C) $2.50
   (D) $5.50

6. The scholarship board of a certain college lent a student $200 at an annual rate of 6% from September 30 until December 15. To repay the loan and accumulated interest, the student must give the college an amount closest to which one of the following?
   (A) $202.50
   (B) $203.00
   (C) $203.50
   (D) $212.00

7. If $300 is invested at simple interest so as to yield a return of $18 in nine months, the amount of money that must be invested at the same rate of interest so as to yield a return of $120 in six months is
   (A) $3,000
   (B) $3,300
   (C) $2,000
   (D) $2,300

8. When the principal is $600, the difference over the course of one year between simple interest at 12% per annum and interest compounded semiannually at 12% per annum is
   (A) $2.16
   (B) $21.60
   (C) $ .22
   (D) $0.00

9. What is the compound interest on $600, compounded quarterly, at 6% for nine months?
   (A) $27.38
   (B) $27.40
   (C) $27.41
   (D) $27.42

10. A ninety-day note for $1,200 is signed on May 12. Seventy-five days later the note is deposited at a bank that charges 8% discount on notes. The bank discount is
    (A) $8.40
    (B) $2.60
    (C) $2.00
    (D) $4.00

ANSWERS AND EXPLANATIONS

1. C	**3.** B	**5.** A	**7.** A	**9.** C
2. C	**4.** B	**6.** A	**8.** A	**10.** D

1. The correct answer is (C).

Principal = $460

$$\text{Rate} = 8\frac{1}{2}\% = .085$$

Time = 2 years

$$\text{Interest} = \$460 \times .085 \times 2 = \$78.20$$

2. The correct answer is (C).

Principal = $300

Interest = $6

$$\text{Time} = \frac{1}{12}\text{ year}$$

$$\$300 \times \frac{1}{12} = \$25$$

$$\$6 \div \$25 = .24 = 24\%$$

3. The correct answer is (B).

Rate = 5% = .05

Interest = $12.50

$$\text{Time} = \frac{1}{2}\text{ year}$$

$$.05 \times \frac{1}{2} = .025$$

$$\$12.50 \div .025 = \$500$$

4. The correct answer is (B).

$$\text{Time} = 2\text{ months }15\text{ days} = 75\text{ days or }\frac{75}{360}\text{ of a year}$$

$$\text{Rate} = 10\frac{1}{2}\% = \frac{21}{2}\% = \frac{21}{200}\%$$

$$\text{Interest} = 480 \times \frac{21}{200} \times \frac{75}{360} = \frac{21}{2} = \$10.50$$

5. The correct answer is (A).

Principal = $300

$$\text{Rate} = .06 = \frac{6}{100}$$

$$\text{Time} = \frac{10}{360} = \frac{1}{36}$$

$$\text{Interest} = \$\overset{3}{\cancel{300}} \times \frac{\overset{1}{\cancel{6}}}{\underset{1}{\cancel{100}}} \times \frac{1}{\underset{6}{\cancel{36}}}$$

$$= \frac{3}{6} = \$.50$$

6. The correct answer is (A).

$$\text{Principal} = \$200$$

$$\text{Rate} = .06 = \frac{6}{100}$$

Time from Sept. 30 until Dec. 15 is 76 days. (31 days in October, 30 days in November, 15 days in December)

$$76 \text{ days} = \frac{76}{360} \text{ year}$$

$$\text{Interest} = \$\overset{2}{\cancel{200}} \times \frac{\overset{1}{\cancel{6}}}{\underset{1}{\cancel{100}}} \times \frac{76}{\underset{60}{\cancel{360}}}$$

$$= \$\frac{152}{60} = \$2.53$$

$$\$200 + \$2.53 = \$202.53$$

The correct answer is (A), \$202.50.

7. The correct answer is (A).

$$\text{Principal} = \$300$$

$$\text{Interest} = \$18$$

$$\text{Time} = \frac{9}{12} \text{ years} = \frac{3}{4} \text{ year}$$

$$\$300 \times \frac{3}{4} = \$225$$

$$\$18 \div 225 = .08$$

Rate is 8%

To yield \$120 at 8% in 6 months:

$$\text{Interest} = \$120$$

$$\text{Rate} = .08$$

$$\text{Time} = \frac{1}{2} \text{ year}$$

$$.08 \times \frac{1}{2} = .04$$

$\$120 \div .04 = \$3{,}000$ must be invested

8. The correct answer is (A).

Simple interest:

$$\text{Principal} = \$600$$

$$\text{Rate} = .12$$

$$\text{Time} = 1 \text{ year}$$

$$\text{Interest} = \$600 \times .12 \times 1$$

$$= \$72.00$$

Compound Interest:

$$\text{Principal} = \$600$$

$$\text{Period of compounding} = \frac{1}{2} \text{ year}$$

$$\text{Rate} = .12$$

For the first period,

$$\begin{aligned} \text{Interest} &= \$600 \times .12 \times \frac{1}{2} \\ &= \$36 \\ \text{New principal} &= \$600 + \$36 \\ &= \$636 \end{aligned}$$

For the second period,

$$\begin{aligned} \text{Interest} &= \$636 \times .12 \times \frac{1}{2} \\ &= \$38.16 \\ \text{New principal} &= \$636 + \$38.16 \\ &= \$674.16 \\ \text{Total interest} &= \$74.16 \\ \text{Difference} &= \$74.16 - \$72.00 \\ &= \$2.16 \end{aligned}$$

9. The correct answer is (C).

$$\text{Principal} = \$600$$

$$\text{Rate} = 6\% = \frac{6}{100}$$

$$\text{Time (period of compounding)} = \frac{3}{12}\text{ year} = \frac{1}{4}\text{ year}$$

In 9 months, the interest will be computed 3 times.

For the first quarter,

$$\begin{aligned} \text{Interest} &= \$600 \times \frac{6}{100} \times \frac{1}{4} \\ &= \$9 \end{aligned}$$

New principal at end of first quarter:

$\$600 + \$9 = \$609$

For second quarter,

$$\begin{aligned} \text{Interest} &= \$609 \times \frac{6}{100} \times \frac{1}{4} \\ &= \$\frac{3654}{400} = \$9.135,\ \text{or } \$9.14 \end{aligned}$$

New principal at end of second quarter:

$\$609 + \$9.14 = \$618.14$

For third quarter,

$$\begin{aligned} \text{Interest} &= \$618.14 \times \frac{6}{100} \times \frac{1}{4} \\ &= \$\frac{3708.84}{400} \\ &= \$9.27 \end{aligned}$$

Total interest for the 3 quarters:

$\$9 + \$9.14 + \$9.27 = \$27.41$

10. The correct answer is (D).

$$\text{Principal} = \$1{,}200$$

$$\text{Time} = 90 \text{ days} - 75 \text{ days} = 15 \text{ days}$$

$$15 \text{ days} = \frac{15}{360} \text{ year}$$

$$\text{Rate} = 8\% = \frac{8}{100}$$

$$\text{Bank discount} = \overset{12}{\cancel{\$1{,}200}} \times \frac{\overset{1}{\cancel{8}}}{\underset{1}{\cancel{100}}} \times \frac{15}{\underset{45}{\cancel{360}}}$$

$$= \$\frac{180}{45} = \$4$$

TAXATION

1. The following facts should be taken into consideration when solving taxation problems:
   a. Taxes may be expressed as a percent or in terms of money based on a certain denomination.
   b. A **surtax** is an additional tax besides the regular tax rate in percent.
2. In taxation, there are usually three items involved: the amount taxable, which is called the base, the tax rate, and the tax itself.
3. To find the tax when given the base and the tax rate in percent:
   a. Rename the tax rate as a decimal.
   b. Multiply the base by the tax rate.

Problem: How much would be realized on $4,000 if taxed at 15%?

SOLUTION: 15% = .15
$4,000 × .15 = $600

Answer: Tax = $600

4. To find the tax rate in percent form when given the base and the tax:
   a. Divide the tax by the base.
   b. Rename as a percent.

Problem: Find the tax rate at which $5,600 would yield $784.

SOLUTION: $784 ÷ $5,600 = .14
.14 = 14%

Answer: Tax rate = 14%

5. To find the base when given the tax rate and the tax:
   a. Rename the tax rate as a decimal.
   b. Divide the tax by the tax rate.

Problem: What amount of money taxed 3% would yield $75?

SOLUTION: 3% = .03
$75 ÷ .03 = $2,500

Answer: Base = $2,500

6. When the tax rate is fixed and expressed in terms of money, take into consideration the denomination upon which it is based; that is, consider whether it is based on every \$100, or \$1,000, etc.

7. To find the tax when given the base and tax rate in terms of money:

   a. Divide the base by the denomination upon which the tax rate is based.

   b. Multiply this quotient by the tax rate.

   Problem: If the tax rate is \$3.60 per \$1,000, find the tax on \$470,500.

   SOLUTION: \$475,500 ÷ \$1,000 = 470.5
   470.5 × \$3.60 = \$1,693.80

   Answer: \$1,693.80

8. To find the tax rate based on a certain denomination when given the base and the tax derived:

   a. Divide the base by the denomination indicated.

   b. Divide the tax by this quotient.

   Problem: Find the tax rate per \$100 that would be required to raise \$350,000 on \$2,000,000 of taxable property.

   SOLUTION: \$2,000,000 ÷ \$100 = \$20,000
   \$350,000 ÷ 20,000 = \$17.50

   Answer: Tax rate = \$17.50 per \$100

9. Since a surtax is an additional tax besides the regular tax, to find the total tax:

   a. Rename the regular tax rate as a decimal.

   b. Multiply the base by the regular tax rate.

   c. Rename the surtax rate as a decimal.

   d. Multiply the base by the surtax rate.

   e. Add both taxes.

   Problem: Assuming that the tax rate is $2\frac{1}{3}\%$ on liquors costing up to \$3, and 3% on those costing from \$3 to \$6, and $3\frac{1}{2}\%$ on those from \$6 to \$10, what would be that tax on a bottle costing \$8 if there is a surtax of 5% on all liquors above \$5?

   SOLUTION: An \$8 bottle falls within the category of \$6 to \$10. The tax rate on such a bottle is

   $3\frac{1}{2}\% = .035$
   \$8.00 × .035 = \$.28
   surtax rate = 5% = .05
   \$8.00 × .05 = \$.40
   \$.28 + \$.40 = \$.68

   Answer: Total tax = \$.68

PRACTICE TEST

1. Mr. Jones' income for a year is $15,000. He pays $2,250 for income taxes. The percent of his income that he pays for income taxes is

(A) 9%
(B) 12%
(C) 15%
(D) 22%

2. If the tax rate is $3\frac{1}{2}$% and the amount to be raised is $64.40, what is the base?

(A) $1,800
(B) $1,840
(C) $1,850
(D) $1,860

3. What is the tax rate per $1,000 if a base of $338,500 would yield $616.07?

(A) $1.08
(B) $1.90
(C) $1.95
(D) $1.82

4. A man buys an electric light bulb for 54¢, which includes a 20% tax. What is the cost of the bulb without the tax?

(A) 43¢
(B) 44¢
(C) 45¢
(D) 46¢

5. What tax rate on a base of $3,650 would raise $164.25?

(A) 4%
(B) 5%
(C) $4\frac{1}{2}$%
(D) $5\frac{1}{2}$%

6. A piece of property is assessed at $22,850 and the tax rate is $4.80 per $1,000 of assessed valuation. What is the amount of tax that must be paid on the property?

(A) $109
(B) $112
(C) $109.68
(D) $112.68

7. $30,000 of land is assessed at 120% of its value. If the tax rate is $5.12 per $1,000 assessed valuation, the amount of tax to be paid is

(A) $180.29
(B) $184.32
(C) $190.10
(D) $192.29

8. Of the following real estate tax rates, which is the greatest?

(A) $31.25 per $1,000
(B) $3.45 per $100
(C) 32¢ per $10
(D) 3¢ per $1

9. A certain community needs $185,090.62 to cover its expenses. If its tax rate is $1.43 per $100 of assessed valuation, what must be the assessed value of its property?

(A) $12,900,005
(B) $12,943,400
(C) $12,940,000
(D) $12,840,535

10. A man's taxable income is $14,280. The state tax instructions tell him to pay 2% on the first $3,000 of his taxable income, 3% on each of the second and third $3,000, and 4% on the remainder. What is the total amount of income tax that he must pay?

(A) $265.40
(B) $309.32
(C) $451.20
(D) $454.62

ANSWERS AND EXPLANATIONS

1. C	**3.** D	**5.** C	**7.** B	**9.** B
2. B	**4.** C	**6.** C	**8.** B	**10.** C

1. The correct answer is (C).

Tax = \$2,250
Base = \$15,000
Tax Rate = Tax ÷ Base
Tax Rate = \$2,250 ÷ \$15,000 = .15
Tax rate = .15 = 15%

2. The correct answer is (B).

$$\text{Tax Rate} = 3\frac{1}{2}\% = .035$$

Tax = \$64.40
Base = Tax ÷ Tax rate
Base = \$64.40 ÷ .035
= \$1,840

3. The correct answer is (D).

Base = \$338,500
Tax = \$616.07
Denomination = \$1,000
\$338,500 ÷ \$1,000 = 338.50
\$616.07 ÷ 338.50 = \$1.82 per \$1,000

4. The correct answer is (C). 54¢ is 120% of the base (cost without tax).

Base = 54 ÷ 120%
= 54 ÷ 1.20
= 45¢

5. The correct answer is (C).

Base = \$3,650
Tax = \$164.25
Tax rate = Tax ÷ Base
= \$164.25 ÷ \$3,650
= .045

$$= 4\frac{1}{2}\%$$

6. The correct answer is (C).

Base = \$22,850
Denomination = \$1,000
Tax rate = \$4.80 per thousand

$$\frac{\$22,850}{\$1,000} = 22.85$$

22.85 × \$4.80 = \$109.68

7. **The correct answer is (B).**

$$\begin{aligned}\text{Base} &= \text{Assessed valuation} = 120\% \text{ of } \$30{,}000\\ &= 1.20 \times \$30{,}000\\ &= \$36{,}000\\ \text{Denomination} &= \$1{,}000\\ \text{Tax rate} &= \$5.12 \text{ per thousand}\\ \frac{\$36{,}000}{\$1{,}000} &= 36\\ 36 \times \$5.12 &= \$184.32\end{aligned}$$

8. **The correct answer is (B).** Express each tax rate as a decimal:

$$\$31.25 \text{ per } \$1{,}000 = \frac{31.25}{1{,}000} = .03125$$

$$\$3.45 \text{ per } \$100 = \frac{3.45}{100} = .0345$$

$$32¢ \text{ per } \$10 = \frac{.32}{10} = .0320$$

$$3¢ \text{ per } \$1 = \frac{.03}{1} = .0300$$

The greatest decimal is .0345

So the correct answer is (B), \$3.45 per \$1,000.

9. **The correct answer is (B).**

$$\begin{aligned}\text{Tax rate} &= \$1.43 \text{ per } \$100\\ &= \frac{1.43}{100} = .0143\\ &= 1.43\%\\ \text{Tax} &= \$185{,}090.62\\ \text{Base} &= \text{Tax} \div \text{Rate}\\ &= 185{,}090.62 \div .0143\\ &= \$12{,}943{,}400\end{aligned}$$

10. **The correct answer is (C).**

$$\begin{aligned}\text{First } \$3{,}000\text{: } .02 \times \$3{,}000 &= \$60.00\\ \text{Second } \$3{,}000\text{: } .03 \times \$3{,}000 &= \$90.00\\ \text{Third } \$3{,}000\text{: } .03 \times \$3{,}000 &= \$90.00\\ \text{Remainder } (\$14{,}280 - \$9{,}000)\text{: } .04 \times \$5{,}280 &= \underline{\$211.20}\\ \text{Total Tax} &= \$451.20\end{aligned}$$

PROFIT AND LOSS

1. The following terms may be encountered in profit and loss problems:

   a. The **cost price** of an article is the price paid by a person who wishes to sell it again.

   b. There may be an **allowance** or **trade discount** on the cost price.

   c. The **list price** or **marked price** is the price at which the article is listed or marked to be sold.

   d. There may be a **discount** or **series of discounts** on the list price.

   e. The **selling price** or **sale price** is the price at which the article is finally sold.

   f. If the selling price is greater than the cost price, there has been a **profit**.

   g. If the selling price is less than the cost price, there has been a **loss**.

   h. If the article is sold at the same price as the cost, there has been no loss or profit.

   i. Profit or loss may be based either on the cost price or on the selling price.

   j. Profit or loss may be stated in terms of dollars and cents, or in terms of percent.

   k. **Overhead** expenses include such items as rent, salaries, etc. Overhead expenses may be added to cost price to determine total cost when calculating profit or assigning selling price.

2. The basic formulas used in profit and loss problems are:

   Selling price = cost price + profit
   Selling price = cost price − loss

   Example: If the cost of an article is \$2.50, and the profit is \$1.50, then the selling price is \$2.50 + \$1.50 = \$4.00.

   Example: If the cost of an article is \$3.00, and the loss is \$1.20, then the selling price is \$3.00 − \$1.20 = \$1.80.

3. a. To find the profit in terms of money, subtract the cost price from the selling price, or selling price − cost price = profit.

   Example: If an article costing \$3.00 is sold for \$5.00, then the profit is \$5.00 − \$3.00 = \$2.00.

   b. To find the loss in terms of money, subtract the selling price from the cost price, or cost price − selling price = loss.

   Example: If an article costing \$2.00 is sold for \$1.50, then the loss is \$2.00 − \$1.50 = \$.50.

4. To find the selling price if the profit or loss is expressed in percent based on cost price:

   a. Multiply the cost price by the percent of profit or loss to find the profit or loss in terms of money.

   b. Add this product to the cost price if a profit is involved, or subtract for a loss.

Problem: If an article costing \$2 is sold at a loss of 5 percent of the cost price, find the selling price.

SOLUTION: 5% of \$2.00 = .05 × \$2.00
= \$.10 loss
\$2.00 − \$.10 = \$1.90

Answer: Selling price = \$1.90

5. To find the cost price when given the selling price and the percent of profit or loss based on the selling price:

   a. Multiply the selling price by the percent of profit or loss to find the profit or loss in terms of money.

   b. Subtract this product from the selling price if profit, or add the product to the selling price if a loss.

Problem: If an article sells for \$12 and there has been a profit of 10 percent of the selling price, what is the cost price?

SOLUTION: 10% of \$12.00 = .10 × \$12.00
= \$1.20 profit
\$12.00 − \$1.20 = \$10.80

Answer: Cost price = \$10.80

Problem: What is the cost price of an article selling for \$2 on which there has been a loss of 6 percent of the selling price?

SOLUTION: 6% of \$2.00 = .06 × \$2.00
= \$.12 loss
\$2.00 + \$.12 = \$2.12

Answer: Cost price = \$2.12

6. To find the percent of profit or percent of loss based on cost price:

   a. Find the profit or loss in terms of money.

   b. Divide the profit or loss by the cost price.

   c. Rename as a percent.

Problem: Find the percent of profit based on cost price of an article costing \$2.50 and selling for \$3.

SOLUTION: \$3.00 − \$2.50 = \$.50 profit

$$2.50\overline{).50} = 250\overset{.20}{\overline{)50.00}}$$

.20 = 20%

Answer: Profit = 20%

Problem: Find the percent of loss based on cost price of an article costing \$5 and selling for \$4.80.

SOLUTION: \$5.00 − \$4.80 = \$.20 loss

$$5.00\overline{).20} = 500\overline{)20.00}^{\;.04}$$

$$.04 = 4\%$$

Answer: Loss = 4%

7. To find the percent of profit or percent of loss on selling price:
   a. Find the profit or loss in terms of money.
   b. Divide the profit or loss by the selling price.
   c. Rename as a percent.

Problem: Find the percent of profit based on the selling price of an article costing \$2.50 and selling for \$3.

SOLUTION: \$3.00 − \$2.50 = \$.50 profit

$$3.00\overline{).50} = 300\overline{)50.00} = .1\overline{6}$$

$$= 16\frac{2}{3}\%$$

Answer: Profit = $16\frac{2}{3}\%$ [This notation ($\overline{6}$) indicates a non-terminating decimal.]

Problem: Find the percent of loss based on the selling price of an article costing \$5 and selling for \$4.80.

SOLUTION: \$5.00 − \$4.80 = \$.20 loss

$$4.80\overline{).20} = 480\overline{)20.00} = .041\overline{6}$$

$$= 4\frac{1}{6}\%$$

Answer: Loss = $4\frac{1}{6}\%$

8. To find the cost price when given the selling price and the percent of profit based on the cost price:
   a. Establish a relation between the selling price and the cost price.
   b. Solve to find the cost price.

Problem: An article is sold for \$2.50, which is a 25 percent profit of the cost price. What is the cost price?

SOLUTION: Since the selling price represents the whole cost price plus 25 percent of the cost price,

2.50 = 125% of the cost price
2.50 = 1.25 of the cost price
Cost price = 2.50 ÷ 1.25
= 2.00

Answer: Cost price = \$2.00

9. To find the selling price when given the profit based on the selling price:
   a. Establish a relation between the selling price and the cost price.
   b. Solve to find the selling price.

Problem: A merchant buys an article for \$27 and sells it at a profit of 10 percent of the selling price. What is the selling price?

SOLUTION: \$27.00 + profit = selling price

Since the profit is 10 percent of the selling price, the cost must be 90 percent of the selling price.

$$27.00 = 90\% \text{ of the selling price}$$
$$= .90 \text{ of the selling price}$$
$$\text{Selling price} = 27.00 \div .90$$
$$= 30.00$$

Answer: Selling price = \$30.00

TRADE DISCOUNTS

10. A **trade discount**, usually expressed in percent, indicates the part that is to be deducted from the list price.
11. To find the selling price when given the list price and the trade discount:
    a. Multiply the list price by the percent of discount to find the discount in terms of money.
    b. Subtract the discount from the list price.

Problem: The list price of an article is \$20. There is a discount of 5 percent. What is the selling price?

SOLUTION: $\$20.00 \times 5\% = 20.00 \times .05 = \$1.00$ discount

$\$20.00 - \$1.00 = \$19.00$

Answer: Selling price = \$19.00

An alternate method of solving the above problem is to consider the list price to be 100 percent. Then, if the discount is 5 percent, the selling price is $100\% - 5\% = 95\%$ of the list price. The selling price is

$$95\% \text{ of } \$20.00 = .95 \times \$20.00$$
$$= \$19.00$$

SERIES OF DISCOUNTS

12. There may be more than one discount to be deducted from the list price. This is called a **discount series**.
13. To find the selling price when given the list price and a discount series:
    a. Multiply the list price by the first percent of discount.
    b. Subtract this product from the list price.
    c. Multiply the difference by the second discount.
    d. Subtract this product from the difference.
    e. Continue the same procedure if there are more discounts.

Problem: Find the selling price of an article listed at $10 on which there are discounts of 20 percent and 10 percent

SOLUTION:

$$\$10.00 \times 20\% = 10.00 \times .20 = \$2.00$$
$$\$10.00 - \$2.00 = \$8.00$$
$$\$8.00 \times 10\% = \$8.00 \times .10 = \$.80$$
$$\$8.00 - \$.80 = \$7.20$$

Answer: Selling price = $7.20

14. Instead of deducting each discount individually, it is often more practical to find the **single equivalent discount** first and then deduct. It does not matter in which order the discounts are taken.

15. The single equivalent discount may be found by assuming a list price of 100 percent. Leave all discounts in percent form.

    a. Subtract the first discount from 100 percent, giving the net cost factor (NCF) had there been only one discount.

    b. Multiply the NCF by the second discount. Subtract the product from the NCF, giving a second NCF that reflects both discounts.

    c. If there is a third discount, multiply the second NCF by it and subtract the product from the second NCF, giving a third NCF that reflects all three discounts.

    d. If there are more discounts, repeat the process.

    e. Subtract the final NCF from 100 percent to find the single equivalent discount.

Problem: Find the single equivalent discount of 20 percent, 25 percent, and 10 percent.

SOLUTION:

	100%	
	−20%	first discount
	80%	first NCF
− 25% of 80% =	20%	
	60%	second NCF
− 10% of 60% =	6%	
	54%	third NCF
100% − 54% =	46%	single equivalent discount

Answer: 46%

Problem: An article lists at $750. With discounts of 20 percent, 25 percent, and 10 percent, what is the selling price of this article?

SOLUTION: As shown above, the single equivalent discount of 20 percent, 25 percent, and 10 percent is 46 percent.

$$46\% \text{ of } \$750 = .46 \times \$750$$
$$= \$345$$
$$\$750 - \$345 = \$405$$

Answer: Selling price = $405

PRACTICE TEST

1. Dresses sold at $65 each. The dresses cost $50 each. The percentage of increase of the selling price over the cost is

   (A) 40%
   (B) $33\frac{1}{3}\%$
   (C) $33\frac{1}{2}\%$
   (D) 30%

2. A dealer bought a ladder for $27. What must it be sold for if he wishes to make a profit of 40 percent on the selling price?

   (A) $38.80
   (B) $43.20
   (C) $45.00
   (D) $67.50

3. A printer was listed at $120 and was bought for $96. What was the rate of discount?

   (A) $16\frac{2}{3}\%$
   (B) 20%
   (C) 24%
   (D) 25%

4. A dealer sells an article at a loss of 50 percent of the cost. Based on the selling price, the loss is

   (A) 25%
   (B) 50%
   (C) 100%
   (D) None of these

5. What would be the marked price of an article if the cost was $12.60 and the gain was 10 percent of the cost price?

   (A) $11.34
   (B) $12.72
   (C) $13.86
   (D) $14.28

6. A stationer buys notepads at $.75 per dozen and sells them at 25 cents apiece. The profit based on the cost is

   (A) 50%
   (B) 300%
   (C) 200%
   (D) 100%

7. An article costing $18 is to be sold at a profit of 10 percent of the selling price. The selling price will be

   (A) $19.80
   (B) $36.00
   (C) $18.18
   (D) $20.00

8. A calculating machine company offered to sell a city agency four calculating machines at a discount of 15 percent from the list price, and to allow the agency $85 for each of two old machines being traded in. The list price of the new machines is $625 per machine. If the city agency accepts this offer, the amount of money it will have to provide for the purchase of these four machines is

   (A) $1,785
   (B) $2,295
   (C) $1,955
   (D) $1,836

9. Pencils are purchased at $9 per gross and sold at six for 75 cents. The rate of profit based on the selling price is

   (A) 100%
   (B) 67%
   (C) 50%
   (D) 25%

10. The single equivalent discount of 20 percent and 10 percent is

    (A) 15%
    (B) 28%
    (C) 18%
    (D) 30%

ANSWERS AND EXPLANATIONS

1. D	**3.** B	**5.** C	**7.** D	**9.** C
2. C	**4.** C	**6.** B	**8.** C	**10.** B

1. The correct answer is (D).

$$\text{Selling price} - \text{cost} = \$65 - \$50$$
$$= \$15$$
$$\frac{\$15}{\$50} = .30 = 30\%$$

2. The correct answer is (C). Cost price = 60% of selling price, since the profit is 40 percent of the selling price, and the whole selling price is 100 percent.

$$\$27 = 60\% \text{ of selling price}$$
$$\text{Selling price} = \$27 \div 60\%$$
$$= \$27 \div .6$$
$$= \$45$$

3. The correct answer is (B).

$$\text{The discount was } \$120 - \$96 = \$24$$
$$\text{Rate of discount} = \frac{\$24}{\$120} = .20$$
$$= 20\%$$

4. The correct answer is (C). Loss = cost − selling price. Considering the cost to be 100 percent of itself, if the loss is 50 percent of the cost, the selling price is also 50 percent of the cost (50% = 100% − 50%). Since the loss and the selling price are therefore the same, the loss is 100 percent of the selling price.

5. The correct answer is (C).

$$\text{Gain (profit)} = 10\% \text{ of } \$12.60$$
$$= .10 \times \$12.60$$
$$= \$1.26$$
$$\text{Selling price} = \text{cost} + \text{profit} = \$12.60 + \$1.26$$
$$= \$13.86$$

6. The correct answer is (B). Each dozen notepads cost $.75 and are sold for

$$12 \times \$.25 = \$3.00$$
$$\text{The profit is } \$3.00 - \$.75 = \$2.25$$
$$\text{Profit based on cost} = \frac{\$2.25}{\$.75}$$
$$= 3$$
$$= 300\%$$

7. The correct answer is (D).

$$\text{If profit} = 10\% \text{ of selling price,}$$
$$\text{then cost} = 90\% \text{ of selling price}$$
$$\$18 = 90\% \text{ of selling price}$$
$$\text{Selling price} = \$18 \div 90\%$$
$$= \$18 \div .90$$
$$= \$20$$

8. The correct answer is (C).

$$\text{Discount for each new machine: } 15\% \text{ of } \$625 = .15 \times \$625 = \$93.75$$

$$\text{Each new machine will cost } \$625 - \$93.75 = \$531.25$$

$$\text{Four new machines will cost } \$531.25 \times 4 = \$2{,}125$$

But there is an allowance of \$85 each for 2 old machines:

$\$85 \times 2 = \$170$

Final cost to city:

$\$2{,}125 - \$170 = \$1{,}955$

9. The correct answer is (C).

$$1 \text{ gross} = 144 \text{ units}$$

$$\text{Selling price for 6 pencils} = \$.75$$

$$\text{Selling price for 1 pencil} = \frac{\$.75}{6}$$

$$\text{Selling price for 1 gross of pencils} = \frac{\$.75}{\cancel{6}_{1}} \times \cancel{144}^{24} = \$18.00$$

$$\text{Cost for 1 gross of pencils} = \$9.00$$

$$\text{Profit for 1 gross of pencils} = \$18.00 - \$9.00 = \$9.00$$

$$\frac{\text{profit}}{\text{selling price}} = \frac{\$9.00}{\$18.00} = .5 = 50\%$$

10. The correct answer is (B).

$$\begin{array}{rr} & 100\% \\ & \underline{-20\%} \\ & 80\% \\ -\ 10\% \text{ of } 80\% = & \underline{-\ 8\%} \\ & 72\% \end{array}$$

$100\% - 72\% = 28\%$ single equivalent discount.

PAYROLL

1. **Salaries** are computed over various time periods: hourly, daily, weekly, biweekly (every two weeks), semimonthly (twice each month), monthly, and yearly.

2. **Overtime** is usually computed as "time and a half," that is, each hour in excess of the number of hours in the standard workday or workweek is paid $1\frac{1}{2}$ times the regular hourly rate. Some companies pay "double time," twice the regular hourly rate, for work on Sundays and holidays.

Problem: An employee is paid weekly, based on a 40-hour workweek, with time and a half for overtime. If the employee's regular hourly rate is $6.50, how much will he earn for working 47 hours in one week?

SOLUTION: Overtime hours = 47 − 40 = 7 hours

$$\text{Overtime pay} = 1\frac{1}{2} \times \$6.50 = \$9.75 \text{ per hour}$$

Overtime pay for 7 hours: 7 × $9.75 = $68.25

Regular pay for 40 hours: 40 × $6.50 = $260.00

Total pay = $68.25 + $260.00 = $328.25

Answer: $328.25

3. a. In occupations such as retail sales, real estate, and insurance, earnings may be based on **commission**, which is a percent of the sales or a percent of the value of the transactions that are completed.

   b. Earnings may be from straight commission only, from salary plus commission, or from a commission that is graduated according to transaction volume.

Problem: A salesman earns a salary of $200 weekly, plus a commission based on sales volume for the week. The commission is 7 percent for the first $1,500 of sales and 10 percent for all sales in excess of $1,500. How much did he earn in a week in which his sales totaled $3,200?

SOLUTION:

$3,200 − $1,500 = $1,700 excess sales
.07 × $1,500 = $105 commission on first $1,500
.10 × $1,700 = $170 commission on excess sales
+ $200 weekly salary
$475 total earnings

Answer: $475

4. **Gross pay** refers to the amount of money earned whether from salary, commission, or both, before any deductions are made.

5. There are several deductions that are usually made from gross pay:

   a. **Withholding tax** is the amount of money withheld for income tax. It is based on wages, marital status, and number of exemptions (also called allowances) claimed by the employee. The withholding tax is found by referring to tables supplied by the federal, state, or city governments.

   Example

MARRIED PERSONS—WEEKLY PAYROLL PERIOD						
Wages		Number of Withholding Allowances Claimed				
		0	**1**	**2**	**3**	**4**
At least	**But less than**	**Amount of Income Tax to Be Withheld**				
390	400	41	32	24	16	7
400	410	42	34	25	17	9
410	420	44	35	27	19	10
420	430	45	37	28	20	12
430	440	47	38	30	22	13
440	450	48	40	31	23	15
450	460	50	41	33	25	16
460	470	51	43	34	26	18
470	480	53	44	36	28	19
480	490	54	46	37	29	21

   Based on the above table, an employee who is married, claims three exemptions, and is paid a weekly wage of $434.50 will have $22 withheld for income tax. If the same employee earned $440 weekly, it would be necessary to look on the next line for "at least $440 but less than $450" to find that $23 would be withheld.

b. The FICA (Federal Insurance Contribution Act) tax is also called the Social Security tax. In 2001, the FICA tax was 7.65 percent of the first $84,000 of annual wages; the wages in excess of $84,000 were subject to 1.45 percent tax.

The FICA may be found by multiplying wages up to and including $84,000 by .0765 or by using tables such as the one below.

Example

SOCIAL SECURITY EMPLOYEE TAX TABLE

If wage payment is	The employee tax to be deducted is	If wage payment is	The employee tax to be deducted is
$61	$4.67	$ 81	$6.20
62	4.74	82	6.27
63	4.82	83	6.35
64	4.90	84	6.43
65	4.97	85	6.50
66	5.45	86	6.58
67	5.13	87	6.66
68	5.20	88	6.73
69	5.28	89	6.81
70	5.36	90	6.89
71	5.43	91	6.96
72	5.51	92	7.04
73	5.58	93	7.11
74	5.66	94	7.19
75	5.74	95	7.27
76	5.81	96	7.34
77	5.89	97	7.42
78	5.97	98	7.50
79	6.04	99	7.57
80	6.12	100	7.65

According to the table above, the Social Security tax, or FICA tax, on wages of $84 is $6.43. The FICA tax on $85 is 6.50.

Problem: Based on 2001 tax figures, what is the total FICA tax on an annual salary of $30,000?

SOLUTION: .0765 × $30,000 = $2,295

Answer: $2,295

c. Other deductions that may be made from gross pay are deductions for pension plans, loan payments, payroll savings plans, and union dues.

6. The **net pay,** or **take-home pay**, is equal to the gross pay less the total deductions.

Problem: Mr. Jay earns $550 salary per week with the following deductions: federal withholding tax, $106.70; FICA tax $41.31; state tax, $22.83; pension payment, $6.42; union dues, $5.84. How much take-home pay does he receive?

SOLUTION:

Deductions	$106.70
	41.31
	22.83
	6.42
	+ 5.84
	$183.10

Gross pay	=	$550.00
Deductions	=	− 183.10
Net pay	=	$366.90

Answer: His take-home pay is $366.90

PRACTICE TEST

1. Jane Rose's semimonthly salary is $750. Her yearly salary is

(A) $9,000
(B) $12,500
(C) $18,000
(D) $19,500

2. John Doe earns $300 for a 40-hour week. If he receives time and a half for overtime, what is his hourly overtime wage?

(A) $7.50
(B) $9.25
(C) $10.50
(D) $11.25

3. Which salary is greater?

(A) $350 weekly
(B) $1,378 monthly
(C) $17,000 annually
(D) $646 biweekly

4. A factory worker is paid on the basis of an 8-hour day, with an hourly rate of $7 and time and a half for overtime. Find his gross pay for a week in which he worked the following hours: Monday, 8; Tuesday, 9; Wednesday, 9½; Thursday 8½; Friday, 9.

(A) $280
(B) $308
(C) $322
(D) $462

Questions 5 and 6 refer to the following table.

SINGLE PERSONS—WEEKLY PAYROLL PERIOD						
		Number of Withholding Allowances Claimed				
Wages		**0**	**1**	**2**	**3**	**4**
At least	**But less than**	**Amount of Income Tax to Be Withheld**				
340	350	49	43	37	32	26
350	360	50	45	39	33	28
360	370	52	46	40	35	29
370	380	55	48	42	36	31
380	390	58	49	43	38	32
390	400	60	51	45	39	34
400	410	63	53	46	41	35
410	420	66	55	48	42	37
420	430	69	58	49	44	38
430	440	72	61	51	45	40

5. If an employee is single and has one exemption, the income tax withheld from his weekly salary of $389.90 is

(A) $51
(B) $58
(C) $49
(D) $43

6. If a single person with two exemptions has $51 withheld for income tax, his weekly salary could NOT be

(A) $430.00
(B) $435.25
(C) $437.80
(D) $440.00

7. Sam Richards earns $1,200 monthly. The following deductions are made from his gross pay monthly: federal withholding tax, $188.40; FICA tax, $91.80; state tax, $36.78; city tax, $9.24; savings bond, $37.50; pension plan, $5.32; and repayment of pension load, $42.30. His monthly net pay is

(A) $788.66
(B) $797.90
(C) $798.90
(D) $799.80

8. A salesman is paid a straight commission that is 23 percent of his sales. What is his commission on $1,260 of sales?

(A) $232.40
(B) $246.80
(C) $259.60
(D) $289.80

9. Ann Johnson earns a salary of $150 weekly plus a commission of 9 percent of sales in excess of $500 for the week. For a week in which her sales were $1,496, her earnings were

(A) $223.64
(B) $239.64
(C) $253.64
(D) $284.64

10. A salesperson is paid a 6 percent commission on the first $2,500 of sales for the week, and $7\frac{1}{2}$ percent on that portion of sales in excess of $2,500. What is the commission earned in a week in which sales were $3,280?

(A) $196.80
(B) $208.50
(C) $224.30
(D) $246.00

ANSWERS AND EXPLANATIONS

1. C	**3.** A	**5.** C	**7.** A	**9.** B
2. D	**4.** C	**6.** D	**8.** D	**10.** B

1. **The correct answer is (C).** A semimonthly salary is paid twice a month. Jane Rose receives $750 × 2 = $1,500 each month, which is $1,500 × 12 = $18,000 per year.

2. **The correct answer is (D).**

   The regular hourly rate is $300 ÷ 40 = $7.50

   $$\text{The overtime rate is } \$7.50 \times 1\tfrac{1}{2} = \$7.50 \times 1.5 = \$11.25$$

3. **The correct answer is (A).** Write each salary in its yearly equivalent:

   $350 weekly = $350 × 52 yearly
   = $18,200 yearly
   $1,378 monthly = $1,378 × 12 yearly
   = $16,536 yearly
   $17,000 annually = $17,000 yearly
   $646 biweekly = $646 ÷ 2 weekly
   = $323 weekly
   = $323 × 52 yearly
   = $16,796 yearly

   So the correct answer is (A), $350 weekly.

4. **The correct answer is (C).**

   The factory worker's overtime hours were:

Monday	0
Tuesday	1
Wednesday	$1\frac{1}{2}$
Thursday	$\frac{1}{2}$
Friday	1
Total	4 hours overtime

   $$\text{Overtime rate per hour} = 1\tfrac{1}{2} \times \$7.00 = 1.5 \times \$7.00 = \$10.50$$

   Overtime pay = 4 × $10.50
   = $42

   Regular pay for 8 hours per day for 5 days or 40 hours.

   Regular pay = 40 × $7.00
   = $280
   Total wages = $280 + $42
   = $322

5. **The correct answer is (C).** The correct amount is found on the line for wages of at least $380 but less than $390, and in the column "1" withholding allowance. The amount withheld is $49.

6. **The correct answer is (D).** In the column for 2 exemptions, or withholding allowances, \$51 is found on the line for wages of at least \$430, but less than \$440. Choice (D) does not fall within that range.

7. **The correct answer is (A).**

Deductions:	\$188.40
	91.80
	36.78
	9.24
	37.50
	5.32
	+ 43.30
Total	\$411.34

Gross pay =	\$1,200.00
Total deductions =	− 411.34
	\$788.66

8. **The correct answer is (D).**

23% of \$1260 = .23 × \$1,260
= \$289.80

9. **The correct answer is (B).**

\$1496 − \$500 = \$996 excess sales
9% of \$996 = .09 × \$996
= \$89.64 commission

\$150.00 salary
+ 89.64 commission
\$239.64 total earnings

10. **The correct answer is (B).**

\$3,280 − \$2,500 = \$780 excess sales

Commission on \$2,500: .06 × \$2,500 =	\$150.00
Commission on \$780: .075 × \$780 =	+ 58.50
Total =	\$208.50

SEQUENCES

1. A **sequence** is a list of numbers based on a certain pattern. There are three main types of sequences:

   a. If each term in a sequence is increased or decreased by the same number to form the next term, then it is an **arithmetic sequence**. The number being added or subtracted is called the **common difference**.

   Examples: 2, 4, 6, 8, 10 . . . is an arithmetic sequence in which the common difference is 2.

   14, 11, 8, 5, 2 . . . is an arithmetic sequence in which the common difference is 3.

   b. If each term of a sequence is multiplied by the same number to form the next term, then it is called a **geometric sequence**. The number multiplying each term is called the **common ratio**.

   Examples: 2, 6, 18, 54 . . . is a geometric sequence in which the common ratio is 3.

   64, 16, 4, 1 . . . is a geometric sequence in which the common ratio is $\frac{1}{4}$.

   c. If the sequence is neither arithmetic nor geometric, it is a miscellaneous sequence. Such a sequence may have each term a square or a cube, or the difference may be squares or cubes; or there may be a varied pattern in the sequence that must be determined.

2. A sequence may be ascending, that is, the numbers increase; or descending, that is, the numbers decrease.

3. To determine whether the sequence is arithmetic:

   a. If the sequence is ascending, subtract the first term from the second, and the second term from the third. If the difference is the same in both cases, the sequence is arithmetic.

   b. If the sequence is descending, subtract the second term from the first, and the third term from the second. If the difference is the same in both cases, the sequence is arithmetic.

4. To determine whether the sequence is geometric, divide the second term by the first, and the third term by the second. If the ratio is the same in both cases, the sequence is geometric.

5. To find a missing term in an arithmetic sequence that is ascending:

   a. Subtract any term from the one following it to find the common difference.

   b. Add the common difference to the term preceding the missing term.

c. If the missing term is the first term, it may be found by subtracting the common difference from the second term.

Problem: What number follows $16\frac{1}{3}$ in this sequence?

$$3, 6\frac{1}{3}, 9\frac{2}{3}, 13, 16\frac{1}{3} \ldots$$

SOLUTION: $6\frac{1}{3} - 3 = 3\frac{1}{3}, 9\frac{2}{3} - 6\frac{1}{3} = 3\frac{1}{3}$

The sequence is arithmetic; the common difference is $3\frac{1}{3}$.

$$16\frac{1}{3} + 3\frac{1}{3} = 19\frac{2}{3}$$

Answer: The missing term, which is the term following $16\frac{1}{3}$, is $19\frac{2}{3}$.

6. To find a missing term in an arithmetic sequence that is descending:

a. Subtract any term from the one preceding it to find the common difference.

b. Subtract the common difference from the term preceding the missing term.

c. If the missing term is the first term, it may be found by adding the common difference to the second term.

Problem: Find the first term in the sequence:

$$\_\_\_\_\_, 16, 13\frac{1}{2}, 11, 8\frac{1}{2}, 6 \ldots$$

SOLUTION: $16 - 13\frac{1}{2} = 2\frac{1}{2}, 13\frac{1}{2} - 11 = 2\frac{1}{2}$

The sequence is arithmetic; the common difference is $2\frac{1}{2}$.

$$16 + 2\frac{1}{2} = 18\frac{1}{2}$$

Answer: The term preceding 16 is $18\frac{1}{2}$.

7. To find a missing term in a geometric sequence:

a. Divide the term by the one preceding it to find the common ratio.

b. Multiply the term preceding the missing term by the common ratio.

c. If the missing term is the first term, it may be found by dividing the second term by the common ratio.

Problem: Find the missing term in the sequence:

2, 6, 18, 54, _____

SOLUTION: $6 \div 2 = 3, 18 \div 6 = 3$

The sequence is geometric; the common ratio is 3.

$$54 \times 3 = 162$$

Answer: The missing term is 162.

Problem: Find the missing term in the sequence:

______, 32, 16, 8, 4, 2

SOLUTION: $16 \div 32 = \frac{1}{2}$ (common ratio)

$$32 \div \frac{1}{2} = 32 \times \frac{2}{1}$$
$$= 64$$

Answer: The first term is 64.

8. If, after trial, a sequence is neither arithmetic nor geometric, it must be of a miscellaneous type. Test to see whether it is a sequence of squares or cubes or whether the difference is the square or cube of the same number; or the same number may be first squared, then cubed, etc.

PRACTICE TEST

Find the missing term in each of the following sequences:

1. ______, 7, 10, 13

2. 5, 10, 20, ______, 80

3. 49, 45, 41, ______, 33, 29

4. 1.002, 1.004, 1.006, ______

5. 1, 4, 9, 16, ______

6. 10, $7\frac{7}{8}$, $5\frac{3}{4}$, $3\frac{5}{8}$, ______

7. ______, 3, $4\frac{1}{2}$, $6\frac{3}{4}$

8. 55, 40, 28, 19, 13, ______

9. 9, 3, 1, $\frac{1}{3}$, $\frac{1}{9}$, ______

10. 1, 3, 7, 15, 31, ______

ANSWERS AND EXPLANATIONS

1. 4
2. 40
3. 37
4. 1.008
5. 25
6. $1\frac{1}{2}$
7. 2
8. 10
9. $\frac{1}{27}$
10. 63

1. This is an ascending arithmetic sequence in which the common difference is 10 − 7, or 3. The first term is 7 − 3 = 4.

2. This is a geometric sequence in which the common ratio is 10 ÷ 5, or 2. The missing term is 20 × 2 = 40.

3. This is a descending arithmetic sequence in which the common difference is 49 − 45, or 4. The missing term is 41 − 4 = 37.

4. This is an ascending arithmetic sequence in which the common difference is 1.004 − 1.002, or .002. The missing term is 1.006 + .002 = 1.008.

5. This sequence is neither arithmetic nor geometric. However, if the numbers are rewritten as 1^2, 2^2, 3^2, and 4^2, it is clear that the next number must be 5^2, or 25.

6. This is a descending arithmetic sequence in which the common difference is $10 - 7\frac{7}{8} = 2\frac{1}{8}$. The missing term is $3\frac{5}{8} - 2\frac{1}{8} = 1\frac{4}{8}$, or $1\frac{1}{2}$.

7. This is a geometric sequence in which the common ratio is:

$$4\frac{1}{2} \div 3 = \frac{9}{2} \times \frac{1}{3}$$
$$= \frac{3}{2}$$

The first term is $3 \div \frac{3}{2} = 3 \times \frac{2}{3}$
$$= 2$$

Therefore, the missing term is 2.

8. There is no common difference and no common ratio in this sequence. However, note the differences between terms:

$$\underbrace{55 \quad 40}_{\substack{15 \\ 5 \times 3}} \quad \underbrace{40 \quad 28}_{\substack{12 \\ 4 \times 3}} \quad \underbrace{28 \quad 19}_{\substack{9 \\ 3 \times 3}} \quad \underbrace{19 \quad 13}_{\substack{6 \\ 2 \times 3}}$$

The differences are multiples of 3. Following the same pattern, the difference between 13 and the next term must be 1×3, or 3. The missing term is then $13 - 3 = 10$.

9. This is a geometric sequence in which the common ratio is $3 \div 9 = \frac{1}{3}$. The missing term is $\frac{1}{9} \times \frac{1}{3} = \frac{1}{27}$.

10. This sequence is neither arithmetic nor geometric. However, note the difference between terms:

$$\underbrace{1 \quad 3}_{\substack{2 \\ 2^1}} \quad \underbrace{3 \quad 7}_{\substack{4 \\ 2^2}} \quad \underbrace{7 \quad 15}_{\substack{8 \\ 2^3}} \quad \underbrace{15 \quad 31}_{\substack{16 \\ 2^4}}$$

The difference between 31 and the next term must be 2^5, or 32. The missing term is $31 + 32 = 63$.

ARITHMETIC REVIEW EXAM 1

Directions: Mark the letter of the choice that best answers the question.

1. A cashier can count 1,286 coins in one hour. How many coins can he count in $3\frac{1}{2}$ hours?

(A) 3,880
(B) 3,902
(C) 4,253
(D) 4,501

2. Jane has two pieces of ribbon. One piece is $2\frac{3}{4}$ yards; the other $2\frac{2}{3}$ yards. To make the two pieces equal she must cut off from the longer piece

(A) 9 in.
(B) 8 in.
(C) 6 in.
(D) 3 in.

3. The present size of a dollar bill in the United States is 2.61 inches by 6.14 inches. The number of square inches of paper used for one bill is closest to which of the following?

(A) 160 sq. in.
(B) 17.8 sq. in.
(C) 16 sq. in.
(D) 1.78 sq. in.

4. The total saving in purchasing 30 fifty-cent rulers at a reduced rate of \$4.60 per dozen is

(A) \$1.20
(B) \$1.75
(C) \$2.85
(D) \$3.50

5. The difference between one hundred five thousand eight-four and ninety-three thousand seven hundred nine is

(A) 11,375
(B) 12,131
(C) 56,294
(D) 56,375

6. If a distance estimated at 150 feet is really 140 feet, the percent of error in this estimate is

(A) $6\frac{2}{3}\%$
(B) $7\frac{1}{7}\%$
(C) 10%
(D) 14%

7. Assuming that on a blueprint $\frac{1}{4}$ inch equals 12 inches, the actual length in feet of a steel bar represented on the blueprint by a line $3\frac{3}{8}$ inches long is

(A) $3\frac{3}{8}$
(B) $6\frac{3}{4}$
(C) $12\frac{1}{2}$
(D) $13\frac{1}{2}$

8. The difference between 320 centimeters and 3 meters is

(A) 20 cm
(B) 31.7 cm
(C) 200 cm
(D) 317 cm

9. If two of the angles of a triangle measure 30° and 60°, the triangle is

(A) right
(B) acute
(C) obtuse
(D) equilateral

10. If A can do a job in three hours and B can do the same job in five hours, then both working together can finish the job in

(A) 4 hr.
(B) $1\frac{2}{3}$ hr.
(C) $2\frac{1}{8}$ hr.
(D) $1\frac{7}{8}$ hr.

11. If Mrs. Jones bought $3\frac{3}{4}$ yards of muslin at $1.16 per yard and $4\frac{2}{3}$ yards of polyester at $3.87 per yard, then the amount of change she received from $25 is

(A) $2.12
(B) $2.28
(C) $2.59
(D) $2.63

12. A piece of cardboard in the shape of a 15-inch square is rolled so as to form a cylindrical surface, without overlapping. The number of inches in the diameter of the cylinder is approximately

(A) 45
(B) 23
(C) 5
(D) 2.5

13. The single commercial discount that is equivalent to successive discounts of 10 percent and 10 percent is

(A) 20%
(B) 19%
(C) 17%
(D) 15%

14. The value of forty-thousand nickels is

(A) $20
(B) $200
(C) $2,000
(D) $20,000

15. A checking account has a balance of $253.36. If deposits of $36.95, $210.23, and $7.34 and withdrawals of $117.35, $23.37, and $15.98 are made, what is the new balance of the account?

(A) $155.54
(B) $351.18
(C) $364.58
(D) $664.58

16. Six percent simple interest for one year on $2,436.18 is most nearly

(A) $145.08
(B) $145.17
(C) $146.08
(D) $146.17

17. Suppose that a pile of ninety-six file cards measures 1 inch in height and that it takes you $\frac{1}{2}$ hour to file these cards. If you are given three piles of cards that measure $2\frac{1}{2}$ inches high, $1\frac{3}{4}$ inches high, and $3\frac{3}{8}$ inches high respectively, the time it would take to file the cards is most nearly

(A) 2 hr. 30 min.
(B) 3 hr. 50 min.
(C) 6 hr. 45 min.
(D) 8 hr. 15 min.

18. If the sum of the lengths of the edges of a cube is 48 inches, the volume of the cube is.

(A) 512 cu. in.
(B) 96 cu. in.
(C) 64 cu. in.
(D) 12 cu. in.

19. If the sum of 42.83 and 72.9 is subtracted from 200, the result is

(A) 230.07
(B) 169.93
(C) 48.12
(D) 84.27

20. Assuming there are 28.4 grams per ounce, the number of kilograms in 3 pounds is closest to

(A) .45
(B) .85
(C) 1.36
(D) 1.92

21. A drawer contains five red pens and three blue pens. If Mr. Jones takes a pen from the drawer without looking, what is the probability that he will take a blue pen?

(A) $\frac{3}{8}$
(B) $\frac{1}{2}$
(C) $\frac{3}{5}$
(D) $\frac{5}{8}$

22. If $1\frac{1}{2}$ cups of cereal are used with $4\frac{1}{2}$ cups of water, the amount of water needed with $\frac{3}{4}$ of a cup of cereal is:

(A) 2 cups
(B) $2\frac{1}{4}$ cups
(C) $2\frac{1}{8}$ cups
(D) $2\frac{1}{2}$ cups

23. The regular price of a TV set that sold for $118.80 at a 20 percent reduction sale is

(A) $148.50
(B) $142.60
(C) $138.84
(D) $ 95.04

24. The number missing in the sequence 2, 6, 12, 20, ?, 42, 56, 72 is

(A) 30
(B) 40
(C) 36
(D) 28

25. A rectangular flower bed whose dimensions are 16 yards by 12 yards is surrounded by a walk 3 yards wide. The area of the walk is

(A) 93 sq. yd.
(B) 204 sq. yd.
(C) 96 sq. yd.
(D) 150 sq. yd.

26. John drives 60 miles to his destination at an average speed of 40 mph and makes the return trip at an average speed of 30 mph. His average speed for the entire trip is

(A) $32\frac{1}{5}$ mph
(B) $34\frac{2}{7}$ mph
(C) 35 mph
(D) $43\frac{1}{3}$ mph

Questions 27 and 28 refer to the following graph.

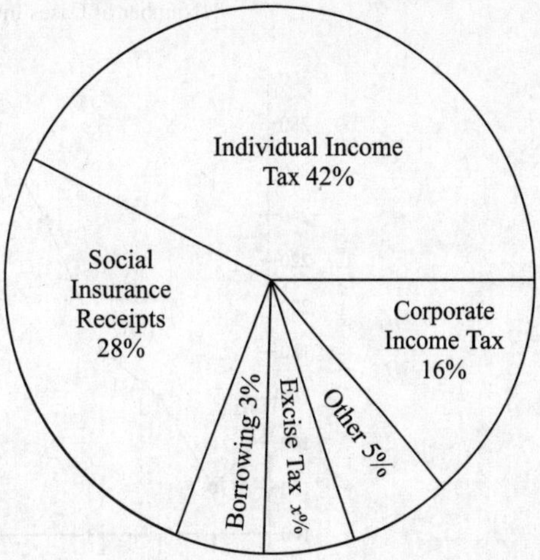

Origin of Federal Revenues of $352.6 Billion

27. The total individual income tax and corporate income tax revenues were, to the nearest billion dollars,

(A) 58
(B) 123
(C) 205
(D) 256

28. The revenue from excise tax was, to the nearest billion dollars,

(A) 14 billion
(B) 15 billion
(C) 20 billion
(D) 21 billion

29. If a worker has completed $\frac{5}{8}$ of a job, what percent of the job remains to be completed?

(A) $37\frac{1}{2}\%$
(B) 40%
(C) 60%
(D) $62\frac{1}{2}\%$

30. After one year, Mr. Richards paid back a total of $1,695 as payment on a $1,500 loan. All the money paid over $1,500 was simple interest. The interest charge was most nearly

(A) 13%
(B) 11%
(C) 9%
(D) 7%

31. If the City Department of Purchase bought 190 calculators for $79.35 each and 208 calculators for $83.99 each, then the total price paid for these calculators is

(A) $31,581.30
(B) $32,546.42
(C) $33,427.82
(D) $33,586.30

Questions 32 and 33 refer to the following graph.

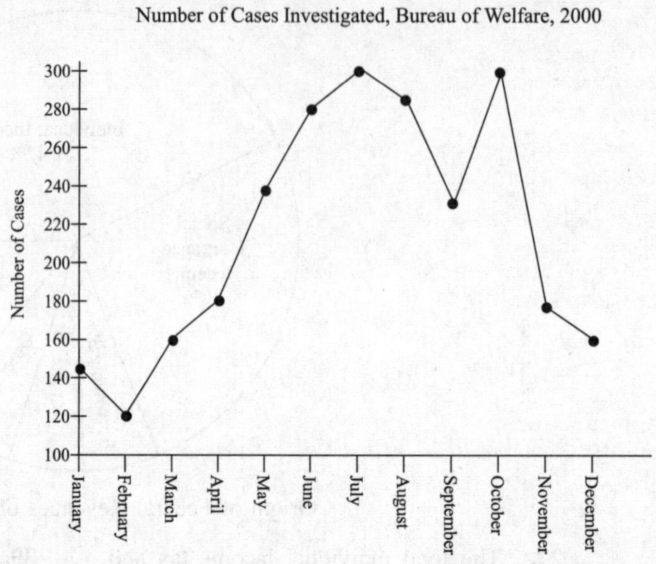

32. In which month were approximately 270 cases investigated?

(A) May
(B) June
(C) July
(D) August

33. The total number of cases investigated during the first three months of the year was approximately

(A) 330
(B) 350
(C) 390
(D) 430

34. Twelve clerks are assigned to enter certain data on index cards. This number of clerks could perform the task in eighteen days. After these clerks have worked on this assignment for six days, 4 more clerks are added to the staff to do this work. Assuming that all the clerks work at the same rate of speed, the entire task, instead of taking eighteen days, will be performed in

(A) 9 days
(B) 12 days
(C) 15 days
(D) 16 days

35. Mr. Smith earns $7.20 per hour for a 40-hour week, with time and a half for overtime hours. In a week in which he worked 46 hours, he earned

(A) $331.20
(B) $352.80
(C) $424.20
(D) $496.80

36. In the Fahrenheit scale, the temperature that is equivalent to 50° Celsius is

(A) 122°
(B) 90°
(C) 106°
(D) 87°

37. The circumference of a circle is 10π. The area of the same circle is

(A) 5π
(B) 10π
(C) 25π
(D) 100π

38. A bank pays 6 percent interest, compounded quarterly, on savings accounts. How much interest will $300 earn in nine months?

(A) $13.31
(B) $13.51
(C) $13.71
(D) $13.91

39. A champion runner ran the 100-yard dash in three track meets. The first time, he ran it in 10.2 seconds; the second in 10.4 seconds; and the third time in 10 seconds. What was his average time?

(A) 10.2 sec.
(B) 10.3 sec.
(C) 10.35 sec.
(D) 10.4 sec.

40. Joshua Howard is paid a yearly salary of $54,000. His monthly paycheck shows the following deductions: federal income tax, $675.20; FICA, $345.15; state tax, $225.45; pension, $135.32. What is his yearly take-home pay?

(A) $37,426.56
(B) $37,561.88
(C) $37,907.03
(D) $38,132.48

41. Two adjacent walls of a 40′ by 35′ office are to be painted. The walls are 8′ high and include no doors or windows. If each gallon of the paint to be used covers 450 square feet, how many gallons are needed?

(A) $1\frac{1}{3}$
(B) $1\frac{1}{2}$
(C) $2\frac{1}{3}$
(D) $2\frac{1}{2}$

42. Mr. Harvey receives a salary of $300 per week plus 2 percent commission on sales. What were his total earnings for a week in which his sales were $5,846?

(A) $406.92
(B) $416.92
(C) $426.92
(D) $436.92

43. If real estate tax is $1.62 per $100 assessed valuation, the tax that must be paid on property assessed at $82,200 is closest to

(A) $152
(B) $694
(C) $1,086
(D) $1,332

44. *A* worked five days on overhauling an old car. *B* worked four days more to finish the job. After the sale of the car, the net profit was $243. They wanted to divide the profit on the basis of the time spent by each. *A*'s share of the profit was

(A) $108
(B) $135
(C) $127
(D) $143

45. Mr. Jones wishes to purchase one item priced at $24.50 and another item priced at $43.28. If sales tax is 5 percent, what is the total amount he must pay for the two items?

(A) $67.78
(B) $67.79
(C) $71.16
(D) $71.17

46. A circle graph shows that 32 percent of the tourists to a city are German, 28 percent are Spanish, 20 percent are English, 10 percent are miscellaneous, and the rest are French. How many degrees of the circle should be devoted to the French?

(A) 12
(B) 24
(C) 30
(D) 36

47. Of the following readings of rainfall—1.2 inches, 2.4 inches, 2.2 inches, 3.5 inches, 4.3 inches, 2.3 inches, 4.2 inches, 3.9 inches, 3.0 inches, 3.3 inches, 2.9 inches, 3.6 inches, 4.5 inches, 4.7 inches, 4.6 inches—the median is

(A) 3.5 inches
(B) 3.3 inches
(C) 3.4 inches
(D) 3.0 inches

48. If FICA tax is 7.65 percent, then the FICA tax on wages of $450.70 is closest to

(A) $34.48
(B) $34.58
(C) $34.68
(D) $34.78

49. In a particular company, 2 employees received hourly wages of $4.50, 3 employees received hourly wages of $4.15, and 5 employees received hourly wages of $4.75. The average hourly wage of this group of employees is

(A) $4.37
(B) $4.47
(C) $4.52
(D) $4.63

50. *A* invested $7,000 in a business venture and his partner, *B*, invested $8,000. They agreed to share the profits in the same ratio. What was *A*'s share of a profit of $2,250?

(A) $1,050.00
(B) $1,200.00
(C) $1,968.75
(D) $2,250.00

ANSWERS AND EXPLANATIONS

1. D	**11.** C	**21.** A	**31.** B	**41.** A
2. D	**12.** C	**22.** B	**32.** B	**42.** B
3. C	**13.** B	**23.** A	**33.** D	**43.** D
4. D	**14.** C	**24.** A	**34.** C	**44.** B
5. A	**15.** B	**25.** B	**35.** B	**45.** D
6. B	**16.** D	**26.** B	**36.** A	**46.** D
7. D	**17.** B	**27.** C	**37.** C	**47.** A
8. A	**18.** C	**28.** D	**38.** C	**48.** A
9. A	**19.** D	**29.** A	**39.** A	**49.** C
10. D	**20.** C	**30.** A	**40.** A	**50.** A

1. The correct answer is (D).

$$1{,}286 \times 3\frac{1}{2} = \overset{643}{\cancel{1{,}286}} \times \frac{7}{\underset{1}{\cancel{2}}}$$

$$= 4{,}501$$

2. The correct answer is (D).

$$\begin{array}{rcr} 2\frac{3}{4} & = & 2\frac{9}{12} \\ -2\frac{2}{3} & = & -2\frac{8}{12} \\ \hline & & \frac{1}{12} \end{array}$$

One piece is $\frac{1}{12}$ of a yard longer than the other.

$$\begin{aligned} 1 \text{ yd.} &= 36 \text{ in.} \\ \frac{1}{12} \text{ of } 1 \text{ yd.} &= \frac{1}{12} \times 36 \text{ in.} \\ &= 3 \text{ in.} \end{aligned}$$

3. The correct answer is (C).

$$\begin{array}{r} 2.61 \text{ in.} \\ \times\ 6.14 \text{ in.} \\ \hline 1044 \\ 261 \\ 1566 \\ \hline 16.0254 \text{ sq. in.} \end{array}$$

4. **The correct answer is (D).**

$$30 = 2\frac{1}{2} \text{ dozen}$$

At the reduced rate, $2\frac{1}{2}$ dozen rulers cost

$$2\frac{1}{2} \times \$4.60 = \$11.50$$

At the regular rate, 30 rulers cost

$$30 \times \$.50 = \$15.00$$

The saving is

$$\begin{array}{r} \$15.00 \\ -\ 11.50 \\ \hline \$\ 3.50 \end{array}$$

5. **The correct answer is (A).**

$$\begin{array}{r} 105{,}084 \\ -\ 93{,}709 \\ \hline 11{,}375 \end{array}$$

6. **The correct answer is (B).**

$$\begin{aligned} \text{Estimated distance} &= 150 \text{ ft} \\ \text{Real Distance} &= 140 \text{ ft} \\ \text{Amount of Error} &= 10 \text{ ft} \\ 10 \text{ ft} \div 140 \text{ ft} &= .07\frac{1}{7} = 7\frac{1}{7}\% \end{aligned}$$

7. **The correct answer is (D).** 12 inches = 1 foot, therefore each $\frac{1}{4}$ inch on the blueprint represents 1 foot. $3\frac{3}{8}$ inches represent:

$$\begin{aligned} 3\frac{3}{8} \text{ in} \div \frac{1}{4} \text{ in} &= \frac{27}{\cancel{8}_{2}} \times \frac{\cancel{4}^{1}}{1} \text{ ft} \\ &= \frac{27}{2} \text{ ft} \\ &= 13\frac{1}{2} \text{ feet} \end{aligned}$$

8. **The correct answer is (A).**

$$\begin{aligned} 3 \text{ meters} &= 300 \text{ centimeters} \\ 320 \text{ cm} - 300 \text{ cm} &= 20 \text{ cm} \end{aligned}$$

9. **The correct answer is (A).** The sum of the measures of the angles of a triangle is 180°. If two of the angles measure 30° and 60°, the third must measure 90°, which is a right angle. The triangle is therefore a right triangle.

10. The correct answer is (D). *A* can do $\frac{1}{3}$ of the job in one hour. *B* can do $\frac{1}{5}$ of the job in one hour. In each hour working together, they will complete $\frac{1}{3} + \frac{1}{5}$ of the job.

$$\frac{1}{3} + \frac{1}{5} = \frac{5}{15} + \frac{3}{15}$$
$$= \frac{8}{15}$$

It will take $\frac{15}{8}$ hours to complete the job working together.

$$\frac{15}{8} = 1\frac{7}{8} \text{ hr.}$$

11. The correct answer is (C).

Cost of muslin: $\$1.16 \times 3\frac{3}{4} = \$1.16 \times \frac{15}{4} = \$4.35$

Cost of polyester: $\$3.87 \times 4\frac{2}{3} = \$3.87 \times \frac{14}{3} = \$18.06$

Total cost: $4.35 + $18.06 = $22.41
Change: $25.00 − $22.41 = $2.59

12. The correct answer is (C). The circumference is 15″. To find the diameter, divide the circumference by $\pi \left(\frac{22}{7}\right)$.

$$15 \div \frac{22}{7} = 15 \times \frac{7}{22}$$
$$= \frac{105}{22}$$
$$= 4\frac{17}{22}$$

The diameter is approximately 5″.

13. The correct answer is (B).

$$\begin{array}{rr} & 100\% \\ & -\ 10\% \\ \hline & 90\% \\ -10\% \text{ of } 90\% = & -9\% \\ \hline & 81\% \end{array}$$

100% − 81% = 19% single equivalent discount.

14. The correct answer is (C).

$$\begin{array}{r} 40{,}000 \\ \times \quad .05 \\ \hline \$2{,}000.00 \end{array}$$

15. The correct answer is (B).

$$\begin{array}{lr} \text{Deposits:} & \$36.95 \\ & 210.23 \\ & +\ 7.34 \\ \hline & \$254.52 \end{array}$$

$$\begin{array}{lr} \text{Withdrawals:} & \$117.35 \\ & 23.37 \\ & +\ 15.98 \\ \hline & \$156.70 \end{array}$$

$$\begin{array}{rl} \$253.36 & \text{original balance} \\ +\ 254.52 & \text{deposits} \\ \hline 507.88 & \\ -\ 156.70 & \text{withdrawals} \\ \hline \$351.18 & \text{new balance} \end{array}$$

16. The correct answer is (D).

$$\begin{array}{r} \$2436.18 \\ \times\ .06 \\ \hline \$146.1708 \end{array}$$

So the correct answer is (D), $146.17.

17. The correct answer is (B). The cards total $2\frac{1}{2} + 1\frac{3}{4} + 3\frac{3}{8}$ inches in height.

$$\begin{aligned} 2\frac{1}{2} &= 2\frac{4}{8} \\ 1\frac{3}{4} &= 1\frac{6}{8} \\ +\,3\frac{3}{8} &= +\,3\frac{3}{8} \\ \hline 6\frac{13}{8} &= 7\frac{5}{8} \end{aligned}$$

Each inch takes $\frac{1}{2}$ hour to file. $7\frac{5}{8}$ inches will take $7\frac{5}{8} \times \frac{1}{2}$ hours.

$$\begin{aligned} 7\frac{5}{8} \times \frac{1}{2} &= \frac{61}{8} \times \frac{1}{2} \\ &= \frac{61}{16} \\ &= 3\frac{13}{16} \end{aligned}$$

1 hour = 60 minutes

$$\frac{13}{16} \text{ of } 60 = \frac{13}{\cancel{16}_{4}} \times \cancel{60}^{15} = \frac{195}{4} = 48\frac{3}{4} \text{ min}$$

Therefore, it will take 3 hours and $48\frac{3}{4}$ minutes to file the cards.

Note that only one of the answer choices is possible once you know that it will take 3+ hours. It is not really necessary to solve for the exact number of minutes. Also note that the fact that ninety-six file cards equal one inch is not needed.

So the correct answer is (B), 3 hr. 50 min.

18. The correct answer is (C). A cube has twelve edges. If the sum of the edges is 48 inches, each edge is 48 inches ÷ 12 = 4 inches.

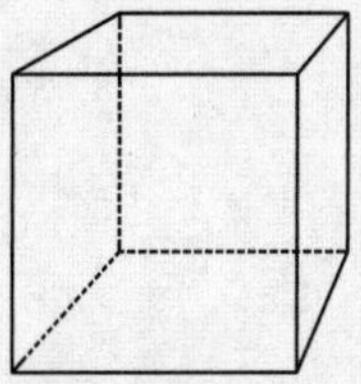

$$\begin{aligned} \text{The volume of the cube} &= 4^3 \text{ cubic inches} \\ &= 4 \times 4 \times 4 \text{ cu in} \\ &= 64 \text{ cu. in.} \end{aligned}$$

19. The correct answer is (D).

Sum of 42.83 and 72.9:

$$\begin{array}{r} 42.83 \\ +\,72.9 \\ \hline 115.73 \end{array}$$

Subtract from 200:

$$\begin{array}{r} 200.00 \\ -\,115.73 \\ \hline 84.27 \end{array}$$

20. The correct answer is (C).

$$\begin{aligned}
3\text{ pounds} &= 3 \times 16\text{ ounces}\\
&= 48\text{ ounces}\\
48\text{ ounces} \times 28.4\text{ grams per ounce} &= 1{,}363.2\text{ grams}\\
1\text{ kilogram} &= 1{,}000\text{ grams}\\
1{,}363.2\text{ grams} \div 1{,}000 &= 1.3632\text{ kilograms}
\end{aligned}$$

The correct answer is (C), 1.36.

21. The correct answer is (A). There is a total of eight pens in the drawer. The probability that the pen is blue is $\frac{3}{8}$.

22. The correct answer is (B). If the cereal is reduced by one half, then the water must also be halved.

$$\begin{aligned}
\frac{1}{2} \times 4\frac{1}{2} &= \frac{1}{2} \times \frac{9}{2}\\
&= \frac{9}{4}\\
&= 2\frac{1}{4}\text{ cups}
\end{aligned}$$

23. The correct answer is (A). The sale price is 80 percent of the regular price.

$$\begin{aligned}
\text{Regular price} &= \$118.80 \div .80\\
&= \$148.50
\end{aligned}$$

24. The correct answer is (A). Find the differences between the terms of the sequence:

2 6 12 20 ____ 42 56 72

4 6 8 14 16

The difference between 20 and the missing term must be 10. Therefore, the missing term is 30.

25. The correct answer is (B).

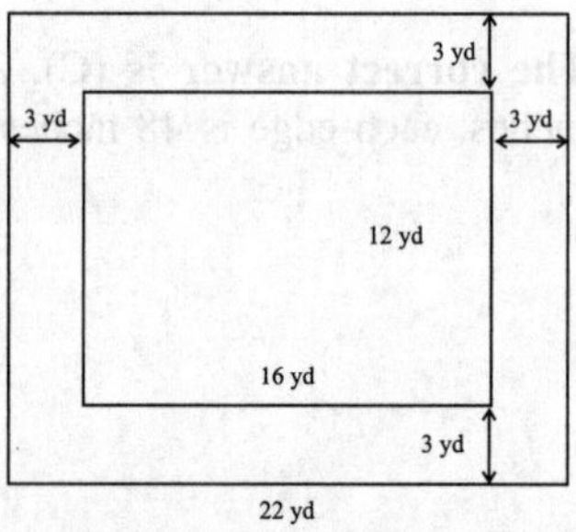

Area of large rectangle is: 22 yd × 18 yd = 396 sq yd

Area of small rectangle is: 16 yd × 12 yd = 192 sq yd

Area of path is difference or 396 sq yd − 192 sq yd = 204 sq yd

26. The correct answer is (B). John took 60 miles ÷ 40 mph = $1\frac{1}{2}$ hours to drive to his destination. The return trip took 60 miles ÷ 30 mph = 2 hours. The entire trip was 120 miles and took $3\frac{1}{2}$ hours.

$$\begin{aligned}\text{Average speed} &= 120 \text{ mi} \div 3\tfrac{1}{2} \text{ hr}\\ &= 120 \div \tfrac{7}{2} \text{ mph}\\ &= 120 \times \tfrac{2}{7} \text{ mph}\\ &= \tfrac{240}{7} \text{ mph}\\ &= 34\tfrac{2}{7} \text{ mph}\end{aligned}$$

27. The correct answer is (C).

$$\begin{aligned}\text{Individual income tax} &= 42\%\\ \text{Corporate income tax} &= +16\%\\ \text{Total} &= 58\%\end{aligned}$$

$$\begin{aligned}58\% \text{ of } \$352.6 \text{ billion} &= .58 \times \$352.6 \text{ billion}\\ &= \$204.508 \text{ billion}\end{aligned}$$

The correct answer is (C), 205.

28. The correct answer is (D). The total of all the sectors of the graph except excise tax is 94%. Therefore, excise tax revenues are 100% − 94%, or 6%.

$$\begin{aligned}6\% \text{ of } \$352.6 \text{ billion} &= .06 \times \$352.6 \text{ billion}\\ &= \$21.156 \text{ billion}\end{aligned}$$

The correct answer is (D), 21.

29. The correct answer is (A). The whole job is $\frac{8}{8}$. If $\frac{5}{8}$ is completed, $\frac{3}{8}$ remains.

$$\begin{aligned}\tfrac{3}{8} &= 3 \div 8\\ &= .375\\ &= 37\tfrac{1}{2}\%\end{aligned}$$

30. The correct answer is (A).

$$\begin{aligned}&\$1{,}695.00\\ -\;&1{,}500.00\\ \hline &\$195.00 \text{ interest}\end{aligned}$$

$$\begin{aligned}\text{Rate of interest} &= \frac{195}{1{,}500}\\ &= .13\\ &= 13\%\end{aligned}$$

31. The correct answer is (B).

$$\begin{aligned}190 \times \$79.35 &= \$15{,}076.50\\ 208 \times \$83.99 &= +\$17{,}469.92\\ \text{Total} &= \$32{,}546.42\end{aligned}$$

32. The correct answer is (B). The dot for June lies between 260 and 280.

33. The correct answer is (D).

January:	145
February:	125
March:	+ 160
	430

34. The correct answer is (C). The first 12 clerks complete $\frac{6}{18}$, or $\frac{1}{3}$ of the job in 6 days, leaving $\frac{2}{3}$ of the job to be completed. One clerk would require $12 \times 18 = 216$ days to complete the job, working alone. Sixteen clerks require $216 \div 16$, or $13\frac{1}{2}$ days for the entire job. But only $\frac{2}{3}$ of the job remains. To do $\frac{2}{3}$ of the job, 16 clerks require:

$$\frac{2}{3} \times 13\frac{1}{2} = \frac{2}{3} \times \frac{27}{2}$$
$$= 9 \text{ days}$$

The entire job takes 6 days + 9 days = 15 days.

35. The correct answer is (B). Smith worked 46 − 40 hours = 6 hours overtime. For each overtime hour he earned:

$$1\frac{1}{2} \times 7.20 = \$10.80$$

Overtime pay: $10.80 × 6 =	$64.80
Regular pay: $7.20 × 40 =	288.00
	$352.80

36. The correct answer is (A). The formula for changing Celsius to Fahrenheit is:

$$F = \frac{9}{5}°C + 32$$

$$F = \frac{9}{\cancel{5}_1} \times \cancel{50}^{10} + 32$$

$$F = 90 + 32 = 122$$

37. The correct answer is (C). If the circumference of a circle is 10π, its diameter is 10 and its radius is $10 \div 2$, or 5.

The area of a circle $= \pi r^2$
$= \pi \times 5^2$
$= 25\pi$

38. The correct answer is (C). The interest will be compounded three times in nine months.

First period: $.06 \times \frac{1}{\cancel{4}_1} \times \cancel{300}^{75} = \$4.50$ interest

New principal: $300 + $4.50 = $304.50

Second period: $.06 \times \frac{1}{4} \times \$304.50 = \$4.57$ interest

New principal: $304.50 + $4.57 = $309.07

Third period: $.06 \times \frac{1}{4} \times \$309.07 = \$4.64$ interest

Total interest: $4.50
4.57
+ 4.64
$13.71

39. The correct answer is (A).

10.2
10.4
+ 10
30.6

Average = 30.6 ÷ 3 = 10.2 sec.

40. The correct answer is (A).

Monthly deductions: $675.20
345.15
225.45
+ 135.32
$1,381.12
× 12

Deductions for year: $16,573.44

Gross pay: $54,000.00
− 16,573.44

Take-home pay: $37,426.56

41. The correct answer is (A).

Area of 40′ wall = 40′ × 8′ = 320 sq ft
Area of 35′ wall = 35′ × 8′ = + 280 sq ft
Total area = 600 sq ft

$600 \div 450 = 1\frac{1}{3}$ gallons

42. The correct answer is (B).

Commission = 2% of $5,846
= .02 × $5,846
= $116.92

Salary + commission = $300 + 116.92
= $416.92

43. The correct answer is (D).

$$\frac{1.62}{100} = 1.62\%$$

$$1.62\% \text{ of } \$82{,}200 = .0162 \times \$82{,}200$$
$$= \$1{,}331.64$$

So the correct answer is (D), $1,332.

44. The correct answer is (B). *A* and *B* worked in the ratio of 5:4.

$$5 + 4 = 9$$
$$\$243 \div 9 = \$27$$
$$A\text{'s share} = 5 \times 27 = \$135$$

45. The correct answer is (D).

The two items together cost:

$$\begin{array}{r} \$24.50 \\ +\ 43.28 \\ \hline \$67.78 \end{array}$$

$$\begin{array}{rr} 5\% \text{ tax} & \times\ \ .05 \\ \hline & \$3.3890 \end{array}$$

The tax for the two items was $3.39.

$$\begin{array}{rr} \text{Total cost:} & \$67.78 \\ & +\ 3.39 \\ \hline & \$71.17 \end{array}$$

46. The correct answer is (D). The total must be 100 percent.

$$\begin{array}{rr} \text{German} & 32\% \\ \text{Spanish} & 28\% \\ \text{English} & 20\% \\ \text{Miscellaneous} & 10\% \\ \hline & 90\% \end{array}$$

Therefore, 100% − 90%, or 10%, are French.

A circle contains 360°.

$$10\% \text{ of } 360° = .10 \times 360°$$
$$= 36°$$

47. The correct answer is (A). To find the median arrange the values in order:

1.2, 2.2, 2.3, 2.4, 2.9,
3.0, 3.3, 3.5, 3.6, 3.9,
4.2, 4.3, 4.5, 4.6, 4.7

The median is the middle value in the list, or 3.5 inches.

48. The correct answer is (A).

$$\begin{array}{r} \$450.70 \\ \times\ .0765 \\ \hline 225350 \\ 270420 \\ 315490 \\ \hline \$34.478550 \end{array}$$

So the correct answer is (A), $34.48.

49. The correct answer is (C).

$$\begin{aligned} 2 \times \$4.50 &= \$\,9.00 \\ 3 \times \$4.15 &= \quad 12.45 \\ 5 \times \$4.75 &= +\,23.75 \\ &\quad \overline{\$45.20} \\ \$45.20 \div 10 &= \$4.52 \end{aligned}$$

50. The correct answer is (A). *A* and *B* invested in the ratio 7:8.

$$\begin{aligned} 7 + 8 &= 15 \\ \$2{,}250 \div 15 &= \$150 \\ A\text{'s share} &= 7 \times \$150 = \$1{,}050 \end{aligned}$$

ARITHMETIC REVIEW EXAM 2

Directions: Mark the letter of the choice that best answers the question.

1. A bag of nickels and dimes contains \$11.50. If there are seventy-three dimes, how many nickels are there?

(A) 78
(B) 80
(C) 82
(D) 84

2. A shipment consists of 340 ten-foot pieces of conduit with a coupling on each piece. If the conduit weighs 0.85 lb. per foot and each coupling weighs 0.15 lb., then the total weight of the shipment is

(A) 340 lb.
(B) 628 lb.
(C) 2,941 lb.
(D) 3,400 lb.

3. A carton contains 9 dozen file folders. If a clerk removes 53 folders, how many are left in the carton?

(A) 37
(B) 44
(C) 55
(D) 62

4. What tax rate on a base of \$4,782 would yield \$286.92?

(A) 6%
(B) $8\frac{1}{4}\%$
(C) 12%
(D) $16\frac{2}{3}\%$

5. *A* can type 500 form letters in 5 hours. *B* can type 400 of these forms in 5 hours. If *A* and *B* are to work together, the number of hours it will take them to type 540 form letters is most nearly

(A) 2
(B) 3
(C) 4
(D) 5

6. The difference between one tenth of 2,000 and one-tenth percent of 2,000 is

(A) 0
(B) 18
(C) 180
(D) 198

7. If the fractions $\frac{5}{7}, \frac{1}{2}, \frac{3}{5},$ and $\frac{2}{3}$ are arranged in ascending order of size, the result is

(A) $\frac{1}{2}, \frac{3}{5}, \frac{2}{3}, \frac{5}{7}$
(B) $\frac{3}{5}, \frac{5}{7}, \frac{2}{3}, \frac{1}{2}$
(C) $\frac{1}{2}, \frac{2}{3}, \frac{3}{5}, \frac{5}{7}$
(D) $\frac{5}{7}, \frac{2}{3}, \frac{3}{5}, \frac{1}{2}$

8. An employee has $\frac{2}{9}$ of his salary withheld for income tax. The percent of his salary that is withheld is most nearly

(A) 16%
(B) 18%
(C) 20%
(D) 22%

9. Frank and John repaired an old auto and sold it for \$900. Frank worked on it ten days and John worked eight days. They divided the money in the ratio of the time spent on the work. Frank received

(A) \$400
(B) \$450
(C) \$500
(D) \$720

10. A driver traveled 100 miles at the rate of 40 mph, then traveled 80 miles at 60 mph. The total number of hours for the entire trip was

(A) $1\frac{3}{20}$
(B) $1\frac{3}{4}$
(C) $2\frac{1}{4}$
(D) $3\frac{5}{6}$

11. On a house plan on which 2 inches represent 5 feet, the length of a room measures $7\frac{1}{2}$ inches. The actual length of the room is

(A) $12\frac{1}{2}$ ft.
(B) $15\frac{3}{4}$ ft.
(C) $17\frac{1}{2}$ ft.
(D) $18\frac{3}{4}$ ft.

12. The ratio between .01% and .1 is

(A) 1 to 10
(B) 1 to 100
(C) 1 to 1,000
(D) 1 to 10,000

13. After an article is discounted by 25 percent, it sells for $375. The original price of the article was

(A) $93.75
(B) $350
(C) $375
(D) $500

14. If Mr. Mitchell has $627.04 in his checking account and then writes three checks for $241.75, $13.24, and $102.97, what will be his new balance?

(A) $257.88
(B) $269.08
(C) $357.96
(D) $369.96

15. If erasers cost 8¢ each for the first 250, 7¢ each for the next 250, and 5¢ for every eraser thereafter, how many erasers can be purchased for $50?

(A) 600
(B) 750
(C) 850
(D) 1,000

16. Assume that it is necessary to partition a room measuring 40 feet by 20 feet into eight square rooms of equal size. Allowing no room for aisles, the *minimum* amount of partitioning that would be needed is

(A) 90 ft.
(B) 100 ft.
(C) 110 ft.
(D) 140 ft.

17. As a result of reports received by the Housing Authority concerning the reputed ineligibility of 756 tenants because of above-standard incomes, an intensive check of their employers has been ordered. Four housing assistants have been assigned to this task. At the end of six days at 7 hours each, they have checked on 336 tenants. In order to speed up the investigation, 2 more housing assistants are assigned at this point. If they worked at the same rate, the number of additional 7-hour days it would take to complete the job is, most nearly,

(A) 1
(B) 3
(C) 5
(D) 7

18. A bird flying 400 miles covers the first 100 at the rate of 100 miles an hour, the second 100 at the rate of 200 miles an hour, the third 100 at the rate of 300 miles an hour, and the last 100 at the rate of 400 miles an hour. The average speed was

(A) 192 mph
(B) 212 mph
(C) 250 mph
(D) 150 mph

19. At 5 o'clock, the least angle between the hands of the clock is

(A) 5°
(B) 75°
(C) 120°
(D) 150°

20. $7\frac{2}{3}$ percent of $1,200 is

(A) $87
(B) $92
(C) $112
(D) $920

21. A certain family spends 30 percent of its income for food, 8 percent for clothing, 25 percent for shelter, 4 percent for recreation, 13 percent for education, and 5 percent for miscellaneous items. The weekly earnings are $500. Assuming that any money left over is put into savings, what is the number of weeks it would take this family to save $15,000?

(A) 100
(B) 150
(C) 175
(D) 200

22. A 12-gallon mixture of antifreeze and water is 25 percent antifreeze. If 3 gallons of water are added to it, the strength of the mixture is now

(A) 12%
(B) $16\frac{2}{3}$%
(C) 20%
(D) 35%

23. A cab driver works on a commission basis, receiving $42\frac{1}{2}$ percent of the fares. In addition, his earnings from tips are valued at 29 percent of the commissions. If his average weekly fares equal $520, then his average earnings for a four-week period would be

(A) between $900 and $1,000
(B) between $1,000 and $1,100
(C) between $1,100 and $1,200
(D) more than $1,200

Questions 24 and 25 refer to the following graph.

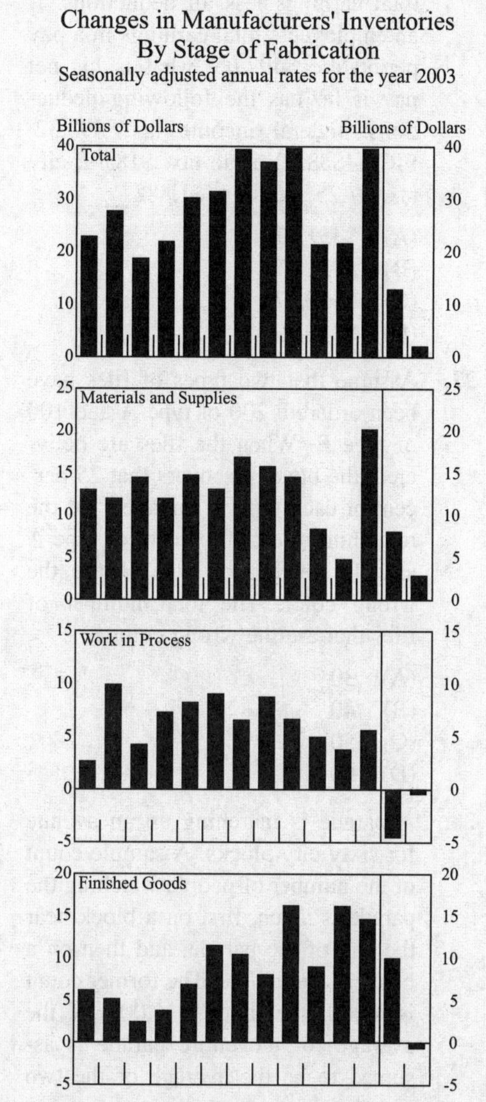

Source: United States Department of Commerce, Bureau of the Census

24. For how many months are materials and supplies inventories exceeding $15 billion at the same time that finished goods inventories are more than $11 billion? (Months January through December are represented by interval marks on the graph going from left to right.)

(A) One
(B) Two
(C) Three
(D) Four

25. In June 2003, the ratio of finished goods to work in process was approximately

(A) 4:7
(B) 3:7
(C) 3:4
(D) 4:3

26. An employee's net pay is equal to his total earnings less all deductions. If an employee's total earnings in a pay period are $497.05, what is his net pay if he has the following deductions: federal income tax, $90.32; FICA, $38.02; state tax, $18.79; city tax, $7.25; pension, $1.88?

(A) $351.17
(B) $351.07
(C) $350.17
(D) $340.79

27. Assume that two types of files have been ordered: 200 of type A and 100 of type B. When the files are delivered, the buyer discovers that 25 percent of each type is damaged. Of the remaining files, 20 percent of type A and 40 percent of type B are the wrong color. The total number of files that are the wrong color is

(A) 30
(B) 40
(C) 50
(D) 60

28. A parade is marching up an avenue for sixty city blocks. A sample count of the number of people watching the parade is taken, first on a block near the end of the parade, and then on a block at the middle. The former count is 4,000, the latter is 6,000. If the average for the entire parade is assumed to be the average of the two samples, then the estimated number of persons watching the entire parade is most nearly

(A) 240,000
(B) 300,000
(C) 480,000
(D) 600,000

29. If *A* takes six days to do a task and *B* takes three days to do the same task, working together they should do the same task in

(A) $2\frac{2}{3}$ days
(B) 2 days
(C) $2\frac{1}{3}$ days
(D) $2\frac{1}{2}$ days

30. The total length of fencing needed to enclose a rectangular area 46 feet by 34 feet is

(A) 26 yd. 1 ft.
(B) $26\frac{2}{3}$ yd.
(C) 52 yd. 2 ft.
(D) $53\frac{1}{3}$ yd.

31. Find the length of time it would take $432 to yield $74.52 in interest at $5\frac{3}{4}$ percent per annum (the amount of interest earned each year is constant).

(A) 2 yr. 10 mo.
(B) 3 yr.
(C) 3 yr. 10 mo.
(D) 4 yr.

32. The price of a radio is $31.29, which includes a 5 percent sales tax. What was the price of the radio before the tax was added?

(A) $29.80
(B) $29.85
(C) $29.90
(D) $29.95

33. If a person in the 19 percent income tax bracket pays $3,515 in income taxes, his taxable income was

(A) $18,500
(B) $32,763
(C) $53,800
(D) $67,785

34. Of the numbers 6, 5, 3, 3, 6, 3, 4, 3, 4, 3, the mode is

(A) 3
(B) 4
(C) 5
(D) 6

35. In a circle graph, a sector of 108 degrees is shaded to indicate the overhead in doing $150,000 gross business. The overhead amounts to

(A) $1,200
(B) $4,500
(C) $12,000
(D) $45,000

36. Two people start at the same point and walk in opposite directions. If one walks at the rate of 2 miles per hour and the other walks at the rate of 3 miles per hour, in how many hours will they be 20 miles apart?

(A) 2
(B) 3
(C) 4
(D) 5

37. In a group of 100 people, 37 wear glasses. What is the probability that a person chosen at random from this group does NOT wear glasses?

(A) .37
(B) .50
(C) .63
(D) 1.00

38. The interest on $148.00 at 6 percent a year for sixty days is

(A) $8.88
(B) $2.96
(C) $14.80
(D) $1.48

39. A man bought a camera that was listed at $160. He was given successive discounts of 20 percent and 10 percent. The price he paid was

(A) $112.00
(B) $115.20
(C) $119.60
(D) $129.60

40. The water level of a swimming pool measuring 75 feet by 42 feet is to be raised 4 inches. If there are 7.48 gallons in a cubic foot, the number of gallons of water that will be needed is

(A) 140
(B) 31,500
(C) 7,854
(D) 94,500

41. A salesman is paid $4\frac{1}{2}$ percent commission on his first $7,000 of sales and $5\frac{1}{2}$ percent commission on all sales in excess of $7,000. If his sales were $9,600, how much commission did he earn?

(A) $432
(B) $458
(C) $480
(D) $528

42. How many boxes 3 inches by 4 inches by 5 inches can fit into a carton 3 feet by 4 feet by 5 feet?

(A) 60
(B) 144
(C) 1,728
(D) 8,640

43. The value of 32 nickels, 73 quarters, and 156 dimes is

(A) $26.10
(B) $31.75
(C) $35.45
(D) $49.85

44. The area of the shaded figure is

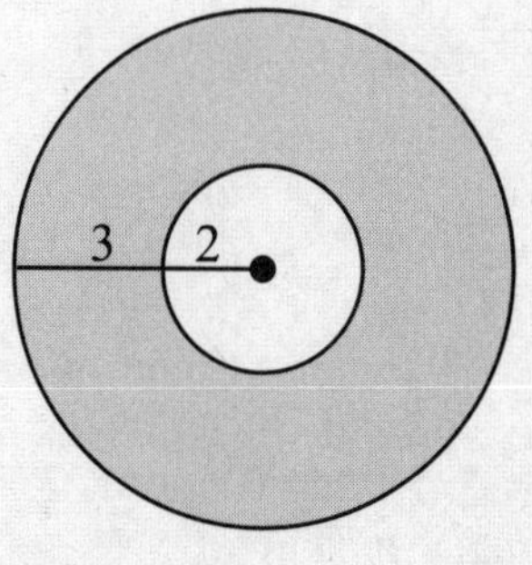

(A) 4π
(B) 5π
(C) 16π
(D) 21π

45. The wage rate at a certain trade is \$8.60 an hour for a 40-hour week and $1\frac{1}{2}$ times the base pay for overtime. An employee who works 48 hours in a week earns

(A) \$447.20
(B) \$498.20
(C) \$582.20
(D) \$619.20

46. Jane Michaels borrowed \$200 on March 31 at the simple interest rate of 8 percent per year. If she wishes to repay the loan and the interest on May 15, what is the total amount she must pay?

(A) \$201
(B) \$202
(C) \$203
(D) \$204

47. How many decigrams are in .57 kilograms?

(A) 57
(B) 570
(C) 5,700
(D) 57,000

48. If candies are bought at \$1.10 per dozen and sold at three for 55 cents, then the total profit on $5\frac{1}{2}$ dozen is

(A) \$5.55
(B) \$6.05
(C) \$6.55
(D) \$7.05

49. The number missing in the sequence 2, 5, 10, 17, ______, 37, 50, 65 is

(A) 22
(B) 24
(C) 26
(D) 27

50. A cylindrical container has a diameter of 14 inches and a height of 6 inches. If 1 gallon equals 231 cubic inches, then the capacity of the tank is approximately

(A) $2\frac{2}{7}$ gal.
(B) 4 gal.
(C) $1\frac{1}{7}$ gal.
(D) 3 gal.

ANSWERS AND EXPLANATIONS

1. D	**11.** D	**21.** D	**31.** B	**41.** B
2. C	**12.** C	**22.** C	**32.** A	**42.** C
3. C	**13.** D	**23.** C	**33.** A	**43.** C
4. A	**14.** B	**24.** B	**34.** A	**44.** D
5. B	**15.** B	**25.** D	**35.** D	**45.** A
6. D	**16.** B	**26.** D	**36.** C	**46.** B
7. A	**17.** C	**27.** D	**37.** C	**47.** C
8. D	**18.** A	**28.** B	**38.** D	**48.** B
9. C	**19.** D	**29.** B	**39.** B	**49.** C
10. D	**20.** B	**30.** D	**40.** C	**50.** B

1. The correct answer is (D).

$$\begin{aligned} 73 \text{ dimes} &= 73 \times \$.10 \\ &= \$7.30 \end{aligned}$$

$$\$11.50 - \$7.30 = \$4.20$$

There are $4.20 worth of nickels in the bag.

$$\$4.20 \div \$.05 = 84 \text{ nickels}$$

2. The correct answer is (C).
Each 10-foot piece weighs:

$$\begin{array}{rr} 10 \times .85 \text{ lb} = & 8.5 \text{ lb} \\ & +\ .15 \text{ lb} \\ \hline & 8.65 \text{ lb} \end{array}$$

The entire shipment weighs:

$$340 \times 8.65 \text{ lb} = 2{,}941 \text{ lb}$$

3. The correct answer is (C). The carton contains 9 × 12 = 108 folders.

$$108 - 53 = 55 \text{ remain in the carton.}$$

4. The correct answer is (A).

$$\text{Rate} = \text{tax} \div \text{base}$$

$$286.92 \div 4782 = 4782\overline{)286.92} = .06$$

$$\begin{array}{r} 286.92 \\ \hline \end{array}$$

$$.06 = 6\%$$

5. The correct answer is (B).

A can type 500 ÷ 5 = 100 letters per hour
B can type 400 ÷ 5 = 80 letters per hour

Together they can type 180 letters per hour.

$$540 \div 180 = 3$$

It will take 3 hours to type 540 letters.

6. The correct answer is (D).

$$\frac{1}{10} \text{ of } 2{,}000 = \frac{1}{10} \times 2{,}000 = 200$$

$$\frac{1}{10}\% \text{ of } 2{,}000 = .001 \times 2{,}000 = 2$$

The difference is 200 − 2 = 198

7. **The correct answer is (A).** To compare the fractions, rename them as fractions having the same denominator.

$$LCD = 7 \times 2 \times 5 \times 3 = 210$$

$$\frac{5}{7} = \frac{150}{210}$$
$$\frac{1}{2} = \frac{105}{210}$$
$$\frac{3}{5} = \frac{126}{210}$$
$$\frac{2}{3} = \frac{140}{210}$$

The correct order is $\frac{105}{210}, \frac{126}{210}, \frac{140}{210}, \frac{150}{210}$.

So the correct answer is (A), $\frac{1}{2}, \frac{3}{5}, \frac{2}{3}, \frac{5}{7}$.

8. **The correct answer is (D).**

$$\frac{2}{9} = 9\overline{)2.00}\quad .22$$
$$\begin{array}{r} 18 \\ \hline 20 \\ 18 \\ \hline 2 \end{array}$$

$22\frac{2}{9} = 22\%$ most nearly

The correct answer is (D), 22%.

9. **The correct answer is (C).** Frank and John worked in the ratio of 10:8.

$$10 + 8 = 18$$
$$\$900 \div 18 = \$50$$
$$\text{Frank's share} = 10 \times \$50 = \$500$$

10. **The correct answer is (D).**

The first part of the trip took:

$$100 \text{ mi} \div 40 \text{ mph} = 2\frac{1}{2} \text{ hours}$$

The second part of the trip took:

$$80 \text{ mi} \div 60 \text{ mph} = 1\frac{1}{3} \text{ hours}$$

$$\begin{array}{rcr} 2\frac{1}{2} & = & 2\frac{3}{6} \\ +\ 1\frac{1}{3} & = & +\ 1\frac{2}{6} \\ \hline & & 3\frac{5}{6} \end{array}$$

11. The correct answer is (D). Let f represent the actual number of feet. The plan lengths and the actual lengths are in proportion. Therefore,

$$\frac{2}{7\frac{1}{2}} = \frac{5}{f}$$

$$f = \frac{5 \times 7\frac{1}{2}}{2}$$

$$= \frac{5 \times \frac{15}{2}}{2}$$

$$= \frac{75}{2} \div 2$$

$$= \frac{75}{2} \times \frac{1}{2}$$

$$= \frac{75}{4} = 18\frac{3}{4} \text{ ft.}$$

12. The correct answer is (C).

$$\frac{.01\%}{.1} = \frac{.0001}{.1}$$

$$= .001$$

$$= \frac{1}{1{,}000}$$

So the correct answer is (C), 1 to 1,000.

13. The correct answer is (D). \$375 is 75 percent of the original price.

The original price = \$375 ÷ 75%
= \$375 ÷ .75
= \$500

14. The correct answer is (B).

Total of checks: \$241.75
13.24
+ 102.97
\$357.96

\$627.04 old balance
−357.96 checks
\$269.08 new balance

15. The correct answer is (B).

First 250 erasers: 250 × \$.08 = \$20.00
Next 250 erasers: 250 × \$.07 = \$17.50
Total for 500 erasers: \$20.00 + \$17.50 = \$37.50
\$50.00 − \$37.50 = \$12.50

\$12.50 remains for 5¢ erasers:
\$12.50 ÷ \$.05 = 250 erasers
500 + 250 erasers = 750

16. **The correct answer is (B).** The room would be partitioned as is shown below:

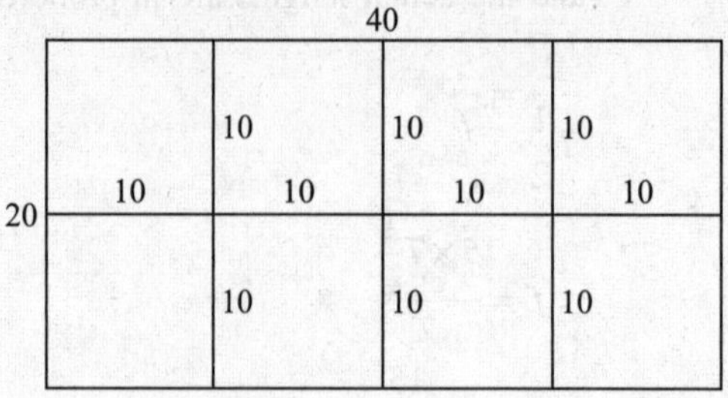

The total amount of partitioning is 100 feet.

17. **The correct answer is (C).** Four assistants completed 336 cases in 42 hours (six days at 7 hours per day). Therefore, each assistant completed 336 ÷ 4, or 84 cases in 42 hours, for a rate of two cases per hour per assistant. After the first six days, the number of cases remaining is

$$756 - 336 = 420$$

It will take 6 assistants, working at the rate of two cases per hour per assistant 420 ÷ 12 or 35 hours to complete the work. If each workday has 7 hours, then 35 ÷ 7 or 5 days are needed.

18. **The correct answer is (A).** At 100 mph, 100 miles will take 1 hour. At 200 mph, 100 miles will take $\frac{1}{2}$ hour. At 300 mph, 100 miles will take $\frac{1}{3}$ hour. At 400 mph, 100 miles will take $\frac{1}{4}$ hour.

$$\begin{aligned}
\text{Total time: } 1 &= \frac{12}{12}\\
\frac{1}{2} &= \frac{6}{12}\\
\frac{1}{3} &= \frac{4}{12}\\
+\frac{1}{4} &= +\frac{3}{12}\\
\hline
& \frac{25}{12} = 2\frac{1}{12} \text{ hours}
\end{aligned}$$

$$\begin{aligned}
400 \text{ miles} \div 2\frac{1}{12} \text{ hours} &= 400 \div \frac{25}{12} \text{mph}\\
&= 400 \times \frac{12}{25} \text{ mph}\\
&= 192 \text{ mph}
\end{aligned}$$

19. **The correct answer is (D).** Each hour is represented by 360° ÷ 12 = 30°.

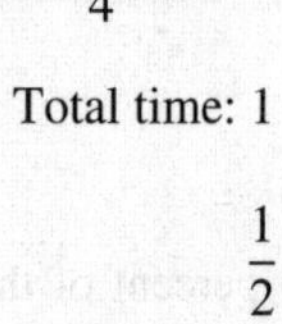

The least angle formed by the hands:

$$= 5 \times 30°$$
$$= 150°$$

20. The correct answer is (B).

$7\frac{2}{3}\%$ of \$1,200 $= \frac{23}{3}\%$ of \$1,200

To rename $\frac{23}{3}\%$ as a fraction, divide by 100:

$$\frac{23}{3} \div 100 = \frac{23}{3} \times \frac{1}{100} = \frac{23}{300}$$

$$\frac{23}{\cancel{300}_{1}} \times \cancel{1200}^{4} = \$92$$

21. The correct answer is (D). The family spends a total of 85 percent of its income. Therefore, 100% − 85%, or 15%, remains for savings.

15% of \$500 = .15 × \$500
= \$75 per week
\$15,000 ÷ \$75 = 200 weeks

22. The correct answer is (C). The mixture contains 25 percent of 12 gallons, or 3 gallons, of antifreeze. The remaining 9 gallons must be water. The new mixture would contain 3 gallons of antifreeze and 9 + 3 = 12 gallons of water, for a total of 15 gallons. The strength would be:

$$\frac{\text{3 gal. antifreeze}}{\text{15 gal. mixture}} = .20 = 20\%$$

23. The correct answer is (C).

Commission $= 42\frac{1}{2}\%$ of fares

$42\frac{1}{2}\%$ of \$520 = .425 × \$520
= \$221 commission

Tips = 29% of commission
29% of \$221 = .29 × \$221
= \$64.09 tips

Weekly earnings:

$$\begin{array}{r} \$221.00 \\ +\ 64.09 \\ \hline \$285.09 \end{array}$$

Four-week earnings:

$$\begin{array}{r} \$285.09 \\ \times\ \ \ \ 4 \\ \hline \$1,140.36 \end{array}$$

24. The correct answer is (B). For this graph, it helps to visualize each bar as representing a calendar month. Finished goods inventories are more than \$11 billion in June, September, November, and December of 2003. Of those months, materials and supplies inventories are more than \$15 billion in September and December. The correct answer is (B), two.

25. The correct answer is (D). In June 2003, finished goods inventories were approximately \$12 billion, and work in process inventories were approximately \$9 billion. The ratio is 12:9, or 4:3.

26. The correct answer is (D).

$$\begin{array}{rr} & \$90.32 \\ & 38.02 \\ & 18.79 \\ & 7.25 \\ & +\ \ 1.88 \\ \hline \text{Total deductions} & \$156.26 \end{array}$$

$$\begin{array}{rl} \$497.05 & \text{total earnings} \\ -156.26 & \text{deductions} \\ \hline \$340.79 & \text{net pay} \end{array}$$

27. The correct answer is (D). If 25 percent are damaged, then 75 percent are not damaged.

Type A:

$$75\% \text{ of } 200 = .75 \times 200 = 150$$

20 percent of 150 are wrong color

$$20\% \text{ of } 150 = .20 \times 150 = 30$$

Type B:

$$75\% \text{ of } 100 = .75 \times 100 = 75$$

40 percent of 75 are wrong color

$$40\% \text{ of } 75 = .40 \times 75 = 30$$

Total wrong color = 30 + 30 = 60

28. The correct answer is (B). Average is $\frac{4{,}000 + 6{,}000}{2} = 5{,}000$ per block. If there are sixty blocks, then there are $60 \times 5{,}000 = 300{,}000$ people.

29. The correct answer is (B). *A* can do $\frac{1}{6}$ of the task in 1 day, and *B* can do $\frac{1}{3}$ in 1 day. Together, in 1 day they can do

$$\begin{array}{rcr} \frac{1}{6} & = & \frac{1}{6} \\ +\frac{1}{3} & = & +\frac{2}{6} \\ \hline & & \frac{3}{6} = \frac{1}{2} \text{ of the job} \end{array}$$

It will take two days to complete the job if they work together.

30. The correct answer is (D).

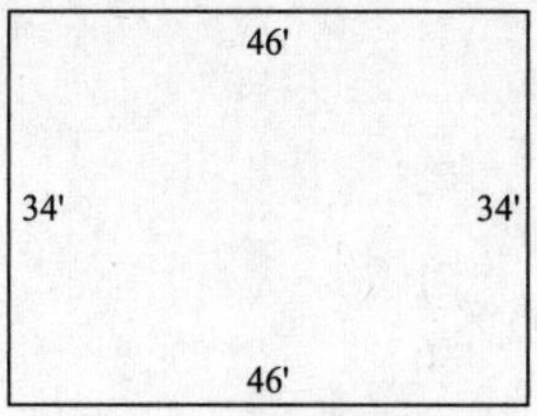

$$\text{Perimeter} = 46' + 34' + 46' + 34'$$
$$= 160'$$

$$160 \text{ ft.} \div 3 \text{ ft. per yd.} = \frac{160}{3} \text{ yd.}$$
$$= 53\frac{1}{3} \text{ yd.}$$

31. The correct answer is (B).

$$\$432 \times 5\frac{3}{4}\% = \overset{108}{\cancel{432}} \times \frac{23}{\underset{100}{\cancel{400}}}$$
$$= \$\frac{2{,}484}{100}$$
$$= \$24.84$$

$$\$74.52 \div \$24.84 = 3$$

32. The correct answer is (A). \$31.29 = 105% of price before tax.

$$\text{Price before tax} = \$31.29 \div 105\%$$
$$= \$31.29 \div 1.05$$
$$= \$29.80$$

33. The correct answer is (A). \$3,515 = 19% of taxable income.

$$\text{Taxable income} = \$3{,}515 \div 19\%$$
$$= \$3{,}515 \div .19$$
$$= \$18{,}500$$

34. The correct answer is (A). The mode is the value appearing most frequently. For the list given, the mode is 3.

35. The correct answer is (D). A sector of 108° is $\frac{108°}{360°} = 30\%$ of the circle.

$$\frac{3}{10} \times \$150{,}000 = \$45{,}000$$

36. The correct answer is (C). After 1 hour, they will be 5 miles apart.

20 mi. ÷ 5 mi. = 4 hr.

It will take 4 hours to be 20 miles apart.

37. The correct answer is (C). If 37 wear glasses, 100 − 37, or 63, do not wear glasses.

The probability is $\frac{63}{100} = .63$

38. The correct answer is (D).

$$60 \text{ days} = \frac{60}{360}$$
$$= \frac{1}{6} \text{ year}$$

$$\text{Interest} = \$148 \times .06 \times \frac{1}{6}$$
$$= \$1.48$$

39. The correct answer is (B).

First discount:

$$20\% \text{ of } \$160 = .20 \times \$160 = \$32$$
$$\$160 - \$32 = \$128$$

Second discount:

$$10\% \text{ of } \$128 = .10 \times \$128 = \$12.80$$
$$\$128.00 - \$12.80 = \$115.20$$

40. The correct answer is (C).

$$4 \text{ in.} = \frac{1}{3} \text{ ft.}$$

$$\text{Volume to be added} = \overset{25}{\cancel{75}} \times 42 \times \frac{1}{\underset{1}{\cancel{3}}}$$
$$= 1{,}050 \text{ cu. ft.}$$
$$= 1{,}050 \times 7.48 \text{ gal.}$$
$$= 7{,}854 \text{ gal.}$$

41. The correct answer is (B).

Commission on first $7,000:

$$4\frac{1}{2}\% \text{ of } \$7{,}000 = .045 \times \$7{,}000$$
$$= \$315$$

Commission on remainder:

$$\$9{,}600 - \$7{,}000 = \$2{,}600$$

$$5\frac{1}{2}\% \text{ of } \$2{,}600 = .055 \times \$2{,}600$$
$$= \$143$$

$$\text{Total commission} = \$315 + \$143$$
$$= \$458$$

42. The correct answer is (C).

$$\text{Volume of the carton} = 3 \text{ ft.} \times 4 \text{ ft.} \times 5 \text{ ft.}$$
$$= 36 \text{ in.} \times 48 \text{ in.} \times 60 \text{ in.}$$
$$= 103{,}680 \text{ cu. in.}$$
$$\text{Volume of each box} = 3 \text{ in.} \times 4 \text{ in.} \times 5 \text{ in.}$$
$$= 60 \text{ cu. in.}$$

$$103{,}680 \div 60 = 1{,}728$$

43. The correct answer is (C).

$$\begin{aligned} 32 \text{ nickels} &= 32 \times \$.05 = \$1.60 \\ 73 \text{ quarters} &= 73 \times \$.25 = \$18.25 \\ 156 \text{ dimes} &= 156 \times \$.10 = \underline{\$15.60} \\ \text{Total} &= \$35.45 \end{aligned}$$

44. The correct answer is (D). The area of the shaded figure equals the area of the greater circle minus the area of the smaller circle:

$$\begin{aligned} \text{Area of larger circle} &= 5^2\pi = 25\pi \\ \text{Minus area of smaller circle} &= 2^2\pi = \underline{4\pi} \\ \text{Equals area of shaded figure} &= 21\pi \end{aligned}$$

45. The correct answer is (A).

$$48 - 40 = 8 \text{ hours overtime}$$

Salary for 8 hours overtime:

$$\begin{aligned} 1\frac{1}{2} \times \$8.60 \times 8 &= \frac{3}{\cancel{2}_1} \times \$8.60 \times \cancel{8}^4 \\ &= \$103.20 \end{aligned}$$

Salary for 40 hours regular time:

$$\begin{aligned} \$8.60 \times 40 &= \$344.00 \\ \text{Total salary} &= \$344.00 + \$103.20 \\ &= \$447.20 \end{aligned}$$

46. The correct answer is (B). From March 31 to May 15 is forty-five days, which is $\frac{45}{360}$ of a year.

$$\begin{aligned} \text{Interest} &= \$200 \times .08 \times \frac{\cancel{45}^1}{\cancel{360}_8} \\ &= \$\frac{16}{8} \\ &= \$2 \end{aligned}$$

She must pay $200 + $2 = $202.

47. The correct answer is (C).

$$\begin{aligned} .57 \text{ kilograms} &= .57 \times 1{,}000 \text{ grams} \\ &= 570 \text{ grams} \\ &= 570 \div .10 \text{ decigrams} \\ &= 5{,}700 \text{ decigrams} \end{aligned}$$

48. The correct answer is (B). The cost of $5\frac{1}{2}$ dozen is

$$5\frac{1}{2} \times \$1.10 = 5.5 \times \$1.10$$
$$= \$6.05$$

The candies sell at three for \$.55. A dozen sells for 4 × \$.55, or \$2.20. The selling price of $5\frac{1}{2}$ dozen is

$$5\frac{1}{2} \times \$2.20 = 5.5 \times \$2.20$$
$$= \$12.10$$
$$\text{Profit} = \$12.10 - \$6.05$$
$$= \$6.05$$

49. The correct answer is (C). Find the differences between terms:

2	5	10	17	___	37	50	65
3	5	7			13	15	

The difference between 17 and the missing term must be 9. The missing term is 17 + 9 = 26.

50. The correct answer is (B). The volume of the cylinder = $\pi r^2 h$. If the diameter is 14, then the radius is 7. Using $\pi = \frac{22}{7}$,

$$\text{Volume} = \frac{22}{\not{7}_1} \times \not{49}^{7} \times 6$$
$$= 924 \text{ cubic inches}$$
$$924 \div 231 = 4 \text{ gallons}$$

PART THREE

VOCABULARY REVIEW

EXPANDING YOUR VOCABULARY SKILLS

This section will help to expand your vocabulary quickly. It will also give you practice in answering vocabulary questions. It is divided into four sections. The first, *Study Aids,* includes an etymology chart and a word list. Read this material carefully, but don't try to absorb it all at once. Becoming familiar with the etymology chart first will help you when you study the word list. Follow the study suggestions. To study effectively, you might want to divide the etymology chart and the word list into sections. Learn each section thoroughly before going on to the next one. To keep your concentration and learning at a maximum level, a half-hour of studying at a time is a good idea. Of course if you feel mentally alert, you can study for a longer period.

The second section gives you practical advice on how to answer synonym (same meaning) questions. There is a series of twelve practice tests on synonyms. The third section teaches you how to answer antonym (opposites) questions. There is a series of eight practice tests on antonyms. The fourth section gives instruction on answering sentence completion questions and concludes with a series of six practice tests. Each section is followed by the answer key to the tests in that section. To get the maximum benefit from the practice tests, do not do them all at once. Take one or two tests; then check to see how you have done. If you need to, go back to the study aids for that section. Then try some more tests. If you keep an honest record of your scores, you'll see how much you've improved.

Use the practice tests to help you learn. When you check your answers, make sure you understand why they were right or wrong. Make a note of any words you're not sure of and look them up in the word list or in a dictionary. The correct answers to the sentence completion practice tests are followed by explanations that clarify the reasoning behind the correct answer choices.

This book is only a starting place. There are many things you can do to increase your vocabulary. Get into the habit of reading as much as you can, and read many different kinds of texts. Reading newspapers, magazines, books, and even the labels and directions on products that you buy can increase your vocabulary. Reading will help you discover the meaning of new words from their use in contexts. When you are reading and you come across a word that you are not familiar with or that you are uncertain about, look it up in a dictionary. Then reread the text to see how the meaning fits. Practice using the word yourself by making up sentences that include the word. This will help to make the word a permanent part of your vocabulary. With a little effort you will find that your knowledge of words grows steadily.

STUDY AIDS

ETYMOLOGY

Etymology is the study of how words are formed and their origins. Many English words, especially those that are long or difficult, are built out of basic word parts. Some word parts usually act as word beginnings. Other word parts, called roots, carry the main meaning of word. One of the most efficient ways to increase your vocabulary is to learn some of these parts. Once you know the basic parts of words, it will be easier to remember words you've learned and to figure out the meaning of unfamiliar words.

Here is an example. The word *biography* is made up of two important parts. *Graphy* comes from a Greek word meaning "writing." Many English words use this root. *Graphology*, for instance, is the study of handwriting. An *autograph* is something written by one's self. The *photograph* is an example of picture writing. The *bio* part of *biography* also comes from Greek, and it means "life." It, too, is a part of many English words, such as *biology* (the study of life) and *biochemistry* (the chemistry of living things). When we put *bio* and *graphy* together, we have a word meaning a writing about the life of a person, or the story of a person's life. We can make another word by adding another part to *biography*. Add the Latin word part *auto*, which means "self," and we have an *autobiography*: a person's written account of his or her own life.

In the last paragraph, the words *graphology* and *biology* appear. Both contain the word part *-logy*. Do you know any other words containing that word part? Reread the paragraph. Can you figure out the meaning of the word part *-logy*? You can check your answer in the etymology chart in this section.

Any good dictionary will provide you with the etymology of words. When you look up an unfamiliar word, make it a habit to look at how it was formed. Does the word have a part that helps to explain its meaning? Is it related to other words you already know?

The following chart lists more than 150 common word parts. Each part is defined, and an example of a word or words in which it appears is given. It will help you to memorize the word parts if you try to make up a sentence using the example words. Don't try to memorize the whole chart at once. If you study only a small section at a time, you'll get better results. When you've learned one of the word parts, remember to look for it in your reading. See if you can think of other words in which the word part appears. Use the dictionary to find out if your choices are right.

To help you find out how much you've learned, there are seven etymology exercises following the chart.

WORD PART	MEANING	EXAMPLE
a, ab, abs	from, away	*abrade*—to wear off
		absent—away, not present
act, ag	do, act, drive	*action*—a doing
		agent—one who acts for another
alter, altr	other, change	*alternate*—to switch back and forth
am, ami	love, friend	*amorous*—loving
anim	mind, life, spirit	*animated*—spirited
annu, enni	year	*annual*—yearly
ante	before	*antediluvian*—before the Flood
anthrop	man	*anthropology*—study of mankind
anti	against	*antiwar*—against war
arbit	judge	*arbiter*—a judge
arch	first, chief	*archetype*—first model
aud, audit, aur	hear	*auditorium*—place where performances are heard
auto	self	*automobile*—self-moving vehicle
bell	war	*belligerent*—warlike
bene, ben	good, well	*benefactor*—one who does good deeds
bi	two	*bilateral*—two-sided
bibli	book	*bibliophile*—book lover
bio	life	*biology*—study of life
brev	short	*abbreviate*—to shorten
cad, cas, cid	fall	*casualty*—one who has fallen
cede, ceed, cess	go, yield	*exceed*—go beyond
		recession—a going backwards
cent	hundred	*century*—hundred years
chrom	color	*monochrome*—having one color

WORD PART	MEANING	EXAMPLE
chron	time	*chronology*—time order
cide, cis	cut, kill	*suicide*—a self-killing *incision*—a cutting into
circum	around	*circumnavigate*—to sail around
clam, claim	shout	*proclaim*—to declare loudly
clin	slope, lean	*decline*—to slope downward
cogn	know	*recognize*—to know
coul, co, col, con, cor	with, together	*concentrate*—to bring closer together *cooperate*—to work with *collapse*—to fall together
contra, contro, counter	against	*contradict*—to speak against *counterclockwise*—against the clock's direction
corp	body	*incorporate*—to bring into a body *corpse*—dead body
cosm	order, world	*cosmos*—universe
cre, crese, cret	grow	*increase*—to grow *accretion*—growth by addition
cred	trust, believe	*incredible*—unbelievable
culp	blame	*culprit*—one who is to blame
cur, curr, curs	run, course	*current*—presently running
de	away from, down, opposite	*detract*—to draw away from
dec	ten	*decade*—ten years
dem	people	*democracy*—rule by the people
dic, dict	say, speak	*dictation*—a speaking *predict*—to say in advance, to foretell
dis, di	not, away from	*dislike*—to not like *digress*—to turn away from the subject
doc, doct	teach, prove	*indoctrinate*—to teach
domin	rule	*domineer*—to rule over
du	two	*duo*—a couple
due, duct	lead	*induct*—to lead in
dur	hard, lasting	*durable*—able to last
equ	equal	*equivalent*—of equal value
ev	time, age	*longevity*—age, length of life
ex, e, ef	from, out	*expatriate*—one who lives outside his native country *emit*—to send out
extra	outside, beyond	*extraterrestrial*—from beyond the earth
fac, fact, feet, fie	do, make	*factory*—place where things are made *fictitious*—made up or imaginary
fer	bear, carry	*transfer*—to carry across
fid	belief, faith	*fidelity*—faithfulness
fin	end, limit	*finite*—limited
flect, flex	bend	*reflect*—to bend back
flu, fluct, flux	flow	*fluid*—flowing substance *influx*—a flowing in
fore	in front of, previous	*forecast*—to tell ahead of time *foreleg*—front leg
form	shape	*formation*—shaping
fort	strong	*fortify*—to strengthen
frag, fract	break	*fragile*—easily broken *fracture*—a break
fug	flee	*fugitive*—one who flees
gen	birth, kind, race	*engender*—to give birth to

WORD PART	MEANING	EXAMPLE
geo	earth	*geology*—study of the earth
grad, gress	step, go	*progress*—to go forward
graph	writing	*autograph*—to write one's own name
her, hes	stick, cling	*adhere*—to cling *cohesive*—sticking together
homo	same, like	*homophonic*—sounding the same
hyper	too much, over	*hyperactive*—overly active
in, il, ig, im, ir	not	*incorrect*—not correct *ignorant*—not knowing *illogical*—not logical *irresponsible*—not responsible
in, il, im, ir	on, into, in	*impose*—to place on *invade*—to go into
inter	between, among	*interplanetary*—between planets
intra, intro	within, inside	*intrastate*—within a state
ject	throw	*reject*—to throw back
junct	join	*juncture*—place where things join
leg	law	*legal*—lawful
leg, lig, lect	choose, gather, read	*legible*—readable *eligible*—able to be chosen *select*—to choose
lev	light, rise	*alleviate*—to make lighter
liber	free	*liberation*—a freeing
loc	place	*location*—place
log	speech, study	*dialogue*—speech for two characters *psychology*—study of the mind
luc, lum	light	*translucent*—allowing light to pass through *luminous*—shining
magn	large, great	*magnify*—to make larger
mal, male	bad, wrong, poor	*maladjusted*—poorly adjusted *malevolent*—ill-wishing
mar	sea	*marine*—sea-dwelling
ment	mind	*demented*—out of one's mind
meter, metr, mens	measure	*chronometer*—time-measuring device *commensurate*—of equal measure
micr	small	*microwave*—small wave
min	little	*minimum*—least
mis	badly, wrongly	*misunderstand*—to understand wrongly
mit, miss	send	*remit*—to send back *mission*—a sending
mono	single, one	*monorail*—train that runs on a single track
morph	shape	*anthropomorphic*—man-shaped
mov, mob, mot	move	*removal*—a moving away *mobile*—able to move
multi	many	*multiply*—to become many
mut	change	*mutation*—change
nase, nat	born	*innate*—inborn *native*—belonging by or from birth
neg	deny	*negative*—no, not
neo	new	*neologism*—new word
nom	name	*nomenclature*—system of naming *nominate*—to name for office
non	not	*nonentity*—a nobody
nov	new	*novice*—newcomer, beginner *innovation*—something new

WORD PART	MEANING	EXAMPLE
omni	all	*omnipresent*—present in all places
oper	work	*operate*—to work *cooperation*—a working together
path, pat, pass	feel, suffer	*patient*—suffering *compassion*—a feeling with
ped, pod	foot	*pedestrian*—one who goes on foot
pel, puls	drive, push	*impel*—to push
phil	love	*philosophy*—love of wisdom
phob	fear	*phobic*—irrationally fearing
phon	sound	*symphony*—a sounding together
phot	light	*photosynthesis*—synthesis of chemical compounds in plants with the aid of light *photon*—light particle
poly	many	*polygon*—many-sided figure
port	carry	*import*—to carry into a country *portable*—able to be carried
pot	power	*potency*—power
post	after	*postmortem*—after death
pre	before, earlier than	*prejudice*—judgment in advance
press	press	*impression*—a pressing into
prim	first	*primal*—first, original
pro	in favor of, in front of, forward	*proceed*—to go forward *prowar*—in favor of war
psych	mind	*psychiatry*—cure of the mind
quer, quir, quis, ques	ask, seek	*query*—to ask *inquisitive*—asking many questions *quest*—a search
re	back, again	*rethink*—to think again *reimburse*—to pay back
rid, ris	laugh	*deride*—to make fun of *ridiculous*—laughable
rupt	break	*erupt*—to break out *rupture*—a breaking apart
sci, scio	know	*science*—knowledge *conscious*—having knowledge
scrib, script	write	*describe*—to write about *inscription*—a writing on
semi	half	*semiconscious*—half conscious
sent, sens	feel, think	*sensation*—feeling *sentient*—able to feel
sequ, secut	follow	*sequential*—following in order
sol	alone	*desolate*—lonely
son, solu, solut	loosen	*dissolve*—to loosen the bonds of *solvent*—loosening agent
son	sound	*sonorous*—sounding
spec, spic, spect	look	*inspect*—to look into *spectacle*—something to be looked at
spir	breathe	*respiration*—breathing
stab, stat	stand	*establish*—to make stand, to found
string, strict	bind	*restrict*—to bind, to limit
stru, struct	build	*construct*—to build
super	over, greater	*superfluous*—overflowing, beyond what is needed
tang, ting, tact, tig	touch	*tactile*—of the sense of touch *contiguous*—touching

WORD PART	MEANING	EXAMPLE
tele	far	*television*—machine for seeing far
ten, tain, tent	hold	*tenacity*—holding power *contain*—to hold together
term	end	*terminal*—last, ending
terr	earth	*terrain*—surface of the earth
test	witness	*attest*—to witness
therm	heat	*thermos*—container that retains heat
tort, tors	twist	*contort*—to twist out of shape
tract	pull, draw	*attract*—to pull toward
trans	across	*transport*—to carry across a distance
un	not	*uninformed*—not informed
uni	one	*unify*—to make one
vac	empty	*evacuate*—to make empty
ven, vent	come	*convene*—to come together
ver	true	*verity*—truth
verb	word	*verbose*—wordy
vid, vis	see	*video*—means of seeing *vision*—sight
viv, vit	life	*vivid*—lively
voc, vok	call	*provocative*—calling for a response *revoke*—to call back
vol	wish, will	*involuntary*—not willed

EXERCISES

Directions: In each of the following exercises, the words in the left-hand column are built on roots given in the etymology chart. Match each word with its definition from the right-hand column. Refer to the chart if necessary. Can you identify the roots of each word? If there is any word you can't figure out, look it up in a dictionary.

EXERCISE 1

mutable	able to be touched
culpable	laughable
interminable	empty of meaning or interest
amiable	of the first age
vacuous	holding firmly
vital	necessary to life
primeval	unending
tenacious	stable, not able to be loosened or broken up
tangible	changeable
inoperable	friendly
risible	blameworthy
indissoluble	not working, out of order

EXERCISE 2

infinity	list of things to be done
duplicity	sum paid yearly
levity	a throwing out or from
brevity	shortness
ejection	endlessness
edict	body of teachings
infraction	killing of a race
genocide	lightness of spirit
agenda	a breaking
annuity	double-dealing
microcosm	official decree; literally, a speaking out
doctrine	world in miniature

EXERCISE 3

recede	state as the truth
abdicate	throw light on
homogenize	forswear, give up a power
illuminate	put into words
supervise	make freer
verbalize	go away
liberalize	bury
legislate	oversee
intervene	make laws
inter	draw out
aver	make the same throughout
protract	come between

EXERCISE 4

abduction	arrival, a coming to
fortitude	a pressing together
consequence	a flowing together
confluence	something added to
compression	a coming back to life
locus	place
status	truthfulness
disunity	that which follows as a result
veracity	strength
revival	lack of oneness
advent	a leading away, kidnapping
adjunct	standing, position

EXERCISE 5

nascent	being born
centennial	before the Civil War
prospective	believing easily
circumspect	going against
multinational	in name only
clamorous	hard, unyielding
antebellum	looking forward
contrary	careful, looking in all directions
impassioned	hundred-year anniversary
credulous	having interests in many countries
obdurate	full of strong feeling
nominal	shouting

EXERCISE 6

dislocation	wrong name
misanthropy	withdrawal
misnomer	a knowing in advance
misconception	denial
negation	power of will
propulsion	forerunner
volition	a putting out of place
retraction	wrong idea
arbitration	a judging
inclination	a pushing forward
precognition	hatred of mankind
precursor	a leaning toward

EXERCISE 7

solitary	measuring time
altruistic	all-powerful
beneficial	badly shaped
benevolent	doing good, favorable
malefactor	alone, single
malformed	of the earth
malodorous	serving others
omniscient	bad-smelling
omnipotent	great-spirited, generous
magnanimous	all-knowing
chronometric	evildoer
terrestrial	well-wishing

WORD LIST

This list contains more than 1,300 words that may appear on the test that you are planning to take. You may know some of them already. Others will sound familiar, although you may not be sure of their exact meaning. Many are words that you will find in the practice tests in this section.

Each word is briefly defined and then used in a sentence. If you want to find the origin of the words and extended definitions, refer to a dictionary. The dictionary may also help by providing synonyms for some of these words.

How can you learn the words on this list that are new to you? Writing a word and its definition can help you remember new vocabulary words and their meanings. While you may not have time to learn every word listed before your exam, you can learn many of them. Divide your work into sections. Choose a moderate number of words whose meanings you do not know. Fifteen to twenty words would be a good choice for most people. Write these words and their definitions on a piece of paper that you can conveniently carry with you. Take the list with you during your normal activities. You can review it whenever you have some spare time. When you know the meanings of the words on this list, prepare another list in the same way.

Another useful way to learn words is to write them on note cards. Again, choose a moderate number of words and write the word on one side of the card and its definition on the other side. After you have studied the words and definitions, test yourself. Arrange the cards so that the sides of the cards with the new vocabulary words are face up. Then, on a separate sheet of paper, write the meaning of the word shown on the top card. Put this card at the bottom of the stack and write the meaning of the next word. Do this until you have gone through the entire stack. Now check yourself by comparing your answers with the definitions on the backs of the cards. Another way to study is to stack the cards with the definition side facing you, and write the word that is defined. These cards can also be used with the help of a friend, who can hold up the cards as you tell him or her the correct meaning of each word or identify the word from its definition.

A

abandon—to give up with the intent of never again claiming a right or interest in: *Abandoned* cars along the highway are unsightly.

abase—to cast down or make humble, to reduce in estimation: He refused to *abase* himself by admitting his mistake in front of the crowd.

abate—to lessen in intensity or number: After an hour, the storm *abated* and the sky began to clear.

abdicate—to give up a power or function: The father *abdicated* his responsibility for the boy.

aberrant—differing from what is right or normal: *Aberrant* behavior is frequently seen as a sign of emotional disturbance.

abet—to encourage or countenance the commission of an offense: Aiding and *abetting* a criminal makes one a party to crime.

abeyance—temporary suspension of an action: The strike motion was held in *abeyance* pending contract negotiations.

abhor—to regard with horror and loathing: The pacifist *abhors* war.

abide by—to live up to, submit to: We will *abide by* the decision of the court.

abject—miserable, wretched: Many people in underdeveloped and overpopulated countries live in *abject* poverty.

abolish—to do away with, as an institution: Slavery was *abolished* in Massachusetts shortly after the American Revolution.

abominate—to loathe: I *abominate* all laws that deprive people of their rights.

abort—to come to nothing, cut short: The mission was *aborted* when several of the helicopters broke down.

abrasive—scraping or rubbing, annoyingly harsh or jarring: The high-pitched whine of the machinery was *abrasive* to my nerves.

abridge—to shorten: The paperback book was an *abridged* edition.

absenteeism—condition of being habitually absent, as from work: *Absenteeism* at the plant becomes more of a problem around holidays.

abstain—to refrain voluntarily from some act: Because I was not sure if I agreed or disagreed with the motion, I *abstained* from voting for it.

abstract—not concrete; not material; not easy to understand; theoretical: His *abstract* ideas are difficult to apply to everyday situations.

absurd—clearly untrue, nonsensical: The parents dismissed the child's story of meeting aliens from outer space as *absurd*.

abundant—plentiful, more than enough: Rich soil and *abundant* rainfall make the region lush and fruitful.

abut—to touch, as bordering property: When estates *abut*, borders must be defined precisely.

accede—to consent: He *acceded* to their request.

accelerate—to increase in speed: Going downhill, a vehicle will naturally *accelerate*.

access—means of approach: Public libraries ensure that the people have *access* to vast stores of information.

acclaim—to applaud, approve loudly: The crowd in the square *acclaimed* their hero as the new president.

accommodate—to make room for, adjust: The room can *accommodate* two more desks. We will *accommodate* ourselves to the special needs of those clients.

accumulate—to gather, pile up: Over the years, she has *accumulated* a large collection of antique bric-a-brac.

accurate—careful and exact; conforming exactly to truth or to a standard; free from error: The witness gave an *accurate* account of the accident.

accustom—to get or be used to: The supervisor was not *accustomed* to having her instructions ignored.

acknowledge—to admit, recognize as true or legitimate: We *acknowledge* the government's authority to make us pay taxes.

acoustic—pertaining to hearing: The *acoustic* qualities of a room may be improved by insulation.

acquiesce—to comply or accept passively: One must often *acquiesce* to the demands of a superior.

acquire—to come into possession or control of: Once *acquired*, the skill of swimming is not easily lost.

acquit—to set free from an accusation: The jury *acquitted* the defendant.

acuity—acuteness, sharpness: His unusual *acuity* of vision allowed him to spot the landmark before it was visible to the others.

acumen—sharpness of mind, keenness in business matters: The *acumen* of many early industrialists accounts for their success.

adamant—inflexible, hard: She was *adamant* in her determination to succeed.

adaptable—able to adjust to new circumstances: Thanks to the intelligence that has made technology possible, humans are more *adaptable* to a variety of climates than any other species.

adept—skilled, well-versed: A journalist is *adept* at writing quickly.

adequate—sufficient, enough: Without *adequate* sunlight, many tropical plants will not bloom.

adhere—to hold, stick to, cling: Many persons *adhere* to their beliefs despite all arguments.

adjacent—adjoining; having a common border: New York and Connecticut are *adjacent* states.

adjourn—to suspend proceedings, usually for the day: Since it is now five o'clock, I move that we *adjourn* until tomorrow morning.

adjunct—something joined to a thing but not necessarily a part of it: A rider is an *adjunct* to a legislative bill.

adroit—skillful in the use of the hands or mental faculties: The *adroit* juggler held the crowd spellbound.

adulterate—to corrupt or to make impure by addition of foreign substances: Many natural foods are *adulterated* when chemicals are added to preserve them.

advantageous—useful, favorable: Our opponent's blunders have been *advantageous* to our campaign.

adverse—opposing, contrary: *Adverse* winds slowed the progress of the ship.

advocate—to plead for or urge: Some politicians *advocate* public ownership of utilities.

affable—amiable, pleasant, easy to talk to: The smiling face and *affable* manner of the teacher put the child at ease.

affect—to influence: The judge did not allow her personal feelings to *affect* her judgment of the case's legal merits.

affectation—artificial behavior or attitudes: His upper-class manner of speaking was nothing but an *affectation.*

affidavit—sworn statement in writing: An *affidavit* may serve in place of a personal appearance.

affiliation—connection, as with an organization: His *affiliation* with the club has been of long standing; he has been a member for ten years.

affinity—relationship, kinship: There is a close *affinity* among many European languages, such as Spanish and Italian.

affirm—to avow solemnly, declare positively: The testimony *affirmed* the defendant's alibi.

affix—to attach, fasten: A price tag was *affixed* to each item.

affluence—wealth: The new *affluence* of the family made them the object of curiosity and envy to their neighbors.

agenda—list of things to be done: The *agenda* of the conference included the problem of taxes.

aggression—unprovoked attack: The invasion of Kuwait was denounced in the press as *aggression.*

agitate—to stir up or disturb: Rumors of change in the government *agitated* the population.

agoraphobia—unreasoning fear of open places: A person suffering from *agoraphobia* may be unable to go outdoors without experiencing panic.

agrarian—having to do with land: *Agrarian* reforms were one of the first measures adopted in the economic rehabilitation of the country.

alarm—disturb, excite: The parents were *alarmed* when their son's temperature rose suddenly.

alien—(adj) strange, foreign: Their customs are *alien* to us. (n) foreigner who has not become a citizen of the country where he lives: It is estimated that there are more than 1 million illegal *aliens* living in New York City.

allay—to pacify, calm: Therapy will often *allay* the fears of the neurotic.

allege—to declare without proof: The *alleged* attacker has yet to stand trial.

alleviate—to lessen, make easier: The medicine helped to *alleviate* the pain.

allocate—to distribute or assign: The new serum was *allocated* among the states in proportion to their population.

allude—to refer to indirectly or by suggestion: The book *alludes* to an earlier document that we have been unable to locate or even to identify.

aloof—distant, reserved, or cold in manner: Her elegant appearance and formal politeness made her seem *aloof,* though in reality she was only shy.

altercation—angry dispute: The *altercation* stopped just short of physical violence.

altitude—height, especially above sea level or the earth's surface: The plane had reached an *altitude* of 4 miles.

altruist—person who acts unselfishly in the interests of others: She proved herself an *altruist* by volunteering to help the flood victims when there was no hope of recompense.

amalgamate—to make into a single unit: The new owners *amalgamated* several small companies into a single corporation.

amass—to collect, pile up: Through careful investment, he had *amassed* a sizable fortune.

ambiguous—having more than one possible meaning: The *ambiguous* wording of some legislative acts requires clarification by the courts.
ambivalent—having conflicting feelings: I am *ambivalent* about the job; although the atmosphere is pleasant, the work itself is boring.
amenable—agreeable, open to suggestion: He was *amenable* to the proposed schedule change.
amicable—friendly: Courts often seek to settle civil suits in an *amicable* manner.
amnesty—pardon for a large group: The judge granted *amnesty* to those who had been arrested for protesting.
amplify—to enlarge, expand: Congressmen may *amplify* their remarks for appearance in the Record.
analogous—having a similarity or partial likeness: Writers have often seen springtime as *analogous* to youth and winter to old age.
analyze—to study or determine the nature and relationship of the parts: After the chemist *analyzes* the powder, she will tell us what it is.
anemia—deficiency of red blood corpuscles or hemoglobin in the blood: Before it was treated, her *anemia* caused her to tire easily.
annals—chronological records: The *annals* of the scientific societies reflect the advances of our era.
annihilate—to destroy completely: If the government did not act to preserve the few remaining herds, the whole species would have been *annihilated* by the end of the century.
annotate—to provide explanatory notes: For the student edition, the editor *annotated* the more difficult passages in the essay.
annual—yearly, once a year: The company holds an *annual* picnic on the Fourth of July.
annuity—amount of money payable yearly: Investment in an *annuity* provides income for their retirement.
annul—to wipe out, make void: The Supreme Court can *annul* a law that it deems unconstitutional.
anomalous—out of place, inappropriate to the surroundings: An *anomalous* jukebox stood rusting in the square of the primitive village.
anonymous—bearing no name, unsigned: Little credence should be given to an *anonymous* accusation.
antecedent—a preceding event, condition, or cause: The bombing of Pearl Harbor was *antecedent* to our entry into World War II.
anticipate—to foresee, give thought to in advance; expect: We *anticipate* that this movie will be a box office hit.
antipathy—dislike: His *antipathy* toward cats almost amounted to a phobia.
apathy—lack of interest or emotion: Voter *apathy* allows a few politically concerned people to influence elections out of proportion to their numbers.
apex—summit, peak: Some people reach the *apex* of their careers quickly.
apparition—phantom, anything that appears suddenly or unexpectedly: Dressed in the antique gown, the woman looked like an *apparition* from her grandmother's era.
appearance—outward aspect; act of coming in sight: The celebrity put in an *appearance* at the awards ceremony.
appease—to give in to satisfy or make peace, to pacify: Only a heartfelt apology will *appease* his rage at having been slighted.
append—to attach as a supplement: Exhibits should be *appended* to the report.
appendix—extra material added at the end of a book: A chronology of the events described may be found in the *appendix*.
applicable—able to be applied, appropriate: Since you are single, the items on the form concerning your spouse are not *applicable*; leave those spaces blank.
appraise—to set a value on: The price at which authorities *appraise* a building determines its taxes.
appreciate—to think well of; to grasp the nature, worth, quality, or significance of: I can *appreciate* the difficulties you are having with your aging parents.
apprehend—to arrest; to understand: The police moved to *apprehend* the suspect. I could not *apprehend* what she was trying to say.
apprehensive—fearing some coming event: The students were *apprehensive* about the examination.
apprise—to give notice to: The shop owners were *apprised* of the new law about closing hours.
approach—to come near to; taking of preliminary steps; a means of access: The *approach* to the haunted house was through a tangled arbor.
approbation—approval: The act was performed with the *approbation* of the onlookers.
apropos—pertinent, to the point: His remarks were *apropos* and well-founded.
arbitrary—despotic, arrived at through will or caprice: An *arbitrary* ruling of the civil commission is being challenged in the courts.
arbitration—settling a dispute by referring it to an outsider for decision: Under the agreement, disputes were to be settled by *arbitration*.
archaic—no longer in use: Some words like "thou," once a common form of address, are now *archaic*.
archives—historic records: A separate building houses the United States *archives* in Washington.
ardent—passionately enthusiastic: Her *ardent* patriotism led her to risk her life in the underground resistance movement.
aroma—fragrance: The *aroma* of good coffee stimulates the salivary glands.
arraign—to bring before a court of law, formally accuse: A person arrested must be *arraigned* within 24 hours.
arrogant—disposed to exaggerate one's own worth and importance: The *arrogant* waiter refused to acknowledge the disheveled man at the counter.
articulate—expressing oneself readily, clearly, or effectively: The *articulate* child told of the day's events in school.
artifact—man-made object: *Artifacts* found by archaeologists allow them to reconstruct the daily lives of ancient peoples.
ascertain—to find out with certainty: Because the woman's story was so confused, we have been unable to *ascertain* whether a crime was committed or not.
ascribe—to attribute, assign as a cause: His death was *ascribed* to poison.
asinine—stupid, silly: The argument was too *asinine* to deserve a serious answer.
asphyxiation—death or loss of consciousness caused by lack of oxygen: The flames never reached that part of the building, but several residents suffered *asphyxiation* from the smoke.
assailant—attacker: Faced with a line-up, the victim picked out his alleged *assailant*.

assemblage—a group or collection of things or persons: Out of the *assemblage* of spare parts in the garage, we found the pieces to repair the bicycle.
assent—to concur, comply, consent: All parties involved *assented* to the statement.
assert—to claim or state positively: She *asserted* her title to the property.
assess—to set a value on: The house has been *assessed* for taxes at far below its market value.
assiduous—performed with constant diligence: *Assiduous* attention to her assignment won her a promotion.
assign—to appoint, prescribe: The new reporters were *assigned* to cover local sports events.
assist—to give aid, help: The laboratory aide *assists* the chemist in researching the properties of chemical substances.
assumption—something taken for granted or supposed to be fact: I prepared dinner on the *assumption* that they would be home by seven.
assure—to make something certain, guarantee; to promise with confidence: The fact that they left their tickets *assures* that they will return. I *assured* her that someone would be there to meet her.
astute—difficult to deceive: An *astute* judge of character, he guessed that his opponent was bluffing.
attain—to get through effort, to achieve or reach: Thanks to their generous contribution, the campaign has *attained* its goal.
attest—to bear witness to by oath or signature: Disinterested witnesses must *attest* to the signing of a will.
attrition—a gradual wearing down: With the armies dug into the trenches, World War I became a war of *attrition*.
atypical—not normal or usual: The usually calm man's burst of temper was *atypical*.
auction—to sell to the highest bidder: Bidding started at 5 dollars, but the chair eventually was *auctioned* for 30.
augment—to increase: He *augments* his wealth with every deal.
aural—of the ear or hearing: Since the sound system was not working properly, the *aural* aspect of the performance was a disappointment.
auspicious—predicting success: The first week's business was an *auspicious* start for the whole enterprise.
austerity—quality of being strict, rigorous, very simple, or unadorned: To save money they went on an *austerity* program, cutting down on nonessential purchases.
authorize—to give official permission: The guard is *authorized* to demand identification from anyone entering the building.
autocratic—despotic, acting without regard for the rights or opinions of others: An *autocratic* attitude on the part of a supervisor is deeply resented by subordinates.
automatically—involuntarily, spontaneously, mechanically: The computer *automatically* records the amount of sales for each month.
autopsy—examination and partial dissection of a body to determine the cause of death: The *autopsy* revealed a brain tumor.
averse—having a dislike or reluctance: The local population disliked tourists and were *averse* to having their pictures taken.
avert—to turn aside or ward off: By acting quickly, we *averted* disaster.
avow—to declare openly: She *avowed* her belief in the political system.

B

baffle—to perplex, frustrate: The intricacies of the game *baffle* description.
banal—commonplace, trite: There was nothing fresh or memorable in their *banal* exchange of opinions.
banter—light, good-natured teasing: The comments were mere *banter*, not intended to wound.
bar—to oppose, prevent, or forbid; to keep out: Conviction of committing a felony will *bar* you from voting.
barren—unfruitful, unproductive: Only a few scrubby trees clung to the rocky soil of that *barren* landscape.
barter—to trade by direct exchange of one commodity for another: At the market I *bartered* my sleeping bag for a handwoven blanket.
basic—fundamental: The teacher explained the *basic* concepts of democracy.
belabor—to beat or attack, especially with words: The speech *belabored* at great length what everyone in the audience already knew.
belie—to lie about, to show to be false: Her laughing face *belied* her pretense of annoyance.
belittle—to make smaller or less important: He *belittled* the actress's talent by suggesting that her beauty, rather than her acting ability, was responsible for her success.
beneficiary—one who benefits, especially one who receives a payment or inheritance: The man named his wife as the *beneficiary* of the insurance policy.
benign—kindly: Her *benign* influence helped to alleviate their depression.
berate—to scold vehemently: The teacher who *berates* his class has lost his temper.
bespeak—to indicate, to speak for, especially in advance: The success of the first novel *bespeaks* a promising career for the young author.
bestow—to grant or confer: The republic *bestowed* great honors upon its heroes.
bibliography—list of sources of information on a particular subject: She assembled a *bibliography* of major works on early American history published since 1960.
biennial—happening every two years: Many state legislatures convene on a *biennial* basis.
bigot—narrow-minded, intolerant person: A *bigot* is not swayed from his beliefs by rational argument.
blatant—too noisy or obtrusive, impossible to ignore: The children's *blatant* disregard for conventional manners appalled their older relatives.
bogus—false, counterfeit: Using a *bogus* driver's license, she had opened an account under an assumed name.
bolster—to prop up, support: The announcement that refreshments were being served *bolstered* the flagging spirits of the company.
bore—to weary by being dull, uninteresting, or monotonous: I get so *bored* when my aunt tells the same stories over and over.
bourgeois—middle-class: Thriftiness, respectability, and hard work are often thought of as *bourgeois* traits.
boycott—to refuse to do business with or use: Consumers *boycotted* the company's products to show support for the striking workers.
brazen—brassy, shameless: The delinquents demonstrated a *brazen* contempt for the law.
breach—opening or gap, failure to keep the terms, as of a promise or law: When they failed to deliver the goods, they were guilty of a *breach* of contract.

brevity—conciseness, terseness: *Brevity* is the essence of journalistic writing.
brochure—pamphlet: *Brochures* on many topics are available free of charge.
brunt—the principal force or shock, greater part: The *brunt* of the attack was absorbed by the infantry.
brusque—blunt, curt in manner: A *brusque* manner displeases many persons.
budget—plan for the spending of income during a certain period: The present *budget* allocates one fourth of our joint income for rent and utilities.
buoyant—rising or floating, cheerful: His *buoyant* nature would not allow him to remain glum for long.

C

cache—hiding place for loot or supplies: The *cache* left by the expedition was found many years later.
cadaver—dead body: The *cadaver* was dissected by the medical students.
cadence—rhythmic flow, modulation of speech, measured movement: The low and musical *cadence* of the actress's voice was a delight to hear.
cadre—framework, skeleton organization: A *cadre* of commissioned and noncommissioned officers was maintained.
cajole—to coax, persuade by artful flattery: He was *cajoled* into betting on the game.
caliber—capacity of mind, quality: It is a crucial and delicate job requiring personnel of the highest *caliber.* Also: **calibre**.
candid—honest, open: She was always *candid* about her feelings; if she liked you, you knew it.
candor—unreserved honest or sincere expression: *Candor* and innocence often go hand in hand.
cant—jargon, secret slang, empty talk: The conversational *cant* of the two social scientists was unintelligible to everyone else at the party.
capacious—roomy, spacious: The travelers had all their possessions in one *capacious* suitcase.
capitulate—surrender: The city *capitulated* to the invaders.
capricious—changing suddenly, willfully erratic: He is so *capricious* in his moods that no one can predict how he will take the news.
captivate—to influence and dominate by some special charm; to hold prisoner: The Frenchman *captivated* the American woman by kissing her hand.
carcinogenic—producing cancer: In tests on laboratory animals, the drug was shown to be *carcinogenic.*
caricature—distorted sketch: *Caricature* is the weapon of the political cartoonist.
carnage—destruction of life: The *carnage* of modern warfare is frightful to consider.
catalyst—substance that causes change in other substances without itself being affected: Platinum is a *catalyst* in many chemical processes.
cataract—a condition of the eye in which the lens becomes opaque: The old man's vision had been impaired by *cataracts.*
category—class or division in a system of classification: Patients are listed according to *categories* that designate the seriousness of their condition.
caustic—biting, burning, stinging: The surface of the wood had been marred by some *caustic* substance.
caveat—legal notice preventing some action; a warning: A *caveat* may be entered to the terms of the product's warranty.
cede—to yield, assign, transfer: A bill of sale will *cede* title of the property.
censure—to disapprove, blame, condemn as wrong: The unprofessional conduct of several of its members has been officially *censured* by the organization.
cerebral—pertaining to the brain: The stroke was the result of a *cerebral* hemorrhage.
chagrin—disappointment, vexation: The failure of the play filled the backers with *chagrin.*
chaos—complete confusion or disorder: By the time the children had finished playing with all the toys, the room was in *chaos.*
characteristic—typical trait, identifying feature: A curved yellow bill is a *characteristic* of this species.
charlatan—one who pretends to know more than he does: *Charlatans* who pretend they can cure cancer have been responsible for many deaths.
chastise—to punish or to censure severely: The disobedient boy was *chastised* by being sent to his room.
chauvinism—zealous, unreasoning patriotism: *Chauvinism* is the cause of many unnecessary wars.
chicanery—unethical methods, legal trickery: He accused the winning candidate of *chicanery* in the campaign.
chide—to rebuke, scold: The parents *chided* the disobedient child.
childish—immature; characteristic of a child: Constant quibbling about the details of past events is *childish.*
chronic—long-lasting, recurring: His *chronic* asthma flares up at certain times of the year.
chronology—arrangement by time, list of events by date: The book included a *chronology* of the poet's life against the background of the major political events of his age.
circumspect—watchful in all directions, wary: A public official must be *circumspect* in all his actions.
circumvent—to go around, frustrate: A technicality allowed people to *circumvent* the intention of the law.
citation—summons to appear in court; an official praise, as for bravery; reference to legal precedent or authority: Caught for speeding, I received a *citation.* Three firefighters received *citations* for the heroic rescue effort. The attorney asked the clerk to check the *citations* to cases in the Supreme Court.
clamor—loud, continuous noise; uproar: The *clamor* of the protesting mob was unbearable.
clandestine—secret: The conspirators held a *clandestine* meeting.
clemency—leniency: The governor granted *clemency* to the prisoners.
cliché—trite, overworked expression: "White as snow" is a *cliché.*
climactic—of a climax: At the *climactic* moment of the film, the heroine walks out and slams the door.
climatic—of a climate: Over eons, *climatic* changes turned the swamp into a desert.
coalition—temporary union of groups for a specific purpose: Various environmentalist groups formed a *coalition* to work for the candidate most sympathetic to their cause.
coerce—to compel, force: He did not sign the confession freely but was *coerced.*

cogent—conclusive, convincing: A debater must present *cogent* arguments to win his point.
cognizant—having knowledge: She was *cognizant* of all the facts before she made a decision.
coherent—logically connected or organized: They were too distraught to give a *coherent* account of the crash.
cohesion—sticking together: The *cohesion* of molecules creates surface tension.
coincide—to be alike, to occur at the same time: This year Thanksgiving *coincides* with her birthday.
collaborate—to work together on a project: The friends decided to *collaborate* on a novel.
collate—to put the pages of a text in order: The photocopies have been *collated* and are ready to be stapled.
colleague—fellow worker in a profession: The biologist enjoyed shoptalk with her *colleagues* at the conference.
colloquial—of speech and informal writing, conversational: Having studied only formal French, she was unable to understand many of her host's *colloquial* expressions.
collusion—secret agreement, conspiracy: Higher prices were set by *collusion* among all the manufacturers.
comatose—lethargic, of or like a coma: The drug left him in a *comatose* state.
comical—causing amusement; funny; humorous: The poodle looked *comical* stepping out in its rubber boots.
commence—to make a beginning: "Open your test booklet and *commence* the exam," the teacher said.
commend—to praise: The supervisor *commended* them for their excellent work.
commensurate—equal, corresponding in measure: He asked for compensation *commensurate* with his experience.
commiserate—to express sympathy for: It is natural to *commiserate* with the innocent victim of an accident.
commission—to authorize, especially to have someone perform a task or to act in one's place: I have *commissioned* a neighbor to collect the mail while I'm away.
commodious—comfortably or conveniently spacious: The *commodious* closets impressed the prospective tenants.
common—ordinary, widespread: Financial difficulty is a *common* problem for young married couples.
commute—to substitute one thing for another; to travel regularly between home and work: The alchemists dreamed of *commuting* lead into gold. *Commuting* is a daily routine for most working people.
comparable—equivalent, able or worthy to be compared: Her degree from a foreign university is *comparable* to our master's degree.
compatible—harmonious, in agreement: Since they have similar attitudes, interests, and habits, they are a *compatible* couple.
compel—to force: He was *compelled* by law to make restitution.
compensate—to be equal to, make up for: Money could not *compensate* him for his sufferings.
competent—fit, capable, qualified: I am not *competent* to judge the authenticity of this document; you should take it to an expert.
competition—rivalry for the same object: The theory of free enterprise assumes an unrestricted *competition* for customers among rival businesses.
complacent—self-satisfied: A *complacent* student seldom attains the heights of success achieved by those who demand more of themselves.
complete—to finish, bring an end to: The project was *completed* in time for the fall science fair.
complex—a whole made up of interconnected or related parts: The school grew from a few classrooms to a *complex* of buildings organized around the computer center.
complicity—partnership in wrongdoing: By withholding evidence, she became guilty of *complicity* in the crime.
comply—to go along with, obey: The crowd *complied* with the order to disperse.
compose—to put together, create: I spent an hour *composing* a formal letter of protest.
comprehensible—able to be understood: The episode was only *comprehensible* to those who knew the story thus far.
comprise—to include, be made up of, consist of: The test will *comprise* the subject matter of the previous lessons.
compromise—a settlement of a difference in which both sides give up something: We are willing to make some concessions in order to reach a *compromise*.
compulsory—required, forced: Attendance is *compulsory* unless one has a medical excuse.
compunction—remorse, uneasiness: He showed no *compunction* over his carelessness.
compute—to figure, calculate: He *computed* the total on his pocket calculator.
concede—to yield, as to what is just or true: When he realized his mistake, he *conceded* gracefully.
concentration—strength or density as of a solution; close or fixed attention: The high *concentration* of frozen orange juice requires that it be diluted with three cans of water before drinking. Studying required all my *concentration*.
concept—idea, general notion: The *concept* that all individuals have inherent and inalienable rights is basic to American political philosophy.
conception—beginning, original idea, mental image: The *conception* of the plan was originally hers.
conciliatory—tending to placate or to gain goodwill: After the quarrel, he sent flowers as a *conciliatory* gesture.
concise—brief, to the point: A summons must be *concise* yet cover the topic.
concoction—combination of various ingredients: The drink was a *concoction* of syrup, soda, and three flavors of ice cream.
concurrent—running together, happening at the same time: *Concurrent* action by the police and welfare authorities reduced juvenile crime.
condole—to express sympathy: His friends gathered to *condole* with him over his loss.
condone—to pardon, overlook an offense: The law will not *condone* an act on the plea that the culprit was intoxicated.
conducive—leading to, helping: I find that a waterbed is *conducive* to restful sleep.
conduct—behavior: Her cool *conduct* in the emergency inspired confidence in those around her.
confidence—a relationship of trust, intimacy or certitude: To relax while skiing, you must have *confidence* in your bindings.
confidential—private, secret: Respondents were assured that the census was *confidential* and would be used for statistical purposes only.

confiscate—to seize, appropriate: The government has no right to *confiscate* private property without just compensation.
conflagration—large fire: New York City was almost destroyed in the 1835 *conflagration*.
conformity—harmony, agreement: In *conformity* with the rule, the meeting was adjourned.
congruent—in agreement or harmony: *Congruent* figures coincide entirely throughout.
conjecture—to make a guess based on information at hand: He *conjectured* that vocabulary questions would appear on the test.
connive—to pretend ignorance of or assist in wrongdoing: The builder and the agent *connived* in selling over-priced homes.
conscientious—honest, faithful to duty or to what is right: He is *conscientious* in his work, and so has won the trust of his employers.
consensus—general agreement: The *consensus* of the jury was that the defendant was not guilty.
consequence—result of an action or process; outcome; effect: The *consequence* of regular exercise is muscular fitness.
conservative—tending to preserve what is, cautious: At the annual conference, they presented their *conservative* views on the future of education.
considerable—important, large, much: The director has *considerable* clout among the members of the board; they value her recommendations highly.
consign—to entrust, hand over: The child was *consigned* to the care of her older sister until the court could appoint a guardian.
consolidate—to combine into a single whole: Let us *consolidate* our forces before we begin our campaign.
consonance—harmony, pleasant agreement: Their *consonance* of opinion in all matters made for a peaceful household.
constant—unchanging, fixed, continual: It is difficult to listen to his *constant* complaining.
constituency—body of voters: The congressman went home to discuss the issue with his *constituency*.
constitute—to set up, make up, compose: In industrialized countries, farmers *constitute* only a small percentage of the population.
constrain—to force, compel: She felt *constrained* to make a full confession.
construe—to interpret, analyze: His attitude was *construed* as one of opposition to the proposal.
consume—to do away with completely; to use up: The fire totally *consumed* the frame dwelling.
contagious—transmittable by direct or indirect contact: Hepatitis is a *contagious* disease.
contaminate—to pollute, to make unclean or unfit: The pesticide seeped into the water table, *contaminating* the wells.
contentious—quarrelsome: One *contentious* student can ruin a debate.
contiguous—next to, adjoining: Alaska is not *contiguous* to other states of the United States.
contingent—depending upon something's happening: Our plans were *contingent* on the check's arriving on time.
contort—to twist out of shape: Rage *contorted* her features into a frightening mask.
contract—a formal agreement, usually written: The company signed a *contract* to operate a bookstore on campus.
contrition—sincere remorse: They were overwhelmed by *contrition* when they realized the damage they had caused.
contrive—to devise, plan: They *contrived* a way to fix the unit using old parts.
controversy—highly charged debate, conflict of opinion: A *controversy* arose over whether to use the funds for highway improvement or for mass transit.
contusion—bruise: He suffered severe *contusions* in the accident.
convene—to gather together, as an assembly: The graduates will *convene* on the campus.
conventional—ordinary; traditional; not unusual: The architecture of the new building is unimaginative and very *conventional*.
converge—to move nearer together, head for one point: The flock *converged* on the seeded field.
convulsion—violent, involuntary contracting and relaxing of the muscles: Epilepsy is accompanied by *convulsions*.
cooperate—to work together for a common goal: If every-one *cooperates* on decorations, entertainment, and refreshments, the party is sure to be a success.
coordinate—to bring different elements into order or harmony: In a well-run office, schedules are *coordinated* so that business is uninterrupted.
corpulent—very fat: The *corpulent* individual must choose clothing with great care.
correlate—to bring into or show relation between two things: Studies have *correlated* smoking and heart disease.
correspondence—letters, communication by letter: A copy of the book order will be found in the *correspondence* file under the name of the publisher.
corroborate—to provide added proof: Laws of evidence require that testimony about a crime be *corroborated* by other circumstances.
counter—to offset or to nullify; to oppose or check: Their fine offense is *countered* by our exceptional defensive line.
countermand—to revoke an order or command: The wise executive will not hesitate to *countermand* an unwise order.
courteous—polite, considerate: A *courteous* manner—friendly but not personal—is essential for anyone who deals with the public.
covert—hidden, secret: To maintain surprise, the general ordered a *covert* military action but publicly denied the invasion would begin.
cranium—skull of a vertebrate: The *cranium* affords great protection to the brain.
crass—stupid, unrefined: The *crass* behavior of some tourists makes them appear foolish to the local population.
craven—cowardly: His *craven* conduct under stress made him the object of many insults.
credence—faith, belief: One could have little *credence* in the word of a known swindler.
credible—worthy or able to be believed: The tale, though unusual, was entirely *credible*, considering the physical evidence.
credulous—inclined to believe on slight evidence: The *credulous* man followed every instruction of the fortune-teller.
creed—statement of faith, system of beliefs: Equal justice for all is part of the American *creed*.

cremate—burn a dead body: He left instructions that he was to be *cremated* upon his death.

criterion—standard of judging: Logical organization was a criterion for grading the essays. Plural: **criteria**.

crucial—of utmost importance: The discovery of the letter was *crucial* to the unraveling of the mystery.

cryptic—having a hidden meaning, mysterious: The *cryptic* message was deciphered by the code expert.

cull—to select, pick out from a group: From the pile we *culled* all the mail for local delivery.

culmination—acme, highest attainment: Graduation with highest honors was the *culmination* of her academic efforts.

culpable—faulty, blameworthy, guilty: The *culpable* parties should not escape punishment.

curative—concerning or causing the cure of disease: The grandmother had faith in the *curative* powers of certain herbs.

cursory—superficial, hurried: *Cursory* examination of the scene revealed nothing amiss, but later we discovered that some jewelry was missing.

curtail—to reduce, shorten: Classes were shortened in the winter to *curtail* heating costs.

customary—usual, according to habit or custom: Because of the traffic jam, she did not take her *customary* route today.

D

dearth—scarcity: A *dearth* of water can create a desert in a few years.

debase—to reduce in dignity or value: Inflation has *debased* the currency so that a dollar now buys very little.

debate—to argue formally for and against: The candidate challenged the incumbent to *debate* the issues on television.

debilitate—to enfeeble, weaken: Constant excesses will *debilitate* even the strongest constitution.

deceive—to trick, be false to: They *deceived* us by telling us that our donations would be used to provide food to the needy; in reality, they pocketed the money.

decelerate—to slow down or to reduce the rate of progress: When you see a stop sign in the distance, it is wise to *decelerate*.

decimate—to destroy a large part (literally, one tenth) of a population: The Black Death had *decimated* London in the 1660s.

decompose—to break up or separate into basic parts or elements: After some time, vegetation that lies on damp ground tends to *decompose*.

decorum—that which is suitable or proper: He had gentlemanly notions of *decorum*; he always held doors open for ladies and held their chairs when they sat down to dinner.

decrepit—broken down by old age: With its crumbling brick and peeling paint, the building had a *decrepit* appearance.

decry—to clamor against: Critics *decry* the lack of clarity in experimental poetry.

deduct—to subtract, take away: Because the package was damaged, the seller *deducted* two dollars from the price.

deem—to judge, think: The newspaper did not *deem* the event worthy of coverage.

de facto—actual as opposed to legal: Although he holds no official position, he is the *de facto* head of the government.

default—failure to do what is required: Because of the *default* of payment, the property was seized by the creditor.

deference—act of respect, respect for another's wishes: Out of *deference* to her age, we rose when she entered.

deficient—not up to standard, inadequate: The child is *deficient* in reading but excels in arithmetic.

definition—description, explanation, or meaning: Look in the dictionary for *definitions* of words you do not know.

defoliate—to strip of leaves: All the trees in the yard had been *defoliated* by an infestation of moths.

defray—to pay (costs): The company *defrayed* the costs of a vacation trip for the winner of the sales contest.

defunct—dead, no longer functioning: The business has been *defunct* since the big fire.

defy—to oppose or resist openly or boldly; to challenge; to dare: Some people *defy* No Smoking rules and light up a cigarette.

degenerate—to decline from a higher or normal form: The discussion eventually *degenerated* into a shouting match.

degrade—to lower in status, value, or esteem: The celebrity refused interviews, feeling that it was *degrading* to have her personal life publicly discussed.

de jure—according to law: Although they had successfully seized power, the rebels were not recognized as the *de jure* government by the neighboring countries.

delegate—to authorize or assign to act in one's place: Since I will be unable to attend the conference, I have *delegated* my assistant to represent me.

delegation—group of persons officially authorized to act for others: Our *delegation* to the United Nations is headed by the ambassador.

delete—to strike out, erase: Names of those who fail to pay their dues for over a year are *deleted* from the membership rolls.

deleterious—injurious, harmful: Alcoholic beverages have a *deleterious* effect on the body.

deliberate—intended, meant: It was no accident but a *deliberate* act.

delineate—to mark off the boundary of: They asked him to *delineate* the areas where play was permitted.

delinquent—delaying or failing to do what rules or law require: Since she was *delinquent* in paying her taxes, she had to pay a fine.

demagogue—leader who uses mob passions to gain power: Hitler was a *demagogue* who played on the irrational fears and hatred of the mob.

demean—to degrade, debase: He would not *demean* himself by making personal attacks.

demolish—to destroy, especially a building: The wrecking crew arrived, and within a few hours the structure was *demolished*.

demonstrable—able to be shown: The tests showed that the consumers' preference was justified by that brand's *demonstrable* superiority.

demote—to lower in rank: He was stripped of his rank and *demoted* to private.

denigrate—to blacken, defame: The lawyer tried to *denigrate* the character of the witness by implying that he was a liar.

dense—thick, compact, or crowded; difficult to penetrate: The underbrush was so *dense* that it was impossible to follow the path.

deny—to declare untrue, refuse to recognize: I categorically *deny* the accusation.

deplete—to empty, use up: At the present rates of consumption, the known reserves will be *depleted* before the end of the century.

deplore—to lament, disapprove strongly: Pacifists *deplore* violence even on behalf of a just cause.

deposition—written testimony taken outside court: A *deposition* had to be taken from the hospitalized witness.

deprecate—to plead against; to express disapproval: Do not *deprecate* what you cannot understand.

depreciate—to lessen in value: Property will *depreciate* rapidly unless kept in good repair.

deprive—to take away, often by force: No person may be *deprived* of his liberty without due process of law.

derelict—(adj.) abandoning duty, remiss: The policeman was *derelict* in his duty. (n) thing or person considered worthless: In winter, the city's *derelicts* frequent the bus station to stay warm.

deride—to mock, laugh at: Many passersby *derided* the comical figure of the street-corner speaker.

derogatory—disparaging, disdainful: Her *derogatory* remarks hid feelings of envy.

designate—to name, appoint: We will meet at the time and place *designated* on the agenda.

despicable—contemptible: The villain in melodramas is always a *despicable* character.

despotic—ruling with absolute authority: A *despotic* king is out of place in a constitutional monarchy.

destitute—in extreme want: Three successive years of crop failures had left the farmers *destitute*.

desuetude—lack of use: The law, which had never been repealed, had fallen into *desuetude* and was never enforced.

deteriorate—to get worse: Storing it in a cedar chest will keep the antique fabric from *deteriorating* further.

determine—to find out; to be the cause of, decide: The doctor interviewed the mother to *determine* whether there was a family history of diabetes. The result of this test will *determine* our next step.

deterrent—a thing that discourages: The absolute certainty of apprehension is a powerful *deterrent* to some types of crime.

detonate—to explode: An electrical charge can be used to *detonate* certain explosives.

detract—to take away a part, lessen: The old-fashioned engraving *detracted* from the value of the piece of jewelry.

detrimental—causing damage or harm: Smoking is *detrimental* to health.

deviate—to stray, turn aside from: The honest man never *deviated* from telling the truth as he saw it.

device—a piece of equipment designed to serve a certain purpose: The *device* at the end of the clothes brush serves as a shoe horn.

devious—roundabout, indirect, underhanded: When no one would tell her anything, she resorted to *devious* means to uncover the truth.

devise—to contrive, invent: I will *devise* a plan of escape.

devoid—completely without: The landscape was flat and barren, *devoid* of interest or beauty.

dexterity—quickness, skill, and ease in some act: The art of juggling is one that calls for the highest degree of *dexterity*.

dichotomy—division into two parts, often opposed: The *dichotomy* of her position, half instructor, half administrator, made efficient work in either field impossible.

diffidence—shyness, lack of assertiveness: His *diffidence* before such a distinguished visitor prevented him from expressing his own views.

diffuse—to spread out, scatter widely: When the bottle broke, the fragrance *diffused* throughout the room.

digress—to wander from the subject: To *digress* from the main topic may lend interest to a theme, but at the cost of its unity.

dilate—to expand: Some drugs will cause the pupil of the eye to *dilate*.

dilemma—choice of two unpleasant alternatives, a problem: Even a wrong decision may be preferable to remaining in a *dilemma*.

diminish—to make less: Inflation *diminishes* the value of the dollar.

diplomatic—employing tact and conciliation in dealing with people, especially in stressful situations: It would be *diplomatic* not to constantly refer to his wife's death.

disability—loss of ability: The accident resulted in a temporary *disability*; the employee was out for two weeks.

discard—to throw away: Inactive files more than ten years old may be *discarded*.

discern—to perceive, identify: The fog was so thick we could barely *discern* the other cars.

disciple—follower of a teacher: The renowned economist won over many *disciples* with her startling theories.

disclaim—to renounce, give up claim to: To obtain United States citizenship, one must *disclaim* any title or rank of nobility from another nation.

disclose—to reveal: The caller did not *disclose* the source of her information.

disconcert—to throw into confusion: An apathetic audience may *disconcert* even the most experienced performer.

discordant—harsh, not harmonious: The *discordant* cries of the gulls made me long for the tranquil sound of the waves.

discount—to underestimate the importance of; to minimize; to disregard: Do not *discount* the value of experience.

discretion—power of decision, individual judgment: The penalty to be imposed in many cases is left to the *discretion* of the judge.

disdain—to reject as unworthy: Many beginners *disdain* a lowly job that might in time lead to the position they desire.

disengage—to loosen or break a connection: Depressing the clutch *disengages* the driving force from the wheels.

disinterested—not involved in, unprejudiced: A *disinterested* witness is one who has no personal stake in the outcome of the case.

dismantle—to take apart: The machine must be *dismantled*, cleaned, repaired, and reassembled.

disparage—to speak slightingly of, belittle: A teacher who *disparages* the efforts of beginners is not helping the students.

disparity—inequality, difference in degree: A *disparity* in age need not mean an incompatible marriage.

dispatch—to send on an errand: The bank *dispatched* a courier to deliver the documents by hand.

dispel—to drive away, make disappear: The good-humored joke *dispelled* the tension in the room.

dispense with—to get rid of, do without: Let's *dispense with* the formalities and get right down to business.

disquieting—disturbing, tending to make uneasy: There have been *disquieting* reports of a buildup of forces along the border.

dissemble—to conceal or misrepresent the true nature of something: He *dissembled* his real motives under a pretence of unselfish concern.

disseminate—to spread, broadcast: The company *disseminated* literature about its new product line.

dissension—lack of harmony or agreement: There was *dissension* among the delegates about which candidate to support.

dissipate—to scatter aimlessly, spend foolishly: He soon *dissipated* his inheritance.

dissuade—to advise against, divert by persuasion: Her friends *dissuaded* her from the unwise plan.

distend—to stretch: If you *distend* a balloon beyond a certain point, it breaks.

distinct—clear, notable: There is a *distinct* difference between these two musical compositions.

distortion—a twisting out of shape, misstatement of facts: Each candidate's speech was a *distortion* of the other's positions.

distract—to divert, turn aside: The loud crash *distracted* the attention of the students.

distraught—crazed, distracted: The young woman was *distraught* over her husband's death.

diverge—to extend in different directions from a common point: The map showed a main highway with small roads *diverging* in all directions.

diverse—varied, unlike: A realistic cross-section must include citizens of *diverse* backgrounds and opinions.

divert—to amuse or entertain; to distract attention: A visit from her sister *diverted* the hospital patient.

divest—to deprive, strip: After the court martial, he was *divested* of his rank and decorations.

divisive—tending to divide, causing disagreement: The issue of abortion, on which people hold deep and morally-based convictions, was *divisive* to the movement.

divulge—to reveal, make public: Newspaper reporters have long fought the courts for the right not to *divulge* their sources of information.

docile—easily led: The child was *docile* until he discovered his mother had left the room.

document—an original or official paper serving as proof: The *document* appears to be the legal deed to the property.

dogmatic—arbitrary, believing or believed without proof: The politician, *dogmatic* in his opposition, refused to consider alternative solutions.

domicile—residence: Some people have one *domicile* in winter, another in summer.

dormant—sleeping, inactive: Perennial flowers such as irises remain *dormant* every winter and grow again in the spring.

dossier—file on a subject or person: The French police kept a *dossier* on every person with a criminal record.

dross—waste matter, scum: The process of separating the valuable metal from the *dross* may be so expensive that a mining claim is worthless.

dubious—doubtful: He had the *dubious* distinction of being absent more than any other student.

duplicity—hypocrisy, double-dealing: The *duplicity* of some politicians may shock the naive.

durable—long-lasting, tough: Canvas, unlike lighter materials, is a *durable* fabric.

dwindle—to become steadily less; to shrink: As we consume more oil, our supply *dwindles*.

dynamic—in motion, forceful, energetic: A *dynamic* leader can inspire followers with enthusiasm and confidence.

E

eclectic—drawing from diverse sources or systems: His *eclectic* record collection included everything from Bach cantatas to punk rock.

ecology—science of the relation of life to its environment: Persons concerned about *ecology* are worried about the effects of pollution on the environment.

ecstasy—extreme happiness: The lovers were in *ecstasy*, oblivious to their surroundings.

edict—public notice issued by authority: The *edict* issued by the rebels dissolved the government.

efface—to obliterate, wipe out: The tablets honoring the leader were *effaced* after his fall from power.

effect—(v) to bring about: New regulations have *effected* a shift in policy on applications. (n) a result: The headache was an *effect* of sinus congestion.

effective—producing a decided, decisive, or desired result: The soft lighting in the restaurant was very *effective* in setting a peaceful mood.

efficacious—able to produce a desired effect: The drug is *efficacious* in the treatment of malaria.

effigy—image of a person, especially of one who is hated: They burned his *effigy* in the public square.

effrontery—audacity, rude boldness: He had the *effrontery* to go up to the distinguished guest and call him by his first name.

egocentric—self-centered: The *egocentric* individual has little regard for the feelings of others.

egress—a going out, exit: The building code requires that the apartment has at least two means of *egress*.

elate—to make joyful, elevate in spirit: A grade of 100 will *elate* any student.

elective—filled or chosen by election: Although she had served on several commissions by appointment, she had never held *elective* office.

electorate—body of persons entitled to vote in an election: Less than 50 percent of the *electorate* actually voted in the last election.

elicit—to draw out, evoke: Her direct questions only *elicited* further evasions.

eligible—fit to be chosen, qualified: Veterans are *eligible* for many government benefits, including low-cost loans.

eliminate—to remove, do away with: By consolidating forms, the new procedures have *eliminated* some needless paperwork.

elocution—style of speaking, especially in public: Her *elocution* was so clear that everyone in the assembly could hear every word.

elusive—hard to find or grasp: Because the problem is so complex, a definitive solution seems *elusive*.

emaciated—very thin, wasted away: He had a tall, bony figure, as *emaciated* as a skeleton.

emanate—to derive from, issue forth: American law *emanates* largely from English common law.

embargo—governmental restriction or prohibition of trade: In retaliation for the invasion, the government imposed an *embargo* on grain shipments to the invaders' country.

embellish—to decorate, adorn: She would *embellish* her narratives with fanciful events.

embody—to render concrete, give form to: He tried to *embody* his ideas in his novel's characters.

emendation—change or correction in a text: The author corrected typographical errors and made a few other *emendations* in his manuscripts.

emigrate—to leave a country permanently to settle in another: Many people applied for visas, wishing to *emigrate* and escape persecution at home.

emissary—one sent to influence opponents politically: The rebels sent an *emissary* to negotiate a truce.

empathy—sense of identification with another person: Her *empathy* with her brother was very strong; she generally knew what he was feeling without his having to explain.

employ—to use: The artist *employed* charcoal in many of her sketches.

enable—to make able or possible: A summer job will *enable* you to pay for the course you need to take.

enact—to put into law, do or act out: A bill was *enacted* lowering the voting age to 18.

encounter—to come upon face to face unexpectedly; to meet in conflict: The burglar ran around the corner and suddenly *encountered* a policeman.

encroach—to infringe or invade: Property values fall when industries *encroach* upon residential areas.

encyclopedic—covering a wide range of subjects: The knowledge of a good instructor must be *encyclopedic*, ranging far beyond a specialized field.

endearment—a word or an act expressing affection: "Honey" is used as a term of *endearment.*

endeavor—to attempt by effort, try hard: I *endeavored* to contact them several times but they never returned my calls.

endemic—peculiar to or prevalent in an area or group: Severe lung disease is *endemic* in coal-mining regions.

endocrine—of a system of glands and their secretions that regulate body functions: The thyroid gland is part of the *endocrine* system.

endorse—to declare support or approval for: Community leaders were quick to *endorse* a project that would bring new jobs to the neighborhood.

enervate—to weaken, enfeeble: A poor diet will *enervate* a person.

enforce—to make forceful, to impose by force: Because of the holiday, parking restrictions are not being *enforced* today.

engender—to produce, cause, beget: Angry words may *engender* conflict.

engross—to absorb fully, monopolize: He was so *engrossed* in his hobbies that he neglected his studies.

engulf—to swallow up: The rising waters *engulfed* the village.

enhance—to improve, augment, add to: The neat cover *enhanced* the report.

enigma—riddle, anything that defies explanation: The origin of the statues on Easter Island is an *enigma*.

enlightened—free from prejudice or ignorance, socially or intellectually advanced: No *enlightened* society could condone the exploitation of children as it was once practiced in American industry.

enmity—state of being an enemy, hostility: The *enmity* between cats and dogs is a traditional idea.

enormity—state of being enormous or outrageous: The age of the victim added to the *enormity* of the crime.

ensue—to follow immediately or as a result: One person raised an objection and a long argument *ensued.*

entail—to involve or make necessary: Getting the report out on time will *entail* working all weekend.

entitle—to give a right or claim to: This pass *entitles* the bearer to two free admissions.

entrenched—firmly established: The value of family is deeply *entrenched* in the lives of those people.

enumerate—to count, specify in a list: In her essay she *enumerated* her reasons for wanting to attend the school.

enunciate—to pronounce clearly: He could not *enunciate* certain sounds because of a speech impediment.

envenom—to make poisonous, embitter: Out of jealousy, he tried to *envenom* the relationship between his friend and his rival.

environs—surroundings, suburbs: We searched the campus and its *environs*.

ephemeral—short-lived, temporary: Even *ephemeral* pleasures may leave lasting memories.

epitome—an abstract, part that typically represents the whole: He prepared an *epitome* of his work to show to the editor.

epoch—distinctive period of time: Hemingway's writings marked an *epoch* in American literature.

equanimity—calm temper, evenness of mind: Adversity could not ruffle her *equanimity.*

equivocal—having more than one possible meaning, deliberately misleading while not literally untrue: His *equivocal* statements left us in doubt as to his real intentions.

eradicate—to pluck up by the roots, wipe out: They tried to *eradicate* the hordes of rabbits by introducing predators to the area.

erode—to eat into, wear away: The glaciers *eroded* the land, leaving deep valleys.

ersatz—substitute, imitation: The burger consisted of *ersatz* beef made from soybeans.

escapade—an adventurous prank, reckless adventure for amusement: Relieved from duty at last, the soldiers went on a three-day *escapade*.

esoteric—limited to a few, secret: The *esoteric* rites of the fraternity were held sacred by the members.

espouse—to take up and support, as a cause: Our congressman *espouses* government funding for housing for the homeless.

essential—necessary, basic: A person must eat a variety of foods to obtain all the *essential* vitamins and minerals.

estimate—rough calculation: The contractor submitted a written *estimate* of the cost of a new roof.

estranged—alienated, separated: Her *estranged* husband had moved out six months ago.

etymology—origin and history of a word, study of the changes in words: The *etymology* of "bedlam" has been traced back to "Bethlehem," the name of a London hospital for the mentally ill.

eulogize—to praise highly in speech or writing: The deceased was *eulogized* at his funeral.
euphemism—substitution of an inoffensive or mild expression for a more straightforward one: Like many other people, he used "gone" and "passed away" as *euphemisms* for "dead."
euphoria—extreme sense of well-being: Their *euphoria* at their ascent of the mountain was heightened by their narrow escape from death.
evacuate—to empty, clear out: The authorities ordered the town *evacuated* when the waters rose.
evaluate—to determine the value of: The purpose of the survey is to *evaluate* the effect of the new teaching methods on the students' progress.
evasive—avoiding direct confrontation: She admitted that she had been there but was *evasive* about her reasons.
evince—to make evident, display: His curt reply *evinced* his short temper.
evolution—gradual change: Through the discovery of ancient bones and artifacts, anthropologists hope to chart the *evolution* of the human species.
exacerbate—to make worse, aggravate: A generous portion of french fries is sure to *exacerbate* an upset stomach.
exacting—severe in making demands: She was an *exacting* tutor, never content with less than perfection from her pupils.
examine—to investigate, to test: The doctor *examined* the patient for symptoms of pneumonia.
exceed—to go beyond, surpass: The business's profits for this year *exceeded* last year's profits by $16,000.
excess—amount beyond what is necessary or desired: When the pieces are in place, wipe away the *excess* glue.
excise—to remove by cutting out: The surgeon will have to *excise* the tumor.
exclude—to shut out, not permit to enter or participate: The children made a pact that all adults were to be *excluded* from the clubhouse.
execrable—extremely bad: Although her acting was *execrable*, she looked so good on stage that the audience applauded.
execute—to put into effect, perform: He *executed* the duties of his office conscientiously.
exemplary—serving as a pattern, deserving imitation: The leader's *exemplary* behavior in both her private and public life made her a model for all to follow.
exempt—excused: Having broken his leg, the child was *exempt* from gym for the rest of the term.
exhibit—to show, display: The paintings were *exhibited* in the municipal museum.
exhort—to incite by words or advice: The demagogue *exhorted* the crowd to attack the station.
exonerate—to free from blame: The confession of one prisoner *exonerated* the other suspects.
exorbitant—too much, beyond what is reasonable or acceptable: *Exorbitant* ticket prices have reduced attendance at concerts.
expansion—enlargement in scope or size: The company's *expansion* into foreign markets has increased its profits.
expedient—advantageous, appropriate to the circumstances, immediately useful though not necessarily right or just: Under pressure to reduce the deficit, the mayor found it *expedient* to cut funds for social services.
expedite—to speed, facilitate: In order to *expedite* delivery of the letter, he sent it special delivery.
expel—to push or force out: When a balloon bursts, the air is *expelled* in a rush.
expenditure—a spending: The finished mural more than justified the *expenditure* of time and money necessary for its completion.
experiment—test undertaken to demonstrate or discover something: *Experiments* were devised to test how motor skills were affected by emotional states.
expertise—skill or technical knowledge of an expert: The *expertise* with which she handled the animal delighted the spectators.
explicate—to explain, develop a principle: He *explicated* the parts of the text that the students had found confusing.
explicitly—openly, without disguise: When the annoying visitor refused to take a hint, the host told him *explicitly* that it was time he left.
exploit—to use, especially unfairly or selfishly: Some employers *exploit* the labor of illegal immigrants, who are afraid to complain about long hours and substandard wages.
exposé—exposure of a scandal: Following the newspaper's *exposés* of corruption in the state capitol, the two assemblymen were indicted for influence-peddling.
expressly—specifically, especially: I wrote it *expressly* for you.
exquisite—perfect, especially in a lovely, finely tuned or delicate way: The handmade lace was *exquisite* in every detail.
extend—to stretch out or to prolong in time; to broaden; to present for acceptance: A snow day *extended* Christmas vacation this year.
extensive—broad, of wide scope, thorough: Several hundred persons were interviewed as part of an *extensive* survey.
extenuate—to partially excuse, seem to lessen: His abrupt rudeness was *extenuated* by his distraught state of mind; no one could blame him for it.
extinct—no longer existing; no longer active, having died down or burnt out: Prehistoric animals are now all *extinct*.
extraneous—not forming an essential or vital part; having no relevance; coming from outside; foreign: The lengthy report was filled with *extraneous* information.
extricate—to free from an entanglement: Carefully removing each prickly branch, she *extricated* herself from the briars.

F

facade—front of a building: People travel to Venice to admire the *facade* of St. Mark's Church.
facetious—amusing, joking at an inappropriate time: His *facetious* criticisms were out of place at that moment; we were too upset to see the humor of the situation.
facilitate—to make easy or less difficult, free from impediment, lessen the labor of: This piece of machinery will *facilitate* production.
facility—ease: Her *facility* in reading several languages made her ideal for the cataloguing job.
facsimile—exact copy: A *facsimile* edition of a book is a photographic reproduction of an original manuscript or printed version.
factotum—employee with miscellaneous duties: He was the chief *factotum* of the plant.
faint—feeble, languid, exhausted: The children were *faint* with fatigue and hunger.

fallacious—untrue, misleading, containing a mistake in logic: Her arguments were transparently *fallacious.*

fallible—capable of erring or being deceived in judgment: It is a shock for children to discover that their parents are *fallible.*

falter—to hesitate, stammer, flinch: He speaks in a *faltering* manner.

fanatic—person with an unreasoning enthusiasm: The *fanatics* screamed at their team to beat their opponents.

fantastic—fanciful, produced or existing only in the imagination: Her story was so *fantastic* that no one could believe it.

fastidious—disdainful, squeamish, delicate to a fault: The homeowner was so *fastidious* that she had the exterminator come every week.

fatigue—mental or physical weariness: After a full day's work, their *fatigue* was understandable.

favoritism—unfair favoring of one person over others: *Favoritism* in the office based on personal friendship is resented.

feasible—able to be performed or executed by human means or agency, practicable: It is *feasible* to plan to complete the project by July.

fickle—likely to change: Young children often have *fickle* food preferences.

finalize—to make final: A notarized signature will *finalize* the agreement.

finesse—artifice, subtlety of contrivance to gain a point: She directed the conversation with such *finesse* that in the end he not only agreed to the plan but thought it was his own idea.

finite—having a limit, bounded: There were only a *finite* number of applicants to be considered.

fiscal—financial, having to do with funds: The administration's *fiscal* policy entailed tighter controls on credit.

fissure—crack: The earthquake created a *fissure* 2 feet wide down the center of the street.

flammable—capable of being kindled into flame: They were careful to keep the material away from sparks because it was *flammable.*

flaunt—to display freely, defiantly, or ostentatiously: *Flaunting* expensive jewelry in public may be an invitation to robbery.

flourish—to achieve success; to prosper or thrive: A baby needs much loving attention in order to truly *flourish.*

flout—to mock, show contempt for: He *flouted* public opinion by wearing jeans to a formal dinner.

fluctuate—to change continually from one direction to another: Stock market prices *fluctuate* unpredictably when the economy is unstable.

foray—plundering raid: The bandits made a *foray* into town to steal supplies.

foreclose—to rescind a mortgage for failure to keep up payments: The bank *foreclosed* the mortgage and repossessed the house, putting it up for sale.

foresight—a looking ahead: She had the *foresight* to realize that the restaurant would be busy, so she called ahead for reservations.

forfeit—to lose because of a fault: The team made a couple of decisive errors and so *forfeited* their lead.

formality—fixed or conventional procedure, act or custom; quality of being formal: Skipping the *formality* of a greeting, she got straight to the point. The *formality* of his attire was entirely appropriate to the ceremonious occasion.

formidable—causing fear or awe: He had a *formidable* enemy.

fortuitous—occurring by chance; bringing or happening by luck: It was *fortuitous* that I chose the winning lottery numbers.

forum—place for public business or discussion: A television interview would be the best *forum* for bringing our views to the attention of the public.

forward—to promote, send, especially to a new address: The secretary promised to *forward* the request to the person in charge.

fracture—a break, split: He sustained a compound *fracture* of the left leg.

frail—physically weak: Very old people are often *frail.*

fraud—intentional deceit for the purpose of cheating: The land development scheme was a *fraud* in which gullible investors lost tens of thousands of dollars.

fraudulent—false, deceiving for gain: His claim to be the true heir was exposed as *fraudulent.*

frenetic—frenzied: *Frenetic* studying is evident in the dormitory just before exam time.

frivolous—not serious: The atmosphere of the gathering was entirely *frivolous* as everyone got dressed up in costumes and played children's games.

fundamental—basic: Education is *fundamental* to your future security.

furious—full of madness, raging, transported with passion: I was *furious* at my cat when it scratched me.

furnish—to provide with what is needed: The army recruit will be *furnished* with uniforms and other equipment.

fuse—to blend thoroughly by melting together: The plastic parts were heated and *fused* to make a unit.

futile—trifling, useless, pointless: The entire matter was dropped because the arguments were *futile.*

G

gall—to chafe, rub sore, annoy, vex: That saddle will *gall* the horse's back.

gamut—complete range: The singer demonstrated the entire *gamut* of her vocal skills in her performance of the operetta.

garish—excessively vivid, flashy, glaring, or gaudy: His gold tuxedo was *garish.*

gauche—without social grace, tactless: It is considered *gauche* to ask acquaintances how much they earn or how much they paid for something.

genealogy—history of family descent, a family tree: They were able to trace their *genealogy* back four generations to a small village in Sicily.

generalization—induction, a general conclusion drawn from specific cases: From his experience with his own pets, he made the *generalization* that all kittens love paper bags.

generate—to beget, procreate, produce: Every animal *generates* its own species.

generic—pertaining to a race or kind: The *generic* characteristics of each animal allow us to identify its species.

genial—pleasant, friendly: The president's rotund and *genial* face made him the perfect Santa Claus.

genus—kind or class: Biologists classify these related species as members of the same *genus*.

geriatrics—science of care for the aged: Our longer life span has made the study of *geriatrics* increasingly important.

germane—pertinent, on the subject at hand: The point, though true, was not *germane* to the argument.

gist—essential part, core: That success requires effort was the *gist* of his speech.

glutton—person habitually greedy for food and drink: The man was too much of a *glutton* to stick to any diet.

goad—to drive with a stick, urge on: Although she was naturally lax, she was *goaded* on by her parents' ambitions.

gorge—to eat greedily: The neighborhood children *gorged* themselves on Halloween candy.

gracious—socially graceful, courteous, kind: A *gracious* host puts his guests at ease and is concerned only that they enjoy themselves.

graft—illegal use of position of power for gain: He was charged with *graft* in selling contracts for public works projects.

grandeur—splendor, magnificence, stateliness: The *grandeur* of the lofty mountains was admired by all.

grant—to bestow or transfer formally: The bright student was *granted* a scholarship.

graphic—described in realistic or vivid detail: The soldiers returned with *graphic* descriptions of the battle.

grapple—to seize, lay hold of, either with the hands or with mechanical devices: He *grappled* with the man who had attacked him.

gratuitous—free, voluntary, unasked for or unnecessary: Her spiteful temper expressed itself in *gratuitous* insults.

gratuity—tip: He left a *gratuity* for the cleaning crew.

gregarious—fond of company: They are a *gregarious* couple who cultivate many friendships among diverse people.

grueling—exhausting: The labor was so *grueling* that two workers fainted.

gruff—rough: His manner was so *gruff* that most of the children feared him.

guile—deceit, cunning: His brief success was due to flattery and *guile* rather than to genuine talent.

gullible—easily deceived: Naive people are often *gullible*.

gyrate—to revolve around a point, whirl: The tornado *gyrates* around a moving center.

gyroscope—rotating wheel apparatus that maintains direction regardless of position of surrounding parts: The automatic *gyroscope* holds an airplane on its course even when the machine is upside down.

H

habitable—capable of being inhabited or lived in, capable of sustaining human beings: The climate of the North Pole makes it scarcely *habitable*.

haggard—gaunt, careworn, wasted by hardship or terror: After three days of being lost on the mountain, the *haggard* campers staggered into the village.

hallucination—apparent perceiving of things not present: In her *hallucinations,* she saw bizarre faces and heard voices calling to her.

haphazard—random, without order: He studied in such a *haphazard* manner that he learned nothing.

harass—to annoy with repeated attacks: The students perpetually *harassed* the teacher with unnecessary questions.

harp—to dwell constantly on a particular subject: The employee *harped* so continually on the difficulty of his job that he was eventually fired.

harrowing—severely hurtful or trying, emotionally or physically: The survivors of the crash went through a *harrowing* ordeal before their rescue.

hazardous—dangerous: Trucks carrying *hazardous* materials such as explosives are not permitted on the bridge.

hectic—fevered, hurried, and confused: The tour turned out to be somewhat *hectic*, covering three cities in as many days.

hegemony—predominance: Hitler's aim was German *hegemony* over the world.

heinous—hateful, atrocious: The deed was so *heinous* that the perpetrator was despised for it.

herald—to announce the arrival of, usher in: Budding flowers *herald* the advent of spring.

heterodox—not orthodox, not conforming, especially in religious belief: Her *heterodox* opinions and outlandish behavior earned her a reputation as an eccentric.

heterogeneous—composed of unlike elements: Since the school favored *heterogeneous* groupings, there was a wide range of ability and achievement in every class.

hinder—to retard, slow down, prevent from moving forward: Cold weather has *hindered* the growth of the plants.

hindsight—a looking backward: With *hindsight,* I realize that everything she said to me was true, though I couldn't accept it at the time.

historical—famous in history: We can gain insights into the present by relating current to *historical* events.

holocaust—great destruction of living beings, especially by fire: As the fire raged out of control, thousands of lives were lost in the *holocaust*.

homage—respect, expression of veneration or extreme admiration: She paid *homage* to her mentor by dedicating her book to him.

homicide—killing of one person by another: Killing in self-defense is considered justifiable *homicide*.

homily—discourse on a moral problem, sermon: The judge read the boy a *homily* on his conduct before sentencing him.

homogeneous—same, uniform throughout: The entering class was fairly *homogeneous*; nearly all the students were the same age and from similar middle-class homes.

horizontal—flat, parallel to the horizon: *Horizontal* stripes are frequently unflattering because they make the figure appear wider.

hospitable—welcoming, generous to guests: It was a *hospitable* room, with a soothing color scheme and deep, comfortable chairs.

hostile—conflicting, antagonistic, expressing enmity: Many tribes were *hostile* to the white settlers, just as the settlers viewed the Indians as enemies and rivals for the land.

huddle—to crowd together, press together without order or regularity: The crowd *huddled* under the shelter to get out of the rain.

humanities—branch of learning concerned with philosophy, literature, the arts, etc., as distinguished from the sciences and sometimes the social sciences: The essence of the *humanities* is a concern with human nature, experience, and relationships.

humble—insignificant or unpretentious; not proud or self-assertive; conscious of one's shortcomings: I feel very *humble* in the presence of wealthy or powerful people.

humility—humbleness of spirit: The minister spoke to the members of his congregation with sincere *humility* about his own failings.

hyperbole—obvious exaggeration as a figure of speech: "He was as big as a house" is a common *hyperbole.*

hypertension—high blood pressure: *Hypertension* is often linked with serious diseases.

hypochondria—abnormal anxiety about health: Although no one could find anything wrong with him, his *hypochondria* drove him to get frequent checkups.

hypothesis—theory, tentative explanation yet to be proved: The *hypothesis* that life is common throughout the universe cannot as yet be supported by direct evidence.

I

identify—to establish the distinguishing characteristics of a group of individuals or activities: Can you *identify* the special skills needed by golfers?

ideologue—one who believes in and propagates a social doctrine: The *ideologue* argued that the state was more important than any individual.

idiosyncrasy—peculiar tendency of an individual: Her *idiosyncrasy* of dropping in on her friends without warning has proved embarrassing on more than one occasion.

idolatry—worship of idols or false gods: His awestruck respect for the older boy amounted to *idolatry.*

ignominy—a discrediting, disgrace: After the *ignominy* of his impeachment, he retired from public life.

illicit—not licensed: *Illicit* love is the root of many divorce actions.

illuminate—to throw light on, explain: The editor's notes *illuminated* the more obscure passages in the text.

illusion—false appearance, vision that is misleading: The optical *illusion* made the lines of equal length appear to be unequal.

illusory—unreal, only apparent: The money we hope to make is *illusory* until we have it in hand.

immolate—to kill as a sacrifice: The Buddhist monk *immolated* himself in a public square as a gesture of protest.

immune—not susceptible, protected, as from disease: An inoculation for smallpox makes one *immune* to the disease.

impalpable—not able to be felt: The seismograph can measure tremors in the earth's crust *impalpable* to humans.

impartial—not favoring one side or another: The squabbling children appealed to the baby-sitter for an *impartial* judgment.

impassioned—animated, excited, expressive of passion or ardor: The *impassioned* performance of the actor was moving and convincing.

impeach—to discredit: A president can be *impeached* for his crimes and misdemeanors. An eyewitness *impeached* the defendant's testimony.

impeccable—faultless: Successful comedy depends on *impeccable* timing.

impediment—hindrance, something that delays or stops progress: Lack of training may be an *impediment* to advancement.

impel—to drive forward, push, incite: Although she was not personally involved, her sense of justice *impelled* her to speak out.

imperative—of greatest necessity or importance: This is an emergency; it is *imperative* that I reach them at once.

imperceptible—not easily seen or observed: The daily growth of the plant was *imperceptible.*

imperil—to put in danger: The incompetence of the pilot *imperiled* the safety of all on board.

imperishable—not subject to decay, indestructible: Through thousands of years, his fame as a philosopher has been *imperishable.*

imperturbable—unshakable, calm; His *imperturbable* expression made it hard to know what he thought.

impervious—not to be penetrated or passed through: Heavy cardboard is *impervious* to light.

impetuous—impulsive, acting suddenly and without forethought: The *impetuous* girl leaped before she looked.

implement—to put into effect, to realize in practice: When they *implemented* the program, they realized that some of the planned procedures were not practicable and would have to be modified.

imply—to suggest, say without stating directly: Although they said nothing about it, their cool manner *implied* strong disapproval of the scheme.

imponderable—not capable of being weighed or measured: The results of the negotiations constitute an *imponderable* outcome at this time.

importune—to beg: Do not *importune* me for another loan; you never paid back the last one.

impotent—lacking power, helpless: The disease left him *impotent* to walk across the room.

impoverish—to make poor: She was an exceptionally effective administrator; the company has been *impoverished* by her loss.

imprecise—not precise, vague, inaccurate: The description was *imprecise* because the witness had had only a fleeting glimpse of the man.

impressive—having the power of affecting or of exciting attention and feeling: The view was so *impressive* that we'll never forget it.

imprimatur—license to publish: He was given an *imprimatur* for all the works of Benjamin Franklin.

impromptu—spontaneous, not planned or prepared in advance: *Impromptu* remarks, spoken on the spur of the moment, often tell voters more about a candidate's real opinions than carefully edited speeches do.

improvise—to make, invent, or arrange offhand, using what is conveniently available: If we do not have all of the proper ingredients, we shall have to *improvise.*

impudence—shamelessness, want of modesty, assurance accompanied by a disregard for the opinions of others: His *impudence* in denying having made the promise left us flabbergasted.

impugn—to cast doubt on someone's motives or veracity: Do not *impugn* his testimony unless you can substantiate your charges.

impunity—exemption from punishment, penalty, injury, or loss: No person should be permitted to violate the laws with *impunity.*

impute—to attribute, ascribe: The difficulties were *imputed* to the manufacturer's negligence.

inadequate—not equal to the purpose, insufficient to effect the object: He could not maintain his car because of *inadequate* funds.

inalienable—not transferable, not able to be taken away: As humans, we are endowed with certain *inalienable* rights.

inarticulate—not able to speak or speak clearly, not distinct as words: The *inarticulate* noises of the infant soon give way to recognizable words.

incarcerate—to imprison: The sheriff ordered the prisoner *incarcerated*.

inception—beginning: The scheme was foolish from its *inception*; it was no surprise when it was abandoned.

incessant—unceasing, uninterrupted, continual: The *incessant* rain kept the children indoors all day.

incidence—range of occurrence or effect: The *incidence* of reported alcoholism among teenagers is increasing.

incision—cut: The surgeon made an *incision* above the navel.

incognito—with identity concealed: The prince was traveling *incognito*.

incompatibility—inconsistency, lack of agreement, inability to get along: The *incompatibility* of their tastes made for endless disagreement.

inconsiderable—not worthy of consideration or notice, unimportant, small, trivial: The distance between Minneapolis and St. Paul is *inconsiderable*.

incontestable—not able to be disputed or denied: That oxygen is necessary for human life is *incontestable*.

inconvenience—to cause trouble or bother to; to incommode: We were *inconvenienced* but not injured by the accident directly in front of us on the highway.

incorrigible—beyond reform, not capable of being corrected: The dog's viciousness was *incorrigible*, so it had to be put to sleep.

increase—to enlarge, become greater, multiply: Class attendance *increased* by 30 percent after the flu epidemic ended.

incriminate—to accuse or implicate in a crime or fault: Picked up by the police, the suspect *incriminated* his companions by naming them as accomplices in the theft.

inculcate—to instill, to impress on the mind by repetition: From earliest childhood, they had been *inculcated* with the tenets of the community's belief.

incur—to acquire or meet with through one's own actions: The debts *incurred* in the legal proceedings were to be paid off in monthly installments.

indelible—not able to be erased, blotted out, or washed away: The form must be signed in *indelible* ink; pencil is not acceptable.

indict—to accuse formally: The grand jury *indicted* two of the company's executives.

indigenous—native to a country: The *indigenous* trees of the Rockies are mostly evergreens.

indigent—poor, penniless: The home is for the *indigent* aged who depend on the state for support.

indiscriminate—not selective: The police made *indiscriminate* arrests, taking into custody scores of people who had broken no law.

indoctrinate—to instruct in a set of principles or beliefs: Children are sent to Sunday school to be *indoctrinated* in the basic tenets of a particular religion.

indolent—lazy: An *indolent* student rarely completes assignments.

induct—to bring in, initiate a person: A volunteer must pass a physical before being *inducted* into the army.

inept—incompetent, clumsy, inefficient: The basketball team's center is tall and powerful but so physically *inept* that he frequently loses the ball.

inexhaustible—unfailing: The city has an *inexhaustible* supply of water.

inexorable—relentless: The *inexorable* forces of erosion flatten mountains.

infer—to conclude from reasoning or implication: From hints that the student dropped, the instructor *inferred* that she was having problems at home.

infiltrate—to pass through or into, especially secretly or as an enemy: The organization had been *infiltrated* by agents who monitored its membership and activities.

inflammable—easily set on fire, excited, or provoked: The tanker truck bore a warning: "Caution: *inflammable* substance!"

inflammatory—tending to arouse to anger or violence: An *inflammatory* speech incited the crowd to riot.

inflate—to blow up or swell, to increase beyond what is right or reasonable: The store is able to get away with charging *inflated* prices because of its convenient location and long hours.

infraction—violation, breaking of a law or regulation: The building inspector noted several *infractions* of the health and safety codes.

ingenuous – lacking in trickery, frank, clever: An *ingenuous* approach is often better than deception.

ingratiate—to establish in favor: He tried to *ingratiate* himself with his teacher by bringing her apples.

inherent—inborn, existing as a basic or natural characteristic: A love of hunting is *inherent* in cats.

initiate—to begin, introduce: The fraternity *initiates* new members every semester.

innocuous—harmless: His words were *innocuous* but his look could have killed.

innovation—something new, a change, as in custom or method: Computers are an *innovation* that has changed many job requirements.

innuendo—indirect intimation, hint, especially of something negative: There was an *innuendo* of threat in the phrases she chose.

inopportune—inconvenient or unseasonable; not appropriate: To suggest a change of itinerary at this time would be *inopportune*.

input—anything put in, such as power into a machine or information into a discussion: The *input* of time and money in market analysis paid off in a profitable investment.

inquest—judicial investigation: The state held an *inquest* to examine the cause of the disaster and determine whether charges should be brought against any parties.

inquisitive—curious, asking questions: Private eyes in detective fiction often get into trouble for being too *inquisitive*.

insatiable—never satisfied, always greedy: His appetite for wealth was *insatiable*; no matter how rich he became, he always craved more.

insert—to put into something else: The nurse *inserted* the needle into the patient's arm.

insidious—secretly dangerous, tending to entrap: The casino games were *insidious*; before he realized it, he had gambled away all of his savings.

insignificant—not important, too small to matter: The difference in scores between the two groups was statistically *insignificant.*

insinuate—to suggest subtly, especially something negative: When you say I remind you of Frankenstein, are you *insinuating* that I'm ugly or a monster?

inspect—to examine, view closely: She *inspected* the cloth for rips or tears.

instigate—to urge a bad action: The propaganda was designed to *instigate* a riot against the members of a rival group.

instill—to impart gradually: A skillful teacher can *instill* in children a love of learning.

instruct—to teach, direct: The employees were *instructed* in the use of the computers during the training session.

insubordinate—failing to obey: Ignoring a direct order is an *insubordinate* act with grave consequences.

insufficient—inadequate to a need, use, or purpose: The provisions are *insufficient* in quantity.

insular—pertaining to an island: Puerto Rico is an *insular* commonwealth.

insure—to make certain, guarantee: Bail is set to *insure* the defendant's appearance in court. Also: **ensure**.

intact—entire or uninjured: Though he is past 80, my father's mental faculties are *intact*.

intangible—not able to be touched or easily defined: The company's goodwill among its customers is a genuine but *intangible* asset.

integral—necessary to the whole: The woodwind section is an *integral* part of an orchestra.

integrate—to absorb into an organization or group: Company orientation programs help to *integrate* new employees into an existing organization.

intelligible—capable of being understood or comprehended; clear: The baby's gibberish is *intelligible* only to its parents.

intend—to mean, signify, plan: They *intend* to make repairs on their old car.

intensive—concentrated, intense: *Intensive* private tutoring is needed to take care of this student's reading problem.

intent—firmly directed or fixed; concentrated attention on something or some purpose; act or instance of intending: The tailor was very *intent* at his sewing machine.

intercede—to interpose in behalf of: She asked the arbitrator to *intercede* with her employer.

intercept—to cut off, meet something before it reaches its destination: The missile was *intercepted* and destroyed before it reached its target.

interpolate—to change a text by inserting new material: The editor *interpolated* the latest news into the proofs.

intractable—stubborn, unruly: An *intractable* person is slow to learn a new way of life.

intransigent—uncompromising: Their *intransigent* attitude antagonized the opposition and made negotiations difficult.

intravenous—through a vein: The patient was given *intravenous* feedings of glucose because he could not swallow.

intrepid—brave, fearless: The *intrepid* explorers stepped out onto the lunar surface.

intrinsic—belonging naturally: An *intrinsic* property of diamonds is their hardness.

inundate—to flood: When the craze was at its height, the police were *inundated* daily with reports of UFO sightings.

inventory—the stock or goods of a business, list of stock or property: The annual *inventory* check showed that several cartons of paper had been damaged by water.

investigation—close examination and observation, inquiry: The *investigation* showed that arson was the cause of the blaze.

inveterate—firmly established over a long period; habitual: The early alarm was a rude shock, for he was an *inveterate* late sleeper.

invoice—a bill, itemized list of goods sent to a buyer: The book was packed with the *invoice* charging $24, including shipping.

irate—intensely angry: The *irate* farmer shot the fox in his barnyard.

irradiate—to spread out, expose to radiant energy, heat by radiant energy: The heat from the fireplace *irradiated* the room, warming the company.

irreconcilable—unable to be harmonized: His statements about liking school were *irreconcilable* with the distaste he expressed for books in general.

irreplaceable—not able to be replaced: The painting is priceless in the sense that it is *irreplaceable*; it is the only one of its kind.

irritate—to annoy, inflame: The harsh cleansers used in the job can *irritate* the skin.

isotopes—chemical elements differing in atomic weight but having the same atomic number: Radioactive *isotopes* are used to follow the flow of oil in a pipeline.

itinerary—plan or schedule of travel: Our *itinerary* includes three days in Florence and a week in Rome.

J

jaded—wearied, sated with overuse: *Jaded* by the pleasures of the idleness, she decided to find a useful occupation.

jargon—confusing unintelligible talk, usually a specialized language used by experts: The computer programmers spoke a *jargon* filled with undecipherable acronyms.

jeopardy—risk or danger, especially the legal situation of a person on trial: Do not put your health in *jeopardy* by exposing yourself to infection needlessly. A person shall not be put in *jeopardy* twice for the same offense.

jettison—to cast overboard: They had to *jettison* the cargo to lighten the plane.

judicial—having to do with courts or judges: Chief Justice of the Supreme Court is the highest *judicial* position in the United States.

judicious—prudent: His policy was *judicious*; he got results without taking great risks.

jurisprudence—philosophy or theory of law: The courses for the most part emphasize the practical application of the law rather than *jurisprudence* or legal history.

justify—to prove by evidence, verify, absolve: The defendant was able to *justify* her statement with evidence.

juxtaposition—a placing close together: The *juxtaposition* of the Capitol and White House was avoided by the planners to emphasize the separation of the branches of government.

K

kindred—alike, related: Though from diverse backgrounds, they were *kindred* spirits, alike in intellect and ambition.

kinetic—of or caused by motion: *Kinetic* energy is produced by a stream turning a water wheel.

knead—to mix, squeeze, and press with the hands: She *kneaded* the dough before shaping it into four loaves for baking.

L

labyrinth—maze, complex and confusing arrangement: The ancient town within the city walls was a *labyrinth* of narrow, winding streets.

lacerate—to tear tissue roughly: When I fell while skating, I *lacerated* my knee.

laconic—terse, pithy: Her *laconic* replies conveyed much in few words.

lament—to bewail, mourn for: The boy *lamented* the death of his father.

languid—listless, slow, lacking energy: His *languid* walk irritated his companions, who were in a hurry.

lapse—slip, minor or temporary fault or error: I was embarrassed by a momentary *lapse* of memory when I couldn't recall her name.

larceny—legal term for theft: The shoplifter was apprehended and charged with petty *larceny*.

lassitude—feeling of weariness, languor: The *lassitude* caused by the intense heat led them to postpone their sightseeing.

laudable—praiseworthy: The girl listened to the old man's endless and repetitive stories with *laudable* patience.

lavish—to give generously or extravagantly: The doting grandfather *lavished* his grandchild with gifts.

laxity—looseness, lack of strictness: In summer, when business was slow, the manager allowed the employees some *laxity* in their hours.

legacy—something inherited: She acquired the house as a *legacy* from her grandmother.

legible—written clearly, able to be read: Please print or type if your handwriting is not easily *legible*.

legislature—lawmaking body: The federal *legislature* of the United States, the Congress, has two houses.

legitimate—lawful, genuine: The government is a *legitimate* one, duly elected by the people in free elections.

leisurely—without haste; slow: The lovers took a *leisurely* stroll around the pond.

leniency—mercy, gentleness, lack of strictness: The *leniency* of the court in suspending the sentence was well repaid by the convicted man's later contribution to the community.

lethargic—drowsy, slothful, sleepy: The convalescent moved in a *lethargic* manner.

levity—lightness of spirit, frivolity, playfulness: The party toys and silly costumes epitomized the *levity* of the occasion.

liability—debt, something disadvantageous: An older person returning to the job market may find his or her age a *liability*.

liable—legally responsible; likely, in a negative sense: If you trip and hurt yourself on the stairs because the light is out, the landlord is *liable*. She is *liable* to lose her temper when she hears the news.

liaison—connection, linking: The lead worker had served as a *liaison* between the management and union.

libel—written defamation, anything tending to lower reputation: The report was a *libel* on the man's professional standing.

limitation—restriction, finitude: There is a *limitation* on the time in which you can redeem the ticket.

lithe—gracefully flexible: Her *lithe* figure suggested that she was a dancer.

litigation—lawsuit, process of carrying on a lawsuit: As long as the estate is tied up in *litigation* by the would-be heirs, no one has use of the property.

loathe—to dislike with disgust; to detest; to hate: I *loathe* people who mistreat animals.

logical—according to reason or logic: Using the data from the experiment, she made a *logical* conclusion about the eating habits of white mice.

longevity—life span, long life: A healthy diet and exercise can increase *longevity*.

longitudinal—pertaining to length: They measured the *longitudinal* distance carefully.

loyal—faithful and unswerving in allegiance: His *loyal* friend stood by the disgraced politician.

lucid—clear, transparent: The directions were written in a style so *lucid* that a child could follow them.

lucrative—profitable: A *lucrative* enterprise is attractive to investors.

ludicrous—apt to raise laughter, ridiculous: The scene was so *ludicrous* that the audience roared with laughter.

lugubrious—excessively mournful in a way that seems exaggerated or ridiculous: The bloodhound had an endearingly *lugubrious* look.

luminous—emitting or reflecting a glowing light: In total darkness, a cat appears to have *luminous* eyes.

lurid—shocking, sensational, tastelessly violent or passionate: The cheap novel told a *lurid* tale of murder and lust.

M

machination—scheme or secret plot, especially an evil one: The *machinations* of his influential uncle landed him a well-paid job in a prestigious company.

maelstrom—whirlpool: The ship was twisted in the *maelstrom*.

magisterial—authoritative, arrogant, dogmatic: In front of a class, the normally humble man assumed a *magisterial* air.

magma—molten rock within the earth: Far beneath the solid crust, the *magma* flows.

magnanimous—noble-minded, extremely generous, especially in overlooking injury: The painter was *magnanimous* enough to praise the work of a man he detested.

magnate—important businessperson: The steel *magnate* refused to approve the consolidation.

magnitude—size: The apparent *magnitude* of the moon is greater near the horizon than at the zenith.

maladroit—tactless in personal relations: His *maladroit* remarks embarrassed the hostess.

malaise—general bodily weakness: She complained of a *malaise* that caused her to sleep 10 hours a day.

malfeasance—wrongdoing, especially in public office: The governor was accused of acts of *malfeasance*, including taking bribes.

malign—(adj.) evil, malicious, very harmful: *Malign* comments are often motivated by jealousy. (v) to speak ill of: The students often *maligned* the strict professor.

malleable—able to be shaped, adaptable: Children are more *malleable* than adults and adapt to new environments more readily.

malpractice—improper professional conduct: The surgeon was sued for *malpractice* after a sponge was found in the patient's abdomen.

mandate—specific order: Some islands are still ruled by United Nations *mandate.*

manifest—to appear, make clear, show: He claims a greater devotion to that cause than his actions *manifest.*

manual—(adj.) involving the hands: In my neighborhood bank, the tellers still use *manual* typewriters. (n.) a handbook: Each new employee is issued a *manual* of office procedures.

mar—to damage: The floor has been *marred* by scratches and scuff marks.

margin—edge, border: Cattails grow in the swampy area at the *margin* of the pond.

marquee—roof projecting from a building over the sidewalk: The theater's *marquee* protects patrons from the rain.

martinet—rigid, petty disciplinarian: The captain was a *martinet* who considered an unpolished button criminal negligence.

matriarch—mother who rules a family or clan: All important decisions were referred to the *matriarch* of the tribe.

matrix—something that gives form, as a mold: The linotype machine is equipped with a brass *matrix* for each letter so that a line can be assembled and cast in lead.

mawkish—slightly nauseating, insipidly sentimental: Her constant display of fawning affection was *mawkish.*

maximum—most: In this course, the *maximum* number of cuts allowed is six.

meager—deficient in quality and quantity; inadequate: It is impossible to feed a family of four on that *meager* salary.

median—middle, middle item in a series: In a series of seven items, the fourth is the *median.*

medicinal—having the property of healing: The plants had a high *medicinal* value.

mediocre—of average or middle quality: A *mediocre* student in high school will rank low among candidates for college.

memorandum—written reminder, informal written interoffice communication. The office manager circulated a *memorandum* outlining the procedures to be followed in the fire drill. Plural: **memoranda**.

menace—to threaten, express an intention to inflict injury: The periodic floods *menaced* the city with destruction.

mend—to improve; to correct; to reform: The naughty child was warned to *mend* her ways.

merchant—shopkeeper, one who buys and sells goods for a profit: The *merchants* who operate businesses in the mall have formed an association.

meritorious—deserving reward: Medals were awarded for *meritorious* service.

metamorphose—to transform: Two months abroad *metamorphosed* him into a man of the world.

meticulous—showing careful attention to detail, very precise: The sewing in the jacket was so *meticulous* that one could hardly see the stitches.

militant—defiant, ready to fight, especially for a cause: *Militant* in their political beliefs, they considered any compromise a sellout.

militate—to have weight or effect: A poor appearance at the interview will *militate* against your being hired.

mingle—to mix, join a group: The mayor *mingled* with the crowd at the reception, shaking hands and thanking her supporters.

miniature—very small, done on a scale smaller than usual: The *miniature* microphone could be concealed in a piece of jewelry.

minuscule—tiny, minute (after a small cursive script): Such *minuscule* particles cannot be viewed with the usual classroom microscope.

minute—tiny; very precise: The device records the presence of even *minute* amounts of radiation. The writer's *minute* attention to the refinements of style resulted in an elegantly worded essay.

misanthropy—dislike or distrust of mankind: The *misanthropy* of the hermit was known to all.

misappropriation—act of using for a wrong or illegal purpose: The *misappropriation* of the funds was uncovered and those responsible were formally charged.

miscalculate—to calculate erroneously: *Miscalculating* the distance, he fell short.

miscellany—collection of various or unlike things: The old steamer trunk contained a *miscellany* of papers, clothes, and assorted junk.

misconstruction—wrong interpretation of words or things, a mistaking of the true meaning: His *misconstruction* of the situation caused him to act unjustly.

misdemeanor—a misbehaving, a minor legal offense: The *misdemeanor* resulted in a $50 fine.

misnomer—wrong or inaccurate name: At this season, Muddy River is a *misnomer*; the waters are sweet and clear.

mitigate—to lessen, make milder: He sought to *mitigate* their grief with soothing words.

modicum—a little, a small quantity: The girl had only a *modicum* of learning, having never finished the fifth grade.

modulation—adaptation or variance in pitch, intensity, volume, musical key: The mother told the noisy children to *modulate* their voices.

molest—to disturb, annoy, bother: The children were warned not to *molest* the bulldog.

mollify—to soothe, placate: The irate customer was *mollified* by the manager's prompt action and apology.

monetary—pertaining to money, consisting of money, financial: A penny is the smallest *monetary* unit in this country.

monitor—to watch over, check on: An office was set up to *monitor* all radio broadcasts originating within the country.

monolith—large piece of stone: The obelisk in New York's Central Park is a *monolith* brought here from Egypt.

montage—picture made up of pictures or material from several sources: The illustration was a *montage* of various urban scenes.

morale—level of spirits, mental or emotional condition: After a landslide victory at the polls, *morale* in the party was at a peak.

morass—swamp, bog, messy or troublesome state: The application became mired in a *morass* of paperwork; there was no response for several weeks.

mores—customs, principles of conduct of a culture: The *mores* of any group are enforced by indoctrination and social pressure to conform.

moribund—dying: The *moribund* tree put out fewer and fewer leaves each spring.

morose—gloomy, sulking, unreasonably unhappy: The boy was *morose* for days over his failure to get tickets for the concert.

mortgage—to pledge property as security for a loan: Few people can afford to buy a house without taking a *mortgage* on it.

motivation—reason for doing something: The *motivation* for her questions was not mere curiosity but a genuine desire to help.

motley—variegated, composed of clashing elements: A *motley* crowd attended the county fair.

muddle—to confuse or stupefy: The liquor had gotten him badly *muddled*.

mundane—worldly, humdrum, unexciting: The film was undistinguished, a *mundane* exercise in horror movie clichés.

mutation—change, especially a sudden one: He deplored the *mutations* of fortune that had altered his position so drastically.

mutilate—to cut up, damage severely: The computer cannot read a *mutilated* card.

mutiny—forcible resistance to lawful authority; revolt; rebellion: The sailors threatened their overbearing captain with *mutiny*.

myopia—nearsightedness: The optometrist prescribed glasses for the patient's *myopia*.

N

nadir—lowest point: Enrollment hit its *nadir* last year, but it has been rising slowly since.

naive—unsophisticated, artless: He was *naive* as the result of a sheltered life in the country.

nape—back of the neck: The collar chafed his *nape*.

nascent—coming into being; being born; beginning to develop: I am afraid that I have a *nascent* cold.

nauseate—to cause disgust and nausea to: Food *nauseates* the patient.

navigation—the science of locating position and plotting course of ships; ship traffic or commerce: The invention of radar was a wonderful *navigational* aid.

nebulous—hazy, indistinct: He had a *nebulous* theory about how life on Earth began.

necessitate—to render unavoidable, compel: Sickness *necessitated* a long hospital stay.

negate—to make nothing, undo, or make ineffective: The witness's full confession *negated* the need for further questions.

neglectful—careless, heedless: Because he was *neglectful* of his duties as principal, he was asked to resign by the board of education.

negligible—too small or insignificant to be worthy of consideration: The difference in their ages is *negligible*.

negotiate—to bargain, confer with the intent of reaching an agreement: As long as both sides are willing to *negotiate* in good faith, a strike can be avoided.

nepotism—favoritism shown to a relative: The civil service system helped to do away with *nepotism* in hiring.

neuralgia—pain along the course of a nerve: *Neuralgia* is often confused with rheumatism.

neurotic—suffering from or typical of neurosis, a range of mental disorders less severe than psychosis: Hysterical pain—physical discomfort without organic cause—is a common *neurotic* symptom.

neutralize—to reduce to a state of indifference between different parties, make inactive: The marine territory was *neutralized* by the nations through a treaty.

node—knot or protuberance: A *node* appears at the joints of a plant.

nomadic—roaming from place to place without a fixed home: People who enjoy adventure may choose a *nomadic* lifestyle.

nomenclature—names of things in any art or science, whole vocabulary of technical terms appropriate to any particular branch of science: The *nomenclature* used in medical science is almost entirely derived from Latin.

nonchalant—indifferent, cool, unconcerned: The woman acted in a *nonchalant* manner, pretending not to notice the celebrities.

noncompliance—failure to comply: His *noncompliance* with the terms of the contract forced them to sue.

nonsensical—meaningless, characterized by nonsense: Until analyzed and interpreted, dreams often seem *nonsensical*.

normal—regular, average, usual: The doctor found that her blood pressure and temperature were *normal*.

notary—person empowered to attest signatures, certify documents, etc.: The signature is valid if witnessed by a *notary*.

notify—to let know, inform: Applicants will be *notified* of the results by mail.

notorious—famous in an unfavorable way: The official was *notorious* among his associates for failing to keep appointments.

novice—person new to a job or activity, someone inexperienced: A *novice* in the job, she needed more time than an experienced worker to complete the same tasks.

noxious—harmful, injurious, unwholesome: The *noxious* fumes from the refinery poisoned the air.

null and void—legal expression for not valid, without legal force: If it is not properly signed, the will may be declared *null and void*.

nullify—to make void or without effect: The new contract *nullifies* their previous agreement.

numerical—expressed in or involving numbers or a number system: Please arrange all of your test papers in *numerical* order.

numerous—consisting of great numbers of units or individuals: The grains of sand on the beach are too *numerous* to count.

O

obesity—excessive fatness: Her *obesity* was due to her love of rich foods.

obituary—account of the death of a person: Newspapers keep files on famous people to use when an *obituary* is published.

objective—(adj) unbiased, not influenced by personal involvement, detached: It is extremely difficult to be *objective* about one's own weaknesses. (n) aim, goal: Our *objective* is greater efficiency; we must study the possible means to that goal.

obligatory—required, morally or legally binding: He feels nothing in common with his family, yet he makes an *obligatory* visit to them once or twice a year.

obliterate—to demolish, destroy all trace of: The building had been *obliterated*; we could not even be sure exactly where it had stood.

oblivious—so preoccupied as not to notice: The patron, absorbed in her reading, was *oblivious* to the librarian's question.

obnoxious—odious, hateful, offensive, repugnant: They left because of the *obnoxious* remarks by the speaker.

obscure—dim, murky, not easily seen or understood: Despite attempts at interpretation, the meaning of the passage remains *obscure*.

obsequious—servile, overly willing to obey: Their *obsequious* obedience to the conquerors turned our stomachs.

observable—able to be seen, noticeable: There has been no *observable* change in the patient's condition.

obsess—to beset, haunt the mind: He was *obsessed* with the idea that he was being followed.

obsolete—outmoded, no longer in use or appropriate: Since several offices have been relocated, the old directory is *obsolete*.

obstacle—hindrance, something that bars a path or prevents progress: She refused to think of her handicap as an *obstacle* to a fulfilling career.

obtain—to gain; to attain or get by means of effort or planned action; to reach or achieve: *Obtain* a Social Security number by applying for one at your local Social Security office.

obtrude—to enter when not invited or welcome: It was unfair to *obtrude* upon their privacy.

obtuse—not sharp or pointed; slow to understand or perceive; dull or insensitive: The bigot feels no sympathy for others because of his *obtuse* perception.

obvious—self-evident: The truth was *obvious* to the well-informed.

occasionally—sometimes, from time to time: We go to the theater *occasionally*.

occidental—pertaining to the Western Hemisphere: The finest gems come from *occidental* countries, according to some experts.

ocular—of the eye: An *ocular* injury impaired her vision temporarily.

odious—deserving hatred or repugnance: Publicly comparing the talents of children is an *odious* habit.

omit—to leave out, pass by, neglect: He *omitted* an important passage when he read his speech.

omnipotent—all-powerful: By the end of the third match, the champion felt *omnipotent*.

onerous—difficult and unpleasant, burdensome: The work was so *onerous*, she often thought of quitting.

onus—burden, responsibility: The *onus* of proof is on the accuser; the defendant is presumed innocent until proven guilty.

operational—in working order, able to be operated: The elevator will not be *operational* until tomorrow; it is being repaired.

opportune—suitable or appropriate: Since I have just made an impressive sale, this is an *opportune* time to ask for a raise.

opprobrium—reproach for disgraceful conduct, infamy: He deserved all the *opprobrium* he received for turning his back on his friend.

optimum—best for a purpose, most favorable: Under *optimum* conditions of light and moisture, the plant will grow to more than 3 feet.

option—(v) to purchase the right to buy or sell something within a specified time: For a thousand dollars she *optioned* the novel for one year, wrote a script, and sold it to the movies. (n) choice, power of right to choose: Before acting, consider your *options*.

optional—not required, open to choice: Air conditioning is *optional*; its cost is not included in the sticker price.

ordinance—city statute: The city council passed an *ordinance* requiring all dogs to be leashed.

ordure—filth, excrement: As soon as he entered the hut, he could smell the stench of *ordure*.

orifice—opening into a cavity: The surgeon worked through an *orifice* below the ribs.

origin—beginning, source: The *origin* of the irrational fear was in a childhood trauma.

oscillate—to swing in regular motion: The pendulum continued to *oscillate*, but the clock hands did not move.

ostensible—avowed, apparent: The *ostensible* purpose of the withdrawal was to pay a debt, but actually the money was used for entertainment.

ostentatious—pretentious, showy: Some people think large diamonds are too *ostentatious*.

ostracize—to exclude from a group by common consent: The family of the gangster was *ostracized* by the community.

outcome—result, end: The *outcome* of the race was never in doubt.

P

pacific—calm, tranquil, placid: On vacation, I prefer a *pacific* experience to a busy one.

pacify—to make peaceful; to soothe; to settle; to subdue: Perhaps a bottle of juice will *pacify* the crying baby.

painstaking—very careful or diligent: The search for the lost ring was long and *painstaking*.

palliate—to make an offense seem less grave: She attempted to *palliate* her error by explaining the circumstances that led to her mistake.

palpitate—to beat rapidly, flutter, or move with slight throbs: Her heart *palpitated* with fright.

pamper—to gratify to the full, coddle, spoil: She *pampered* her pet dog by feeding him steaks.

pamphlet—very brief, paperbound book or treatise: The library has a pile of *pamphlets* explaining how to apply for Social Security.

panacea—remedy for all ills: Aspirin was once considered the *panacea* for all kinds of pain.

panic—sudden and overwhelming terror, exaggerated alarm: When the children heard the noise, they fled the old house in *panic*.

panoramic—offering a broad or unlimited view: From the summit of the mountain one has a *panoramic* view of the whole range.

paradigm—model, pattern to be copied: The teacher handed out a sample letter as a *paradigm* of the correct form.

paradox—internal contradiction, statement that appears to contradict itself: "If he doesn't watch his health, he's going to wake up dead" is an example of a *paradox*.

paralyze—to unnerve or render ineffective: The catastrophe *paralyzed* the community.

paraphrase—a rewording, repetition of the meaning of something in different words: To *paraphrase* someone's work without acknowledging the source of one's information is a form of plagiarism.

parasite—person or creature who lives at the expense of another without giving anything in return: Fleas are common *parasites* on cats and dogs.

parity—comparative equality: Municipal employees demanded wage *parity* with workers in the private sector.

parochial—narrow in viewpoint: Having no acquaintance with other cultures and ways of life made his outlook *parochial*.

parole—conditional release, release from prison before full sentence is served: Freed on *parole*, the convict was required to report periodically to an officer assigned to his case.

parsimonious—frugal or stingy: The extravagant person may consider the average man to be *parsimonious*.

partially—in part: Bald tires were *partially* responsible for the skid; slick road conditions also contributed.

participate—to take part in: At the meet, all contestants will *participate* in the opening ceremonies.

partisan—devoted or committed to a party or cause, especially blindly or unreasonably so: *Partisan* loyalty can no longer be taken for granted; voters are now attracted to individuals more than to parties.

partition—division into parts: The *partition* of the staff permits efficient assignment of tasks.

passionate—expressing intense feeling; enthusiastic; intense; easily angered: The *passionate* young musician practiced 5 hours each day.

patent—(adj) obvious, easily seen: The promise of tax relief was a *patent* attempt to win last-minute support from the voters. (n) exclusive right, as to a product or invention: The company's *patent* on the formula expires after a certain number of years.

peculiar—odd, special, unique, not ordinary: The fragrance is *peculiar* to roses; no other flower smells the same.

pecuniary—financial: She had no *pecuniary* interest in the project.

pedantic—making a needless display of learning: The *pedantic* lecturer made several allusions to literary works that his audience had no acquaintance with.

peevish—fretful, hard to please: The girl was unpopular because she was so *peevish*; she was always complaining about something.

pejorative—disparaging: Calling a man a rat is *pejorative*.

penal—concerning legal punishment: The *penal* code defines crimes and their legal penalties.

penchant—strong inclination: He has a *penchant* for making friends.

pending—waiting to be decided: Our petition is still *pending*; we don't know what will be decided.

penetrate—to pierce or to pass into or through: The stiff cloth was hard to *penetrate* with an ordinary needle.

pension—regular payments to someone who has fulfilled certain requirements: After twenty years of service, she retired on a full *pension*.

per capita—for each person: The country has a *per capita* income of under $800.

perceive—to feel, comprehend, note, understand: I *perceived* that the dog was harmless in spite of his barking.

perception—act of receiving impressions by the senses: *Perception* is that act of the mind whereby the mind becomes aware of anything, such as hunger or heat.

peremptory—imperative, dictatorial: He announced his opinions in a *peremptory* tone that was extremely offensive to his listeners.

perforate—to make holes in: The top of the box had been *perforated* to allow the air to circulate.

peripheral—of an edge or boundary: People who notice people almost behind them have excellent *peripheral* vision.

permeable—capable of having fluids or gases pass through: Most clay dishes are *permeable* unless glazed.

permutation—rearrangement of the order of a group of items: The sequences CBA and BCA are *permutations* of ABC.

pernicious—causing much harm: Excessive drinking is a *pernicious* habit.

perpendicular—in an up-and-down direction, vertical, upright, at a right angle: The lamp post, having been grazed by the truck, was no longer *perpendicular*.

perpetrate—to do something evil, to commit, as a crime: The actors *perpetrated* the hoax in an attempt to gain publicity.

perquisite—benefit of a position other than salary: A chauffeured car is one of the *perquisites* of a commissioner's position.

persist—to continue, especially against opposition: Despite the rebuffs, he *persisted* in his efforts to befriend the disturbed youngster.

pertinent—relevant, concerning the matter at hand: Since those circumstances were vastly different, that example is not *pertinent* to this case.

perturb—to disturb greatly; to disquiet: We were greatly *perturbed* by strange noises in the night.

peruse—to read carefully, study: She *perused* the text, absorbing as much information as she could.

petty—small, trivial, unimportant, small-minded: Don't bother the supervisor with *petty* problems but try to handle them yourself.

petulance—petty fretfulness, peevishness: Her *petulance* in demanding her own way reminded me of a 2-year-old's behavior in demanding parental attention.

picturesque—having a rough, unfamiliar, or quaint natural beauty: The mountains with their rugged crags and steep ravines present a *picturesque* landscape.

pinnacle—peak, acme: She had reached such a *pinnacle* of fame that everywhere in the country her name was a household word.

piquant—stimulating the sense of taste, agreeably pungent: Mustard and chutney are both *piquant* in different ways.

pique—fit of resentment: His *pique* at being scolded lasted all day.

placate—to soothe the anger of, pacify: A quick temper is often easily *placated*.

placid—peaceful, calm: The drug had relieved her anxiety, leaving her in a *placid* mood.

platitude—trite remark: He spouts *platitudes* constantly revealing that he has no ideas of his own.

plausible—seeming credible, likely, trustworthy: Since his clothes were soaked, his story of falling into the creek seemed *plausible*.

plenary—full, fully attended: The issue was so serious that the committee called a *plenary* meeting of the board to decide on a course of action.

plethora—oversupply: The *plethora* of oil supplies caused a drop in gasoline prices.

pliable—flexible, able to bend, readily influenced, yielding: Having no preconceived opinion on the matter, we were *pliable*, ready to be swayed by a forceful speech.

podium—raised platform, as for use by speakers or musical conductors: The poet stepped to the *podium* to address the audience.

pogrom—organized massacre of a certain class of people: The Russian *pogroms* in the 1880s forced a huge exodus of Jews.

poignant—having sharp emotional appeal, moving: Reading the *poignant* story, he began to cry.

polemics—art of disputing: She is an expert at *polemics,* so a career in law seemed to suit her.

polymer—compound of high molecular weight: *Polymers* are basic to the creation of plastics.

pontificate—to speak pompously: He would rise slowly, *pontificate* for half an hour, and sit down without having said a thing we didn't know before.

portable—able to be carried easily: Laptops are *portable* computers.

portentous—foreshadowing future events, especially somber ones: The thunderstorm that broke as we were leaving seemed *portentous,* but in fact the weather was lovely for the rest of the trip.

posterity—succeeding generations: Many things we build today are for *posterity.*

postmark—official mark on a piece of mail showing the post office from which it was delivered and the date: Although the letter had been written in Tulsa, the *postmark* showed that it had been mailed from Omaha.

potent—powerful or effective in action: Antibiotics are *potent* medicine that should be administered with care.

potential—possible, not yet realized: If she qualifies for the promotion, her *potential* earnings for the next year might be close to $50,000.

pragmatic—concerned with practical values: He has a *pragmatic* mind, willing to try whatever promises to get results.

precarious—insecure: The cat had a *precarious* perch on the window ledge.

precedent—similar earlier event, especially one used as a model or justification for present action: The lawyer's brief argued that the legal *precedents* cited by the opposition were not relevant because of subsequent changes in the law.

precipitous—steep like a precipice: The road had a *precipitous* drop on the south side.

precise—exact: The coroner could not determine the *precise* time of murder by examining the victim.

preclude—to make impossible: Obeying the speed limit would *preclude* my getting home in 5 minutes.

precocious—advanced in development: *Precocious* children should be given enriched programs of study to develop their talents.

precursor—predecessor, forerunner: The Continental Congress was the *precursor* of our Senate and House of Representatives.

predatory—plundering, hunting: The hawk is a *predatory* bird.

predecessor—one who has preceded or gone before another in a position or office: In his inaugural address, the new president of the association praised the work done by his *predecessor.*

predicament—troublesome or perplexing situation from which escape seems difficult: Having promised to balance the budget, cut taxes, and increase defense spending, the newly-elected president found himself in a hopeless *predicament.*

predilection—preference, liking: She had a *predilection* for spicy food.

predominantly—for the most part: Although there are a few older students, the class is *predominantly* made up of 18-year-olds.

preeminent—outstanding: Notable above all others, she is the *preeminent* authority in her field.

preempt—to exclude others by taking first: Regularly scheduled programs were *preempted* by a news bulletin about the storm.

prejudiced—biased, judging in advance without adequate evidence: Since I have never liked Westerns, I was *prejudiced* against the film before I ever saw it.

preliminary—going before the main event or business, introductory: A few easy *preliminary* questions put the applicant at ease.

premature—not yet mature or ripe, happening too soon: As she got to know him better, she decided that her initial judgment of him had been *premature.*

premeditation—act of meditating beforehand, previous deliberation: The *premeditation* of the crime was what made it so hideous.

premise—proposition or idea on which an argument or action is based: I waited to call on the *premise* that they wouldn't be home until evening.

preoccupied—having one's thoughts elsewhere, inattentive: *Preoccupied* by her dilemma, she missed her stop on the train.

preposterous—very absurd: The idea of the president's visiting our class was *preposterous.*

prerogative—exclusive privilege or right: As the child's guardian, she had the *prerogative* of deciding whether he would attend private or public school.

prescribe—to recommend, especially in a professional capacity: For the headache, the physician *prescribed* aspirin.

presume—to accept as true without proof; to anticipate or take for granted, overstep bounds: An accused person is *presumed* innocent until proven guilty. I was furious that she had *presumed* to take the car without permission.

prevalent—current, widely found, common: Feelings of anger and helplessness are *prevalent* among the voters in that district.

preventive—aiming to prevent or keep from happening: *Preventive* measures must be taken to guard against malaria.

previous—occurring before in time or order: The *previous* month's electric bill included only twenty-nine days.

primary—first, most important: Our *primary* goal is to train people for jobs that are actually available; other aspects of the program are secondary.

prime—of highest quality, value, or importance: The *prime* reason for donating to charity should be to help others.

principal—main, most important: The *principal* city economically is also the most populous in the state.

prior—earlier, and therefore usually taking precedence: The director will not be able to meet with you today due to a *prior* engagement.

privileged—exempt from usual conditions, receiving special benefit; not to be made known, confidential: Only a few *privileged* outsiders have been permitted to observe the ceremony. Since communications between spouses are *privileged,* a man cannot be compelled to testify against his wife.

probability—likelihood: The *probability* that your plane will crash is practically nil.

probation—period of testing or evaluation: After a week's *probation,* the employee was hired permanently.

proceed—to go forward, continue: Because of numerous interruptions, the work *proceeded* slowly.

proclaim—to announce loudly, publicly, and with conviction: When the victory was announced, a holiday was *proclaimed* and all work ground to a halt.

proclivity—tendency: The child has a *proclivity* for getting into trouble.

procrastinate—to delay doing something, put off without reason: Since you'll have to get it done eventually, you might as well stop *procrastinating* and get started.

procure—to get, obtain, cause to occur: At the last minute, the convict's attorney *procured* a stay of execution.

prodigal—extravagant, spending freely: She is more *prodigal* with her advice than with financial aid.

prodigious—very large: He had a *prodigious* nose and a tiny mouth.

profit—valuable return, income, or gain: We hope to realize a nice *profit* from the sale of our home.

profligate—utterly immoral: The *profligate* son was a regular source of income for his father's attorney.

prohibit—to prevent by authority; to forbid: The law *prohibits* unleashed dogs on the beach.

prolong—to draw out to greater length: The treatment *prolongs* life but cannot cure the disease, which is terminal.

promote—to help bring about; to raise or advance to a higher position: The object of many service clubs is to *promote* athletic events for the handicapped.

prompt—quick, following immediately: Correspondents appreciate *prompt* replies to their inquiries.

promulgate—to announce publicly as a law or doctrine: The revolutionary government *promulgated* some of the promised reforms.

proofread—to read and mark corrections: Always *proofread* and correct your work before you turn it in.

proper—suitable, appropriate: It is *proper* to write a letter of thanks to someone who has given you a present.

proportionate—in correct proportion or relation of amount, fairly distributed: An area's representation in the House of Representatives is *proportionate* to its population.

proscribe—to outlaw, forbid by law: Theft is *proscribed* mostly by state law.

prosecute—to carry on legal proceedings against: In return for information, the attorney general has agreed not to *prosecute* your client.

prospectus—booklet describing a business enterprise, investment or forthcoming publication distributed to prospective buyers: The *prospectus* for the real estate development was mailed to potential investors.

prosper—to thrive, do well, grow richer: An expensive suit and a new car suggested that the man's business was *prospering*.

protagonist—leading character: Mike Hammer is the *protagonist* of a whole series of detective stories.

protocol—rigid code of correct procedure, especially in diplomacy: *Protocol* demands that we introduce the ambassador before the special envoy; to fail to do so would be interpreted as an insult.

prototype—original model, first example: Homer's Iliad became the *prototype* for much of the later epic poetry of Europe.

protract—to draw out in time or space, lengthen: The jury's deliberations were *protracted* by confusion over a point of law.

provisional—temporary, for the time being only: The *provisional* government stepped down after the general elections.

provocation—a provoking, a cause for resentment or attack: The attack, coming without *provocation*, took them by surprise.

proximity—nearness: The *proximity* of the shopping mall is a great advantage to those residents who don't drive.

psychic—of the mind, acting outside of known physical laws: He claimed special *psychic* powers, including the ability to foresee the future.

punctuality—being on time: The train had an excellent record for *punctuality*; it almost always arrived precisely at 8:15.

purchase—to buy: We need to *purchase* or borrow a tent before we can go camping.

putative—supposed, reputed: Her *putative* wealth was an exaggeration of what she really owned.

Q

quadrennial—lasting four years, occurring once in four years: The *quadrennial* games were anticipated eagerly.

qualification—that which makes one qualified or eligible: The applicant's *qualifications* for the position are a degree in library science and two years' experience in a small branch library.

quandary—doubt, uncertainty, state of difficulty or perplexity: She was in a *quandary* because the problem was so complex.

quantity—amount: Speeding up the process would result in an increased *quantity* but a poorer quality.

queasy—causing or affected by nausea; squeamish: The thought of riding the subway at night makes me *queasy*.

quench—to extinguish, put out: She *quenched* the flames with water.

query—to question: He *queried* the witness about his alibi.

quirk—turn, twist, caprice: A sudden *quirk* of fancy caused her to change her mind.

quiver—to shake, tremble, shudder: The dog *quivered* with excitement.

quorum—minimum number of members that must be present for an assembly to conduct business: No votes may be taken until there are enough representatives present to constitute a *quorum*.

quota—proportional share: The school had an unwritten *quota* system that set limits on the proportion of applicants accepted from different geographical areas.

quote—to cite word for word, as a passage from some author; to name or repeat: He *quoted* the words of Woodrow Wilson in his acceptance speech.

quotient—in arithmetic, the number resulting from the division of one number by another: The *quotient* of ten divided by five is two.

R

rabid—furious, raging; suffering from rabies: The *rabid* animal was put to sleep before it could bite anyone.

radiation—divergence in all directions from a point, especially of energy: Solar *radiation* is the *radiation* of the sun as estimated from the amount of energy that reaches the earth.

rambunctious—wild; marked by uncontrollable exuberance; unruly: When the children get together with all of their cousins, the group tends to get *rambunctious*.

ramification—breakdown into subdivisions, a branching out: The *ramifications* of the subject were complex.

rampant—springing or climbing unchecked, rank in growth: The *rampant* growth of the weeds made the lawn look extremely unsightly.

ramshackle—tumbling down, shaky, out of repair: It was impossible to be comfortable in such a *ramshackle* house.

rancor—malice, ill will, anger: In spite of the insults of his opponent, the man remained calm and spoke without *rancor*.

randomly—in an unplanned or haphazard way, without order or pattern: The papers had been strewn *randomly* about the room.

rapidity—speed: The *rapidity* with which her hands flew over the piano keys was too great to follow with the eye.

ratify—to give formal approval to: The proposed amendment must be *ratified* by the states before it can become law.

ratio—proportion, fixed relation of number or amount between two things: The *ratio* of women to men in middle-level positions in the firm is only one to seven.

rationale—rational basis, explanation or justification supposedly based on reason: They defended their discrimination with the *rationale* that women were incompetent physically to handle the job.

raze—to destroy down to the ground, as a building: Buildings in the path of the highway construction will be *razed*.

reactionary—extremely conservative, marked by opposition to present tendencies and advocating a return to some previous or simpler condition: The pamphlet expressed a *reactionary* hatred of innovation and a nostalgia for "the good old days."

rebuff—a snub, repulse, blunt or impolite refusal: When overtures of friendship are met with *rebuff*, they are not likely to be renewed.

rebuke—to reprimand, criticize sharply: He *rebuked* the puppy in stern tones for chewing up the chair.

rebuttal—contradiction, reply to a charge or argument: Each side was allowed 5 minutes for *rebuttal* of the other side's arguments.

recalcitrant—stubborn, refusing to obey: A *recalcitrant* child is difficult to teach.

recapitulate—to mention or relate in brief, summarize: The abstract *recapitulated* the main points of the argument.

recede—to go back or away: The waters *receded* and left the beach covered with seaweed.

receptive—able and tending to receive and accept, open to influence: The manager, unsatisfied with the store's appearance, was *receptive* to the idea of a major remodeling.

recessive—tending to recede or not make itself felt: The characteristic encoded in a *recessive* gene may be passed on to an individual's offspring even though it is not apparent in the individual.

recipient—one who receives: The *recipient* of the award had been chosen from among 200 candidates.

reciprocal—done in return, affecting both sides, mutual: The United States has *reciprocal* trade agreements with many nations.

reckless—not thinking of consequences, heedless, causing danger: People who feel they have nothing to lose often become *reckless*.

recondite—profound; obscure; concealed: Anthropologists try to discover the *recondite* facts about human origins.

reconsider—to think over again: When she refused the appointment, the committee asked whether she would *reconsider* her decision if more money was offered.

recourse—seeking of aid or remedy in response to some action or situation: Unless you correct this error immediately, I will have no *recourse* but to complain to the manager.

recreation—relaxation, play: Physical *recreation* often relieves tension and improves the emotional outlook.

recriminate—to return accusation for accusation: They *recriminated* constantly over the most trivial setbacks, each blaming the other whenever anything went wrong.

rectitude—honesty, integrity, strict observance of what is right: Her unfailing *rectitude* in business dealings made her well trusted among her associates.

recumbent—lying down: The painting depicted the goddess *recumbent* on a sumptuous couch.

recuperate—to become well, get better: It is best to stay home from work until you have *recuperated* completely.

recur—to happen again: Unless social conditions are improved, the riots are bound to *recur*.

redeem—to save, ransom, free by buying back: Though the film is boring in parts, it is *redeemed* by a gripping finale.

redress—compensation for a wrong done: The petitioners asked the state for a *redress* of grievances for which they had no legal recourse.

reduce—diminish in size, amount, extent, or number: His campaign included a promise to *reduce* taxes.

redundant—wordy, repeating unnecessarily: The expressions "more preferably" and "continue to remain" are *redundant*.

referral—a being referred from one person or agency to another, as for employment: A *referral* service arranged appointments for people who have excellent clerical skills.

refinement—act of clearing from extraneous matter, purification: The *refinement* of the metals freed them from the impurities that made them unfit for commercial use.

refrain—to keep from doing something, to not do: Considerate parents *refrain* from criticizing their children in front of others.

refuse—to decline to accept; reject: If you *refuse* this assignment, you may not be offered another.

regal—pertaining to a monarch, royal: He had a *regal* air that impressed even those who knew him for an imposter.

regimen—routine manner of living: The *regimen* of army life bored him.

rehabilitate—to restore to a former state or capacity: The stated object of the program is to *rehabilitate* accident victims.

reimburse—to refund, pay back: The company found it difficult to *reimburse* the salesman for all his expenses.

reiterate—to repeat: The instructions were *reiterated* before each new section of the test.

related—connected by some common relationship: The circumstances of this fire are closely *related* to those of the hotel fire that occurred last week.

relegate—to transfer to get rid of, assign to an inferior position: The chief *relegated* the policeman to a suburban beat.

relevant—concerning the matter at hand, to the point, related: Her experience in government is *relevant* to her candidacy; her devotion to her family is not.

relinquish—to give up, hand over: The aunt *relinquished* custody of the child to its mother.

reluctant—opposing or unwilling: The bank is *reluctant* to give further loans until all obligations are paid.

reminisce—to remember, talk about the past: When old friends get together, they love to *reminisce*.

remit—to pay, to send payment: The invoice was *remitted* by check; you should be receiving it shortly.

remuneration—reward, payment, as for work done: Health benefits are part of the *remuneration* that goes with the position.

renege—to go back on a promise or agreement: Their assurances of good faith were hollow; they *reneged* on the agreement almost at once.

renounce—to give up or disown, usually by formal statement: The nation was urged to *renounce* its dependence on imports and to buy more American products.

replenish—to supply again, to make full or complete again something that has been depleted: Some natural resources, such as lumber, can be *replenished*.

reprehensible—deserving rebuke or blame: Conduct that selfishly endangers the safety of others is *reprehensible*.

repress—to subdue, hold back, keep down, keep from expression or consciousness: We could not *repress* a certain nervousness as the plane bumped along the runway.

reprieve—postponement of some evil, such as punishment: You have a *reprieve*; the test has been put off for a week.

reprimand—severe criticism, especially a formal rebuke by someone in authority: Since it was a first offense, the judge let the teenager off with a *reprimand*.

reprisal—injury in return for injury: The enemy launched a raid in *reprisal* for the night attack.

reprove—to censure, rebuke, find fault with: The instructor *reproved* the student for failing to hand in the assignments on time.

repudiate—to refuse to accept, reject: The candidate *repudiated* the endorsement of the extremist group.

request—to ask for: The students *requested* a meeting with the college president to discuss the new policy.

requisite—required, necessary: Employees may take vacation time as soon as they have worked the *requisite* number of weeks.

requisition—formal written order or request: The office manager sent in a *requisition* for another desk and chair.

requite—to give in, return, to repay: The man's sympathy and good humor were *requited* by the enthusiastic affection of his nephews.

rescind—to cancel formally or take back: They *rescinded* their offer of aid when they became disillusioned with the project.

reserve—to keep back or save for use at a later time; to set aside for the use of a particular person: The runner had *reserved* energy for a burst of speed in the final lap. Call the restaurant to *reserve* a table for four.

residence—place where a person lives, fact of living in a place: According to the phone company, that number is a *residence*, not a business.

residue—something left over, remainder: A *residue* of coffee grounds was left at the bottom of the cup.

resilient—able to spring back: The down pillow was still *resilient* after years of use.

resplendent—very bright, shining: She was *resplendent* in the jewelry and sequined dress.

respondent—person who responds or answers: Several *respondents* refused to answer some of the questions in the survey.

response—a reply or reaction: His *response* to my question was another question.

restitution—restoration to a rightful owner, reparation for an injury: He agreed to make *restitution* for the money he had stolen.

restrict—to confine, keep within limits: Use of the computer room is *restricted* to authorized personnel.

resume—to begin again after an interruption: The courtroom proceedings *resumed* after an hour's recess for lunch.

resurgent—rising again: The *resurgent* energy of youth kept him studying for hours.

resuscitate—to bring back to life: Artificial respiration was used to *resuscitate* the swimmer.

retain—to keep: Throughout the grueling day, she had managed somehow to *retain* her sense of humor.

retaliate—to give injury for injury: The boxer *retaliated* for the punch with a stunning blow to the head.

retard—to slow: Drugs were successfully used to *retard* the progress of the disease.

reticent—restrained in speech, unwilling to talk: People are *reticent* to confess such anxieties for fear of appearing weak.

retroactive—applying to what is past: A law cannot be made *retroactive*; it can only apply to future actions.

retrogress—to go backward, lose ground: Because of the devastation of the recent earthquakes, living conditions in the region have *retrogressed*.

reveal—to make known, display: His dishonesty was *revealed* during the trial.

reverence—feeling of deep respect or awe, as for something sacred: The great novelist was disconcerted by the *reverence* with which her students greeted her most casual remark.

revision—a correction or a change; revised form or version: A playwright makes many *revisions* to the script before the play is produced.

revive—to come or bring back to life: A cool drink and a bath *revived* her spirits.

revolutionize—to change fundamentally or completely: The internet has *revolutionized* research procedures.

rheostat—electrical resistor with changeable resistance: A *rheostat* is used to make lights dimmer.

rife—widespread, prevalent, filled with: The city was *rife* with rumors that a coup was imminent.

robust—hardy, strong, healthy: Her *robust* health was apparent in her springy walk and glowing skin.

rouse—to stir up; to excite or to awaken: Let us *rouse* the citizenry to a new era of patriotism.

rubicund—ruddy; reddish: The heavy drinker has a bulbous, *rubicund* nose.

rue—to be sorry for, regret: He *rued* the day he made that mistake.

ruminate—to chew the cud; to think over at leisure: A cow *ruminates* after it eats. I will *ruminate* on your proposal and let you know my decision later this week.

rupture—a breaking off, breach: Difficulties over trade policy led to a *rupture* of diplomatic relations between the two nations.

S

saccharine—pertaining to sugar, having the qualities of sugar, overly sweet: The *saccharine* sentimentality of the film is cloying to any audience over the age of 12.

sacrament—sacred rite: The Roman Catholic Church recognizes seven *sacraments*, including baptism, matrimony, and anointing of the sick.

sagacious—wise, discerning: The *sagacious* writing of Greek philosophers survive to the present day.

salient—conspicuous, noticeable, prominent: The *salient* points of the speech could not be forgotten by the audience.

salutary—promoting health, conducive to good: Regular exercise is a *salutary* practice.

salvage—to save or recover from disaster, such as shipwreck or fire: Divers *salvaged* gold coins and precious artifacts from the sunken Spanish galleon.

salvation—act of preserving from danger, destruction, or great calamity: Prompt attention to an injury can be the victim's *salvation.*

sanction—to authorize, approve, support: The parent organization refused to *sanction* the illegal demonstration staged by the splinter group.

sanguine—ardent, confident, optimistic: The leader was *sanguine* about the movement's chances for success.

satiate—to gratify completely, surfeit: After eating a pound of chocolate, I was so *satiated* that I never wanted to see candy again.

saturate—to fill fully, soak, cause to become completely penetrated: The cloth was thoroughly *saturated* with the soapy water.

scant—barely or scarcely sufficient; inadequate: They made do with the *scant* rations in the lifeboat for two days.

schematic—in the form of an outline or diagram: A *schematic* drawing of the circuitry illustrated how the radio worked.

schism—a split, breakup: The Great *Schism* created two rival Christian churches, the Eastern and the Western.

scintillating—sparkling, brilliant, witty: Absorbed in the *scintillating* conversation, the guests lost track of the time.

scrupulous—having scruples, conscientiously honest and upright: That attorney is too *scrupulous* to get involved in criminal cases.

secular—not religious, not concerned with religion: In some nations, the *secular* authorities have differences with religious leaders.

secure—(adj.) safe, reliable, free from fear or danger: Her *secure* job assured her of a steady income for as long as she chose to work. (v) to make safe, to obtain: I have *secured* two tickets for tonight's performance.

sedition—incitement to rebel against the government: *Sedition* is an offense punishable under state laws.

seismic—caused by earthquake: A *seismograph* measures the strength of seismic tremors in the earth.

semantics—study of the meanings of words: In English *semantics*, many synonyms have quite different connotations.

semester—a period of six months; either of the two approximately 18-week periods into which the academic year is commonly divided: Each *semester,* every student must produce at least two lengthy research papers.

seminar—a group of students working under the direction of a professor, each doing original research and sharing results through group discussions, a meeting, or a conference for the exchange of ideas: The advanced psychology class enjoyed its *seminars* concerning personality disorders.

sentimental—having or showing tender feelings; such feelings in excess; influenced more by emotion than reason or thought: The *sentimental* actress wept when she watched herself in her old movies.

sequester—to seize by authority, set apart in seclusion: The jury was *sequestered* until the members could reach a verdict.

severe—harsh, extreme, serious: The tough drug laws required *severe* penalties for repeat offenders.

shibboleth—password, identifying phrase of a group or attitude: "Power to the people" was a popular *shibboleth* of the 1960s.

silicosis—lung disease resulting from inhaling silica dust: Blasters are often victims of *silicosis* and resultant tuberculosis.

simulate—to pretend, imitate, give a false appearance of: Although she had guessed what the gift would be, she *simulated* surprise when she unwrapped the package.

simultaneous—happening or existing at the same time: There were *simultaneous* broadcasts of the game on local television and radio stations.

sinecure—job requiring little work: The person who is looking for a *sinecure* should avoid working here; this job is very demanding.

site—piece of land considered as a location for something, such as a city: The archaeologists began excavations at the *site* of the ancient city.

skepticism—doubt, partial disbelief: He listened to the fantastic story with patent *skepticism*. Also: **scepticism**.

slander—spoken false statement damaging to a person's reputation: The witness was guilty of *slander* when he falsely testified that his partner had connived in the tax fraud scheme.

slate—to put on a list, to schedule: The meeting is *slated* for next Tuesday.

slipshod—shabby; careless in appearance or workmanship: *Slipshod* work habits tend to lead to faulty products.

slovenly—untidy in personal and work habits: The *slovenly* housekeeper had to be fired.

smirk—annoyingly smug or conceited smile: His arrogant behavior and *smirk* of satisfaction whenever he won made him unpopular with the fans.

smother—to destroy life by depriving of air; to suppress expression or knowledge: One way to extinguish a small fire is to *smother* it with thick foam.

solicitude—concern, anxiety, uneasiness of mind occasioned by the fear of evil or the desire for good: The teacher had great *solicitude* for the welfare of her students.

solution—in chemistry, a homogeneous molecular mixture in which a substance is dissolved in a liquid: To relieve her sore throat she gargled with a saline *solution*.

somatic—bodily, physical: Psychological disturbances often reveal themselves indirectly as *somatic* symptoms.

sonorous—resonant: His *sonorous* voice helped make him a success as a stage actor.

soporific—causing sleep: Because of the drug's *soporific* effect, you should not try to drive after taking it.

sparkling—glittering or shining; brilliant or lively: The sailors polished the brass until it was *sparkling*.

spartan—very simple, frugal, hardy, disciplined, or self-denying: In addition to the usual classes, the military school imposed a *spartan* regimen of physical training.

specialize—to adapt to a special condition, concentrate on only one part of a field or endeavor: The assembly line caused labor to become more *specialized* as each worker performed only a small part of the whole manufacturing process.

specific—precise, well-defined, not general: The patron was not looking for any *specific* book but had just come in to browse.

specious—deceptively plausible: He advanced his cause with *specious* arguments and misinformation.

spontaneous—coming from natural impulse, having no external cause, unplanned: Oily rags improperly disposed of may cause a fire by *spontaneous* combustion. When questioned by the teacher, the student's answer was *spontaneous*.

sporadic—occasional, happening at random intervals: He made *sporadic* attempts to begin an executive program.

spurious—false, counterfeit, phony: The claim that the new device would make cars run for 150 miles on a gallon of gas was *spurious*.

spurt—a sudden brief burst of activity; a squirt or shooting forth: There is a *spurt* of extra retail business right before Christmas.

squalid—wretched, filthy, miserable: The *squalid* shantytown was infested with rats and fleas.

stalemate—deadlock, situation in which neither side in a game or contest can make a move: Talks have reached a *stalemate*; neither side is authorized to make the necessary concessions.

stamina—power of endurance, physical resistance to fatigue or stress: While younger swimmers tend to be faster over short distances, older swimmers often have more *stamina*.

stature—height, elevation (often used figuratively): His work in physics was widely admired in the profession and his *stature* as an expert in his field unquestioned.

status—position, rank, present condition: Her *status* as vice president allows her to take such action without prior approval by the board of directors.

stealthy—furtive, secret: While their grandfather was distracted by the phone, the children made a *stealthy* raid on the refrigerator.

sterile—free from germs, barren, infertile, unproductive, lacking in liveliness or interest: The room was depressingly *sterile* with its drab colors, bare walls, and institutional furniture.

stigma—distinguishing blemish inflicted by others: The *stigma* caused by gossip lasted long after the accusation had been disproved.

stipulate—to make an express demand or condition: The lease *stipulated* that the rent could be raised by a certain percentage every year.

stoical—showing calm fortitude: She was *stoical* in the face of great misfortunes.

stratagem—scheme that outwits by cleverness or trickery: His *stratagem* created confusion among the other team and allowed his side to take the lead.

strenuous—rugged, vigorous, marked by great energy or effort: Climbing the volcano was *strenuous* exercise even for the physically fit.

strident—harsh-sounding: She had a *strident* voice that sent shivers down my back.

stringent—severe, strict, compelling: The buying and selling of securities is governed by *stringent* SEC rules.

sturdy—strongly built; hardy: The *sturdy* oak tree has withstood many hurricanes.

suave—smoothly polite: His *suave* manners reflected great confidence and poise.

subdue—to overcome, calm, render less harsh or less intense: The understanding actions of the nurse helped to *subdue* the stubborn and unruly child.

submit—to give in, surrender, yield; to give, hand in: Although the doctors were dubious of his full recovery, the patient refused to *submit* to despair. The couple *submitted* their application to the loan officer.

subordinate—under the power or authority of another; one occupying a lower rank: The private is *subordinate* to his sergeant.

subpoena—writ summoning a witness: They issued *subpoenas* to all necessary witnesses.

subsequent—following in time, order, or place: *Subsequent* to his arrest, the suspect was arraigned before the judge.

subsidy—financial aid granted by the government: Ship operators and airlines receive federal *subsidies* in the form of mail delivery contracts.

substantial—real or actual; of considerable wealth or value; significantly large; ample: Wise parents put aside *substantial* sums of money toward their children's education.

substitute—person or thing put in place of something else: A temporary worker filled in as a *substitute* for personnel on vacation.

subterfuge—deceitful means of escaping something unpleasant: The lie about a previous engagement was a *subterfuge* by which they avoided a distasteful duty.

subversive—tending to undermine or destroy secretly: The editor was accused of publishing propaganda *subversive* to the national security.

successive—following one after another without interruption: Last week it rained on four *successive* days.

successor—one who follows another, as in an office or job: Retiring from office, the mayor left a budget crisis and a transit strike to his *successor*.

succinct—to the point, terse: A *succinct* communiqué summed up the situation in four words.

succor—aid, help in distress: The Red Cross provides *succor* to victims of natural disasters.

succumb—to yield to superior strength or force; to give in; to die: The reluctant novice *succumbed* to the pleading of the swimming counselor and plunged into the water.

sufficient—ample, adequate, enough: Our supplies are *sufficient* to feed a family for a week.

suffuse—to spread over as with liquid or light: Sunlight *suffused* the room when I opened the curtains.

summarize—to cover the main points: The newscaster *summarized* the content of the president's speech.

sundry—miscellaneous, various: *Sundry* errands can be consolidated into a single trip in order to save gas.

supercilious—proud and haughty: The *supercilious* attitude of the old and wealthy families has contributed to many social upheavals.

superficial—on or concerned with the surface only, shallow: The *superficial* review merely gave a synopsis of the movie's plot.

superfluous—extra, beyond what is necessary: It was clear from the scene what had happened; his lengthy explanations were *superfluous*.

superior—one who is above another in rank, station, or office; placed higher up; good or excellent in quality: The manager of the division is *superior* to the other employees.

supersede—to take the place of: The administration appointed new department heads to *supersede* the old.

supervise—to oversee, direct work, superintend: A new employee must be carefully *supervised* to insure that he learns the routine correctly and thoroughly.

supine—lying on the back, passive, inactive: The girls were *supine* on the beach, baking in the sun.

supplant—to take the place of, especially unfairly: The mother claimed that her sister had deliberately tried to *supplant* her in the daughter's affections.

supple—capable of being bent or folded without creases, cracks, or breaks; limber; easily changed or influenced: The *supple* gymnast danced on the exercise bar.

supplement—to add to, especially in order to make up for a lack: The dietician recommended that she *supplement* her regular meals with iron pills.

supplicate—to beg: He *supplicated* the emperor for a pardon.

support—to uphold, assist: I *support* our country's policy of aid to underdeveloped nations.

surcharge—an additional tax or cost above the usual: There is a *surcharge* for buying tickets online.

surfeit—excess: There was a *surfeit* of food at the table, and no one could finish the meal.

surpass—to excel, go beyond: The success of our program *surpassed* even our high expectations.

surreptitious—secret, unauthorized, clandestine: A *surreptitious* meeting in the basement of one of the conspirators was arranged for midnight.

surrogate—acting in place of another, substituting: The housekeeper acted as *surrogate* mother for the children after their own mother died.

surveillance—a watching: The suspect was kept under *surveillance*.

susceptible—easily affected, liable: She is *susceptible* to colds because of her recent illness.

suspend—to stop or cause to be inactive temporarily; to hang: Service on the line was *suspended* while the tracks were being repaired. The light fixture was *suspended* from the beam by a chain.

suture—stitch on a wound: The surgeon made several *sutures* to close the wound.

syllabus—a summary or outline containing main points; a course of study or examination requirements: The course *syllabus* should give an overview of what is to be taught in that course.

symposium—meeting for discussion of a subject: They listened to a television *symposium* on the subject of better schools.

synthesis—combination of parts into a whole: The decor was an artful *synthesis* of traditional and contemporary styles.

systematic—orderly, following a system: A *systematic* review of hiring in the past two years revealed discrepancies between official policy and actual practice.

T

tabulate—to arrange data in some order: The election results were *tabulated* by district.

tachometer—instrument for measuring rotational speed: They watched the *tachometer* closely, keeping an eye on the engine's rpm's.

tacitly—silently, without words, by implication: He *tacitly* assented to his friend's arguments but wouldn't admit to being convinced.

tangential—digressing, off the point, not central: Facts about the author's life, while they may be fascinating, are *tangential* to an evaluation of her works.

tangible—capable of being touched, having objective reality and value: The new position offered an opportunity for creativity as well as the more *tangible* reward of a higher salary.

taper—progressively narrowed toward one end; to lessen; diminish: The *tapered* shape of a funnel makes it suitable for transferring liquids into narrow-neck containers.

tardiness—lateness: His *tardiness* was habitual; he was late getting to class most mornings.

taxonomy—science of classification: The *taxonomy* of the law first separates the civil from the criminal.

tedious—boring, long and tiresome: The film was so *tedious* that we walked out in disgust before it was half over.

temerity—contempt for danger or opposition; recklessness; nerve; audacity: The arsonist had the *temerity* to offer to help fight the fire.

temporize—to evade immediate action, to stall for time: The child wanted to *temporize* when told it was bed time.

tenable—capable of being held or defended: The club had no *tenable* reasons for the exclusion; it was purely a case of prejudice.

tenacity—persistence, quality of holding firmly: His *tenacity* as an investigator earned him the nickname "Bulldog."

tenancy—state or time of being a tenant: We observed nothing unusual during the first few weeks of our *tenancy* at the cottage.

tendon—in anatomy, a hard, insensible cord or bundle of connective tissue by which a muscle is attached to a bone: The Achilles *tendon* connects the heel with the calf of the leg.

tenement—dwelling place, apartment, especially a building that is run-down, dirty, etc.: Rows of dilapidated *tenements* lined the streets of the impoverished neighborhood.

tension—tautness or stress; mental or nervous strain: The intense hostility between the opposing sides created a great deal of *tension* in the room.

tentative—done as a test, experiment, or trial: The negotiators have reached a *tentative* agreement, the details of which have yet to be worked out.

tenuous—held by a thread, flimsy: The business survived on a *tenuous* relationship with a few customers.

terminate—to end: She *terminated* the interview by standing up and thanking us for coming.

terminology—special vocabulary used in a field of study: Use proper *terminology* in technical writing so that your meaning will not be ambiguous.

terse—to the point, using few words: The official's *terse* replies to our questions indicated that he did not welcome being interrupted.

textile—cloth, woven material: New England in the nineteenth century was dotted with *textile* mills operated by water power.

theory—speculative truth, proposition to be proved by evidence or chain of reasoning: The professor emphasized that the explanation was only a *theory* subject to verification, not an established fact.

thesaurus—dictionary of synonyms: A good *thesaurus* distinguishes the shades of meaning among words with similar definitions.

thesis—essay, proposition to be debated: She completed her doctoral *thesis*.

thorough—done to the end; omitting nothing; complete; very exact: The search for the missing airplane was *thorough* and painstaking.

timorous—fearful; timid: The abused child was a *timorous* little waif.

tirade—vehement speech: He shouted a long *tirade* at the driver who had hit his car from behind.

tolerate—to permit, put up with: We *tolerate* ignorance in ourselves because we are too lazy to study.

torrent—a swift, violent stream of liquid; rush of words or mail; heavy rain: When a dam breaks, it releases a *torrent* of water.

torsion—twisting or wrenching: Too much bodily *torsion* may lead to backaches.

total—complete, entire, whole: The *total* cost of our European vacation will be more than $4,000.

toxic—poisonous: Alcohol consumed in very large quantity may prove highly *toxic*.

tractable—easily led: A *tractable* worker is a boon to a supervisor but is not always a good leader.

tradition—handing down of beliefs and customs from generation to generation; long established customs or practice: Our family *tradition* is to sing at the table at Sunday dinner.

tranquil—quiet, calm, peaceful: The *tranquil* morning was disturbed by the appearance on the lake of a motorboat.

transcribe—to make a written copy of: These almost illegible notes must be *transcribed* before anyone else will be able to use them.

transcript—written copy: The court reporter read from the *transcript* of the witness's testimony.

transfusion—a pouring from one container into another: They gave the victim a blood *transfusion*.

transgression—a breaking of a law or commandment or duty: Some people think that experimental art is a *transgression* of good taste.

transition—change, passage from one place or state to another: The weather made a quick *transition* from sweltering to freezing.

transitory—fleeting, passing, not permanent: It is normal to feel a *transitory* depression over life's setbacks.

translate—to change from one medium to another, especially from one language or code to another: The flight attendant *translated* the announcement into Spanish for the benefit of some of the passengers.

transverse—lying across: They placed the ties *transversely* on the tracks and waited for the train to crash.

trauma—wound: Many emotional ailments in adults are related to psychic *traumas* in childhood.

travesty—imitation of a serious work so as to make it seem ridiculous: His production of Shakespeare in modern language was a *travesty*.

treaty—formal agreement between nations: An economic alliance between the governments was established by *treaty*.

trenchant—sharp, penetrating, forceful: His *trenchant* remarks cut to the heart of the matter.

trepidation—involuntary trembling, as from fear or terror: The ghost story caused them to feel a certain *trepidation* walking home late at night.

tribulation—great trouble or hardship: The settlers faced many *tribulations* before the colony was firmly established.

tribunal—court of justice: The decision was left to an international *tribunal*.

truculent—ferocious, savage, harsh in manner: The champion affected a *truculent* manner to intimidate the young challenger.

truncate—to shorten by cutting: The shrubs were uniformly *truncated* to form a neat hedge.

truncheon—club: British police are armed with *truncheons*.

truss—to support, tie up in a bundle: The chicken should be *trussed* with string before roasting.

turbulent—violent, in wild motion, agitated: The *turbulent* stream claimed many lives.

turgid—swollen: The river was *turgid* from the incessant rains.

tutelage—guardianship: She grew up under her cousin's *tutelage*.

tyro—novice, beginner: He is a *tyro* in finance.

U

ubiquitous—existing everywhere: Papaya trees, *ubiquitous* in the region, bear large yellow fruits.

ultimate—final, last: After hours of soul-searching, her *ultimate* decision was no different from her original one.

unaccountable—mysterious, not able to be explained: The *unaccountable* disappearance of the family led to wild stories of flying saucers.

unavoidable—not preventable: Because he likes dogs and she prefers cats, their disagreement about choice of a pet is *unavoidable*.

uncanny—weird, so acute as to appear mysterious: After a lifetime of fishing those waters, the old man was able to predict weather changes with *uncanny* precision.

uncouth—unrefined, awkward: The girl was so *uncouth* she could hardly handle a knife and fork and had no notion of table manners.

unethical—without or not according to moral principles: Although she did not break any law, her actions in taking advantage of naive people were *unethical.*

ungainly—not expert or dexterous, clumsy, physically awkward: She walked in an *ungainly* way, as if her shoes were two sizes too large.

uniformity—sameness, lack of variation: Although the temperature is pleasant, the *uniformity* in weather from season to season can become boring.

unilateral—one-sided, coming from or affecting one side only: The decision to separate was *unilateral*; one spouse moved out against the other's wishes.

unique—without a like or equal, unmatched, single in its kind: The statue was valuable because of its *unique* beauty.

unkempt—uncombed, not cared for, disorderly: He was recognized by his *unkempt* beard.

unmitigated—not lessened, not softened in severity or harshness: The strong earthquake was an *unmitigated* disaster.

unprecedented—never before done, without precedent: The first manned voyage to the moon accomplished *unprecedented* feats.

unravel—to untangle, explain, clear from complication: The detective was able to *unravel* the mystery.

unreliable—not dependable: Because of his *unreliable* attendance at conferences, the professor was not asked to prepare a speech.

unscrupulous—unprincipled, not constrained by moral feelings: The *unscrupulous* landlord refused to return the security deposit, claiming falsely that the tenant had damaged the apartment.

unwieldy—ponderous, too bulky and clumsy to be moved easily: I need help moving this *unwieldy* mattress.

upbraid—to charge with something disgraceful, reproach, reprove with severity: The husband *upbraided* his wife for her extravagance.

urbane—smoothly polite, socially poised and sophisticated: He travels in *urbane* circles and is as suave as any of his friends.

urgent—pressing, having the nature of an emergency: We received an *urgent* message to call the hospital.

utensil—implement, tool: Forks and other *utensils* are in the silverware drawer.

utilize—to use, put to use: We will *utilize* all the resources of the department in the search for the missing child.

V

vacant—empty, unoccupied: The *vacant* lot was overgrown with weeds.

vacate—to leave empty: The court ordered the demonstrators to *vacate* the premises.

vacillate—to fluctuate, change back and forth, be inconsistent: The employer's manner *vacillated* between oppressive friendliness and curt command.

vacuity—dullness of comprehension, lack of intelligence, stupidity: The *vacuity* of her mind was apparent to all who knew her.

vacuous—empty, without substance: His *vacuous* promises were forgotten as soon as they were uttered.

vain—unsuccessful, useless: A *vain* rescue attempt only made the situation worse.

valid—well-grounded or justifiable on principle or evidence; correctly derived; sound: On the basis of the evidence, the verdict appears to be *valid.*

validity—strength, force; being supported by fact, proof or law: The bill was never paid because its *validity* could not be substantiated.

valor—worthiness, courage, strength of mind in regard to danger: His *valor* enabled him to encounter the enemy bravely.

vandal—one who deliberately disfigures or destroys property: *Vandals* broke all the windows in the vacant building.

vanguard—troops who march in front of any army, advance guard: The uniforms of the *vanguard* were the most colorful of all.

vanquish—to conquer, overcome, overpower: Napoleon *vanquished* the Austrian army.

vapid—tasteless, dull, lifeless, flat: Their conversation was so *vapid* and predictable that I lost interest in talking to them.

variable—changing, fluctuating: The weather report stated that winds would be *variable.*

varicose—swollen, said of veins: *Varicose* veins sometimes cause large bulges on the legs.

variegate—to diversify in external appearance, mark with different colors: The builder created a *variegated* facade with marble of different hues.

various—dissimilar; characterized by variety; numerous; separate: We visited *various* national parks on our trip across the United States.

venal—able to be corrupted or bribed: The *venal* judge privately offered to hand down the desired verdict for a price.

vendetta—blood feud: The two families carried on a *vendetta* through three generations.

venerate—to respect: She was a great philanthropist whose memory deserves to be *venerated.*

venial—forgivable; pardonable; excusable: A *venial* sin stands in marked contrast to a mortal sin, which is extreme, grave, and totally unpardonable.

venous—pertaining to a vein or veins: *Venous* blood is carried by the veins to the right side of the heart.

verbatim—word for word, in the same words: The lawyer requested that the defendant repeat the speech *verbatim.*

verbose—using more words than are necessary, tedious because of wordiness: The paper is well-organized but *verbose*; it should be cut to half its present length.

verdant—green, fresh: The *verdant* lawn made the old house look beautiful.

verdict—decision, especially a legal judgment of guilt or innocence: In our legal system, the *verdict* of a jury in convicting a defendant must be unanimous.

verge—to be on the border or edge: Their behavior *verged* on hysteria.

verify—to prove to be true, establish the proof of: You should *verify* the rumor before acting on it; it may not be true at all.

verisimilitude—appearance of truth: The movie set reproduced the ancient city with great *verisimilitude*; every detail seemed correct.

verity—truthfulness, honesty, quality of being real or actual: The *verity* of the document could not be questioned.

vernacular—native language: He spoke in the *vernacular* of southern Germany.

vernal—pertaining to spring: The *vernal* influence was everywhere, as trees blossomed and lovers strolled hand in hand.
versatile—competent in many things, subjects, fields; flexible: *Versatility* is the hallmark of the good handyman.
vertex—top, highest point, apex: The view from the *vertex* of the hill was breathtaking.
vertical—upright, in an up-and-down position: A graph is constructed around a *vertical* and a horizontal axis.
vertigo—dizziness, giddiness, sense of apparent rotary movement of the body: The physician explained that the *vertigo* was due to an inner ear infection.
verve—enthusiasm; energy; vitality: The optimist greets each new day with *verve* and a big smile.
vestige—remnant, remainder, trace: The appendix is a useless *vestige* of an earlier human form.
veterinary—concerning the medical treatment of animals: Reliable *veterinary* services are indispensable in areas where people raise animals for their livelihood.
vex—to irritate, distress, cause disquiet: She was periodically *vexed* by anonymous phone calls.
viability—capacity to live, survival ability: The chart compared the *viability* of male and female infants.
vibrate—to swing or oscillate rapidly: The strings of the instrument produce sound waves by *vibrating*.
vicarious—experienced secondhand through imagining another's experience: She took *vicarious* pleasure in the achievements of her daughter.
vigilant—watchful, on guard: As a Supreme Court justice, he has always been *vigilant* against any attempt to encroach on the freedoms guaranteed by the Bill of Rights.
vilify—to defame, attempt to degrade by slander: She was sued for attempting to *vilify* her neighbor.
vindicate—to uphold, confirm: The judgment of the editor was *vindicated* by the book's success.
vindictive—unforgiving, showing a desire for revenge: Stung by the negative reviews of his film, in the interview the director made *vindictive* personal remarks about critics.
viscosity—in physics, the resistance to flow of a fluid: Motor oil has a greater *viscosity* than water.
vitality—life, energy, liveliness, power to survive: She had been physically active all her life and at the age of 80 still possessed great *vitality*.
vocation—regular occupation or work: My son's *vocation* is carpentry; his avocation (hobby) is fishing.
volatile—changing to vapor, quickly changeable, fickle: She had a *volatile* temper—easily angered and easily appeased.
volition—deliberate will: He performed the act of his own *volition*.
voracious—ravenous, very hungry, eager to devour: The *voracious* appetite of the man startled the other guests.
vulnerable—open to attack or danger; easily wounded or physically hurt; sensitive: A person undergoing chemotherapy is very *vulnerable* to infection.

W

waive—to forego, give up voluntarily something to which one is entitled: In cases of unusual hardship, the normal fee may be *waived*.
warp—to bend slightly throughout: The board had *warped* in the sun.
warrant—to deserve, justify: The infraction was too minor to *warrant* a formal reprimand.
wayward—perverse, capricious, willful, erratic: The apparently *wayward* flight of the bat was difficult to follow.
weaken—to lose strength or effectiveness: His argument was *weakened* by the evidence.
weld—to join pieces of metal by compression and great heat: Steel bars were *welded* to make a frame.
welter—a wallowing, wavelike rolling; commotion: She took the *welter* of the crowd in stride, slipping down the street as quickly as she could.
wield—to use with full command or power: The soldier was skilled at *wielding* his sword.
wily—artful, cunning: He was *wily* enough to avoid being caught.
wince—to shrink, as from a blow or from pain, flinch: She *winced* when the dentist touched the tooth.
winch—crank with a handle that is turned, usually for hoisting or hauling: They couldn't hoist the cargo onto the deck because the *winch* was too rusty to turn.
winnow—to examine, sift for the purpose of separating the bad from the good: Her statement was so garbled that it was impossible to *winnow* the falsehoods from the truth.
wooden—stiff; lifeless; dull; insensitive; made of wood: His *wooden* facial expression led us to believe that he was not at all interested in what we were telling him.
worthless—having no value or use: His suggestions are *worthless* because he has not studied the problems thoroughly.
wrest—to take by violence: It was impossible for the child to *wrest* the toy from the hands of the bigger boy.

X

xenophobia—fear and hatred of strangers or foreigners: The *xenophobia* of the candidate expressed itself in his extreme and unrealistic isolationism.

Y

yearn—to feel longing or desire: The parents *yearned* for their recently deceased child.

Z

zeal—ardor, fervor, enthusiasm, earnestness: She left a record for *zeal* that cannot fail to be an inspiration.
zenith—point directly overhead, highest point: The sun reaches its *zenith* at noon.

SYNONYMS

Two words are synonyms if they mean the same thing. A word or phrase can replace another word or phrase in a sentence without changing the meaning of the sentence. In a synonym question, you must pick the word or phrase closest in meaning to the given word. This is the simplest kind of vocabulary question.

Synonym questions on civil service exams have two forms. One form of question lists a key word followed by a number of choices. You are to select the word or phrase that is exactly the same as or closest in meaning to the key word. If you are not sure about the meaning of the word, try to eliminate some choices by recalling where you have seen or heard the word. Perhaps you will recognize a part of the word from your study of word parts. This can help you figure out the synonym. You may try to make up a sentence using the word, and this can help you to decide which answer is the best choice.

The other form of synonym question presents a sentence with one word printed in italics. You select, from the choices following the sentence, the best synonym for the word printed in italics. Sentence questions offer more clues than key word questions. The meaning of the sentence may give you a clue about the word's meaning, even if you do not know the word. The word's use in the sentence also lets you see if the word is used as a noun, a verb, or a modifier. When synonym questions are in the form of sentences, and you do not know the word or cannot eliminate some of the choices, begin by substituting each choice for the word in italics. This will help you to eliminate some of the choices because they are the wrong part of speech or because they do not make sense in the sentence. Then, unless you already know the answer, try to decide which word makes the *most* sense in the context of the sentence.

HOW TO ANSWER SYNONYM QUESTIONS

1. Read each question carefully.
2. Eliminate answer choices that you know are wrong.
3. Use all of the clues to decide on the best answer. If the question is a sentence, consider the part of speech and the context of the word. For both sentence and nonsentence items, see if there are any word parts that you are familiar with. Recall where you have seen or heard the word used. Make up your own sentence using the word.
4. From the answer choices that seem possible, select the one that *most nearly* means the same as the given word, even if this choice is not part of your normal vocabulary. The correct answer may not be a perfect synonym, but it is the *closest* in meaning to the given word.
5. Test your answer by putting it in the place of the given word in the question sentence or the sentence you have made up. The meaning of the sentence should be the same, even though you have changed a word.
6. Answer the questions that you know the answers to first. Then go back to work on the questions with answers you did not immediately recognize.
7. When all else fails, guess, based on your best hunches.

Here are some examples of synonym questions presented as sentences.

SAMPLE QUESTIONS

1. *Remedial* measures need to be taken to clean up air pollution in the area.

(A) reading
(B) slow
(C) corrective
(D) graceful

The correct answer is (C). First eliminate choice (A), *reading*. Its use in this sentence does not make sense, although you may associate *remedial* with remedial reading. Because pollution is a serious problem, choice (B), *slow,* would not be a good choice. Why would one delay solving such a problem? Choice (D), *graceful,* describes a physical trait, so it is not appropriate in this sentence. After you eliminate these choices, even if you are not sure of exactly what *remedial* means, you should be able to choose (C) as the best synonym in this context.

2. The increased use of word processing equipment has greatly *reduced* the need for typewriters.

(A) enlarged
(B) canceled
(C) lessened
(D) expanded

The correct answer is (C). The meaning of the sentence should cause you to immediately rule out choice (A), *enlarged,* and choice (D), *expanded*. Choice (B), *canceled*, implies that there is no need at all for typewriters. If this were the case, then the modifier *greatly* would be unnecessary. Therefore, choice (C), *lessened*, is the best synonym for *reduced.*

3. Although a complex response was required to the difficult question, she answered with *equanimity.*

(A) composure
(B) anger
(C) pauses
(D) doubts

The correct answer is (A). Even if you are not sure what *equanimity* means, you can eliminate choices (C) and (D) because the word *although* in the first part of the sentence tells you that the response was not affected by the difficulty of the question. Choice (B) is not a good choice because the emotion of the person answering is not related to difficulty of the question.

4. The *uniformity* of the students' answers suggested they had not considered the many possible responses.

(A) military appearance
(B) slowness
(C) great variety
(D) sameness

The correct answer is (D). Although *uniform* may make you think of the armed forces, clothing has nothing to do with the meaning of this sentence, so choice (A) is not a possible choice. Choice (C) is an incorrect choice because the sentence says *not* many were considered. Choice (B) fits grammatically, but *slowness* changes the meaning of the sentence. Thus, the best choice based on the meaning of the sentence is (D), *sameness.*

5. The surface of the *tranquil* lake was as smooth as glass.

(A) cold
(B) muddy
(C) deep
(D) calm

The correct answer is (D). Any one of these choices might substitute for the word *tranquil*, and the sentence would still make sense. However, if the surface of the lake was as smooth as glass, the water would have to be very *calm*. Thus, while a *cold, muddy,* or *deep* lake could have a smooth surface, it is most reasonable to assume, on the basis of the sentence, that *tranquil* means *calm* and that choice (D) is the answer.

6. The manager ordered a *gross* of pencils from the office supplies store.

(A) disgusting
(B) all inclusive
(C) twelve dozen
(D) monster

The correct answer is (C). In this example, the sentence is absolutely necessary to the definition of the word. Without the sentence, you could not know if the word *gross* is the noun, which means "twelve dozen," or the adjective, which can mean "crude and disgusting" or "total" depending on the context. The sentence tells you *gross* is a noun. Choices (A) and (B) are adjectives, so they cannot be correct. Choice (D) is tricky. *Monster* is sometimes used as slang for "many" or "a large amount," but this is an incorrect use of the word. *Monster* does not appear in dictionaries as an adjective. As a noun, a *monster* suggests something disgusting, but that would not fit in a sentence about pencils. Therefore, choice (C), *twelve dozen,* is the only possible correct answer.

7. To send a note of apology is the only *decent* thing to do in these circumstances.

(A) proper
(B) going down
(C) children
(D) inclination

The correct answer is (A). As in the previous example, the sentence helps you to decide on the best synonym because *decent* is an adjective describing what someone will do. Thus, you will know not to confuse *decent* with the noun that sounds the same, although spelled differently, *descent*, which means a downward path, or another similar sounding noun, *descendants,* which means one's children.

Sometimes a sentence may be of little or no use in helping you to choose the best synonym. The sentences may help you to determine the part of speech of the indicated word, but not its meaning.

8. The speaker had an *abrasive* voice.

(A) tuneful
(B) high pitched
(C) loud
(D) harsh

The correct answer is (D). The sentences shows that *abrasive* is used to describe a voice, but it gives you no clue that *abrasive* means *harsh*, choice (D).

9. Her *domicile* was very well maintained.

(A) clothing
(B) residence
(C) appearance
(D) office

The correct answer is (B). In this example, it is clear that a *domicile* is something that belongs to someone, but there is no information in the sentence to help you decide what that is. Although any of the choices could be substituted for *domicile*, the correct answer is choice (B), *residence*.

In examples 8 and 9, because the sentence is of no help to you, you must either know the meaning of the word, or you must guess.

If the word is not part of a sentence, or the sentence does not help you to define the word, you must rely on other clues. Perhaps you have seen or heard the word but were never sure of its meaning. Look at the word carefully. Is there any part of the word whose meaning you know?

10. disinterested

(A) sympathetic
(B) young
(C) objective
(D) poor

The correct answer is (C). When you see the word *disinterested*, you will recognize the word part "interested," which means concerned. Since the prefix *dis* often means "not," you can eliminate choice (A). A *sympathetic* person is interested in a person or situation. You cannot immediately eliminate choice (D), *poor*, but before selecting an answer, consider all the possibilities. Since *dis* is a negative prefix, look for a negative word as the meaning of *disinterested*. There is no choice meaning "not interested," so you should look for a negative kind of interest. To be objective is to have no interest in the outcome of a situation. An objective person is one who makes decisions without considering personal consequences; thus to be *objective,* choice (C), means to be *disinterested*.

11. temporize

(A) increase
(B) consider
(C) flatter
(D) stall

The correct answer is (D). When you see *temporize*, you will recognize the word part *tempo*, which means time. You may think of a word like "temporary" which means for a short period of time. Thus, you should look for an answer that involves the concept of time. Choice (D), *stall,* is to hesitate or delay before responding, so it involves time. Therefore, choice (D) is the correct choice.

Sometimes it helps to make up your own sentence using the given word. Then try substituting the answer choices in your sentence.

12. abominate

(A) adore
(B) help
(C) abide
(D) hate

The correct answer is (D). *Abominate* means to loathe. In your sentence "Good people *abominate* injustice," you could put *hate,* choice (D), in the place of *abominate* without changing the meaning. Because the sentence mentions good people, choice (A), *adore*, which means to admire strongly, would not make sense. Nor would choice (C), *abide*, which means to submit to. And logically, good people would not *help,* choice (B), injustice, so choice (B) is incorrect.

13. salient

(A) prominent
(B) true
(C) meaningful
(D) respectable

The correct answer is (A). *Salient* means conspicuous or highly noticeable. In the sentence "The *salient* points of the mayor's program were noted by the reporters," you could put choice (A), *prominent,* in place of *salient* without changing the sentence's meaning. Although choice (B), *true,* might seem like a good choice, it means actually existing. Since the sentence is about a program or plan for action, *true* would not make sense. Choice (C) is misleading. It means *significant*, but not every point that is a significant part of a program is a *prominent* one. Choice (D), *respectable,* means conforming to appropriate behavior or standards; it describes a person's behavior, not a program. You might logically guess, then, that choice (A), *prominent,* is the correct answer. To avoid problems with examples like this one, think of how you have heard or seen the word used. You never see *salient* used to mean *respectable.*

The next seven examples use several of the techniques from examples 1 through 13 to help you to discover the correct synonym.

14. The president nominates candidates for *judicial* positions in the federal courts.

(A) engineer
(B) philosophical
(C) technician
(D) judge

The correct answer is (D). Because the sentence tells you that these positions are in courts, you need to find a synonym for someone who works in a court. While *engineers* or *technicians* might be important witnesses in a case, they're not court employees. Some people who work in courts may have a *philosophical*, choice (B), character or turn of mind, but that is not a description of a job. Thus you can decide that choice (D), *judge*, is the best answer.

15. When hula-hoops were a fad, these toys were *ubiquitous* in school playgrounds.

(A) rare
(B) enjoyed
(C) abundant
(D) broken

The correct answer is (C). The word in the sentence that most helps in choosing the correct answer is *fad.* A *fad* is something that is enjoyed by many people. Thus choice (C), *abundant,* is the best choice. While choice (B), *enjoyed*, makes sense in the sentence, there are many toys that children enjoy that do not become *ubiquitous*. Choice (A), *rare*, contradicts the idea of a fad. And while toys may get broken while they are being played with, choice (D), *broken,* changes the meaning of the sentence.

16. An efficient manager knows how to *delegate* responsibilities.

(A) representative
(B) give to a subordinate
(C) hire
(D) elect to office

The correct answer is (B). Looking at the sentence, it is clear that *delegate* is a verb. Therefore, although you may have heard of a delegate as a person who attends a convention, choice (A), *representative*, is not a correct choice. While choice (C), *hiring,* may be one of a manager's duties, responsibilities are duties, not persons who can be hired. Similarly, responsibilities cannot be *elected to office*, so choice (D) is a poor choice. To *delegate* means to authorize someone to act in one's place or take over one's responsibilities. Choice (B), *give to a subordinate*, is the best answer.

17. transcript

(A) journey
(B) videotape
(C) correction
(D) written copy

The correct answer is (D). When you see the word *transcript*, you will probably recognize the word part *script* that means writing. You may think of a script for a movie. Since the word includes writing, choice (B), *videotape,* which is not a writing, could be eliminated. Although *tran* may make you think of trains or transportation, there is no choice that means anything like moving writing, so choice (A), *journey*, can be eliminated. This leaves you with choices (C) and (D). Think about where you have heard or seen the word. Newspapers often print *transcripts* of speeches, which give a complete text of what a speaker said. Thus, a *transcript* is a written copy.

18. The city purchased a *site* for the new public library building.

(A) reference
(B) location
(C) job
(D) book

The correct answer is (B). When you read the sentence, you may be confused because there are two words that sound exactly the same, *site* and *cite*, but their meanings are not similar. A *cite* is a reference to some other document or piece of writing found within a text. Since *reference* does not fit the meaning of the sentence, you can eliminate choice (A). Choice (C), *job*, is a synonym for a *situation,* which sounds like *site,* but a building cannot hold a job. While you would find a *book*, choice (D), in a library, it does not make sense to buy a book to create a new building. Since these choices can be eliminated, choice (B), *location*, will be the answer you would choose.

19. insufficient

(A) excessive
(B) having enough
(C) lacking
(D) nonexistent

The correct answer is (C). You recognize the word *sufficient*, meaning *enough,* as a part of the word, and you know that the prefix *in* often means not. So *insufficient* means *not enough.* Choices (A) and (B) are opposites of not enough. Choice (D) means *having none at all*, which does not mean the same thing as *not enough.* Thus, a choice meaning *not enough* is the best answer, and choice (C), *lacking,* means not enough.

20. detrimental

(A) favorable
(B) lasting
(C) harmful
(D) temporary

The correct answer is (C). Making up your own sentence may help you to find the best synonym for this word. Choice (A), *favorable*, and choice (C), *harmful*, are about the quality of an experience. Choice (B), *lasting*, and choice (D), *temporary*, are about how long the experience continues. If you think of the sentence "Poor study habits are *detrimental* to remembering new material," you will realize that synonyms having to do with how long the experience took would not fit in your sentence. The subject of the sentence, "poor study habits," is a negative term, so the synonym should be a negative word, and choice (C), *harmful,* is the correct answer.

PRACTICE TESTS

PRACTICE TEST 1

Directions: Select the word or phrase *closest* in meaning to the given word.

1. retain

(A) pay out
(B) play
(C) keep
(D) inquire

2. endorse

(A) sign up for
(B) announce support for
(C) lobby for
(D) renounce

3. intractable

(A) confused
(B) misleading
(C) instinctive
(D) unruly

4. correspondence

(A) letters
(B) files
(C) testimony
(D) response

5. obliterate

(A) praise
(B) doubt
(C) erase
(D) reprove

6. legitimate

(A) democratic
(B) legal
(C) genealogical
(D) underworld

7. deduct

(A) conceal
(B) withstand
(C) subtract
(D) terminate

8. mutilate

(A) paint
(B) damage
(C) alter
(D) rebel

9. egress

(A) extreme
(B) extra supply
(C) exit
(D) high price

10. horizontal

(A) marginal
(B) in a circle
(C) left and right
(D) up and down

11. controversy

(A) publicity
(B) debate
(C) revolution
(D) revocation

12. preempt

(A) steal
(B) empty
(C) preview
(D) appropriate

13. category

(A) class
(B) adherence
(C) simplicity
(D) cataract

14. apathy

(A) sorrow
(B) indifference
(C) aptness
(D) sickness

15. tentative

(A) persistent
(B) permanent
(C) thoughtful
(D) provisional

16. per capita

(A) for an entire population
(B) by income
(C) for each person
(D) for every adult

17. deficient

(A) sufficient
(B) outstanding
(C) inadequate
(D) bizarre

18. inspect

(A) disregard
(B) look at
(C) annoy
(D) criticize

19. optional

(A) not required
(B) infrequent
(C) choosy
(D) for sale

20. implied

(A) acknowledged
(B) stated
(C) predicted
(D) hinted

21. presumably

(A) positively
(B) helplessly
(C) recklessly
(D) supposedly

22. textile

(A) linen
(B) cloth
(C) page
(D) garment

23. fiscal

(A) critical
(B) basic
(C) personal
(D) financial

24. stringent

(A) demanding
(B) loud
(C) flexible
(D) clear

25. proceed

(A) go forward
(B) parade
(C) refrain
(D) resume

PRACTICE TEST 2

Directions: Select the word or phrase *closest* in meaning to the given word.

1. brochure
(A) ornament
(B) flowery statement
(C) breakage
(D) pamphlet

2. permeable
(A) penetrable
(B) durable
(C) unending
(D) allowable

3. limit
(A) budget
(B) sky
(C) point
(D) boundary

4. scrupulous
(A) conscientious
(B) unprincipled
(C) intricate
(D) neurotic

5. stalemate
(A) pillar
(B) deadlock
(C) maneuver
(D) work slowdown

6. competent
(A) inept
(B) informed
(C) capable
(D) caring

7. somatic
(A) painful
(B) drowsy
(C) indefinite
(D) physical

8. obstacle
(A) imprisonment
(B) hindrance
(C) retaining wall
(D) leap

9. redundant
(A) concise
(B) reappearing
(C) superfluous
(D) lying down

10. supplant
(A) prune
(B) conquer
(C) uproot
(D) replace

11. haphazard
(A) devious
(B) without order
(C) aberrant
(D) risky

12. commensurate
(A) identical
(B) of the same age
(C) proportionate
(D) measurable

13. accelerate
(A) drive fast
(B) reroute
(C) decline rapidly
(D) speed up

14. purchased
(A) charged
(B) bought
(C) ordered
(D) supplied

15. zenith
(A) depths
(B) astronomical system
(C) peak
(D) solar system

16. succor
(A) assistance
(B) Mayday
(C) vitality
(D) distress

17. restrict

(A) limit
(B) replace
(C) watch
(D) record

18. strident

(A) booming
(B) austere
(C) swaggering
(D) shrill

19. dispatch

(A) omit mention of
(B) send out on an errand
(C) hurry up
(D) do without

20. inventory

(A) catalog of possessions
(B) statement of purposes
(C) patent office
(D) back order

21. assiduous

(A) untrained
(B) unrestricted
(C) diligent
(D) negligent

22. portable

(A) drinkable
(B) convenient
(C) having wheels
(D) able to be carried

23. annual

(A) yearly
(B) seasonal
(C) occasional
(D) infrequent

24. endeavored

(A) managed
(B) expected
(C) attempted
(D) promised

25. acumen

(A) caution
(B) strictness
(C) inability
(D) keenness

PRACTICE TEST 3

Directions: Select the word or phrase *closest* in meaning to the given word.

1. excess

(A) surplus
(B) exit
(C) inflation
(D) luxury

2. verbose

(A) vague
(B) brief
(C) wordy
(D) verbal

3. collusion

(A) decision
(B) connivance
(C) insinuation
(D) conflict

4. subversive

(A) secret
(B) foreign
(C) evasive
(D) destructive

5. vacillating

(A) changeable
(B) equalizing
(C) decisive
(D) progressing

6. coincide

(A) agree
(B) disregard
(C) collect
(D) conflict

7. petty

(A) lengthy
(B) communal
(C) small
(D) miscellaneous

8. concede

(A) confess
(B) ebb
(C) enact
(D) give in

9. intrepid

(A) willing
(B) fanciful
(C) cowardly
(D) fearless

10. prolonged

(A) refined
(B) drawn out
(C) tiresome
(D) ardent

11. transcribe

(A) write a copy
(B) invent
(C) interpret
(D) dictate

12. negotiate

(A) suffer
(B) think
(C) speak
(D) bargain

13. credible

(A) believable
(B) correct
(C) intelligent
(D) gullible

14. objective

(A) strict
(B) courteous
(C) fair
(D) pleasant

15. examine

(A) file
(B) collect
(C) distribute
(D) inspect

16. quantity

(A) flow
(B) type
(C) amount
(D) difficulty

17. expedite

(A) obstruct
(B) advise
(C) accelerate
(D) demolish

18. coordinator

(A) enumerator
(B) organizer
(C) spokesman
(D) advertiser

19. reprisal

(A) retaliation
(B) warning
(C) advantage
(D) denial

20. relevant

(A) controversial
(B) recent
(C) applicable
(D) impressive

21. sterile

(A) antique
(B) germ-free
(C) unclean
(D) perishable

22. imperative

(A) impending
(B) impossible
(C) compulsory
(D) logical

23. assist

(A) malign
(B) incur
(C) advise
(D) aid

24. maximum

(A) greatest
(B) limited
(C) oldest
(D) smallest

25. construe

(A) violate
(B) contradict
(C) question
(D) interpret

PRACTICE TEST 4

Directions: Select the word or phrase *closest* in meaning to the given word.

1. customary
(A) methodical
(B) usual
(C) curious
(D) procedural

2. minute
(A) quick
(B) protracted
(C) tiny
(D) shrunken

3. preclude
(A) arise from
(B) account for
(C) prevent
(D) define

4. abundant
(A) plentiful
(B) accessible
(C) concentrated
(D) scattered

5. invoice
(A) speech
(B) bill
(C) offense
(D) liability

6. recreation
(A) sport
(B) recess
(C) diversion
(D) escapade

7. futile
(A) medieval
(B) unfortunate
(C) wasteful
(D) useless

8. expenditure
(A) exhaustion
(B) budgeting
(C) conservation
(D) spending

9. stamina
(A) part of a flower
(B) incentive
(C) staying power
(D) reservation

10. advantageous
(A) profitable
(B) winning
(C) enterprising
(D) shrewd

11. merchant
(A) producer
(B) executive
(C) advertiser
(D) storekeeper

12. observable
(A) noticeable
(B) understandable
(C) keen
(D) blatant

13. parole
(A) sentence
(B) conditional release
(C) good behavior
(D) granting of privileges

14. reveal
(A) describe fully
(B) make known
(C) guess at
(D) question seriously

15. fraud
(A) guilt
(B) criminality
(C) cheating
(D) disguise

16. asserted
(A) decided
(B) agreed
(C) contradicted
(D) declared

17. durable

(A) thick
(B) waterproof
(C) lasting
(D) costly

18. vindictive

(A) revengeful
(B) boastful
(C) aggressive
(D) impolite

19. bourgeois

(A) middle-class
(B) affluent
(C) decadent
(D) prevalent

20. absurd

(A) careless
(B) foolish
(C) impulsive
(D) regrettable

21. hospitable

(A) careful
(B) incurable
(C) relaxed
(D) welcoming

22. graft

(A) undercover activity
(B) political influence
(C) illegal payment for political favor
(D) giving jobs to relatives

23. emendations

(A) illustrations
(B) new problems
(C) unexplained actions
(D) corrections

24. punctuality

(A) partiality
(B) being on time
(C) precision
(D) being delayed

25. fatigue

(A) illness
(B) worry
(C) weariness
(D) indolence

PRACTICE TEST 5

Directions: Select the word or phrase *closest* in meaning to the given word.

1. affluence

(A) persuasion
(B) power
(C) inspiration
(D) wealth

2. related

(A) subordinated
(B) connected
(C) detached
(D) finished

3. designate

(A) name
(B) illustrate
(C) accuse
(D) change

4. chagrin

(A) enjoyment
(B) disappointment
(C) smirk
(D) disgust

5. anomalous

(A) out of place
(B) vague
(C) similar
(D) unknown

6. altitude

(A) outlook
(B) height
(C) distance
(D) magnitude

7. precise

(A) short
(B) picky
(C) exact
(D) trivial

8. ignominy

(A) fame
(B) disgrace
(C) bad luck
(D) despair

9. normal

(A) comfortable
(B) right
(C) usual
(D) necessary

10. increase

(A) decline
(B) plenty
(C) quantity
(D) growth

11. collate

(A) destroy
(B) separate
(C) assemble
(D) copy

12. authorize

(A) permit
(B) write
(C) train
(D) constrain

13. platitude

(A) data
(B) length
(C) theory
(D) trite remark

14. entrenched

(A) firmly established
(B) at war
(C) eternal
(D) earthy

15. constant

(A) absent
(B) unchanging
(C) perpetrated
(D) tiring

16. misnomer

(A) wrong address
(B) mistaken identity
(C) crime
(D) wrong name

17. monitor

(A) preserve
(B) warn
(C) keep ahead of
(D) keep track of

18. sufficient

(A) interesting
(B) enough
(C) excessive
(D) accepting

19. prior

(A) previous
(B) official
(C) conflicting
(D) important

20. anticipated

(A) required
(B) revised
(C) expected
(D) extraordinary

21. substitute

(A) excuse
(B) replacement
(C) arrangement
(D) pretense

22. rapidity

(A) idleness
(B) delay
(C) speed
(D) efficiency

23. verify

(A) control
(B) line up
(C) confirm
(D) decide

24. attain

(A) mar
(B) exhaust
(C) reach
(D) attack

25. requisition

(A) payment
(B) written order
(C) formality
(D) cancellation

PRACTICE TEST 6

Directions: Select the word or phrase *closest* in meaning to the given word.

1. fundamental

(A) serious
(B) emphasized
(C) essential
(D) difficult

2. experiment

(A) refinement
(B) test
(C) patent
(D) plan

3. sporadic

(A) occasional
(B) restless
(C) unpredictable
(D) seeded

4. forwarded

(A) returned to sender
(B) detained
(C) sent on
(D) canceled

5. larceny

(A) homicide
(B) levity
(C) theft
(D) corruption

6. bibliography

(A) list of books on a subject
(B) spelling dictionary
(C) geographical index
(D) thesaurus

7. disclose

(A) lock up
(B) uncover
(C) unhinge
(D) set free

8. chronological

(A) in time order
(B) recent
(C) schematic
(D) in order of importance

9. participate

(A) supervise
(B) depend on
(C) divide up
(D) join in

10. vacant

(A) empty
(B) preoccupied
(C) quiet
(D) available

11. remit

(A) confess
(B) send a bill
(C) pay
(D) delete

12. sundry

(A) valuable
(B) specific
(C) miscellaneous
(D) general

13. irritating

(A) unnerving
(B) annoying
(C) unbearable
(D) nervous

14. secure

(A) convenient
(B) nearby
(C) safe
(D) secret

15. document

(A) outline
(B) agreement
(C) blueprint
(D) record

16. reprehensible

(A) censurable
(B) above reproach
(C) dim-witted
(D) without precedent

17. assemble

(A) mark
(B) put in order
(C) bring together
(D) locate

18. compelled

(A) tempted
(B) forced
(C) persuaded
(D) commanded

19. affiliation

(A) connection
(B) juncture
(C) parental guidance
(D) sincere affection

20. privileged

(A) covert
(B) indoctrinated
(C) autocratic
(D) honored

21. deliberate

(A) clever
(B) considerate
(C) intentional
(D) daring

22. slate

(A) schedule
(B) postpone
(C) diagram
(D) quench

23. disclaim

(A) cry out
(B) query
(C) argue
(D) deny

24. principal

(A) main
(B) only
(C) authoritarian
(D) current

25. vandalism

(A) boyish prank
(B) willful destruction
(C) petty thievery
(D) juvenile delinquency

PRACTICE TEST 7

Directions: Select the word or phrase *closest* in meaning to the given word.

1. supervise
(A) acquire
(B) oppress
(C) oversee
(D) restrain

2. mitigate
(A) lessen
(B) incite
(C) measure
(D) prosecute

3. logical
(A) reasoned
(B) calm
(C) fixed
(D) cold

4. peculiar
(A) sensitive
(B) special
(C) arbitrary
(D) indefensible

5. effect
(A) raise
(B) put on
(C) bring about
(D) pass

6. utilize
(A) offer
(B) employ
(C) ponder
(D) enjoy

7. analogous
(A) similar
(B) hidden
(C) metallic
(D) unreasonable

8. uniformity
(A) costume
(B) sameness
(C) custom
(D) boredom

9. legible
(A) printed
(B) allowed
(C) typed
(D) readable

10. augment
(A) adopt
(B) increase
(C) modify
(D) predict

11. complex
(A) group of buildings
(B) tower
(C) neighborhood
(D) corporation

12. request
(A) tell
(B) ask
(C) suspect
(D) complain

13. courteous
(A) fast
(B) polite
(C) impersonal
(D) royal

14. tenacity
(A) firmness
(B) temerity
(C) sagacity
(D) discouragement

15. insignificant
(A) useless
(B) unrewarding
(C) low
(D) unimportant

16. execute
(A) resign
(B) affect
(C) carry out
(D) harm

17. unique

(A) sole
(B) odd
(C) certain
(D) valuable

18. utensil

(A) machine
(B) fork
(C) tool
(D) object

19. outcome

(A) result
(B) aim
(C) premise
(D) statistic

20. dogmatic

(A) manual
(B) doctrinaire
(C) canine
(D) unprincipled

21. basic

(A) fundamental
(B) outstanding
(C) simplistic
(D) strange

22. plenary

(A) progressive
(B) unusual
(C) temporary
(D) full

23. insert

(A) put in
(B) copy
(C) fold up
(D) mail

24. accumulate

(A) get used to
(B) shut off
(C) pile up
(D) care for

25. median

(A) midpoint in a series
(B) numerical score
(C) bar graph
(D) first item in a series

PRACTICE TEST 8

Directions: Select the word or phrase *closest* in meaning to the given word.

1. discard
(A) ignore
(B) throw away
(C) refuse
(D) fire

2. capitulate
(A) repeat
(B) surrender
(C) finance
(D) retreat

3. extenuating
(A) excusing
(B) opposing
(C) incriminating
(D) distressing

4. degraded
(A) assorted
(B) declassified
(C) receded
(D) debased

5. dynamic
(A) noisy
(B) static
(C) forceful
(D) magnetic

6. criterion
(A) charge
(B) theater
(C) standard
(D) requirement

7. intercept
(A) cut off
(B) speak
(C) ask
(D) break away

8. memorandum
(A) formal letter
(B) command
(C) note
(D) minutes of a meeting

9. instruct
(A) teach
(B) work
(C) build
(D) study

10. assure
(A) normalize
(B) insist
(C) persist
(D) make certain

11. affidavit
(A) arraignment
(B) written statement made under oath
(C) enforceable promise
(D) invoice

12. determine
(A) convince
(B) find fault with
(C) find out
(D) bring about

13. xenophobic
(A) susceptible to disease
(B) fearing strangers
(C) opposed to gambling
(D) fearing dogs

14. extensive
(A) thorough
(B) arbitrary
(C) superficial
(D) leisurely

15. unreliable
(A) late
(B) untrustworthy
(C) independent
(D) temporary

16. compensation
(A) remuneration
(B) fulfillment
(C) appreciation
(D) promotion

17. common
(A) occasional
(B) frequent
(C) rare
(D) debased

18. affected
(A) influenced
(B) arrogant
(C) reduced
(D) caused

19. employ
(A) restore
(B) use
(C) use up
(D) plan

20. exempt
(A) excused
(B) withdrawn
(C) selected
(D) honored

21. liaison
(A) connection
(B) lie
(C) opportunity
(D) officer

22. recur
(A) get well
(B) run away
(C) happen again
(D) give back

23. engender
(A) make inanimate
(B) imperil
(C) manage skillfully
(D) produce

24. pamphlet
(A) novel
(B) prospectus
(C) advertisement
(D) booklet

25. corroborate
(A) connect
(B) confirm
(C) cooperate
(D) rust

PRACTICE TEST 9

Directions: Select the word or phrase *closest* in meaning to the given word.

1. sanctioned
(A) standardized
(B) carefully planned
(C) officially approved
(D) publicly announced

2. proper
(A) many
(B) appropriate
(C) straight
(D) obsolete

3. reprimand
(A) engraved invitation
(B) investigation
(C) formal rebuke
(D) revocation of privileges

4. demonstrable
(A) describable
(B) able to be shown
(C) under control
(D) able to be taught

5. insure
(A) determine
(B) pay for
(C) retain
(D) assure against loss

6. alarm
(A) frighten
(B) confuse
(C) endanger
(D) insult

7. obligatory
(A) optional
(B) advisable
(C) inconsequential
(D) compulsory

8. tangential
(A) on target
(B) merely approximate
(C) off the main subject
(D) geometrical

9. legacy
(A) game of chance
(B) tax-free gift
(C) inheritance
(D) benefit

10. diffidence
(A) disgust
(B) confidence
(C) shyness
(D) lack of harmony

11. mingle
(A) visit
(B) dance
(C) mix
(D) sing

12. explicitly
(A) exclusively
(B) specifically
(C) casually
(D) intelligibly

13. infraction
(A) violation
(B) uneven division
(C) minor fracture
(D) fraying

14. urgent
(A) desirous
(B) sudden
(C) startling
(D) pressing

15. residue
(A) remainder
(B) tenant
(C) refund
(D) delta

16. distinct
(A) impressive
(B) loud
(C) regular
(D) clear

17. procure
(A) legalize
(B) serve
(C) obtain
(D) possess

18. neglectful
(A) unworthy
(B) inattentive
(C) unfit
(D) abandoned

19. cull
(A) separate out
(B) deceive
(C) search out
(D) think over

20. plausible
(A) hesitant
(B) seeming reasonable
(C) evoking applause
(D) tranquil

21. recapitulate
(A) surrender again
(B) seize again
(C) be insubordinate
(D) summarize

22. deceive
(A) trick
(B) undermine
(C) mitigate
(D) infuriate

23. exorbitant
(A) alien
(B) eccentric
(C) excessive
(D) modest

24. origin
(A) direction
(B) model
(C) beginning
(D) end

25. exhibit
(A) suppress
(B) promote
(C) publicize
(D) display

PRACTICE TEST 10

Directions: Select the word or phrase *closest* in meaning to the given word.

1. culpable
(A) dangerous
(B) soft
(C) blameworthy
(D) easily perceived

2. status
(A) departure
(B) position
(C) stature
(D) interference

3. rehabilitate
(A) restore
(B) reiterate
(C) realize
(D) parole

4. eligible
(A) incompetent
(B) unreadable
(C) suitable
(D) lawless

5. annul
(A) make a commitment
(B) recall
(C) make void
(D) subscribe

6. contract
(A) formal agreement
(B) license
(C) commission
(D) influence

7. partially
(A) seemingly
(B) always
(C) particularly
(D) not entirely

8. abridged
(A) linked
(B) expanded
(C) shortened
(D) alphabetized

9. unethical
(A) morose
(B) dishonest
(C) fine
(D) bent

10. considerable
(A) large
(B) frequent
(C) common
(D) potential

11. assume
(A) argue
(B) display
(C) suppose
(D) hope

12. feasible
(A) impossible
(B) payable
(C) guilty
(D) practicable

13. deplete
(A) omit
(B) exhaust
(C) deposit
(D) replenish

14. delegate
(A) fire an employee
(B) give to a subordinate
(C) notify
(D) elect to an office

15. deny
(A) injure
(B) hinder
(C) blockade
(D) refuse

16. legislature
(A) court of appeals
(B) high office
(C) lawmaking body
(D) session

17. complete

(A) mediocre
(B) fancy
(C) entire
(D) retired

18. forum

(A) majority rule
(B) place for public discussion
(C) means of escape
(D) consensus

19. motivation

(A) intervention
(B) reservation
(C) argument
(D) reason

20. arbitrary

(A) responsible
(B) despotic
(C) conciliatory
(D) argumentative

21. auspicious

(A) questionable
(B) well-known
(C) free
(D) favorable

22. recipient

(A) receiver
(B) donor
(C) carrier
(D) borrower

23. premature

(A) too easy
(B) too small
(C) too early
(D) too late

24. probability

(A) guess
(B) theory
(C) preference
(D) likelihood

25. adequate

(A) long
(B) acceptable
(C) required
(D) equal

PRACTICE TEST 11

Directions: Select the word or phrase *closest* in meaning to the italicized word in the sentence.

1. To say that the work is *tedious* means, most nearly, that it is

(A) technical
(B) interesting
(C) tiresome
(D) confidential

2. An *innocuous* statement is one that is

(A) forceful
(B) harmless
(C) offensive
(D) brief

3. To say that the order was *rescinded* means, most nearly, that the order was

(A) revised
(B) canceled
(C) misinterpreted
(D) confirmed

4. A *recurring* problem is one that

(A) replaces a problem that existed previously
(B) is unexpected
(C) has long been overlooked
(D) comes up from time to time

5. A *homogeneous* group of persons is characterized by its

(A) similarity
(B) teamwork
(C) discontent
(D) differences

6. Courage is a trait difficult to *instill.*

(A) measure exactly
(B) impart gradually
(C) predict accurately
(D) restrain effectively

7. A *conscientious* person is one who

(A) feels obligated to do what he or she believes right
(B) rarely makes errors
(C) frequently makes suggestions for procedural improvements
(D) has good personal relationships with others

8. There was much *diversity* in the suggestions submitted.

(A) similarity
(B) value
(C) triviality
(D) variety

9. The survey was concerned with the problem of *indigence.*

(A) poverty
(B) corruption
(C) intolerance
(D) morale

10. He was surprised at the *temerity* of the new employee.

(A) shyness
(B) enthusiasm
(C) rashness
(D) self-control

11. A *vindictive* person is one who is

(A) prejudiced
(B) unpopular
(C) petty
(D) revengeful

12. The vehicle was left *intact.*

(A) a total loss
(B) unattended
(C) where it could be noticed
(D) undamaged

13. The *remuneration* was unsatisfactory.

(A) payment
(B) summary
(C) explanation
(D) estimate

14. The faculty members of the Anthropology Department agreed that the departmental program was *deficient.*

(A) excellent
(B) inadequate
(C) demanding
(D) sufficient

15. His friends had a *detrimental* influence on him.

(A) favorable
(B) lasting
(C) harmful
(D) short-lived

16. When you study from an ARCO book, you get *accurate* information.

(A) correct
(B) good
(C) ample
(D) much

17. The speaker was urged to *amplify* his remarks.

(A) soften
(B) simplify
(C) enlarge upon
(D) repeat

18. An 18-year-old is legally *competent* to enter into a contract.

(A) expert
(B) ineligible
(C) rival
(D) able

19. There is a specified punishment for each *infraction* of the rules.

(A) violation
(B) use
(C) interpretation
(D) part

20. The aims of the students and the aims of the faculty members often *coincide*.

(A) agree
(B) are ignored
(C) conflict
(D) are misinterpreted

21. The secretary of the Sociology Department was responsible for setting up an index of *relevant* magazine articles.

(A) applicable
(B) controversial
(C) miscellaneous
(D) recent

22. One of the secretary's duties consisted of sorting and filing *facsimiles* of student term papers.

(A) bibliographical listings
(B) exact copies
(C) summaries
(D) supporting documentation

23. Your *numerical* rating is based upon your test score, education, experience, and veteran's status.

(A) orderly
(B) actual
(C) employment
(D) number

24. Please consult your office *manual* to learn the proper operation of our copying machine.

(A) labor
(B) handbook
(C) typewriter
(D) handle

25. No computational *device* may be used during the exam.

(A) calculator
(B) adding
(C) mathematical
(D) machine

PRACTICE TEST 12

Directions: Select the word or phrase *closest* in meaning to the italicized word in the sentence.

1. The secretary *complied* with the boss's wishes.

(A) objected to
(B) agreed with
(C) followed
(D) disobeyed

2. A passing grade on the special exam may *exempt* the applicant from the experience requirements for that job.

(A) excuse
(B) prohibit
(C) subject
(D) specify

3. The civil service dictation test differs from the *conventional* dictation test.

(A) agreeable
(B) public
(C) large-scale
(D) usual

4. Improper office lighting may cause *fatigue*.

(A) uniform
(B) eyestrain
(C) tiredness
(D) overweight

5. The professor explained that the report was too *verbose* to be submitted.

(A) brief
(B) specific
(C) general
(D) wordy

6. The faculty meeting *preempted* the conference room in the dean's office.

(A) appropriated
(B) emptied
(C) filled
(D) reserved

7. The professor's credentials became a subject of *controversy*.

(A) annoyance
(B) debate
(C) envy
(D) review

8. The professor developed a different central theme during every *semester*.

(A) biannual period of instruction
(B) orientation period
(C) slide demonstration
(D) weekly lecture series

9. The College offered a variety of *seminars* to upperclass students.

(A) reading courses with no formal supervision
(B) study courses for small groups of students engaged in research under a teacher
(C) guidance conferences with grade advisers
(D) work experiences in different occupational fields

10. The person who is *diplomatic* in his relations with others is

(A) well dressed
(B) very tactful
(C) somewhat domineering
(D) deceitful and tricky

11. Action at this time would be *inopportune*.

(A) untimely
(B) premeditated
(C) sporadic
(D) commendable

12. An incentive that is *potent* is

(A) impossible
(B) highly effective
(C) not immediately practicable
(D) a remote possibility

13. He presented a *controversial* plan.

(A) subject to debate
(B) unreasonable
(C) complex
(D) comparable

14. He sent the *irate* employee to the personnel manager.

(A) irresponsible
(B) untidy
(C) insubordinate
(D) angry

15. The secretary was asked to type a rough draft of a college course *syllabus*.

(A) directory of departments and services
(B) examination schedule
(C) outline of a course of study
(D) rules and regulations

16. Information may be *obtained* at your public library.

(A) learned
(B) read
(C) gotten
(D) distributed

17. Lateness will *bar* you from taking the test.

(A) stick
(B) prevent
(C) harm
(D) assist

18. An *ambiguous* statement is one that is

(A) forceful and convincing
(B) capable of being understood in more than one sense
(C) based upon good judgment and sound reasoning processes
(D) uninteresting and too lengthy

19. A solvent will assist the paint in the *penetration* of porous surfaces.

(A) covering
(B) protection
(C) cleaning
(D) entering

20. Iron oxide makes a very *durable* paint.

(A) cheap
(B) long-lasting
(C) easily applied
(D) quick-drying

21. For precision work, center punches are ground to a fine *tapered* point.

(A) conical
(B) straight
(C) accurate
(D) smooth

22. There are *limitations* to the drilling of metals by hand power.

(A) advantages
(B) restrictions
(C) difficulties
(D) benefits

23. A painter should make sure there is *sufficient* paint to do the job.

(A) enough
(B) the right kind of
(C) the proper color of
(D) mixed

24. The investigation unit began an *extensive* search for the information.

(A) complicated
(B) superficial
(C) thorough
(D) leisurely

25. They were not present at the *inception* of the program.

(A) beginning
(B) discussion
(C) conclusion
(D) rejection

ANSWER KEY

Test 1	Test 2	Test 3	Test 4	Test 5	Test 6
1. C	1. D	1. A	1. B	1. D	1. C
2. B	2. A	2. C	2. C	2. B	2. B
3. D	3. D	3. B	3. C	3. A	3. A
4. A	4. A	4. D	4. A	4. B	4. C
5. C	5. B	5. A	5. B	5. A	5. C
6. B	6. C	6. A	6. C	6. B	6. A
7. C	7. D	7. C	7. D	7. C	7. B
8. B	8. B	8. D	8. D	8. B	8. A
9. C	9. C	9. D	9. C	9. C	9. D
10. C	10. D	10. B	10. A	10. D	10. A
11. B	11. B	11. A	11. D	11. C	11. C
12. D	12. C	12. D	12. A	12. A	12. C
13. A	13. D	13. A	13. B	13. D	13. B
14. B	14. B	14. C	14. B	14. A	14. C
15. D	15. C	15. D	15. C	15. B	15. D
16. C	16. A	16. C	16. D	16. D	16. A
17. C	17. A	17. C	17. C	17. D	17. C
18. B	18. D	18. B	18. A	18. B	18. B
19. A	19. B	19. A	19. A	19. A	19. A
20. D	20. A	20. C	20. B	20. C	20. D
21. D	21. C	21. B	21. D	21. B	21. C
22. B	22. D	22. C	22. C	22. C	22. A
23. D	23. A	23. D	23. D	23. C	23. D
24. A	24. C	24. A	24. B	24. C	24. A
25. A	25. D	25. D	25. C	25. B	25. B

Test 7	Test 8	Test 9	Test 10	Test 11	Test 12
1. C	1. B	1. C	1. C	1. C	1. C
2. A	2. B	2. B	2. B	2. B	2. A
3. A	3. A	3. C	3. A	3. B	3. D
4. B	4. D	4. B	4. C	4. D	4. C
5. C	5. C	5. D	5. C	5. A	5. D
6. B	6. C	6. A	6. A	6. B	6. A
7. A	7. A	7. D	7. D	7. A	7. B
8. B	8. C	8. C	8. C	8. D	8. A
9. D	9. A	9. C	9. B	9. A	9. B
10. B	10. D	10. C	10. A	10. C	10. B
11. A	11. B	11. C	11. C	11. D	11. A
12. B	12. C	12. B	12. D	12. D	12. B
13. B	13. B	13. A	13. B	13. A	13. A
14. A	14. A	14. D	14. B	14. B	14. D
15. D	15. B	15. A	15. D	15. C	15. C
16. C	16. A	16. D	16. C	16. A	16. C
17. A	17. B	17. C	17. C	17. C	17. B
18. C	18. A	18. B	18. B	18. D	18. B
19. A	19. B	19. A	19. D	19. A	19. D
20. B	20. A	20. B	20. B	20. A	20. B
21. A	21. A	21. D	21. D	21. A	21. A
22. D	22. C	22. A	22. A	22. B	22. B
23. A	23. D	23. C	23. C	23. D	23. A
24. C	24. D	24. C	24. D	24. B	24. C
25. A	25. B	25. D	25. B	25. D	25. A

ANTONYMS

An antonym is a word with the opposite meaning of another word. Antonym questions on civil service tests are sometimes called "opposites." Antonym questions, like synonym questions, test your knowledge of the meaning of words. The task may appear simple; you need to define the key word and choose its opposite. But antonym questions challenge you to demonstrate thinking abilities as well as verbal skills. When none of the answer choices are true opposites, as *alive* is the opposite of *dead*, you must find the word or phrase that is *most nearly* opposite. While the word *dirty* might not be the first word you would think of as the opposite of *shiny*, if there is no answer choice that says *dull*, and the other choices are not appropriate, *dirty* would be the correct answer.

Be careful not to choose a word or phrase that has a *different* meaning than the key word but is not its opposite. Another difficulty can occur when you have concentrated on thinking of the definition of the key word; you may mistakenly choose its synonym rather than its antonym.

You can make antonym questions easier to answer by using the following strategy.

HOW TO ANSWER ANTONYM QUESTIONS

Antonym questions can be answered by using a step-by-step approach. Read each word and its possible opposites very carefully. Then, beginning with step one, find your answer. This process may lead you through a number of different steps, depending on your initial ideas about the word.

STEP 1

You know the meaning of the word. You read all of the choices and the *best* opposite is clear to you. Mark your answer quickly and go on. Do this for all of the words you are sure of. Then return to the more puzzling questions.

STEP 2

You know the meaning of the key word but none of the answer choices seem correct. Think about additional ways of looking at the key word.

Perhaps you misread the word. Is there another word that looks very much like it with a different meaning? For example, did you read *president* for *precedent* or *decent* for *desçent*?

Did you read the word correctly but accent the wrong syllable? Some words have more than one pronunciation, and each pronunciation has a different meaning. A *desert* is something eaten at the end of a meal, but a *dessert* is an area with a very dry climate.

Is the word one that has different meanings when used as different parts of speech? A *rank* (noun) is a position. To *rank* (verb) can mean to classify. And *rank* (adjective) means very smelly.

Is the word one that not only can be used as many parts of speech but also has different shades of meaning within each of them? *Fair* (adjective) can mean of pleasing appearance, light in color, consistent with rules, or serving justice. A *fair* (noun) can be a market or an exhibition. As an adverb, *fair* can mean legally or directly. Your task is to choose an answer that is the opposite of *one* of those meanings of the word *fair*.

STEP 3

You do not know the meaning of the word, but it contains a word part that is a clue to its meaning. Here is an example of that type of word.

circumspect

(A) invisible
(B) hidden
(C) careless
(D) dangerous

The correct answer is (C). You do not know the meaning of the word *circumspect*. But you recognize *spect* as being part of spectacles, which you know are eyeglasses. You also know that the prefix *circum* means around. Therefore, you can determine *circumspect* means something like looking around. But be careful. This is where your reasoning may lead you to the wrong conclusion. If you associate the word with eyeglasses, you may think the opposite of seeing something is *not* seeing it, so choice (A), *invisible,* is the best choice. But these are not direct opposites. Or you might think that if you don't see something when you look around, it is choice (B), *hidden*. But an object that is hidden can't look at something, so that choice is incorrect. Choice (C), *careless,* is the correct choice because one who does not look around is acting carelessly. That might result in danger, so choice (D), *dangerous,* is a possible choice, but not the best answer.

STEP 4

You do not know the meaning of the word and can see no clues, but you have the feeling that the word has some specific connotation or emotional overtone—positive, unhappy, funny. Use this feeling. Choose a word with a connotation that is *opposite* to what you think the connotation of the key word is.

STEP 5

You are stumped. You have no choice but to guess and move on. Do not waste time on a question for which you cannot figure out an answer. However, you should make a note in the question book so that you can return to this question and try to answer it again if you have time after completing the other questions.

The sample questions that follow provide examples of different steps in the process for answering antonym questions.

SAMPLE QUESTIONS

1. light

(A) dim
(B) shaded
(C) dark
(D) black

The correct answer is (C). *Dark,* choice (C), is the accepted opposite of *light* when referring to the amount of visibility. Choice (A), *dim,* is a quality between dark and light, and choice (D), *black,* is a specific dark color rather than a description of the amount of visibility.

2. cold

(A) chilly
(B) freezing
(C) fury
(D) hot

The correct answer is (D). *Hot*, choice (D), is the opposite of *cold.* Choices (A) and (B), *chilly* and *freezing,* are degrees of coldness and not direct opposites. *Fiery* is a synonym for *hot*, but choice (C) is not *fiery*, but *fury*, which means anger.

3. somatic

(A) sick
(B) healthy
(C) psychological
(D) imaginative

The correct answer is (C). *Psychological*, choice (C), means "of the mind." It is the opposite of *somatic*, which means "of the body." You may have heard the word *somatic* applied to diseases. That should be a clue in helping you to decide its opposite. You can eliminate choices (A) and (B), because they are the best antonyms of each other! Thus, neither is likely to be the *best* antonym for the key word.

4. stand

(A) lean
(B) climb
(C) sit
(D) sleep

The correct answer is (C). Among these choices, the absolute opposite of *stand* is *sit*. Remember, you must choose the *best* opposite.

5. wise

(A) brave
(B) foolish
(C) strong
(D) weak

The correct answer is (B). A person may be both *wise* and *brave, wise* and *strong,* or *wise* and *weak*. But a person cannot be both *wise* and *foolish*. Choice (B) is the correct answer.

6. indolent

(A) charitable
(B) careful
(C) awake
(D) ambitious

The correct answer is (D). Someone who is *indolent* is lazy. Someone who is lazy may be sleeping, but the word *awake* is not the opposite of *indolent.* Choice (D), *ambitious*, is the opposite of lazy.

7. toxic

(A) healthful
(B) disgusting
(C) poisonous
(D) obscene

The correct answer is (A). Although you may not be sure what *toxic* means, you recall seeing the word used with *negative* connotations. Therefore, you can eliminate choices (B), (C), and (D), which are also negative, with confidence that choice (A), *healthful*, which is *positive*, is the correct antonym.

8. mingle

(A) untangle
(B) separate
(C) mix
(D) confuse

The correct answer is (B). To *mingle* means to mix or join with. When things are mixed, they may become confused; choice (D) is closer to a synonym than an antonym of *mingle*. To *untangle* means to take things apart that are twisted together. Objects that are mingled are not necessarily tangled. Although *untangle* is a possible choice, choice (B), *separate*, is the best antonym for *mingle*.

9. antipathy

(A) abstraction
(B) attraction
(C) altercation
(D) affiliation

The correct answer is (B). You may recognize that *anti* means against, so *antipathy* means a feeling against something, a dislike for. The opposite of *dislike* is *admire*, so choice (B) is the best answer. One is *attracted* to things one admires. While choice (D), *affiliation,* means a connection with, it does not refer to a feeling. An *altercation*, choice (C), is a fight or argument, so it is closer to a synonym than an antonym of *antipathy.*

10. gamut

(A) ration
(B) monster
(C) game
(D) portion

The correct answer is (D). The *gamut* is the full range or complete number of choices or possibilities, so choice (D), *portion*, is the best answer.

11. placid

(A) flexible
(B) beautiful
(C) disturbed
(D) pleasing

The correct answer is (C). You may recall seeing the word *placid* used with positive connotations. Therefore, a positive word cannot be its opposite, and only choice (C), *disturbed*, remains as the correct choice.

12. detract

(A) improve
(B) concentrate
(C) focus
(D) develop

The correct answer is (A). Be careful not to confuse *distract*, which means to divert or turn aside, with *detract*, which means to lessen. Choices (B) and (C), *concentrate* and *focus*, would be good choices for *distract,* but not for *detract*. Choice (D), *develop,* might be a possible choice, but choice (A), *improve,* is the best antonym for *detract.*

13. ephemeral

(A) usual
(B) occasional
(C) permanent
(D) standard

The correct answer is (C). *Ephemeral* means *temporary* or short-lived, so choice (C), *permanent*, is the best choice. The other choices refer to segments of time when things may occur, but they are not opposite of *temporary.*

14. evince

(A) visualize
(B) hide
(C) evict
(D) consider

The correct answer is (B). When you see *evince*, you may think of *evidence*, and that is a helpful clue. To *evince* means to *display* or make evident. Therefore, its opposite is choice (B), *hide.*

15. sanguine

(A) melodic
(B) genuine
(C) anguished
(D) pessimistic

The correct answer is (D). If you don't know that *sanguine* means *cheerful*, there is little to assist you in choosing an antonym. Even knowing that the word part *sangui* means blood is of little help. The incorrect answers are tricky! *Sanguine* contains *sang*, but it has nothing to do with music or *melody*. It rhymes with *genuine*, choice (B), but has nothing to do with truth or falsehood. It looks like choice (C), *anguished*, but doesn't mean worried or upset. The opposite of *cheerful* is *gloomy*, and *pessimistic* means the same thing as *gloomy*, so choice (D) is the best answer. When you see a word like this, you may have no choice but to use *Step 5* in the process of answering antonyms: guess, and come back to the question later if you have time.

PRACTICE TESTS

PRACTICE TEST 1

Directions: Select the word that means the *opposite* or *most nearly the opposite* of the given word.

1. affluent
(A) glamorous
(B) scanty
(C) stable
(D) charitable

2. trepidation
(A) fearlessness
(B) anger
(C) honesty
(D) vigor

3. commodious
(A) disengaged
(B) rich
(C) mourned
(D) small

4. endearment
(A) attachment
(B) strangeness
(C) hostility
(D) thriftiness

5. affectation
(A) hatred
(B) vanity
(C) security
(D) modesty

6. credulity
(A) doubt
(B) understanding
(C) muscularity
(D) commendation

7. alienate
(A) unfurl
(B) befriend
(C) banish
(D) encourage

8. vulnerable
(A) reverent
(B) innocent
(C) unassailable
(D) inflated

9. abatement
(A) addition
(B) lessening
(C) guarantee
(D) denial

10. estrange
(A) allow
(B) release
(C) recognize
(D) reconcile

11. frivolity
(A) distraction
(B) seriousness
(C) warmth
(D) exactness

12. imperturbable
(A) disrespectful
(B) relaxed
(C) rattled
(D) penetrable

13. abhorrence
(A) revelation
(B) detachment
(C) engagement
(D) admiration

14. garish
(A) dull
(B) sweet
(C) damp
(D) closed

15. gregarious

(A) sour
(B) unsociable
(C) free
(D) shortened

16. diverse

(A) happy
(B) understandable
(C) definite
(D) similar

17. unkempt

(A) tidy
(B) tied
(C) sloppy
(D) enclosed

18. luminous

(A) solar
(B) unknown
(C) unimaginative
(D) dim

19. rescind

(A) provide
(B) reinstate
(C) cancel
(D) mutilate

20. affable

(A) unbent
(B) untruthful
(C) unfriendly
(D) unable

21. caustic

(A) sleepy
(B) sharp
(C) soothing
(D) unintelligent

22. adamant

(A) effeminate
(B) prayerful
(C) yielding
(D) courageous

23. unadulterated

(A) diluted
(B) childlike
(C) destroyed
(D) disgraced

24. mundane

(A) livable
(B) spiritual
(C) unprotected
(D) critical

25. rectitude

(A) disillusionment
(B) dishonesty
(C) decisiveness
(D) wholesomeness

PRACTICE TEST 2

Directions: Select the word that means the *opposite* or *most nearly the opposite* of the given word.

1. timorous
(A) timid
(B) tardy
(C) punctual
(D) bold

2. debilitate
(A) harass
(B) annoy
(C) strengthen
(D) affix

3. mutable
(A) changeable
(B) lovable
(C) constant
(D) spiteful

4. deprecate
(A) plead for
(B) dishonor
(C) contrive
(D) aver

5. secular
(A) musical
(B) worldly
(C) sacred
(D) hospitable

6. vocation
(A) purification
(B) novitiate
(C) silencing
(D) hobby

7. recondite
(A) confused
(B) hidden
(C) clear
(D) unpaid

8. parsimonious
(A) frugal
(B) obdurate
(C) officious
(D) extravagant

9. nascent
(A) terminating
(B) commencing
(C) erecting
(D) halting

10. culpable
(A) blameless
(B) childless
(C) courteous
(D) trustworthy

11. nepotism
(A) favoritism
(B) indifference
(C) impartiality
(D) apathy

12. surfeit
(A) plenty
(B) insufficiency
(C) distaste
(D) affect

13. odious
(A) hateful
(B) sinful
(C) inoffensive
(D) spiteful

14. inveterate
(A) habitual
(B) experienced
(C) dauntless
(D) inexperienced

15. indolent
(A) industrious
(B) lazy
(C) opulent
(D) corpulent

16. venial
(A) sacrificial
(B) unrealistic
(C) unpardonable
(D) sanguine

17. rubicund
(A) ruddy
(B) pale
(C) rotund
(D) roseate

18. espouse
(A) support
(B) relate
(C) sue
(D) oppose

19. lugubrious
(A) doleful
(B) mournful
(C) happy
(D) malicious

20. emend
(A) improve
(B) worsen
(C) correct
(D) ignore

21. accelerate
(A) stop
(B) slow
(C) quicken
(D) hasten

22. docile
(A) active
(B) healthy
(C) probable
(D) teachable

23. candor
(A) frankness
(B) doubt
(C) deception
(D) enthusiasm

24. nomadic
(A) secret
(B) anonymous
(C) stationary
(D) famous

25. humble
(A) simple
(B) just
(C) hurt
(D) proud

PRACTICE TEST 3

Directions: Select the word that means the *opposite* or *most nearly the opposite* of the given word.

1. succumb
(A) arrive
(B) yield
(C) eat
(D) conquer

2. divert
(A) instruct
(B) include
(C) bore
(D) amuse

3. assent
(A) agree
(B) disagree
(C) climb
(D) fall

4. diminish
(A) lessen
(B) begin
(C) complete
(D) expand

5. brazen
(A) frozen
(B) humble
(C) rustproof
(D) leaky

6. intent
(A) alfresco
(B) busy
(C) disinterested
(D) shy

7. smother
(A) cuddle
(B) expel
(C) aerate
(D) rescue

8. lavish
(A) filthy
(B) elegant
(C) squander
(D) conserve

9. aloof
(A) sociable
(B) humble
(C) public
(D) ignorant

10. elated
(A) on time
(B) tardy
(C) ideal
(D) depressed

11. furnish
(A) dress
(B) decorate
(C) remove
(D) polish

12. ostracize
(A) include
(B) shun
(C) hide
(D) delight

13. exorbitant
(A) priceless
(B) worthless
(C) fair
(D) straight

14. chastise
(A) dirty
(B) cleanse
(C) praise
(D) straighten

15. profit
(A) gain
(B) money
(C) suffer
(D) disgust

16. defy
(A) desire
(B) embrace
(C) fight
(D) abscond

17. gorge

(A) duck
(B) diet
(C) stuff
(D) valley

18. curtail

(A) curry
(B) open
(C) shorten
(D) extend

19. initiate

(A) instruct
(B) begin
(C) terminate
(D) invade

20. grant

(A) confiscate
(B) money
(C) land
(D) swamp

21. clamor

(A) ugliness
(B) beauty
(C) silence
(D) dishonor

22. rouse

(A) lull
(B) alarm
(C) complain
(D) weep

23. credible

(A) believable
(B) unbelievable
(C) honorable
(D) dishonorable

24. thorough

(A) around
(B) circumvented
(C) sloppy
(D) slovenly

25. wooden

(A) iron
(B) slippery
(C) rubbery
(D) green

PRACTICE TEST 4

Directions: Select the word that means the *opposite* or *most nearly the opposite* of the given word.

1. sparkling
(A) military
(B) festive
(C) lethal
(D) grimy

2. loyal
(A) lovely
(B) unfaithful
(C) unlucky
(D) unusual

3. refuse
(A) reheat
(B) accept
(C) reveal
(D) tidy

4. acquire
(A) solo
(B) buy
(C) release
(D) collect

5. scant
(A) sparse
(B) scoundrel
(C) abundant
(D) straight

6. pinnacle
(A) bridge
(B) base
(C) wall
(D) rummy

7. corpulent
(A) bulky
(B) singular
(C) company
(D) slender

8. naive
(A) rural
(B) dull
(C) sophisticated
(D) funny

9. depression
(A) incline
(B) valley
(C) hill
(D) oppression

10. diminish
(A) trim
(B) augment
(C) decorate
(D) decrease

11. abandon
(A) abdicate
(B) keep
(C) refer
(D) encourage

12. abhor
(A) pour
(B) waft
(C) desire
(D) hate

13. finite
(A) endless
(B) final
(C) done
(D) galaxy

14. homogeneous
(A) similar
(B) foolish
(C) mixed
(D) pasteurized

15. detrimental
(A) favorable
(B) harmful
(C) lasting
(D) short

16. divergent
(A) spontaneous
(B) differing
(C) apparent
(D) alike

17. sporadic

(A) perpetual
(B) irregular
(C) sudden
(D) disturbing

18. opportune

(A) convenient
(B) premeditated
(C) commendable
(D) untimely

19. flourish

(A) nourish
(B) blossom
(C) flounder
(D) wave

20. candid

(A) predictable
(B) written
(C) frank
(D) confidential

21. meager

(A) overdue
(B) valuable
(C) abundant
(D) scanty

22. commencement

(A) graduation
(B) end
(C) beginning
(D) diploma

23. reluctance

(A) eagerness
(B) consultation
(C) consolation
(D) energy

24. potent

(A) practical
(B) weak
(C) possible
(D) impossible

25. cogent

(A) convincing
(B) confusing
(C) opposite
(D) unintentional

PRACTICE TEST 5

Directions: Select the word that means the *opposite* or *most nearly the opposite* of the given word.

1. vindictive

(A) forgiving
(B) petty
(C) beautiful
(D) unattractive

2. tedious

(A) technical
(B) boring
(C) interesting
(D) confidential

3. various

(A) dangerous
(B) spotted
(C) uniform
(D) several

4. ambiguous

(A) alike
(B) definite
(C) eager
(D) dexterous

5. precisely

(A) roughly
(B) costly
(C) poorly
(D) doubly

6. sturdy

(A) strong
(B) dark
(C) unintelligent
(D) decrepit

7. response

(A) activity
(B) breath
(C) question
(D) duty

8. rescind

(A) grow
(B) affirm
(C) cancel
(D) burn

9. assistance

(A) handout
(B) aid
(C) insufficiency
(D) hindrance

10. consume

(A) create
(B) sell
(C) want
(D) begin

11. hazardous

(A) annoying
(B) flammable
(C) inflammable
(D) secure

12. decelerate

(A) climb
(B) slide
(C) speed up
(D) unwind

13. subsequently

(A) before
(B) afterward
(C) wisely
(D) stupidly

14. decompose

(A) choose
(B) pick up
(C) create
(D) break

15. restrict

(A) hit again
(B) sit down
(C) limit
(D) activate

16. augment

(A) stop
(B) disagree
(C) decrease
(D) decant

17. utilize
(A) improve
(B) waste
(C) praise
(D) criticize

18. toxic
(A) abnormal
(B) beneficial
(C) improved
(D) ashen

19. sufficient
(A) hurt
(B) choke
(C) better
(D) lacking

20. abatement
(A) reduction
(B) revival
(C) tax
(D) tide

21. analyze
(A) study
(B) submit
(C) accept
(D) dissect

22. adjacent
(A) distant
(B) neighboring
(C) added
(D) subtracted

23. dismantle
(A) inspect
(B) appraise
(C) assemble
(D) cover

24. extensive
(A) prolonged
(B) adulterated
(C) exaggerated
(D) narrow

25. ultimate
(A) penultimate
(B) original
(C) final
(D) most

PRACTICE TEST 6

Directions: Select the word that means the *opposite* or *most nearly the opposite* of the given word.

1. dense
(A) sparse
(B) stupid
(C) cloudy
(D) shallow

2. negligible
(A) careful
(B) serious
(C) loved
(D) abandoned

3. dwindle
(A) extinguish
(B) twinkle
(C) multiply
(D) flirt

4. salient
(A) prominent
(B) salty
(C) bland
(D) unnoticeable

5. improvised
(A) worn out
(B) agreed to
(C) planned
(D) wealthy

6. retained
(A) tied up
(B) educated
(C) debriefed
(D) dismissed

7. contamination
(A) radioactivity
(B) pollution
(C) purification
(D) release

8. approaches
(A) trespasses
(B) disperses
(C) encroaches
(D) exits

9. extricate
(A) intricate
(B) bury
(C) specialize
(D) puzzle

10. facilitate
(A) copy
(B) use
(C) destroy
(D) deter

11. indiscriminate
(A) selective
(B) blind
(C) haphazard
(D) unclear

12. proximity
(A) location
(B) distance
(C) certainty
(D) neighborhood

13. supplement
(A) vitamin
(B) subtraction
(C) addition
(D) diet

14. indigent
(A) healthy
(B) wealthy
(C) wise
(D) active

15. procrastinate
(A) eulogize
(B) invest
(C) expedite
(D) mediate

16. intrepid
(A) surreptitious
(B) monotonous
(C) paranoid
(D) pedestrian

17. mend

(A) give back
(B) change
(C) clean
(D) destroy

18. abstract

(A) art
(B) absurd
(C) concrete
(D) asphalt

19. rambunctious

(A) lazy
(B) friendly
(C) calm
(D) fearful

20. invalid

(A) alert
(B) trusting
(C) brave
(D) true

21. discord

(A) reward
(B) music
(C) punishment
(D) harmony

22. articulate

(A) decisive
(B) direct
(C) general
(D) silent

23. verve

(A) cowardice
(B) ability
(C) lethargy
(D) agility

24. indolent

(A) rich
(B) happy
(C) generous
(D) ambitious

25. queasy

(A) nautical
(B) partial
(C) broken
(D) confident

PRACTICE TEST 7

Directions: Select the word that means the *opposite* or *most nearly the opposite* of the given word.

1. consolidate
(A) strengthen
(B) diversify
(C) liquefy
(D) educate

2. arrogant
(A) meek
(B) exaggerated
(C) clever
(D) inept

3. eulogize
(A) bury
(B) engrave
(C) defend
(D) berate

4. tranquility
(A) harm
(B) concern
(C) discord
(D) knowledge

5. fortuitous
(A) unfortunate
(B) strong
(C) designed
(D) fearful

6. candid
(A) painted
(B) dishonest
(C) unimportant
(D) expected

7. loathe
(A) reprieve
(B) formalize
(C) provoke
(D) love

8. placid
(A) rigid
(B) agitated
(C) pliable
(D) demure

9. graphic
(A) tabular
(B) painted
(C) obscure
(D) incorrect

10. excise
(A) forgive
(B) insert
(C) deny
(D) imprint

11. sentimental
(A) unresponsive
(B) unwilling
(C) unreliable
(D) unpardonable

12. diffident
(A) assertive
(B) happy
(C) companionable
(D) easygoing

13. consequence
(A) truth
(B) plan
(C) cause
(D) retaliation

14. inflammable
(A) soaked
(B) fireproof
(C) on fire
(D) flammable

15. surcharge
(A) commence
(B) receipt
(C) bill
(D) discount

16. lethargic
(A) silky
(B) limpid
(C) vigorous
(D) metallic

17. pacify

(A) assault
(B) tremble
(C) conceal
(D) exhibit

18. incarcerate

(A) remit
(B) extinguish
(C) decline
(D) release

19. temerity

(A) verve
(B) beginning
(C) humility
(D) strength

20. tractable

(A) retarded
(B) brilliant
(C) airborne
(D) stubborn

21. benign

(A) relevant
(B) tumorous
(C) malevolent
(D) precarious

22. soporific

(A) painkilling
(B) narcotic
(C) awakening
(D) drying

23. mutiny

(A) exchange
(B) valor
(C) hesitation
(D) obedience

24. obscure

(A) disclose
(B) dishonor
(C) discover
(D) disavow

25. assail

(A) pretend
(B) conceal
(C) commend
(D) despise

PRACTICE TEST 8

Directions: Select the word that means the *opposite* or *most nearly the opposite* of the given word.

1. tenacity
(A) vacillation
(B) inspiration
(C) retaliation
(D) equalization

2. slovenly
(A) youthful
(B) intelligent
(C) swift
(D) tidy

3. exorbitant
(A) axiomatic
(B) astral
(C) reasonable
(D) disobedient

4. antecedent
(A) opposition
(B) prerequisite
(C) preventive
(D) subsequent

5. captivate
(A) alienate
(B) stipulate
(C) stimulate
(D) indicate

6. compliance
(A) profanity
(B) strictness
(C) approval
(D) rebellion

7. intelligible
(A) dull
(B) unclear
(C) unteachable
(D) faulty

8. consensus
(A) poll
(B) disharmony
(C) convergence
(D) miscount

9. obtuse
(A) sensitive
(B) slim
(C) ill-mannered
(D) angular

10. endorse
(A) allot
(B) invest
(C) elect
(D) denounce

11. fuse
(A) obey
(B) regulate
(C) sever
(D) negate

12. embellish
(A) simplify
(B) overeat
(C) abstain
(D) signify

13. prohibition
(A) amendment
(B) illegality
(C) pretense
(D) endorsement

14. extraneous
(A) immigrant
(B) emigrant
(C) irregular
(D) inherent

15. torsion
(A) compressing
(B) sliding
(C) spinning
(D) straightening

16. cognizant
(A) afraid
(B) ignorant
(C) capable
(D) optimistic

17. magnanimous

(A) insolent
(B) shrewd
(C) selfish
(D) threatening

18. judicious

(A) foolish
(B) biased
(C) illegal
(D) limited

19. zealous

(A) awkward
(B) enthusiastic
(C) reluctant
(D) skillful

20. dubious

(A) cheerful
(B) questionable
(C) unacceptable
(D) assured

21. morose

(A) curious
(B) morbid
(C) impatient
(D) optimistic

22. terse

(A) detailed
(B) harsh
(C) vague
(D) concise

23. spurt

(A) spill
(B) seep
(C) stream
(D) stalk

24. supple

(A) soft
(B) stale
(C) lazy
(D) rigid

25. perturbed

(A) disrespectful
(B) tractable
(C) cheerful
(D) relaxed

ANSWER KEY

Test 1

1. B
2. A
3. D
4. C
5. D
6. A
7. B
8. C
9. A
10. D
11. B
12. C
13. D
14. A
15. B
16. D
17. A
18. D
19. B
20. C
21. C
22. C
23. A
24. B
25. B

Test 2

1. D
2. C
3. C
4. A
5. C
6. D
7. C
8. D
9. A
10. A
11. C
12. B
13. C
14. D
15. A
16. C
17. B
18. D
19. C
20. B
21. B
22. A
23. C
24. C
25. D

Test 3

1. D
2. C
3. B
4. D
5. B
6. C
7. C
8. D
9. A
10. D
11. C
12. A
13. C
14. C
15. C
16. B
17. B
18. D
19. C
20. A
21. C
22. A
23. B
24. C
25. C

Test 4

1. D
2. B
3. B
4. C
5. C
6. B
7. D
8. C
9. C
10. B
11. B
12. C
13. A
14. C
15. A
16. D
17. A
18. D
19. C
20. D
21. C
22. B
23. A
24. B
25. B

Test 5

1. A
2. C
3. C
4. B
5. A
6. D
7. C
8. B
9. D
10. A
11. D
12. C
13. A
14. C
15. D
16. C
17. B
18. B
19. D
20. B
21. C
22. A
23. C
24. D
25. B

Test 6

1. A
2. B
3. C
4. D
5. C
6. D
7. C
8. D
9. B
10. D
11. A
12. B
13. B
14. B
15. C
16. C
17. D
18. C
19. C
20. D
21. D
22. D
23. C
24. D
25. D

Test 7

1. B
2. A
3. D
4. C
5. C
6. B
7. D
8. B
9. C
10. B
11. A
12. A
13. C
14. B
15. D
16. C
17. A
18. D
19. C
20. D
21. C
22. C
23. D
24. A
25. C

Test 8

1. A
2. D
3. C
4. D
5. A
6. D
7. B
8. B
9. A
10. D
11. C
12. A
13. D
14. D
15. D
16. B
17. C
18. A
19. C
20. D
21. D
22. C
23. B
24. D
25. D

SENTENCE COMPLETIONS

In a sentence completion question, you are given a sentence containing one or two blank spaces. The answer choices are words or word pairs. You must select the word or word pair that *best* completes the meaning of the whole sentence.

Sentence completion questions are more complex than synonym questions and antonym questions. They test not only your knowledge of basic vocabulary but also your reading skills. You need the ability to understand how words match the meaning of the sentence. Other words in the sentence indicate what the sentence should mean to help you decide what word best fills in the blank space or spaces. Studying the meanings of individual words is a helpful way to prepare for this type of question, but it is even more important that you read as much as possible. A dictionary or word list will tell you what a word means; reading a great variety of material will teach you how the word is used.

In a typical sentence question, *any* of the answer choices might fit the sentence to make it technically correct, but it might not make sense. However, sometimes one or more of the choices cannot fit in the blank because it is wrong technically or is the wrong part of speech. Usually, more than one of the choices is a possible answer, and if used, the sentence would make sense, *but* only one choice makes the intended meaning of the sentence completely clear. There is only one *best* answer.

HOW TO ANSWER SENTENCE COMPLETION QUESTIONS

STEP 1

Read the sentence. Try to figure out what it means. Look for key words that show the logic of the sentence. A word like *but* or *although* indicates the sentence contains a contrast. A phrase like *as a result* tells you the sentence is about a cause and effect. A word like *before* or *later* indicates the sentence is about a time relationship.

STEP 2

Look at the blank or blanks in relation to the meaning of the sentence. Does the blank space require a word that is positive or negative? If there are two blanks, is there a relationship of comparing, contrasting, or adding to each other? Is the blank a place for a word that best defines a phrase in the sentence?

STEP 3

Look at the answer choices. Eliminate any that will not fit in the sentence because they are the wrong part of speech. Of the remaining possibilities, eliminate those that do not meet the criteria you established by using step 2. Consider the definitions of the words in the choices that are left. Be careful not to confuse words that look similar but have different meanings.

STEP 4

Read the sentence to yourself, trying out each of the remaining possible answers. Which choice is the most exact, appropriate, or likely, considering the information given in the sentence? Which of the choices does the *best* job of completing the meaning of the sentence?

When you begin to look at the sentence completion items, if the best choice for any of the questions is immediately apparent to you, answer those questions first. Then, use steps 1 through 4 for the remaining questions. If this process still leaves you in doubt about the best choice, mark the question and return to it later. Complete the questions where the answer you have chosen seems most probable before returning to questions that leave you in doubt. When you return to these questions, if you are still unsure of the best choice, make an educated guess.

Before trying the practice tests for sentence completions, study the following examples.

SAMPLE QUESTIONS

1. It wasn't astonishing when the outfielder dropped the fly ball; even the best athletes are __________.

(A) surprising
(B) flawless
(C) fallible
(D) fallacious

The correct answer is (C). The best answer is choice (C), *fallible*, which means capable of making mistakes. Choice (D), *fallacious,* which looks like fallible, means false, which doesn't make sense in the sentence. Choice (B), *flawless,* means never making a mistake, and it is clearly opposite to what the sentence intends to say. Choice (A), *surprising,* would be a possible choice, since great athletes often surprise us with their talent, but the sentence says what happened was *not* astonishing.

2. The meeting cannot __________ until the chair of the committee arrives.

(A) proceed
(B) precede
(C) promote
(D) preside

The correct answer is (A). While the chair of a committee *presides* over a meeting, choice (D) doesn't make sense because a meeting cannot preside. The best answer is choice (A), *proceed,* which means to begin. Do not confuse this with choice (B), *precede,* which means to occur before; there is no other action in the sentence, so the meeting cannot precede something else.

3. Mozart, who composed symphonies while a child, is considered a __________.

(A) precocious
(B) prodigy
(C) musician
(D) novice

The correct answer is (B). This sentence calls for a word that defines someone who has exceptional talents. While a child may be a beginner, or *novice,* choice (D), at some activity, that doesn't indicate talent. Since the question tells us Mozart composed symphonies, he obviously was a musician, but that doesn't explain what the sentence indicates is special about Mozart. Choice (A), *precocious,* meaning having abilities beyond what is expected at a young age, is a word describing Mozart, but it is the wrong part of speech. The blank requires a noun, not an adjective. Thus choice (B), *prodigy,* is the best answer.

4. A(n) __________ would probably refuse an invitation to a large social gathering.

(A) misanthropist
(B) philanthropist
(C) anti-social
(D) misogyny

The correct answer is (A). Choice (C) can be eliminated because it is an adjective, and the blank requires a noun. Like the previous example, this question requires a word that names a type of person. Choice (D), *misogyny*, names an attitude—the dislike of women. The definition of the remaining choices helps you select the answer. Choice (B), a *philanthropist,* is a person who is charitable. (The word comes from roots that mean lover of people.) In contrast, choice (A), a *misanthropist,* dislikes people, so choice (A) is the best answer.

5. People who hunt for bargains may think that paying full retail price for an item is _______.

(A) useless
(B) necessary
(C) illegal
(D) foolish

The correct answer is (D). The clue to this answer is the attitude that is expressed. Bargain hunters disapprove of paying the full retail price. It is not choice (C), *illegal,* to pay the amount a price tag states. It might be *necessary,* choice (B), to do so if no bargain was available, and thus it would not be choice (A), *useless,* to pay full price. The remaining choice, choice (D), *foolish,* best indicates that attitude of a bargain hunter as described in this sentence.

6. To run a 26-mile marathon requires great _______.

(A) courage
(B) aptitude
(C) speed
(D) fortitude

The correct answer is (D). The best choice would be a word that distinguishes a marathon runner. All runners are *speedy*, by definition. Choice (B), *aptitude,* is a general word that can apply to any ability. Choice (A), *courage*, is a possibility, because it takes a form of bravery to meet any challenge. However, choice (D), *fortitude*, which means strength that gives one the ability to endure, best describes a marathon runner.

7. A tropical rainstorm, _______ with high tides, resulted in flooding along the coast.

(A) concerned
(B) disenchanted
(C) concurrent
(D) separated

The correct answer is (C). The meaning of the sentence is that the two events occurring at the same time caused the flooding. Therefore, choice (C), *concurrent*, is the best answer. Choice (D), *separated,* contradicts the meaning of the sentence. Choice (A), *concerned,* and choice (B), *disenchanted,* are human attitudes that can't be used to describe a storm.

8. I needed a new car, but I kept _______ between a new and a used vehicle.

(A) contemplating
(B) financing
(C) deciding
(D) vacillating

The correct answer is (D). The word "but" indicates a contrast. Although a car was needed, a choice was not made. Thus, choice (C), *deciding*, contradicts the meaning of the sentence. Choice (A), *contemplating,* means thinking about, but the word *between* indicates there are two possibilities. Choice (D), *vacillating,* means going back and forth between alternatives, so it is the best answer for this question.

9. He realized his dream of becoming an actor was a(n) _______ when he had great difficulties in a public speaking class.

(A) allusion
(B) illusion
(C) fallacy
(D) misdemeanor

The correct answer is (B). This sentence is about a cause (difficulties) and an effect (what was realized). Choice (C), *fallacy*, is a statement contrary to logic. The situation in the sentence is about a person's emotions, so although *fallacy* might be possible, it is not the best choice. Choice (B), *illusion*, means something that is not real like a dream that cannot come true, so it is the best answer. Do not confuse an *illusion* with an *allusion*, which is a reference in a text to another text or to a historical event.

10. The spy attempted to ________ information without ________ her identity.

(A) conceal — hiding
(B) elicit — revealing
(C) illicit — recovering
(D) discover—explaining

The correct answer is (B). The word *spy* is the key to this sentence. Since spies must act secretly, choice (A) doesn't make sense because the spy is not hiding who she is. Choice (C) uses an adjective, *illicit*, where a verb is required, so it cannot be correct. Choice (D) is a good possibility, but *explaining* identity is not exactly the same as permitting it to be known. Therefore, choice (B) is the best answer. To *elicit* means to bring forth or draw out; to *reveal* means to make known.

11. The ________ criticism of the play's initial performance led to its swift _______.

(A) negative — success
(B) bizarre — popularity
(C) pejorative — closing
(D) favorable — demise

The correct answer is (C). Choices (A) and (D) use words that result in a negative having a positive result, and a positive having a negative result. This is not logical, so they can be eliminated. Choice (B) is almost possible, because some people might be attracted to a bizarre play, but according to the sentence, the criticism was bizarre, not the play. Thus, choice (C) is the best choice. *Pejorative* criticism is negative, and such a review of a play would mean it would not attract audiences and would quickly close.

12. Although the dog barked ________ when he saw strangers, he was not _______.

(A) loudly — friendly
(B) aggressively — ferocious
(C) infrequently — seldom
(D) softly — quietly

The correct answer is (B). The clue is that the sentence requires a second word that is a synonym of the first word. The sentence begins with *although*, which tells you a contrast is required. But because the second word is described by *not*, a synonym will contrast with the first word. In choices (C) and (D), the second word choice is the wrong part of speech. In choice (A), *loudly* and *friendly* are not synonyms. To be *aggressive* and to be *ferocious* both mean to be hostile and intense, so choice (B) is the best answer.

13. The defendant ________ the right to a trial before a jury since he trusted the judge's ________.

(A) waived — objectivity
(B) waved — friendliness
(C) bypassed — intelligent
(D) denied — behavior

The correct answer is (A). The sentence requires a word that is used in the context of law to indicate giving up a right. While *bypassed* and *denied* can mean to give something up, they are not the terms used in talking about legal rights. Be careful not to confuse *wave*, to move back and forth, with *waive*. Choice (A) is the best choice for this sentence.

14. A ________ meeting with the personnel manager resulted in an opportunity to ________ for the job.

(A) sudden — beg
(B) diplomatic — concur
(C) favorable — request
(D) fortuitous — interview

The correct answer is (D). Choice (A) is a possibility, but *beg* is not appropriate in a professional situation. While it would be a good idea to be *diplomatic*, choice (B), when talking to a manager, *concur*, which means agree, doesn't make sense. In choice (C), the problem is the incorrect phrasing; one does not *request for* a job. Thus, choice (D) is the best answer. The meeting was *fortuitous*, which means lucky. It could be lucky both that the person met the manager by accident, and that the meeting went well for the person.

15. In spite of their ________ discussion, the members of the committee reached a ________.

(A) harmonious — agreement
(B) acrimonious — consensus
(C) funny — discovery
(D) contentious — impasse

The correct answer is (B). *In spite of* tells you the blanks need to be filled with words with opposite suggestions. Both words in choice (A) suggest getting along well. Both words in choice (D) suggest inability to reach agreement. In choice (C), the words fit in the sentence, but the resulting sentence doesn't convey a specific meaning. Choice (B) is the best answer. An *acrimonious* discussion is a bitter one; even so, a *consensus,* or general agreement, was reached.

PRACTICE TESTS

PRACTICE TEST 1

Directions: Select the word or word pair that *best* completes each sentence.

1. Although her lips wore a smile, her eyes wore a _______.

(A) veil
(B) laugh
(C) shadow
(D) frown

2. Martha's _______ handling of the steaks caused us to amend our plans for dinner and eat out.

(A) ingenious
(B) disingenuous
(C) inverted
(D) inept

3. The stigma attached to this job makes it _______ even at a(n) _______ salary.

(A) unattractive — attractive
(B) attractive — attractive
(C) sybaritic — meager
(D) uninviting — nominal

4. One man's meat is another man's _______.

(A) dairy
(B) flesh
(C) poison
(D) prerogative

5. Joseph's _______ handling of the Thompson account made him the laughingstock of the industry.

(A) proper
(B) maudlin
(C) humorous
(D) incompetent

6. Do not undertake a daily program of _______ exercise such as jogging without first having a physical checkup.

(A) light
(B) spurious
(C) hazardous
(D) strenuous

7. The police received a(n) _______ call giving them valuable information that led to an arrest. The caller refused to give his name out of fear of reprisals.

(A) anonymous
(B) asinine
(C) private
(D) candid

8. He was the chief _______ of his uncle's will. After taxes, he was left with an inheritance of $20,000,000.

(A) exemption
(B) beneficiary
(C) contestant
(D) winner

9. Don't be _______; I don't have time to split hairs with you.

(A) spurious
(B) childish
(C) picayune
(D) erudite

10. When his temperature climbed above 104 degrees, he became _______.

(A) tepid
(B) discordant
(C) deceased
(D) delirious

11. To climb at another's expense is to _______ yourself morally.

(A) upbraid
(B) energize
(C) enervate
(D) abase

12. We waited patiently for the storm to slacken; it refused _______ to _______.

(A) persistently — strengthen
(B) stoutly — abate
(C) wanly — sublimate
(D) sternly — mitigate

13. "Berty" decided to ______ when he found that he couldn't have his love and his throne at the same time; it was 1937.

(A) prevaricate
(B) alter
(C) abrogate
(D) abdicate

14. Although he was not ever at the scene of the crime, his complicity was uncovered; he had ______ and ______ in the robbery by acting as a fence.

(A) stolen — sold
(B) assisted — testified
(C) witnessed — participated
(D) aided — abetted

15. In view of the extenuating circumstances and the defendant's youth, the judge recommended ______.

(A) conviction
(B) a mistrial
(C) leniency
(D) hanging

16. A person who will not take "no" for an answer may sometimes be classified as a ______.

(A) salesperson
(B) persistent
(C) zealot
(D) heretic

17. The children were told that they should be ______ of strangers offering candy.

(A) weary
(B) wary
(C) envious
(D) considerate

18. Politicians are not coerced into taxing the public; they do it of their own ______.

(A) reputation
(B) graft
(C) expediency
(D) volition

19. Elder statesmen used to be ______ for their wisdom when respect for age was an integral part of the value structure.

(A) known
(B) venerated
(C) exiled
(D) abused

20. The 45-minute sermon is a potent ______; it is an absolute cure for ______.

(A) astringent — drowsiness
(B) aphrodisiac — celibacy
(C) soporific — insomnia
(D) therapeutic — malaise

21. His cynicism was ______; it was written all over him.

(A) affected
(B) covert
(C) infamous
(D) manifest

22. Suffering from ______, she was forced to spend most of her time indoors.

(A) claustrophobia
(B) anemia
(C) agoraphobia
(D) ambivalence

23. We were not allowed to ______ our appetite until we had tidied up our living quarters.

(A) fill
(B) whet
(C) sate
(D) flag

24. If you don't badger the child, he may do what you want him to do without ______.

(A) pleasure
(B) pain
(C) pressure
(D) volition

25. You must see the head of the agency; I am not ______ to give out that information.

(A) nervous
(B) authorized
(C) programmed
(D) happy

PRACTICE TEST 2

Directions: Select the word or word pair that *best* completes each sentence.

1. The local tavern was one of the last _______ of male supremacy.

(A) coffins
(B) places
(C) potentials
(D) bastions

2. The ship was in a(n) _______ position; having lost its rudder it was subject to the _______ of the prevailing winds.

(A) unintended — riptides
(B) untenable — vagaries
(C) dangerous — breezes
(D) favored — weaknesses

3. _______ shadows played over her face as the branches above her danced in the sunlight.

(A) Transient
(B) Prolonged
(C) Clandestine
(D) Sedentary

4. Alchemists expended their energies in an attempt to _______ base elements into gold.

(A) transfer
(B) raise
(C) translate
(D) transmute

5. Publication of the article was timed to _______ with the professor's 50th birthday.

(A) coincide
(B) amalgamate
(C) terminate
(D) interfere

6. The chariot _______ around the curve completely out of control when Thessalius dropped the reins.

(A) competed
(B) careened
(C) fell
(D) caromed

7. Don't _______; stick to the _______ of the issue so that we can take it to a vote.

(A) prevaricate — gist
(B) procrastinate — promptness
(C) delay — urgency
(D) digress — crux

8. The more the search proved fruitless, the more _______ the parents of the missing child became.

(A) disconsolate
(B) dislocated
(C) disappointed
(D) disheveled

9. When the unpopular war began, only a few men enlisted; the rest had to be _______.

(A) reassigned
(B) processed
(C) reassured
(D) conscripted

10. The runner advanced one base without stealing, hitting, or getting a walk; the pitcher had committed a _______.

(A) spitball
(B) balk
(C) dropped ball
(D) syllogism

11. They prefer to hire someone fluent in Spanish, since the neighborhood where the clinic is located is _______ Hispanic.

(A) imponderably
(B) sparsely
(C) consistently
(D) predominantly

12. A dark, cloudy sky is a _______ of a storm.

(A) remnant
(B) precursor
(C) belier
(D) proof

13. The Freedom of Information Act gives private citizens _______ government files.

(A) access to
(B) excess to
(C) redress of
(D) release from

14. His remarks were so _______ we could not decide which of the possible meanings was correct.

(A) ambiguous
(B) facetious
(C) improper
(D) congruent

15. His performance was _______; it made a fool of him.

(A) auspicious
(B) ludicrous
(C) luscious
(D) interlocutory

16. The upset furniture and broken window silently _______ to the fact that the apartment had been robbed.

(A) witnessed
(B) confirmed
(C) attested
(D) admitted

17. Although the warrior could cope with blows from swords, he was _______ to gunshots; his armor was not _______ to them.

(A) reachable — proof
(B) vulnerable — susceptible
(C) vulnerable — impervious
(D) invulnerable — susceptible

18. When she addressed the reporters, her beauty, bearing, and elegant garb were belied by the _______ words she uttered.

(A) untrue
(B) uncouth
(C) unemotional
(D) unfettered

19. "A stitch in time saves nine" and other such _______ expressions made his speeches insufferable.

(A) tried
(B) cryptic
(C) redundant
(D) trite

20. The new regulations turned out to be _______, not permissive.

(A) impermissive
(B) liberal
(C) stringent
(D) uniform

21. A person who commits a wrong may be required to _______ his property as a penalty.

(A) confiscate
(B) destroy
(C) forfeit
(D) assess

22. When the desk was placed facing the window, he found himself _______ from his work by the activity in the street.

(A) distraught
(B) destroyed
(C) distracted
(D) decimated

23. He said he didn't get the job done because he was incapacitated; in truth, he was _______.

(A) indigent
(B) indolent
(C) indulgent
(D) insipid

24. The "police" turned out to be clowns; it was all a _______.

(A) mystery
(B) mix-up
(C) fracas
(D) hoax

25. The authorities declared an _______ on incoming freight because of the trucking strike.

(A) impression
(B) immolation
(C) embargo
(D) alert

PRACTICE TEST 3

Directions: Select the word or word pair that *best* completes each sentence.

1. We are indeed sorry to hear of your mother's passing; please accept our sincerest _______.

(A) adulations
(B) congratulations
(C) condolences
(D) concatenations

2. While on a diet I remained lean, but once off it I became _______.

(A) scrawny
(B) remiss
(C) corpulent
(D) corporeal

3. With his gutter language and vile manner he was positively _______.

(A) urbane
(B) rural
(C) liberal
(D) boorish

4. The voters show their _______ by staying away from the polls.

(A) interest
(B) usury
(C) apathy
(D) serendipity

5. Being less than perfectly prepared, I took my exams with _______.

(A) aplomb
(B) confidence
(C) trepidation
(D) indifference

6. The grade was steep and the load heavy; we had to _______ the oxen in order to arrive home on time.

(A) rest
(B) feed
(C) goad
(D) slaughter

7. He was proved guilty; his alibi had been a complete _______.

(A) attestation
(B) fabrication
(C) intonation
(D) litany

8. He claimed to be deathly ill, although he looked perfectly _______ and _______ to us.

(A) fine — fettle
(B) sane — sound
(C) hale — hearty
(D) hectic — healthy

9. Although he had _______ about the weather, he had no _______ about his ability to navigate through it.

(A) doubts — confidence
(B) confidence — qualms
(C) qualms — confidence
(D) misgivings — qualms

10. The police department will not accept for _______ a report of a person missing if his residence is outside the city.

(A) foreclosure
(B) convenience
(C) investigation
(D) control

11. Rabbits, elephants, deer, and sheep are _______; they eat only plants.

(A) omnivorous
(B) herbivorous
(C) carnivorous
(D) ruminants

12. The rivals were fighting tooth and nail when suddenly, in the thick of the _______, the bell rang.

(A) night
(B) day
(C) fray
(D) ring

13. The judge _______ the union from blocking the accesses.

(A) enjoined
(B) ordered
(C) forbade
(D) unfrocked

14. The ______ on the letter showed it had been mailed in North Dakota two weeks previously.

(A) address
(B) stamp
(C) postmark
(D) envelope

15. It is easy to see the difference between the two photographs when they are placed in ______.

(A) disarray
(B) juxtaposition
(C) composition
(D) jeopardy

16. During colonial winters in America, there was a ______ in every ______.

(A) fire — hearth
(B) flintlock — chimney
(C) stokes — pot
(D) tepee — Indian

17. He was a ______ salesman; he could sell refrigerators to Eskimos.

(A) perverse
(B) low-keyed
(C) glib
(D) fruitless

18. When the bomb exploded in front of the building, it destroyed the whole ______.

(A) cellar
(B) pontoon
(C) facade
(D) facet

19. He is expected to testify that he saw the ______ thief fleeing the scene of the crime.

(A) convicted
(B) delinquent
(C) alleged
(D) innocent

20. A child who has not slept well will be anything but ______.

(A) intractable
(B) docile
(C) equine
(D) bovine

21. What we thought was a ______ volcano suddenly erupted.

(A) deceased
(B) dactylic
(C) dormant
(D) disruptive

22. Cigarette smoking is ______ to your health.

(A) disengaging
(B) deleterious
(C) delectable
(D) irrespective

23. My uncle hardly ever needed a telephone; his voice was ______ from a distance of half a mile.

(A) inaudible
(B) audible
(C) suspicious
(D) visible

24. His parents never had to ______ him for being ______.

(A) chide — industrious
(B) ride — superfluous
(C) chide — indolent
(D) punish — independent

25. The current use of "______" in place of "fat" is a euphemism.

(A) ale
(B) portly
(C) porter
(D) beer

PRACTICE TEST 4

Directions: Select the word or word pair that *best* completes each sentence.

1. An accident report should be written as soon as possible after the necessary _______ has been obtained.

(A) bystander
(B) formulation
(C) information
(D) charter

2. A change in environment is very likely to _______ a change in one's work habits.

(A) affect
(B) inflict
(C) effect
(D) prosper

3. With typical diplomatic maneuvering, the State Department used every _______ known to man to avoid expressing the avowed policy in _______ language.

(A) trick — diplomatic
(B) circumlocution — concise
(C) page — gobbledygook
(D) summary — plain

4. The U.N., like the League of Nations before it, is an exercise in _______; it begs the issues and brings no _______ deterrent to the impending cataclysm.

(A) debating — acknowledged
(B) parliamentarianism — neutral
(C) self-rule — realistic
(D) futility — substantive

5. The main reason for the loss of the Alamo was the _______ of Santa Anna's forces.

(A) decline
(B) felicitation
(C) preponderance
(D) isolation

6. A cloudy suspension may be described as _______.

(A) turbid
(B) precipitous
(C) suspicious
(D) auspicious

7. The flamenco dancer stood still, ready to perform, his arms _______.

(A) blazing
(B) akimbo
(C) flailing
(D) deadlocked

8. The woman sued the magazine, claiming that the article _______ her character.

(A) demoted
(B) deplored
(C) defamed
(D) whitewashed

9. To be a "joiner" is to be _______.

(A) gregarious
(B) popular
(C) hilarious
(D) woodworking

10. As a result of constant and unrelenting eating, her figure changed from "pleasingly plump" to _______.

(A) overrun
(B) parsimonious
(C) oblate
(D) obese

11. When you have _______ your palate with pickles, you want no more.

(A) scarred
(B) satiated
(C) imbibed
(D) covered

12. To protect the respondents' privacy, names and Social Security numbers are _______ the questionnaires before the results are tabulated.

(A) referred to
(B) deleted from
(C) retained in
(D) appended to

13. TASS was the _______ for Telegrafnoe Agentsvo Sovietskoyo Soyuza.

(A) homonym
(B) acronym
(C) heteronym
(D) pseudonym

14. Murdered by a crazed derelict who was running amuck, he was the victim of a _______ crime.

(A) gratuitous
(B) gratifying
(C) pathological
(D) demented

15. To put off until tomorrow what you should do today is to _______.

(A) prorate
(B) procrastinate
(C) face
(D) proscribe

16. Being a geologist, he tended to _______ his head as he walked along the path; he didn't want to overlook a single pebble.

(A) mind
(B) cover
(C) shake
(D) incline

17. _______ means an injustice so _______ that it is wicked.

(A) Iniquity — gross
(B) Perjury — mendacious
(C) Lobotomy — inane
(D) Bias — slanted

18. A _______ has a strong _______ to steal.

(A) pyromaniac — urge
(B) dipsomaniac — aversion
(C) megalomaniac — phobia
(D) kleptomaniac — proclivity

19. The _______ assumed for the sake of discussion was that business would improve for the next five years.

(A) labyrinth
(B) hypothesis
(C) outlay
(D) itinerary

20. I wish you wouldn't be so _______; you make faces at everything I say.

(A) supercilious
(B) insubordinate
(C) disconsolate
(D) superficial

21. New York's climate is not very _______; its winters give you colds, and its summers can cause heat prostration.

(A) sanitary
(B) salutary
(C) salubrious
(D) healthy

22. One who _______ another is laughing at him, not with him.

(A) derides
(B) defiles
(C) irks
(D) buffoons

23. The politician hoped to _______ his opponent's negative comments by openly revealing his past mistakes.

(A) encourage
(B) deflate
(C) encounter
(D) assist

24. It is hard to believe that the Trojans could have been so easily deceived by the _______ of the wooden horse.

(A) tragedy
(B) stratagem
(C) strategy
(D) prolixity

25. At the 2004 Academy Awards, there was a veritable _______ of stars.

(A) bevy
(B) collection
(C) galaxy
(D) pride

PRACTICE TEST 5

Directions: Select the word or word pair that *best* completes each sentence.

1. I felt as _____ as a fifth wheel.

(A) rolled
(B) round
(C) superfluous
(D) axillary

2. If we were to _______ our democracy with a _______, there would be no way, short of civil war, to reverse the change.

(A) contrast — parliament
(B) supplant — dictatorship
(C) substitute — constitutional monarchy
(D) reinforce — three-party system

3. A(n) _______ look came into the poodle's eye as a dachshund wandered onto his territory.

(A) feline
(B) bellicose
(C) onerous
(D) canine

4. Always the _______, she spent hours preening herself in the presence of her escort.

(A) prude
(B) croquette
(C) coquette
(D) diplomat

5. The annual ______ in his school attendance always coincided with the first week of fishing season.

(A) sequence
(B) hiatus
(C) accrual
(D) increment

6. His sermon opened with a few _______ remarks about the Golden Rule and closed with a homily that was equally unclear.

(A) nebulous
(B) Old Testament
(C) concise
(D) sanctimonious

7. Giving preference to his brother's son for that office smacks of _______ to me!

(A) chauvinism
(B) sycophancy
(C) nepotism
(D) nihilism

8. A _______'s arms are usually very strong as a result of performing some of the tasks that would be otherwise done by his now _______ legs.

(A) paraplegic — useless
(B) quadriplegic — diplegic
(C) hemiplegic — undependable
(D) somnambulist — comatose

9. Although the wind was quite dependable in those waters, the schooner had an inboard engine as a _______ just in case.

(A) relief
(B) substitute
(C) generator
(D) subsidiary

10. Being perfectly prepared, I took my exams with _______.

(A) aplomb
(B) pugnacity
(C) trepidation
(D) indifference

11. His speech was too _______; its meaning escaped me completely.

(A) protracted
(B) concise
(C) sordid
(D) abstruse

12. The "life" of some subatomic particles is so _______ it has to be measured in nanoseconds.

(A) contrived
(B) finite
(C) ephemeral
(D) circumscribed

13. The president proposed a reduction in income taxes in the new _______.

(A) apocalypse
(B) holocaust
(C) milestone
(D) millennium

14. If you hadn't _______ we might have won the argument; I wish you'd keep your _______ to yourself henceforth.

(A) confessed — hands
(B) obfuscated — deviations
(C) obtruded — opinions
(D) truncated — pruning

15. You'll _______ the day you voted for Zilch; he'll break every promise he's made to you.

(A) regard
(B) eschew
(C) obliterate
(D) rue

16. During the Revolutionary War, Hessian troops fought on the British side not as allies, but as _______. They were paid in money, not glory.

(A) orderlies
(B) valets
(C) hors de combat
(D) mercenaries

17. On and on they came, countless as the blades of grass in a field, _______ of them.

(A) myriads
(B) dryads
(C) dozens
(D) multitudinous

18. If you find peeling potatoes to be _______, perhaps you'd prefer to scrub the floors?

(A) preferable
(B) onerous
(C) infectious
(D) relevant

19. The offenders then prostrated themselves and _______ for mercy.

(A) applauded
(B) supplicated
(C) imprecated
(D) deprecated

20. Her rebelliousness was _______; it was written all over her.

(A) exterior
(B) covert
(C) implicit
(D) manifest

21. If he hasn't yet learned the importance of speaking well of others, he must be quite _______.

(A) loquacious
(B) oblique
(C) arcane
(D) obtuse

22. Louis XIV was the _______ of _______ elegance; he wore a different outfit for practically every hour of the day.

(A) paragon — peripatetic
(B) acme — epicurean
(C) epitome — sartorial
(D) architect — gastronomic

23. Favoring one child over another will only intensify _______ rivalry.

(A) fraternal
(B) sororal
(C) parental
(D) sibling

24. The man _______ the speaker at the meeting by shouting false accusations.

(A) corrected
(B) interfered
(C) disconcerted
(D) collapsed

25. If he continues to _______ liquor at this rate, he will end up as an alcoholic.

(A) buy
(B) imbibe
(C) secrete
(D) accumulate

PRACTICE TEST 6

Directions: Select the word or word pair that *best* completes each sentence.

1. I'm glad to see you have _______; patience is a virtue!

(A) arrived
(B) decided
(C) time
(D) forbearance

2. As the fog came _______, visibility dropped to 5 feet.

(A) often
(B) silently
(C) nigh
(D) damp

3. A(n) _______ jogger, she could do 15 miles a day.

(A) reluctant
(B) indefatigable
(C) outfitted
(D) aged

4. To tame wild horses was what her fierce nature _______.

(A) exuded
(B) precluded
(C) intruded
(D) required

5. Wars seem to be _______; the end of one always tends to precipitate the beginning of the next.

(A) parallel
(B) concatenate
(C) irrelevant
(D) hell

6. If you _______ your energy wisely, you will never lack for it; if you _______ it, you'll remain poor.

(A) burn — cauterize
(B) husband — economize
(C) use — dissipate
(D) expend — spend

7. The only fair way to choose who will have to work over the holiday is to pick someone _______ by drawing lots.

(A) covertly
(B) conspicuously
(C) randomly
(D) painstakingly

8. Richelieu achieved eminence under Louis XIII; few cardinals since have been so politically _______.

(A) retiring
(B) unassuming
(C) prominent
(D) hesitant

9. People started calling him a _______; he had broken a law.

(A) conspirator
(B) transgressor
(C) transient
(D) bystander

10. "_______ and _______," he said with a smile as he met his class for the new term.

(A) Warm — welcome
(B) Hail — farewell
(C) Friends — countrymen
(D) Greetings — salutations

11. Although he is reputed to be aloof, his manner that day was so _______ that everyone felt perfectly at ease.

(A) reluctant
(B) gracious
(C) malign
(D) plausible

12. Speeding may be a ______, but fleeing from the scene of a crime is a ______.

(A) mistake — nuisance
(B) misdemeanor — felony
(C) faux pas — crime
(D) felony — misdemeanor

13. Among his ______ was the skill of escaping from any type of handcuffs.

(A) virtues
(B) crafts
(C) habits
(D) repertories

14. Gold is one of the most ______ elements; it can be hammered into sheets thinner than a human hair.

(A) brittle
(C) soft
(B) adamantine
(D) malleable

15. The impact of the situation failed to touch him; he remained ______ as a stone.

(A) oppressive
(B) reticent
(C) immaculate
(D) impassive

16. A(n) ______ lawyer will help his client ______ the law.

(A) efficient — abrogate
(B) unscrupulous — evade
(C) honest — bend
(D) clever — elect

17. Your banker may look at you ______ if you admit to not wanting to save money.

(A) respectfully
(B) only
(C) askance
(D) directly

18. The gossip-hungry readers combed through the article for every ______ detail.

(A) lurid
(B) common
(C) nagging
(D) recurring

19. Worshipping her every move, he was her most ______ admirer.

(A) beneficent
(B) fatuous
(C) ardent
(D) sophisticated

20. He was stubbornly persistent; nothing or nobody could ______ him from his self-appointed mission.

(A) slow
(B) pervade
(C) arrest
(D) dissuade

21. To be ______ was her lot; she was destined never to earn enough money to support herself.

(A) importune
(B) impulsive
(C) impecunious
(D) innocuous

22. You would not be so ______ if you worked out at the gym; you have loose fat all over!

(A) flaccid
(B) placid
(C) avoirdupois
(D) gaunt

23. A police officer's ______ job is to prevent crime.

(A) primary
(B) compendium
(C) only
(D) infrequent

24. The general couldn't attend; but he sent his ______.

(A) commandant
(B) commander
(C) adjutant
(D) superior

25. You can depend on a malingerer to ______ his duty.

(A) perform
(B) pursue
(C) shirk
(D) lack

ANSWERS AND EXPLANATIONS

Test 1	Test 2	Test 3	Test 4	Test 5	Test 6
1. D	**1.** D	**1.** C	**1.** C	**1.** C	**1.** D
2. D	**2.** B	**2.** C	**2.** C	**2.** C	**2.** C
3. A	**3.** A	**3.** D	**3.** C	**3.** B	**3.** B
4. C	**4.** D	**4.** C	**4.** D	**4.** C	**4.** D
5. D	**5.** A	**5.** C	**5.** C	**5.** B	**5.** B
6. D	**6.** B	**6.** C	**6.** A	**6.** A	**6.** B
7. A	**7.** D	**7.** B	**7.** B	**7.** C	**7.** C
8. B	**8.** A	**8.** C	**8.** C	**8.** A	**8.** C
9. C	**9.** D	**9.** D	**9.** A	**9.** D	**9.** B
10. D	**10.** B	**10.** C	**10.** D	**10.** A	**10.** D
11. D	**11.** D	**11.** B	**11.** B	**11.** D	**11.** B
12. B	**12.** B	**12.** C	**12.** B	**12.** C	**12.** B
13. D	**13.** A	**13.** A	**13.** B	**13.** D	**13.** B
14. D	**14.** A	**14.** C	**14.** A	**14.** B	**14.** D
15. C	**15.** B	**15.** B	**15.** B	**15.** D	**15.** D
16. C	**16.** C	**16.** A	**16.** D	**16.** D	**16.** C
17. B	**17.** C	**17.** C	**17.** A	**17.** A	**17.** C
18. D	**18.** B	**18.** C	**18.** D	**18.** B	**18.** A
19. B	**19.** D	**19.** C	**19.** B	**19.** B	**19.** C
20. C	**20.** C	**20.** B	**20.** A	**20.** D	**20.** D
21. D	**21.** C	**21.** C	**21.** C	**21.** D	**21.** C
22. C	**22.** C	**22.** B	**22.** A	**22.** C	**22.** A
23. C	**23.** B	**23.** B	**23.** B	**23.** D	**23.** A
24. C	**24.** D	**24.** C	**24.** B	**24.** C	**24.** C
25. B	**25.** C	**25.** B	**25.** C	**25.** B	**25.** C

PRACTICE TEST 1

1. **The correct answer is (D).** *Although* means "regardless of the fact that." Hence the missing noun must be contrary to the key word *smile*, that is, *frown*.
2. **The correct answer is (D).** What kind of handling of food would make them decide to forego Martha's cooking? Choice (A) is wrong because such handling would have the opposite effects; it would make people eager to try.
3. **The correct answer is (A).** The word *stigma* indicates that the job puts the jobholder in a disgraceful or unenviable position so that it is *unattractive,* choice (A), or *uninviting,* choice (D). But *even* means "in spite of," so the salary must be quite unlike the job. This eliminates choice (D) and makes choice (A), with its exact opposite adjectives, the best choice.
4. **The correct answer is (C).** The sentence structure, balancing "one" against "another," suggests contrast. Contrast is not provided by choice (D), meaning right or privilege, since the first man already has the meat as his prerogative. Choices (A) and (B) make no sense. Choice (C) is a clear contrast, providing not nourishment but harm.
5. **The correct answer is (D).** What kind of handling of the account would make Joseph an object of jokes and ridicule? Choice (A) would earn him respect. Choice (C) would make the industry laugh *with* him, not *at* him. Choice (B), meaning "effusively sentimental," might well elicit ridicule, but in respect to a business situation, choice (D) is the more logical answer choice.
6. **The correct answer is (D).** Think of how you categorize jogging. It is more than *light* but less than *hazardous.* And it is certainly not *spurious* or *counterfeit.*
7. **The correct answer is (A).** Since the caller refused to give his name, the call was *anonymous*, literally "without a name."

8. **The correct answer is (B).** There is nothing to suggest that he has been omitted from the will or will fight it in court. Although he may be described as a *winner*, the legal term used for an heir is *beneficiary*.
9. **The correct answer is (C).** *Picayune* means "petty," "mean," or "small-minded." It is an appropriate adjective for a *hair-splitter*.
10. **The correct answer is (D).** High fever can produce a state of mental confusion.
11. **The correct answer is (D).** The context implies you would be taking unfair advantage of another and so, in a moral sense, would lower or *abase* yourself. There is no indication that you would scold or censure yourself, as choice (A) would mean, or that it would stimulate, choice (B), or weaken, choice (C), you.
12. **The correct answer is (B).** This is an instance in which you might first try out the second word in each pair. The main idea is that the storm *refused to slacken*, so you must find for the second blank a close synonym for *slacken*. Of the two offered, *mitigate*, meaning "alleviate," sounds too affected; *abate*, meaning "diminish" or "subside," is more idiomatic and is a better choice.
13. **The correct answer is (D).** Which of the four words offered has much to do with deciding between love and the throne? Only *abdicate*, which means "to give up a high position." *Prevaricate*, meaning "to lie," would not be a decision. Choice (B) doesn't tell us how or what he would alter or change; choice (C) wouldn't say which one he would nullify or abolish, which is what *abrogate* would involve.
14. **The correct answer is (D).** A fence, by disposing of and paying for fruits of the crime, serves as an encouraging force to robbers thereby aiding and abetting the crime itself.
15. **The correct answer is (C).** "Extenuating circumstances" are those that make an offense less serious by providing partial excuses. Coupled with "the defendant's youth," such circumstances make it unlikely that the judge would have recommended conviction or hanging. A mistrial results from errors in the course of a trial or from inability of the jury to come to a conclusion. It is the province of a judge to recommend *leniency*, that is, mercy or restraint.
16. **The correct answer is (C).** A fanatical and uncompromising person is by definition a *zealot*. Choice (B) is correct in terms of meaning but is ruled out as a correct answer because the blank requires a noun, not an adjective.
17. **The correct answer is (B).** The word *strangers* and the fact that they would be offering candy to children they do not know strongly suggest that the children be cautious and watchful, that is, *wary*.
18. **The correct answer is (D).** The position taken is that people do things in response either to outer force or to inner will. *Volition* means "free will."
19. **The correct answer is (B).** The phrase "respect for age" calls for a statement of strong positive regard or reverence for elder statesmen. That they were *venerated* fills the requirement. Choice (A) is too mild, while choices (C) and (D) are negative.
20. **The correct answer is (C).** The length of the sermon indicates its effect on the congregation—boredom and resultant passivity. Hence the metaphor of the sermon as a *soporific*, a sleep-inducing drug, that would cure *insomnia*, or chronic wakefulness.
21. **The correct answer is (D).** Since his cynicism was written all over him, it was obvious or *manifest*.
22. **The correct answer is (C).** The result of her condition identifies it as *agoraphobia*, fear of open spaces. *Claustrophobia* is the opposite, a fear of closed spaces. *Anemia*, a blood deficiency, and *ambivalence*, a state of conflicting emotions, do not necessarily keep their sufferers indoors.
23. **The correct answer is (C).** To sate is to "satisfy" or to "indulge." One assumes that the appetite is already *whetted*, and *fill* is simply an unidiomatic usage.
24. **The correct answer is (C).** The missing word must be a synonym for *badgering*. Choice (B) is too strong, choice (A) the opposite, and choice (D) wrong because the speaker *wants* the child to do it on his own volition.

25. **The correct answer is (B).** The speaker is clearly working in a formal relationship to a superior. We learn this from the first clause. *Authorized* is the correct word for describing what he or she is and is not allowed to say.

PRACTICE TEST 2

1. **The correct answer is (D).** The point that the sentence is trying to make is that "male supremacy" is now on the defensive. *Places* is too neutral a word to convey this meaning. *Bastions*, defensive strongholds, is a highly appropriate word choice.
2. **The correct answer is (B).** Choice (D) is ridiculous, and choice (A) cannot be correct because winds do not have riptides. The first blank could easily be filled with *dangerous* of choice (C), but breezes would not contribute to the danger. The *vagaries* or unexpected actions of the winds would make the position of a rudderless boat *untenable*.
3. **The correct answer is (A).** If the branches are moving, so are the shadows they cast. *Transient*, which means "passing," describes the action of the shadows.
4. **The correct answer is (D).** *Transmute* means "to change from one form, nature, or substance into another."
5. **The correct answer is (A).** It would be a nice birthday present to have an article appear in print right on the professor's 50th birthday. The other choices all fit grammatically, but make no sense in context.
6. **The correct answer is (B).** The chariot *careened* out of control; it lurched and swerved rapidly. *Caromed* means "bounced off" or "rebounded." The sentence makes no mention of a collision, so choice (D) does not constitute an acceptable completion.
7. **The correct answer is (D).** The sentence indicates that the speaker is urging someone not to *digress*, not to "stray," from the crux or "heart" of the matter. To *prevaricate* is to "lie." The sentence deals with time pressure, not with truthfulness.
8. **The correct answer is (A).** Under the circumstances, *disappointed* seems rather tame. These parents would surely have been *disconsolate*, that is, "beyond consolation" or "hopelessly sad."
9. **The correct answer is (D).** *Conscripted* means "drafted." Both volunteers and draftees would have to be *processed*, so choice (B) is not a good choice.
10. **The correct answer is (B).** You do not have to know baseball to choose this answer by elimination. A *syllogism* is a tactic in abstract logic. If you try out the verb with choices (A) and (C), you determine that these choices just don't fit well. Choice (B) is the only possible choice even if you do not know that a *balk* is a false move by the pitcher for which the penalty is the award of one base for the runner.
11. **The correct answer is (D).** If everyone in the neighborhood spoke Spanish, as implied by choice (C), hiring a Spanish-speaking person would be mandatory and not a matter of preference.
12. **The correct answer is (B).** Dark clouds tend to come before the storm; they constitute a *precursor* or a forerunner. Sometimes, however, the clouds blow over and there is no storm, so choice (D) is incorrect.
13. **The correct answer is (A).** The title of the act alone is a dead giveaway to the meaning of the correct answer. Incorrect choice (B) is based upon common mispronunciation and misspelling.
14. **The correct answer is (A).** "Possible meanings" is your main clue. Any statement with more than one meaning is, by definition, *ambiguous*.
15. **The correct answer is (B).** A performance by which one makes a fool of one's self causes scornful laughter; it is *ludicrous*.
16. **The correct answer is (C).** The blank requires a verb that is used with *to*. Choice (D) creates an impossible situation. The state of the house gave unspoken testimony, *attested* to the fact that it had been robbed.

17. **The correct answer is (C).** "Although" alerts you to expect a reversal of results: they will be different for "blows" and, "gunshots." Since the warrior could deal with swords, look for problems with gunshots and with his armor. *Vulnerable* means "susceptible to injury" or "not sufficiently protected" from. *Impervious* means "incapable of being penetrated." His armor was NOT impervious; therefore he was *vulnerable*.
18. **The correct answer is (B).** The word "belied" tells you that her words contradicted the beauty and elegance of her appearance. *Uncouth* means "crude, rude, and ungraceful."
19. **The correct answer is (D).** Apparently it is the quality, not the content, of the expressions he uses that makes them "insufferable" or unbearable. *Trite* expressions are so overused, so overfamiliar, that they no longer command our interest.
20. **The correct answer is (C).** The opposite of "permissive" is *stringent*. *Impermissive*, while not incorrect, would create a redundant sentence. Regulations may be both permissive and *uniform*, so there is no contrast in choice (D).
21. **The correct answer is (C).** Destruction of property gives no benefit to either victim or state, so choice (B) is unlikely. The form of the sentence requires the wrongdoer, himself, do something to the property. He cannot *confiscate* or "seize" his own property, but he can *forfeit* it or "give it up."
22. **The correct answer is (C).** The meaning alone should make this an easy completion. In addition, *distracted* is the only past participle here that is used with "from."
23. **The correct answer is (B).** He lied when he said he couldn't do the job because he was physically unable; actually he was *indolent* or just plain "lazy."
24. **The correct answer is (D).** "Police" in quotes is your clue that this was all a big joke, or *hoax*.
25. **The correct answer is (C).** Think of what happens to incoming freight if there is a trucking strike and the cargo is piled up at the unloading dock. An *embargo* or "suspension or prohibition of trade" is the best solution until the strike is settled.

PRACTICE TEST 3

1. **The correct answer is (C).** *Condolences* are expressions of sympathy for another person's grief or pain.
2. **The correct answer is (C).** The "but" signals that an opposite must fill the blank. Logically, coming off an effective diet that kept one lean, one would then become *corpulent* or fat.
3. **The correct answer is (D).** A *boorish* person is rude, crude, and impolite. Being *liberal* has nothing to do with manners but rather with attitude.
4. **The correct answer is (C).** *Apathy* or lack of interest is shown by staying away from the polls; conversely, if the voters flock to the polls, they show interest.
5. **The correct answer is (C).** Being unprepared leaves the student taking exams filled with alarm, apprehension, maybe even some trembling—in short, with *trepidation*.
6. **The correct answer is (C).** The grade is steep and the load heavy; obviously we need those oxen to get home, so we cannot slaughter them. Time appears to be a factor. Resting and feeding the oxen would involve time that we do not have, but if we *goad* them, prod them with a stick, they may move faster.
7. **The correct answer is (B).** He was convicted because his "alibi," his explanation of where he was at the time of the crime, turned out to be false, a lie or *fabrication*.
8. **The correct answer is (C).** People do not tend to "look" perfectly *sane*, so eliminate choice (B). *Hale* means whole or free from defect, and *hearty* means vigorous and robust.
9. **The correct answer is (D).** Only choice (D) fulfills the requirement of the "Although . . ." construction. The others might make more sense with *and*; for example, "He had doubts about the weather *and* he had no confidence."
10. **The correct answer is (C).** If they were to accept a missing person report, the only thing the police could do with it would be to *investigate*.
11. **The correct answer is (B).** By definition, an animal that eats only plants is *herbivorous*; it may also be called a "vegetarian."

12. **The correct answer is (C).** "The thick of the *ring*" does not ring true as an expression. "The thick of the *fray*," of the fight or the heated contest, is the idiomatic expression.
13. **The correct answer is (A).** The first three choices all convey the correct meaning, but structurally only *enjoined* works with "from blocking."
14. **The correct answer is (C).** Only the *postmark* gives date and location of mailing.
15. **The correct answer is (B).** The best way to compare two photographs is to place them in *juxtaposition*, that is, side-by-side.
16. **The correct answer is (A).** You can assume that given the technology of colonial America and the presence of virgin forests from coast to coast that wherever there was a hearth at all, there was a fire burning in it on cold winter days. Furthermore, none of the other choices make any sense at all.
17. **The correct answer is (C).** The sentence depends upon your acceptance of the stereotype cliché that Eskimos, that is, persons who live in cold places, have no use for refrigerators. Then a salesperson who is a fast talker, who is very *glib*, could sell them what they do not need.
18. **The correct answer is (C).** The *facade* is the front of the building, logically the portion most likely to be destroyed by an explosion at the front of the building.
19. **The correct answer is (C).** If a witness is to testify against him, the case is still in the trial stage, and he has not yet been *convicted* or adjudged *innocent*. An *alleged* thief is a person accused of thievery.
20. **The correct answer is (B).** The child who has not slept well will be cranky and unmanageable, in other words, *intractable*. Note the construction of the sentence; it calls for a completion that tells what the child will be "anything BUT." The child then will be the opposite of *intractable*, that is, anything but *docile*.
21. **The correct answer is (C).** If the eruption was unexpected, the volcano must have been considered inactive or *dormant*, literally "sleeping."
22. **The correct answer is (B).** Aside from the tobacco industry and its spokespersons, everyone agrees that cigarette smoking is harmful, that is, *deleterious*, to your health.
23. **The correct answer is (B).** *Audible* means "able to be heard." The sentence calls for a positive statement; choice (A) is the opposite of the meaning required.
24. **The correct answer is (C).** Any one of the choices might fill the first blank, but the second blank must be filled with a reason for which parents might *chide* or *punish* a child. Choice (B) makes no sense, and parents would take great pride in a child who was *industrious* or *independent*. However, parents might well *chide* or scold a child who was *indolent* or lazy.
25. **The correct answer is (B).** A "euphemism" is a word or phrase that is less direct and less expressive but considered less distasteful or offensive than the more blunt word. *Portly* means "stout in a dignified way." It is often used in place of "fat."

PRACTICE TEST 4

1. **The correct answer is (C).** Obviously, you cannot write the report until you have gathered the *information*. Writing the report as soon as possible once you have the information makes sense; you can work with fresh facts, and those who receive the report can act upon it promptly.
2. **The correct answer is (C).** To *effect* is "to bring about or to produce as a result." The incorrect *affect* means "to have an influence on."
3. **The correct answer is (C).** A *circumlocution* is a "roundabout way of saying something." *Circumlocution* is certainly the way of avoiding *concise* expression. Choice (D) is half right. Diplomats do try to avoid *plain* language, but they don't use *summaries* to do it.

4. **The correct answer is (D).** Once you have picked up the sense of the second half of the sentence, even without filling the blank, completing the first half is easy. It is an exercise in *futility* that produces no results. Having filled the first blank, you need only confirm that the second part of choice (D) also makes sense. It logically follows that an exercise in *futility* will bring no *substantive* deterrent to the impending cataclysm.
5. **The correct answer is (C).** If Santa Anna's forces had been in *decline* or *isolation*, the Alamo would not have fallen. Santa Anna won through sheer force of numbers. In fact, what makes the Alamo battle historic is that so small a force held out for so long against an army overwhelmingly superior in numbers, that is, a *preponderant* army.
6. **The correct answer is (A).** *Turbid* is a synonym for "cloudy."
7. **The correct answer is (B).** A process of elimination makes this an easy completion even with no knowledge of flamenco dancing. The dancer stood still, so his arms could not be *flailing*. *Akimbo*, hands on hips with elbows bent outward, is the only position for arms.
8. **The correct answer is (C).** The woman would not sue because her character had been *whitewashed*; she would sue because it had been "blackened" or *defamed*. To *defame* is to maliciously injure a reputation.
9. **The correct answer is (A).** A "joiner," in quotes, is one who joins. A person who joins groups or organizations does so in order to socialize with others of like interests. A *gregarious* person is sociable. Without the quotes, a joiner is a cabinetmaker.
10. **The correct answer is (D).** *Obese* means extremely fat. Here the sentence itself moves from a euphemism to a blunt statement of fact.
11. **The correct answer is (B).** If you want no more, you are *satiated* or satisfied. Your "palate" is the roof of your mouth.
12. **The correct answer is (B).** This is just plain common sense. To protect privacy, the names and Social Security numbers must be removed or *deleted* from the questionnaires.
13. **The correct answer is (B).** A word made up of the initial letters of words in a phrase is an *acronym*. A *homonym* is a word that has the same sound as another word, but a different meaning. A *heteronym* is a word with the same spelling but different meanings with different pronunciations. For example, compare the word tēar, a drop from the eye, to teār, a rip in a piece of clothing. A *pseudonym* is an assumed name.
14. **The correct answer is (A).** A criminal can be *demented*, as indeed this one may have been, or *pathological*, but a crime cannot. *Gratuitous* in this context means unwarranted and unjustified.
15. **The correct answer is (B).** The test sentence itself provides a good definition of the verb to *procrastinate*.
16. **The correct answer is (D).** To accomplish his goal, he would want to lower his head toward the ground, perhaps as if to bow, that is, to *incline* it and to keep it steady. *Shaking* his head would make it harder to focus on individual stones.
17. **The correct answer is (A).** The words chosen must add up to a "wicked injustice." By definition, an *iniquity* is a *grossly* immoral act.
18. **The correct answer is (D).** The first blank requires someone with some feelings about stealing. A *kleptomaniac* has an uncontrollable urge to take things, without regard to need; in fact, a *kleptomaniac* has a strong *proclivity* to steal. A *pyromaniac* starts fires; a *megalomaniac* has delusions of omnipotence; a *dipsomaniac* is an alcoholic. None of these should have strong feelings about stealing stemming from their own peculiarities.
19. **The correct answer is (B).** A *hypothesis* is a proposition stated as the basis for argument or experiment.
20. **The correct answer is (A).** The blank must be filled with a word somehow related to making faces. Only *supercilious* is specifically related to facial expression. It suggests "being disdainful, raising the eyebrows, looking down the nose."
21. **The correct answer is (C).** The climate is allegedly not conducive to good health; it is not *salubrious*. *Sanitary* conditions have no effect on heat prostration. *Salutary*, meaning "conducive to improvement," goes beyond the scope of the second clause. As for *healthy*, climates can be "healthful," but only living things can be *healthy*.

22. **The correct answer is (A).** To *deride* is to "treat with contemptuous mirth"; it clearly refers to laughing *at.* A *buffoon* (noun not verb) is one who makes himself or herself the object of laughter.
23. **The correct answer is (B).** The blank requires a word that relates to the comments of the opponent. An alternate meaning of *deflate* is to reduce in size, importance, or effectiveness. In this sense, choice (B) is the most approriate answer.
24. **The correct answer is (B).** *Strategy* is the overall science of military planning. A *stratagem* is one small part of a strategy, a single maneuver or tactic. The use of the wooden horse to breach the Trojan gates was a clever *stratagem.*
25. **The correct answer is (C).** A large assembly of stars, film or otherwise, is a *galaxy.* A group of larks or bathing beauties is called a *bevy*; a group of lions is a *pride.*

PRACTICE TEST 5

1. **The correct answer is (C).** For purposes of stability, extra wheels are added in pairs to large vehicles. A fifth wheel added to a four-wheel vehicle would serve no useful purpose, would be *superfluous.* A person who feels as *superfluous* as a fifth wheel feels useless.
2. **The correct answer is (C).** *Parliaments, constitutional monarchies,* and *three-party systems* all contain internal mechanisms for legislated change. Only a dictatorship would destroy the mechanism for its own change, requiring civil war for reversal. Once the second blank is filled, completion for the first blank falls into place.
3. **The correct answer is (B).** Animals tend to be territorial, so when the dachshund encroached on its turf, the poodle was ready to fight. *Onerous,* which means "burdensome," would never be used to describe a look.
4. **The correct answer is (C).** Some sentence completions are easier than others. Provided you do not mistake *croquette,* a fried cake, for *coquette,* a vain flirt, you should have no trouble with this sentence.
5. **The correct answer is (B).** The start of the fishing season brings to mind immediately the phrase "Gone fishin'!" A person who has "gone fishin' " is not there. A *hiatus* or gap in attendance is the result of the lure of the fishing season.
6. **The correct answer is (A).** The words "equally unclear" tip you off to the need for a word that means "unclear." *Nebulous,* which means "cloudy" or "vague," is the only choice to meet the test.
7. **The correct answer is (C).** *Nepotism* is showing favoritism to relatives for employment or for appointment to high places.
8. **The correct answer is (A).** Whose arms would be very strong? Not both arms of the *hemiplegic,* who suffers extreme weakness on one side of the body as a result of a stroke or other brain damage; not those of the *quadriplegic,* who suffers paralysis of all four limbs; and not those of the *somnambulist,* the sleepwalker whose legs are far from comatose. The *paraplegic,* who is paralyzed from the waist down, tends to develop extra strength in the arms to compensate for now *useless* legs.
9. **The correct answer is (D).** From "although" you infer the engine is there "just in case" the wind becomes less dependable and the ship needs an additional source of power. The implication is not so much that it needs a complete *substitute* as a *subsidiary,* a "supplement" or an "auxiliary."
10. **The correct answer is (A).** *Aplomb* is the poise that comes from self-confidence.
11. **The correct answer is (D).** The speech was difficult to understand, that is, *abstruse.* If the speech was also *protracted,* long and drawn-out, that might have contributed as well to its being *abstruse.*
12. **The correct answer is (C).** Since the lifetime is being measured in such tiny units, it must be extremely fleeting, short-lived, or *ephemeral.*
13. **The correct answer is (D).** The *millennium* was the eagerly awaited golden age of peace, prosperity, and happiness. None of the other choices make sense.

14. **The correct answer is (B).** Begin with the second blank. What should you keep to yourself? Only choices (A) and (B) are possible. However, keeping one's *hands* to oneself has nothing to do with *confessing*, so choice (A) must be eliminated. To *obtrude* is to force one's *opinions* on others.
15. **The correct answer is (D).** If you are disappointed, you will remember the day regretfully; you will *rue* it.
16. **The correct answer is (D).** Soldiers who rent themselves to foreign armies are called *mercenaries*.
17. **The correct answer is (A).** "Countless" calls for *myriads*, an indefinite number that surpasses *dozens*. *Multitudinous* conveys the correct meaning but is syntactically incorrect; "multitudes" would work here. *Dryads* are wood nymphs.
18. **The correct answer is (B).** Why would you prefer to scrub floors? You must find peeling potatoes to be very *onerous*, burdensome, or oppressive.
19. **The correct answer is (B).** The picture painted here is one of the offenders lying face down on the ground begging humbly, *supplicating*, for mercy.
20. **The correct answer is (D).** Her rebelliousness was written all over her; it was clearly and openly revealed; it was *manifest*. *Exterior* bears the correct meaning but is an inappropriate descriptor.
21. **The correct answer is (D).** A dull, insensitive, or *obtuse* person would be slow to learn basic social niceties.
22. **The correct answer is (C).** The second clause indicates that we are here talking about Louis XIV with respect to elegance of dress. The adjective *sartorial* is used specifically to refer to men's clothing.
23. **The correct answer is (D).** The sentence is gender neutral, so the blank must be filled with a gender-neutral word that includes brothers and sisters, that is, *siblings*.
24. **The correct answer is (C).** "False accusations" do not constitute corrections. The man did indeed *interfere*, but the sentence lacks the necessary preposition to utilize choice (B). To be correct, the completion would need to read "interfered with." What did happen was that the man *disconcerted* the speaker by upsetting, ruffling, or irking him or her.
25. **The correct answer is (B).** He will never become an alcoholic if he just buys, *secretes* (hides), or *accumulates* liquor. He must *imbibe* it; in other words, he must drink it too.

PRACTICE TEST 6

1. **The correct answer is (D).** Turn the sentence around. Patience is a virtue; I'm glad to see that you have (it), that is, *forbearance*. Choice (C) would seem to be irrelevant. If the person has the *time*, then being patient does not represent great virtue. As for choice (A), since "have" can be either an independent verb taking an object or an auxiliary to a main verb, "have *arrived*" seems possible. But choice (A) makes for a self-congratulatory statement; choice (D) is the better choice.
2. **The correct answer is (C).** Only increasing nearness would reduce visibility. *Nigh* means "near" or "close."
3. **The correct answer is (B).** Of the choices offered, only the fact that she was an *indefatigable* or tireless jogger can explain that she covered 15 miles a day.
4. **The correct answer is (D).** The relationship between her nature and the activity described is best explained by saying the first *required* the second.
5. **The correct answer is (B).** *Concatenate* means "linked together as a chain." This is precisely the state of affairs described in the second clause. War is *hell*, but not according to the requirements of this sentence.
6. **The correct answer is (B).** The "if" construction of both clauses indicates that we are seeking two contrasting behaviors each of which produce contrasting results. Both choices (C) and (D) offer synonyms to fill the two blanks, while choice (A) makes no sense at all. To *dissipate* is to waste or to squander, quite the opposite of using wisely.

7. **The correct answer is (C).** "Lots" are "objects used to make a choice by chance," that is, *randomly*.
8. **The correct answer is (C).** "Eminence" is used to describe Richelieu. The only adjective that corresponds to "eminent" is *prominent*.
9. **The correct answer is (B).** A *transgressor* is someone who has simply crossed the boundary between legal and illegal activities.
10. **The correct answer is (D).** "*Greetings* and *salutations*" is a bit redundant, but it is a frequent form of address to a group, especially at an initial meeting. Choice (B) would be ridiculous. The teacher would not begin by saying "Hello and goodbye." The "and" between the two words precludes choice (A). Choice (C) would be acceptable if there were no other choice, but choice (D) is the more likely opener in this context.
11. **The correct answer is (B).** "Although" alerts you to look for the opposite of "aloof," which means "cool, distant, and uninvolved." The only opposite offered is *gracious*, which means "warm, courteous, and sympathetic."
12. **The correct answer is (B).** The "but" tells you that the two activities are being put into different categories. The word "crime" in juxtaposition with "speeding" suggests that the second blank is to be filled with a word carrying more serious import than the first. Choice (A) is clearly wrong, and choice (D) reverses the order of seriousness. As for choice (C), "speeding" is not a social blunder, which is what a *faux pas* is.
13. **The correct answer is (B).** *Craft* is a synonym for "skill"; it implies dexterity with the hands.
14. **The correct answer is (D).** *Malleable* means capable of being shaped, especially by hammering, pounding, or bending. The fact that gold is very *soft* contributes to its malleability, but "most soft element" is not good English.
15. **The correct answer is (D).** *Impassive* has more than one meaning. One meaning is motionless or still. By this meaning, *impassive* is the only choice that can describe a "stone." Another meaning of *impassive* is "devoid of feelings." Here, "failed to touch him" means failed to affect his emotions, making him quite stone-like.
16. **The correct answer is (C).** Fill the second blank first. A client cannot *abrogate* (annul) or *elect* a law, so eliminate choices (A) and (D). Choice (B) fills the blanks so as to make an untrue statement. You are left with choice (C), which does happen now and then.
17. **The correct answer is (C).** To look *askance* is to look sidewise or with suspicion. Certainly a banker would wonder at anyone who claimed no interest in saving money.
18. **The correct answer is (A).** What the readers want is shocking, horrifying, or titillating, that is, *lurid* information.
19. **The correct answer is (C).** "Worshipping her every move" did not of itself make him her kindest, most *beneficent* admirer, nor did it necessarily prove that he was more unconsciously stupid, *fatuous*, or more worldly and *sophisticated* than her other admirers. It qualified him only to be called her most devoted and most *ardent* admirer.
20. **The correct answer is (D).** Once you eliminate the totally irrelevant choice, *pervade*, meaning "to spread through," the other three words all express some degree of opposition. *Dissuade*, meaning "to discourage by persuasion," fits most gracefully into the syntax and conveys the most likely intent of the sentence.
21. **The correct answer is (C).** If she lacked money, she was *impecunious*.
22. **The correct answer is (A).** The main clue is "loose fat," which indicates that the person being spoken to is flabby or *flaccid*. *Avoirdupois* does refer to weight, but it is a noun, and this blank calls for an adjective.
23. **The correct answer is (A).** Common sense is all you need to answer this question. Crime prevention is the officer's *primary*, first, and most important role, but the officer also instructs, assists, and reacts to crime in progress.

24. **The correct answer is (C).** The only person we are certain that the general had the authority to send in his place would have been his *adjutant*, his assistant.
25. **The correct answer is (C).** A "malingerer" is someone who pretends to be ill, hurt, or otherwise unavailable in order to avoid obligations—in other words, in order to *shirk* his duty.

NOTES

NOTES

NOTES

NOTES

NOTES

NOTES